Edition

2

Introduction to Social Work and Social Welfare

Mary W. Macht

Program Director, Short-term Treatment Unit,
Winnebago Mental Health Institute, Wisconsin

José B. Ashford

Arizona State University

Merrill, an imprint of
Macmillan Publishing Company
New York

Collier Macmillan Canada, Inc.
Toronto

Maxwell Macmillan International Publishing Group
New York   Oxford   Singapore   Sydney

Cover photograph: copyright 1990, Tony Freeman/PhotoEdit

Editor: Sally Berridge MacGregor
Developmental Editor: Linda James Scharp
Production Editor: Sheryl Glicker Langner
Art Coordinator: Ruth Ann Kimpel
Photo Editor: Gail Meese
Text Designer: Debra A. Fargo
Cover Designer: Brian Deep

This book was set in Italia.

Macmillan Publishing Company
866 Third Avenue, New York, NY 10022

Collier Macmillan Canada, Inc.

Library of Congress Catalog Card Number: 90–61374
International Standard Book Number: 0–675–21192–1

Photo Credits: p. xvi by Mary Hagler/Merrill; pp. 10, 200, 228, 290, 376 by Gail Meese/Merrill; p. 24 by David S. Strickler; pp. 55, 384 by Student Support Services Publication Center, University of Minnesota; p. 58 by Department of Housing and Urban Development; pp. 62, 88, 92, 116, 127, 137, 143, 147, 151, 167, 183, 186, 256, 283, 297, 310 by Social Welfare History Archives, University of Minnesota; p. 71 by Michelle Lesley; p. 214 by the *Columbus Dispatch*; p. 368 by Mary Hagler/Riverside Methodist Hospital.

Printing: 2   3   4   5   6   7   8   9   Year: 2   3   4

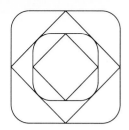

Preface

This book is about social work—its past, present, and potential. It is an invitation to students entering the human service professions to consider social work as a dynamic and vital field. In extending this invitation we have tried to be comprehensive in identifying issues pertinent to the field; traditionally, this is the duty of an introductory course. This conceptual/ philosophical approach has required us to address some tough concepts and complex material in order to present social work in its unique potential.

The authors' pride in being part of this young and promising profession will be apparent throughout the text. No other profession has consistently struggled to improve the functioning of the most oppressed of our society. Throughout this book we strive to convey the excitement we feel about the profession, in terms of what it has accomplished and what a profound difference social work can make in the future.

While recognizing that diversity is a hallmark of our profession, as authors we have tried to be aware of our own biases. We taught together over a five-year period; during this time tremendous professional debate and intellectual growth occurred. While we continue to engage in theoretical debates, we strongly agree that the primary target population of the profession must be the most oppressed groups. While some social workers may legitimately opt to provide counseling to the middle and upper classes from comfortable private offices, the profession must maintain its commitment to the poor, the abused, the criminal, the chronically mentally ill, the chronically disabled, the homeless, as well as seriously dysfunctional families. Our efforts must be focused at both the individual and policy levels.

The very complexity of the problems we deal with demands that we have a theoretically sound knowledge base that is continually tested and refined. Our commitment to and enthusiasm for knowledge-based practice has led us to present some material in more depth than is typical in an introductory textbook; we encourage teachers to expose students to this knowledge even though in-depth comprehension and appreciation may have to wait for advanced educational experiences. For the student who pursues any of the human service professions, this book can continue to serve as a reference on the social work profession.

We have written this text with several objectives in mind—specifically, to:

1. Provide a comprehensive overview of the social work profession
2. Allow students to make a knowledge-based decision about whether social work is an appropriate professional choice
3. Clarify the social work value base
4. Provide illustrative examples of practice in various settings and fields of practice
5. Present the professional organizational structure
6. Illustrate how core social work knowledge such as policy, human behavior, and research are integral components of daily practice
7. Introduce the importance of systemic thinking to social work practice
8. Integrate the person-in-environment concept into all areas of practice
9. Acquaint the student with political and economic variables in social work practice
10. Illustrate generalist practice in casework, group work, and community organization settings, as well as in direct and indirect practice

We have made more explicit the relationship between knowledge and practice. We have added a chapter on practice research and demonstrated throughout the text that research is an integral part of practice that holds the potential for increasing effectiveness and job satisfaction.

Perhaps the major improvement in this edition is Part V, Fields of Practice. In Part I we identify the social work roles, values, functions, and knowledge base. In the Fields of Practice section we translate these concepts into practice. We have greatly increased the number of examples to provide an opportunity to apply what has been learned.

The analytical quality of the first edition has been maintained. In addition, our overt enthusiasm for the field invites students to consider the field of social work. We recognize the tremendous political, social, and economic barriers to effective practice; admittedly, social work has a great deal to learn about how to improve the human social condition. Nevertheless for those who are committed to such improvement, the authors believe that social work is an excellent vehicle to work toward those goals.

We have tried to be sensitive to gender references. Short of writing every reference to people in plural form, one has to confront the he/she referent issue. Because we were unhappy with using he and she in alternate chapters, we chose a different style. It was our goal to alternate the use of gender specific pronouns with each new example. This method, though not perfect, allowed us to avoid the clumsy he/she usage and to have practitioners and clients of both genders within a single chapter.

We are grateful to many people who have contributed to the development of this textbook. Lucy Rowley and Jean Quam worked on the first edition; their contributions continue to strengthen the second edition.

In this edition we have been particularly blessed in working with Linda Scharp of Merrill Publishing Company. Linda's enthusiasm, knowledge, and perseverance have been wonderful. Carol Sykes, Sheryl Langner, and Jan Brittan, also of Merrill, have provided valuable assistance. Copies of the manuscript were read by John M. Herrick, Michigan State University; Katheryn B. Davis, University of Georgia; Margaret M. Dwyer, Loyola University of Chicago; Fred W. Seidl, State University of New York–Buffalo; Jane Macy-Lewis, Luther College, Iowa; Marvin Tossey, Salisbury State University; and David Stoesz, San Diego State University. Their input greatly enhanced the final product.

Contributors to the second edition include Craig LeCroy, Ann Stirling Frisch, Edwin Gonzalez-Santin, Janet Davenport, Toby Ferrell, Ron Cross, and Beverly Gudex. Their endeavors truly enhance our presentation of the respective topics.

In an applied field such as social work, perhaps the most important individuals are those practitioners who continue to implement and test new ideas. Exposure to their accomplishments keeps us excited about the field. Robert Goetter and Phil Gordon are two such individuals. In addition, both of the authors are married to skilled practitioners who provide valuable ideas and suggestions to our thinking and writing; we owe special thanks to Phil Macht and Nancy Disbrow. Theolinda Macht provided much of the research in the health care chapter. Timothy Macht read a number of chapters and strengthened the organization from a student's perspective.

Finally, we would like to thank our parents, Theodore and Grace Wirtz and Joseph and Elva Ashford, for providing the nurturance to develop the creativity and confidence necessary to undertake authoring a textbook.

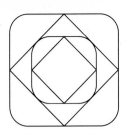

Contents

PART

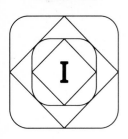

I

AN OVERVIEW OF SOCIAL WORK PRACTICE

S ocial work is an exciting and essential but poorly understood profession. It endures because social and physical needs of a significant portion of the population remain unmet. If we, as a profession, achieved our stated goals, there would be no need for social workers.

In this book we analyze why social work exists, what social workers do, and what values and skills they need to function effectively within the profession.

Our assumption is that as students you are taking this course because you are strongly inclined to enter a human service profession. One reason you may be taking the course is to determine whether your career goals can be met in the field of social work. For this reason, we begin Chapter 1 with an overview of human service professions. Our intent is to allow you to compare and contrast social work with other professions, thereby increasing your ability to make an informed decision. Clearly, this overview cannot be comprehensive, as it would detract from the purpose of the book. However, it does allow the student to see how social work fits into the wider picture. The rest of the book explores social work's uniqueness in considerable detail.

Our analysis of the human service professions in Chapter 1 suggests that each has a unique frame of reference that guides practitioners in problem assessment. The knowledge and experience that flow from this frame of reference determine what knowledge and skills will be used in the intervention. Having implemented an intervention, the professional then assesses whether the intervention was successful. If successful, the theoretical framework of the problem assessment and the intervention method become part of practice knowledge. If the intervention fails, the professional will reassess the problem using alternative theories, which in turn call for different interventions. Through this conscious use of theory and skills, human service professionals greatly increase their theoretical and practice knowledge of their field. Figure I–1 shows a flowchart for professional social work practice.

Chapter 4 discusses values and ideology in greater detail.

The ideological perspective basically comprises the societal and group norms that affect social work practice. The social worker's ideological perspective is the foundation on which social work practice is based. The social

1

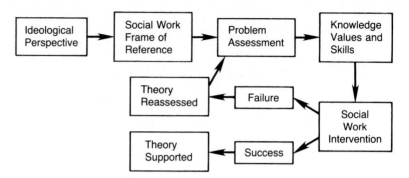

FIGURE I–1

work frame of reference determines the knowledge, values, and skills that will guide the social work intervention. Within this framework you can see how feedback will alter some components of the system, but the ideological base and the social work frame of reference tend to remain stable.

The first chapter addresses how social work is different from other professions by systematically comparing it with other human service professions. Chapter 2 builds on the uniqueness identified in Chapter 1. Chapter 3 identifies a model of practice that is the primary model of social work practice today, the model that is most consistent with social work's unique frame of reference.

In making comparisons with other professions, you should bear in mind that in addition to dealing with the same types of clients and related problems, each profession draws heavily on the theoretical knowledge developed in the other professions.

In Part I we introduce the themes that you will encounter consistently throughout this book.

1. Practice must be knowledge-based. This includes practice knowledge and empirically based knowledge.
2. Practice must be evaluated. To the extent that we can develop our empirical base for practice, we will increase our effectiveness.
3. Understanding the political, social, and economic environment is critical to effective social work practice.
4. Social work has a unique set of knowledge, values, and skills.

Chapter

1

Social Work and Related Professions: A Comparative Analysis

More than any other "helping professional" the social worker is expected to understand the influence of the environment — both the broad societal context and the more immediate environment as they contribute to individual situations.[1]

Economic and scientific development in the industrialized world has created a paradox. As society's ability to provide for the physical needs of the population increases, the ability of the individual to find personal fulfillment tends to decrease. The affluence created by industrialization has provided us with the ability to create disciplines to study and find solutions to these perceived human and social problems. Sociology, anthropology, political science, and economics are just some of the disciplines that have attempted to study the human condition, with the goal of increasing life satisfaction.

Affluence does not create happiness.

Material possessions do not fulfill individual needs. Human service professionals work to increase the quality of life.

While these disciplines *study* human problems, professionals *intervene* in human problems, guided by the knowledge developed by social scientists. Because human behavior is so complex, the social science disciplines frequently overlap. This overlapping phenomenon also takes place within the human service professions. As we learn to appreciate the complexity of human behavior, the tasks, roles, and functions of human service professionals spill over from one discipline to another.

CHOOSING A PROFESSION: WHAT ARE THE DIFFERENCES?

As a student considering the social work profession, you may not fully understand how your choice of a profession will make a difference. This chapter provides a basic survey of the differences among the major human service professions. In spite of the considerable overlap among the human service professions, the variety of services each provides and the specific training and education they require is tremendous.

Different functions re-
quire different educa-
tional preparation.

The longest course of training is that of the psychiatrist, who first completes medical training and then must serve a three-year residency in psychiatry. At the other end of the continuum is the indigenous worker, who is
trained in the "learning by doing" method. Some current examples of learning by doing preparation are drug and alcohol counselors whose primary
training is based in receiving treatment for their own abuse problems, or correctional officers without professional education who are able to assume social work positions by passing a social work exam. (It should be noted that
this cannot happen in states that have social work licensing.)

If we limit our analysis to human service professions that have been
established for some time, we can see that the various professions demand
different kinds of education and training; they reflect different guiding theories
and frames of reference; and they experience different kinds of regulation. In
fact, regulation varies from state to state.

Most important, each of these professions has a unique expertise and
domain that others may or may not have. This expertise is basic to the profession. For instance, throughout this book we emphasize the importance of
the social environment to social work practice. This implies that all social
workers must adopt a person-in-environment emphasis. The psychiatrist or
psychologist may also adopt a community-based approach, but we do not
expect all psychiatrists or psychologists to be knowledgeable about community resources. This is the unique domain of social work practice.

By the same token, pharmacotherapy (treatment using drugs) is the
unique domain of psychiatric practice. Social workers who deal extensively
with the mentally ill may develop an expertise in pharmacology that is essential to their practice. However, we would not expect social workers in general to have such expertise.

COMPETENCE REQUIRES SOCIAL WORK EXPERTISE

Social workers who become too concerned or specialized in the skills and
knowledge of other professions may be operating outside their professional
and legal sanction. This can harm the client in two ways: (1) the social
worker may not have the necessary expertise, and (2) the client may be deprived of the expertise the social worker should have.

To illustrate the first problem, a social worker who tried to suggest
which drugs a client should use would not have the appropriate knowledge to
do so effectively. In the second, a social worker who was overly concerned
with medical issues may ignore the social functioning issues—the very area
in which social workers should be the expert. Since we work at the boundaries of the human service professions, we must always maintain our emphasis on person-in-environment functioning. For example, a relatively new
area of treatment called rage therapy is used with antisocial children to deal

Social workers often work on teams with psychiatrists, psychologists, and paraprofessionals.

with their anger and encourage bonding. For this therapy to be successful, both the parents and the schools must be educated and involved. Social workers may do the therapy themselves, but it is more likely that in a team approach, their role will be to prepare the child's environment to support the new behaviors.

We need to remain flexible. We need to know our own abilities and limitations and effectively use other professionals who are more competent in different areas of expertise. We must keep in mind that the most "glamorous" interventions may not be the most effective. If the environment is not changed, the new behavior is unlikely to continue.

Although specific aspects of our comparisons may raise debate, we believe this general overview can help you understand the basic differences among the human service professions; discover which profession is most compatible with your attitudes, values, and skills; and gain some insight into the expectations that will be made of you depending upon which profession you choose.

Each profession is unique, yet overlaps with other professions in tasks and knowledge.

HOW SOCIAL WORK IS UNIQUE

To illustrate how social work is different from other human service professions we first identify its distinguishing characteristics and then discuss the major activities performed by social workers.

Distinguishing Characteristics

The uniqueness of social work can be better understood by examining its characteristics.

Social work focuses on the totality of the problem situation. The social work assessment requires the social worker to assess the problem from a psychological, sociological, biological, political, and economic perspective. For this reason social work students are required to have a strong grounding in all of the social sciences.

Social workers see the individual or group experiencing the problem as part of a larger social system. Primary support systems such as family, church, community, and neighborhood are important components of this system. Frequently, more formal components of the system, such as schools or places of employment, may be part of the problem or the solution.

Social workers must have comprehensive knowledge of community resources, how to engage appropriate resources, and how to develop them if they do not exist. There has been considerable concern expressed in the professional literature lately that social workers are abandoning this area of expertise for the more esoteric clinical therapy roles. Davis observed negative consequences in the community mental health field when discharge planning for the chronically mentally ill was done poorly.[2] His findings suggested that the social workers studied placed their priority on group therapy and research, and that some were quite ignorant about existing community resources. This gap in service accounted for several failed placements. Social workers in this setting lost sight of the fact that long-term stability of chronic psychiatric patients is more a function of comprehensive community resources than of short-term psychotherapy applied in a hospital or clinical setting.

Social work emphasizes social interaction and resultant social functioning and malfunctioning. To perform effectively, social workers must have considerable knowledge of interpersonal relationships, conflict resolution, and group facilitation. Social workers use these skills constantly in dealing with a variety of systems that affect the client or client group; they are not merely skills applied in the office setting.

Social workers recognize that many individual problems are social. To understand the problem the individual is experiencing requires understanding how that problem is rooted in social institutions. Although individual social workers might disagree about whether the individual or society needs to change, they all recognize the need to address both the individual and the institutional problems. This subject will be addressed more fully as we emphasize the importance of seeing private troubles as public issues.

The basic goal of social work is client empowerment. The term *client empowerment* has been used in a variety of ways. Rappaport suggested that empowerment is most easily understood in its absence.[3] The absence of empowerment is powerlessness, learned helplessness, alienation, lack of a sense of control over one's life. The difficulty in defining it positively comes

Part IV identifies the social work knowledge base and explains the importance of this knowledge to social work practice.

Chapter 4 discusses the societal roots of social problems in more detail.

from the fact that it takes on different forms with different people and different environments.

Perhaps the best positive definition was made by Solomon, who suggested that empowerment is a

> process whereby the social worker engages in a set of activities with the client or client system that aims to reduce the powerlessness that has been created by negative valuations based on membership in a stigmatized group.[4]

All individuals experience powerlessness at some time, in certain situations. Some groups and individuals, however, experience a pervasive sense of powerlessness.

In practice, then, powerlessness can be viewed as an individual's or group's inability to obtain and use resources to achieve goals. Empowerment is the process of developing an effective support system for those who have been blocked from achievement.[5]

Having looked at the characteristics that are basic to practice, we now discuss some of the professional activities that tend to separate social workers from other professionals.

Activities of Social Workers

Guidelines for the Selection and Use of Social Workers, published by the National Association of Social Workers (NASW) in 1981, identifies some of the major activities that social workers perform.[6] Once again, some form of these activities may be performed by other professionals on occasion, but it is expected that all social workers will have the required skills.

Case management consists of those activities required to develop, implement, and monitor a social service plan. It begins with conceptualizing the client system as part of the social environment, providing appropriate services, identifying and referring to services when appropriate, involving the client in the development of the solution to the problem, monitoring the client's progress, and representing or advocating on behalf of the client when necessary.

Psychosocial assessment is the gathering of information needed to determine the type and nature of problems involved, the capacities and resources of the client, and the services needed to solve the problem. This task primarily concerns the basic personal and social characteristics of the client and the significant social and environmental factors, rather than unconscious psychological functioning, which is the domain of the psychiatrist or psychologist.

Psychosocial diagnosis is the process by which relevant facts are organized and conceptualized within a theoretical framework that incorporates psychological and social aspects. The information is analyzed to determine the cause and history of the problem, the interactions among different aspects of the problem, and how potential interventions and goals will work. The outcome of the diagnostic step is a treatment plan.

Information and referral is the process of collecting and distributing information about available resources that will enhance the individual's or group's functioning. Frequently, social workers develop reference materials about services available that can be used by any member of the community (not just identified clients). Crisis hotlines are a good example of a formalized information and referral system. When people call the hotline during times of crisis, counselors have many sources available to identify what kind of service is needed and how the service can be obtained by the caller.

Social workers engage in *resource development* to create new resources when a significant gap in services is identified. Resource development can involve extending or improving existing services, planning and allocating available resources more effectively, or increasing the efficiency of the service delivery system.

Therapy is the use of specific techniques to promote human growth and improve social functioning. In social work practice, therapy is based on a holistic concept of personality. Learned patterns of thinking and behaving are the result of the socialization process. This implies that there is an inseparable relationship between the person and the environment.

Administration involves coordinating or directing the activities and personnel within an agency. Social workers have been involved in programs ranging from cabinet level posts to small private agencies such as rape crisis centers. As NASW uses the term, *administration* means the use of formal and informal authority delegated by the governing body to organize, direct, or control the individual or groups involved in order to coordinate all parts of the organization for the attainment of the organization's purpose.

Group practice, professional supervision, and *consultation* are some of the other activities that social workers accomplish. Most of the activities involved in these tasks are more similar than different from one profession to another.

Now that we have identified the characteristics and activities that make social work unique, we can move on to the differences between social workers and other professionals. Our discussion is limited to a comparison with sociologists, psychologists, psychiatrists, counselors, and attorneys, because these are the professionals with whom you are most likely to work. New human service professions continue to develop, but they have not yet identified unique characteristics necessary to be included in this comparison. We begin the discussion with sociologists, because many students are unsure about the difference between a degree in social work and one in sociology. Sociologists are not included in the comparison in Table 1–1 (see p. 14) because they tend not to be involved in direct practice.

> Eddie Brown, MSW, DSW, is assistant secretary of the Interior for the Bush administration.

SOCIOLOGISTS AND SOCIAL WORKERS

> Sociologists develop knowledge which informs social work practice.

Sociology is the primary discipline involved in the study of the social environment, and sociological theory has made significant contributions to the knowledge base of social work. Succinctly described, a sociologist's primary goal is to develop and test theories about social phenomena, while a social worker's primary goal is to solve human problems. Social workers try to understand the client or the community, making appropriate assessment and proceeding with an intervention that they hope will lead to problem resolution and change.[7]

The educational preparation of each discipline reflects these different goals. Sociology students spend their time studying theory and research methods; social work students spend a greater portion of their education applying those theories in practicums or field experiences. The doctorate is the terminal degree in sociology; the master's degree is generally the terminal degree for social work practitioners. Most sociologists work at universities or other research settings and deal with generating and testing knowledge. Social workers generally work in public or private social welfare agencies and deal directly with clients.

PSYCHIATRISTS AND SOCIAL WORKERS

In contrast to the different settings of the sociologist and the social worker, social workers and psychiatrists frequently work in the same settings, such as community mental health agencies, mental hospitals, general hospitals, and prisons. Some of the roles they play (consultant, therapist, group facilitator, administrator) may overlap. Yet it is important that social workers be cognizant of their unique contributions and not become mere nonmedical extensions of the physician. One text summarized the difference between psychiatry and social work in this way:

> Psychiatry tends to focus on pathology and healing of illness; social work concentrates on strengths and the development of potential. The psychiatrist is particularly interested in the internal dynamic of individual and group behavior. The social worker is especially concerned about social functioning involving community factors and interactions.[8]

Psychiatrists are trained in medicine. Having completed all the requirements of medical school and an internship, a physician can then serve a residency to qualify as a psychiatrist. Psychiatrists are trained to understand the dynamics of family life, personality development, and human functioning, but their treatments focus on illness and are based on the medical model. Psychiatrists have traditionally been the only mental health professionals who can prescribe medication or administer electroconvulsive therapy (ECT). However, in some states nurse practitioners are being sanctioned to prescribe limited psychiatric medication.

If both a psychiatrist and a social worker are dealing with a chronically mentally ill patient, the psychiatrist is likely to prescribe and monitor medications. The social worker provides tangible resources—adequate housing can be just as essential to individual functioning as proper medication. The social worker and psychiatrist could each provide therapy, and they may find

In the school setting, social workers work with a variety of professionals.

it beneficial to do this jointly. The social worker is likely to use more socially oriented types of treatment and assess the problem differently, focusing on problems and strengths in human relationships. The social worker analyzes how the social environment is contributing to the mental illness and attempts to determine how it could be altered to support healthy behavior. The social worker would be expected to have a more comprehensive knowledge of community resources and would be in charge of discharge planning when appropriate.

The psychiatrist concentrates more on the identified patient than on the client's larger social network. The psychiatrist is more likely to be concerned with neurotransmitter dysfunctions, while the social worker is more likely to operate on a behavioral level. The psychiatrist's role as a physician is that of healer; the social worker's role is a combination of enabler, resource developer, case manager, and advocate.

All fifty states protect psychiatrists' professional domain by requiring licensing. Only thirty-five states register or license social workers; regulation within social work flows primarily from the national organization (NASW) and professional values and norms.

Psychiatrists are more likely to be paid on a fee-for-service basis and to receive third party payments. Some social workers are increasingly being paid by third party payments, but their practices tend to be limited to psychotherapy rather than the full range of social work services. While most psychiatrists are in private practice, most social workers are employed within public agencies and receive a salary. Because of psychiatry's association with medicine, the relationship between the service provider and seeker is frequently viewed as a doctor-patient relationship. Rather than seeing patients, social workers are more likely to see clients. The term *client* implies more power and choice for the person receiving the service.

PSYCHOLOGISTS AND SOCIAL WORKERS

Very closely related to the field of psychiatry is clinical psychology. Clinical psychologists may engage in some of the same tasks as psychiatrists or social workers. All engage in some form of psychotherapy, but each profession has a different emphasis. The psychologist draws on psychological theories of human behavior rather than the medical model of the psychiatrist. Both psychiatrists and psychologists concentrate on understanding the individual psyche. Clinical psychologists use the individual psyche as their frame of reference for therapy; experimental psychologists engage in research to increase our understanding of the human psyche. The field of psychology has developed a considerable array of psychological tests to help understand and predict human behavior, and psychologists in general are likely to have expertise in psychological testing. Because the profession places considerable credence in the potential contributions of psychological testing, psychologists are usually trained to administer and interpret such tests. Psychological testing is also an integral part of public and private insurance reimbursement requirements.

Psychologists are more likely to be licensed than social workers.

Psychologists are required to be licensed, although the monopolistic components are not developed to the same degree as in the medical profession. Psychologists work in both private practice and public agencies. Psychologists in private practice tend to have doctorates; psychologists with less academic preparation usually work under the supervision of a doctorally trained psychologist. Psychologists in school systems and state agencies, for instance, are not required to complete the doctorate or be licensed. Psychologists ordinarily assume the role of therapist, and their view of the patient's role tends to parallel the psychiatrist's more closely than the social worker's. However, the patient's role may differ, depending upon which type of psychotherapy is chosen.

COUNSELORS AND SOCIAL WORKERS

Counselors also have areas of overlap with psychologists, psychiatrists, and social workers. Like social workers, most counselors are not licensed by the state. Both psychologists and psychiatrists have their professions regulated by licensure. One advantage of licensing from an academic perspective is that it helps define the boundaries of the profession; psychiatrists and psychologists have not only professional but also legal guidelines that determine the appropriate domain of practice.

Counselors may have very specific roles, depending upon the agencies they serve.

There are many types of counselors. The most common types are marriage and family, employment, school, and rehabilitation counselors; social workers too have been involved in each of these areas. Marriage and family counseling, for example, is not a separate profession, but rather a specialization pursued by psychiatrists, psychologists, and social workers. Few graduate programs prepare marriage counselors who do not have a degree in one of the other professional fields. The American Association of Family and Marriage Counselors has members from all of these disciplines.

Social workers are often confused with school counselors. Ordinarily the school counselor has an undergraduate degree in education, at least some teaching experience, and a graduate degree in counseling. More affluent schools often require students to see a counselor who helps them plan their course schedules and careers. These are usually brief encounters, and it is not unusual for students to visit various school counselors interchangeably. In contrast, students who see a school social worker have usually been sent because their behavior (in the classroom or in the community) has been defined as problematic. The relationship between social worker and student tends to be more extensive and change-oriented. Students voluntarily approach a counselor for information; students are usually required to see a social worker based on something they have done or failed to do.

Employment and rehabilitation counselors ordinarily have at least some training in common. They are qualified to administer and interpret certain aptitude tests; they know what employment suits the individual's capabilities. The rehabilitation counselor usually has additional training in the special needs and abilities of handicapped people. Both employment and rehabilitation counselors have specific training the social worker is unlikely to have, and the social worker frequently works with these professionals to determine clients' academic or employment potential. The social worker then helps activate the resources necessary to allow clients to meet their potential. For example, a social worker may have to work with clients' families to help them get the necessary resources or adjust to allowing their children to risk themselves in the educational or occupational world outside the home.

ATTORNEYS AND SOCIAL WORKERS

Attorneys and social workers frequently work with the same clients, either as members of the same team or as adversaries. The role of attorneys in the legal setting is clear: they act as advocates for their clients' legal defense. They are obliged to advise the clients what they believe is in the clients' best interest, but clients make their own decisions. Legal clients, in theory, have more power in the professional–client relationship than clients of other human service professionals.

Legal practice, like social work practice, is undergoing changes. Attorneys have traditionally been involved in private practice, but more and more are now finding employment in public programs, where they almost always receive a salary rather than a fee for service. Clients of attorneys in private practice usually assume the role of consumer; placing attorneys in public settings changes that role. Individuals who hire an attorney have considerable choice (assuming they have the ability to pay). In public programs, clients are more likely to be assigned an attorney. Nonetheless, attorneys in either setting have the same obligation to their clients.

Attorneys must be licensed. Most states require practicing attorneys to complete law school and pass a state bar exam. Many states also require continuing education credits to retain the license to practice.

Attorneys and social workers may both serve as advocates for clients.

Both attorneys and social workers may work as advocates, but how each profession defines advocacy points up some important differences. The mandate to legal advocates is clear—attorneys must use every means within the legal system to promote and defend their client's position. The responsibility of social work advocates has traditionally been ambiguous. Historically, it was assumed that social work advocates were limited by their responsibility to balance the best interests of society and the client.

SUMMARY

The material presented in this chapter is summarized in Table 1–1.

In this chapter we have assumed that you are considering a social work career or a career in which you will be required to work closely with social workers. For this reason we tried to clarify how the human service professions are similar and how they are different. To do this we focused on differences in emphasis, unique expertise, frame of reference, regulation, educational preparation required, source of sanction, professional goals, and roles.

We feel very strongly that it is in the best interests of both the profession and the clients we serve that students enter the field of social work understanding its potential. To us, social work represents a practical, down-to-earth, problem-solving approach. Social workers must be flexible and willing to do the mundane tasks essential to successful treatment of our client population.

We are concerned about the danger of emphasizing narrow treatment issues to the exclusion of broader existential concerns. As the profession becomes more concerned with third party payments and professional status, we are concerned that social work not drift away from its traditional practical roots to a preoccupation with therapeutic matters that neglects vital, practical client needs. As social workers, we assist clients with tasks of daily living, such as budgeting money, buying clothes and food, maintaining personal hygiene, taking medications, keeping appointments, and finding apartments. We must develop the skill and willingness to connect clients with basic resources and to lobby for such resources when they do not exist.[9] Given the current political, social, and economic conditions, this social work function is more crucial than ever.

TABLE 1-1
A Comparative View of Professions

	Social Worker	Attorney	Psychiatrist	Psychologist	Counselor
Emphasis	Totality of problem	Legal defense	Internal functioning	Psychological adjustment	Education or employment
Unique Expertise	Social environment and resource development	Law; legal representation	Electroshock therapy and pharmacotherapy	Psychological testing	Aptitude testing
Frame of Reference	Psychosocial Political/economic	Statutes/Constitution	Medical model	Psychological theory	Educational psychology
Regulation	35 states licensed; 27 regulated by profession	Licensed	Licensed	Licensed	Unregulated
Education	BSW, MSW, PhD	Doctor of jurisprudence (JD)	Doctor of medicine (MD) and residency	Primarily PhD	BS or BA in various disciplines
Sanction	Salaried public employee (approximately 90 percent)	Primarily private practice (fee for service)	Primarily private practice (fee for service)	Either private practice or salaried public employee	Salaried public employee
Professional Goal	Client empowerment	Legal protection	Cure of (mental) disease	Coping with adjustment	Self support
Professional Role	Enabler, counselor, advocate, broker; resource linkage	Pure advocate	Healer	Therapist	Advice giver
Client Role	Client—limited power or choice	Consumer—considerable power and choice	Patient—limited power	Patient—limited power	Advice seeker

One of the methods we use in this book to make the material more understandable is to present the conceptual material in application form. In this chapter we have chosen to do this by comparing attorneys' and social workers' ethics, roles, and expertise in actual practice. What may seem very clear-cut when first presented becomes much more complex in practice. The following example introduces the value conflict that social workers face in a legal setting. First, we address the debate over whether the best interests of society prevail over advocacy for the client. We compare and contrast the legal profession with social work to illustrate the points made in this chapter. (This issue is discussed further in a recent issue of *Social Work.*[10])

This example also gives you some background to help you apply the material in Chapter 2, where we discuss the social work frame of reference and the uniqueness of social work practice.

CASE STUDY
Social Work in the Legal Setting

Social workers in legal settings receive conflicting messages about what constitutes ethical practice. To clarify the issues surrounding this debate is to answer the most basic questions of all: Does social work have a unique expertise and frame of reference, or is our expertise and role dictated by the agency in which we work? Do our identity and ethics change when we are not the primary professional within the agency? Are we guided by a different knowledge and value base in a legal setting than in a mental health setting?

There are very different and conflicting interpretations of the proper role for social work. Some believe that the only ethical approach is what we define as a "best interests" approach, while others think that "pure advocacy" is the proper approach. Practitioners from both ends of this continuum believe their practice directly embodies the profession's code of ethics.

BEST INTERESTS

The following statement by Compton reflects the "best interests" view.

> Advocacy in social work differs from that found in law in that the social worker is often involved in protecting people from actions of their clients.

Thus, the worker does not become an advocate for the client in situations in which doing so could result in hurt to others. The attorney stands for the client; the social worker stands between the client and other social systems and must be concerned with the totality of the situation.[11]

Proponents of this position view social workers as professionals who as such have a unique expertise and a value base that is neither dictated nor compromised by the setting in which practice takes place, but rather emanates from the norms, values, and code of ethics of the profession.

ADVOCACY

Another view of the social work role is reflected in the "pure advocate" approach. This stance has been taken by some social workers involved in the court system. Reflecting this view, Dickson suggests that if social workers are to be effective in the legal setting they must be "prepared to disregard loyalties to agency goals, social work theory, and ideologies that run counter to the client's goals."[12] In a similar vein, Miller sees the social worker as an equalizer for the client in dealing with agencies and others who control resources.

The sanction of the advocate to act must come from the person whose position s/he is advancing. The advocate must be accountable solely to the client; s/he cannot and should not take a position without the informed consent or authorization of the client. The ability of the social worker to be a client advocate is shaped by the nature of his/her employment. The worker in a setting where there are conflicting sanctions or interests cannot be a true advocate. . . . The advocate needs autonomy from constraint, pressures or responsibilities to any person or authority other than the client.[13]

Joseph Senna found that social workers in a public defender's office face conflicts of interest and professional ethics. For example, the attorney's goal is to win the case; the social worker's goal is to evaluate the offender's behavior. While the advocacy view seems to imply that the social worker must help the client "beat the rap" or at least get the lightest sentence possible, Senna found that the real situation is more complex. Social workers felt that the goals of their agency determined the direction and content of the evaluation, yet they also felt that social workers must exercise independent judgment. Their primary concern was to maintain integrity while at the same time using their professional skills competently. This introduced a strong potential for going against the interests of the client, the attorney, or the agency.[14]

Since the pure advocacy position is less familiar and questions many assumptions basic to the social work profession, the issues underlying this position need to be addressed. To understand the pure advocacy position, however, it is necessary to understand the legal system—a purely adversary system in which there are always at least two sides: a plaintiff or petitioner, and a defendant or respondant. One of the most fundamental tenets of this system is that every person is entitled to legal representation, "and to have his conduct judged and regulated in accordance with the law, to seek any lawful objective through legally permissible means, and to present for adjudication any lawful claim, issue or defense."[15] If the attorney does not exercise every legitimate effort in his client's behalf, then he is betraying a sacred trust.

According to their professional code of ethics, social workers are obligated to be advocates, but two major factors limit social workers as advocates.

First, social workers generally lack the orientation and technical skills necessary to be effective advocates. Secondly, social workers are often employees of agencies and organizations that do not support advocacy. The pure advocate stance suggests that social workers practicing within the legal system must not only fulfill their obligation to be advocates, but must also overcome the two major factors that act as constraints to advocacy. Social workers must gain the orientation and technical competence needed to become effective advocates and must work to encourage the legal system itself to support the advocacy effort.

From this perspective, then, the social work advocate can benefit both social work and the legal profession. New avenues of practice will be opened for the social work profession, and social workers will be better equipped to meet their obligation to become advocates. For the legal profession, social workers can perform valuable services for which they have more training and experience than attorneys. For example, social workers generally have more training and expertise in interviewing and accessing community resources than do attorneys—an expertise that would be valuable to legal programs and attorneys practicing criminal law or family law. By gaining technical competence in legal areas, social workers may very well expand their advocate role.

Without a thorough understanding of the legal system, the advocacy approach may at first appear antithetical to that of other human service agencies and organizations where social workers are traditionally employed. In most settings social workers seek to improve the functioning of clients; regardless of their practice approach, social workers always seek to promote the best interests of the client and society.

When an attorney makes a decision about a legal matter, she must always act in the best interest of the client. However, the decision to follow a particular course of action has to be the client's. If the attorney feels the client's choice is not in the client's best interest, the attorney must inform the client and may request him to forgo such action, but ultimately the decision rests with the client. The attorney or lay advocate represents the client and the client's position regardless of the advocate's personal or professional opinion of the client's best interest.

For example, an attorney may feel it is in the best interest of a client charged with a criminal offense to enter into a plea bargain and may advise the client that there is little probability of prevailing if the case goes to trial. If the client pleads guilty to a lesser charge, he might be placed on probation rather than incarcerated. If convicted of the charges originally brought against him, the client could face several years in prison. The attorney has a duty to inform the client of the options and possible ramifications of each option and to advise the client accordingly. If the client still insists on going to trial after having been advised, however, the attorney must comply with the client's desire even if it works against what the lawyer believes are the best interests of the client.

Social workers rarely participate in actual litigation of a case. Their role is usually limited to the preparation, submission, and/or presentation of a presentence or other court report. From the pure advocacy perspective, irrespective of any mandates social workers might have from the social work profession, they are nevertheless employees of the attorney or other legal services provider. As such, they are an extension of the attorney or provider and must comply with the attorney's code of ethics. In addition to the assumption that the attorney will abide by the client's decision, there is the assumption that support staff within the agency will also act in accordance with the client's judgment. Moreover, the attorney is required by the *Code of Professional Responsibility* to exercise due diligence and control over his employees to prevent them from disclosing confidences or acting in a manner inconsistent with the client's wishes. The attorney is responsible for the actions of employees perceived as extensions of the attorney, and thereby subject to his code of ethics. Given the very nature of the legal system, the conflict involves not so much the social workers' choice of ethics, but rather their choice of employment.

Because of the relationship between employer and employee, social workers could very easily be placed in a position of making some difficult ethical choices. For example, the social worker in a public defender's office preparing a presentence report may believe that the client would benefit from mental health services. Bringing this to the court's attention may put constraints on the client's freedom, and the social worker knows that as an employee, he is expected to prepare a report in the light most favorable to the client. Should he prepare a favorable report, or inform the court of what he feels is in the client's best interest or the best interests of the client's family? However, even this kind of conflict is not irreconcilable.

In the legal or adversary system, each party presents its side in the most favorable light. It is not within the attorney/advocate's purview to embark upon a course of action she sees as in the client's best interests except in the purely legal sense. Determining a client's best interests is, after all, no more than a subjective opinion. It is the court's and the jury's responsibility to determine which side will prevail and what is in the best interests of the plaintiff, the defendant, and society. The social worker in a legal setting need not concern herself with deciding what is in the best interest of the client, because this is the exclusive jurisdiction of the court. In more traditional human services settings, the social worker may act as judge and jury. For instance, in juvenile services a social worker may determine whether the child or the family is the problem and what type of services should be brought to bear in the best interests of the child. Social workers (as well as the social work profession as a whole) must develop a basic trust in the legal system so they can relinquish this territory and eliminate potential conflicts of ethics.

The role of social workers acting as pure advocates raises several questions. Can the social worker legitimately stay in the advocate role in situations that require professional judgment? Can a social worker be an expert and an advocate simultaneously? Is it appropriate for a professional practitioner to serve the exclusive interest of the client while acting as a professional consultant? What are the limits of the pure advocacy role in the legal setting? How do professional concerns for the client's total environment and particularly for individuals in the client's immediate environment limit the social worker's role?

NOTES

1. D. Brieland, L. Costin, and C. Atherton, *Contemporary Social Work,* 2nd ed. (New York: McGraw-Hill, 1980), 13.
2. S. Davis, " 'Soft' Versus 'Hard' Social Work," *Social Work* 33, 4 (July–August 1988): 373.
3. J. Rappaport, "Studies in Empowerment," *Prevention in Human Services* 3, 1: 3.
4. B. Solomon, "Social Work with Afro-Americans," in *Social Work: A Profession of Many Faces,* 3rd ed. (Boston: Allyn & Bacon, 1983), 425–426.
5. R. J. Parsons, S. H. Hernandez, and J. D. Jorgensen, "Integrated Practice: A Framework for Problem Solving," *Social Work* 33, 5 (September–October 1988): 417–421.
6. *Guidelines for the Selection and Use of Social Workers* (New York: NASW, 1981), 2.
7. R. Skidmore and M. G. Thackeray, *Introduction to Social Work,* 3rd ed. (Englewood Cliffs, N.J.: Prentice-Hall, 1982), 14.
8. *Ibid.,* 16.
9. Davis, "Soft vs. Hard," 374.
10. See J. Ashford, M. Macht, and M. Mylym, "Advocacy by Social Workers in the Public Defender's Office," *Social Work* 32, 3 (May–June 1987): 199–204. A version of this paper was also presented at the Council on Social Work Education annual program meeting, Detroit, Michigan, 1984.
11. Beulah Compton, *Introduction to Social Welfare and Social Work* (Homewood, Ill.: Dorsey Press, 1980), 119.
12. Donald T. Dickson, "Law in Social Work: Impact of Due Process," *Social Work* 21, 4 (July 1976): 274–278.
13. Jill Miller, "The Social Worker as Client Advocate," presented at the Council on Social Work Education annual program meeting, Los Angeles, California, March, 1980.
14. Joseph Senna, "Social Workers in Public Defender Programs," *Social Work* 21, 4 (July 1975): 271–277.
15. *The Code of Professional Responsibility and Code of Judicial Conduct* (Chicago: The American Bar Association, 1977), 32.

Chapter

2

Understanding Social Work

INTRODUCTION TO SOCIAL WORK:
"A course designed to instruct the social worker who is interested in going out in the field. Topics include: how to organize street gangs into basketball teams and vice versa; playgrounds as a means of preventing juvenile crime; and how to get potentially homicidal cases to try the sliding pond; discrimination; the broken home; what to do if you are hit with a bicycle chain."[1]

I n this chapter we take a slightly more serious approach to defining social work than Woody Allen did in the quote from *Getting Even* that opens the chapter. We draw upon widely accepted definitions of the profession, expand on what we identified in Chapter 1 as the social work frame of reference, and discuss social work roles.

WHAT IS SOCIAL WORK PRACTICE?

In the early 1900s Jeffrey Brackett, a Charity Organization Society volunteer and first director of Simmons College of Social Work, successfully argued for adopting the term *social work: social* to describe the profession's concern with social forces that shape people's lives; *work* to differentiate between the "ladies bountiful" who went "slumming" as recreational activity and professionals whose activities were orderly, responsible, and disciplined.[2]

Social work practice describes what social workers do, that is, how they apply professional knowledge and skills to problem situations they encounter. Traditionally, social work practice has been broken down into three methodologies: casework, group work, and community organization. More recently, the profession has come to recognize the similarities between these methodologies and has tended to see generalist practice as the social work method.

Methodology is discussed in more detail in Chapter 3.

19

TABLE 2–1
Comparison of Direct and Indirect Services

Field of Practice	Direct Service	Indirect Service
Corrections	Institution social worker	Public Defender Board
Child Welfare	Protective Services worker	Social work supervisor
Health	Family planning counselor	Nursing home administrator
Mental Health	Therapist	Director, Mental Health Board
Gerontology	Nursing home social worker	Area agency administrator

Another way practice has been described is in terms of direct and indirect practice. In *direct practice,* social workers help individuals cope with difficulties they encounter in everyday life: losing a job, marital conflict, divorce, problems in disciplining their children, fear of failure, lack of self-esteem, lack of resources such as gas for heating, or conflict with neighbors. The direct services they provide may include therapy, counseling, education, advocacy, information, referral, or resource development.[3]

These same problems are also met by social workers involved in *indirect practice.* Indirect practice occurs when social workers are involved in the "big picture" — policymaking at the community, state, or nationwide level, for example. Indirect service can also be program planning, development, and evaluation. Probably the most common indirect practice of all is administration of agencies and programs. Table 2–1 compares direct and indirect services in different fields of practice.

Because there are many diverse areas of social work practice, it is not surprising that we have many definitions of social work. Each definition is slightly different, yet there is clearly agreement that social work occurs at the interface between people and their environment and that it involves goal-oriented change.[4]

Defining Social Work

Defining social work requires identifying the goals and boundaries of social work practice. Goals provide meaning for the actions that social workers undertake. You can see how the activities, boundaries, and goals of practice are implied in each of the following definitions:

Social functioning refers to any biological, psychological, or sociocultural response pattern that results from the interactions between individuals and their environment.

Social work seeks to enhance the social functioning of individuals, singularly and in groups, by activities focused upon their social relationships which constitute interaction between individuals and their environments. These activities can be grouped into three functions: restoration of impaired capacity, provision of individual and social resources, and prevention of social dysfunction.[5]

Social work is the professional activity of helping individuals, groups, or communities enhance or restore their capacity for social functioning and creating societal conditions favorable to that goal.[6]

Social work practice (is) a goal-oriented planned change process.[7]

Social work is concerned and involved with the interactions between people and the institutions of society that affect the ability of people to accomplish life tasks, realize aspirations and values, and alleviate distress. These interactions between people and social institutions occur within the context of the larger social good.[8]

In these definitions, we see consensus that the goal of social work practice is to strengthen the ability of people to cope with the tasks and problems they face. A second goal, which supports the first, is to promote improvements in the social environment that enable people to meet their everyday needs. If people cannot meet the demands of their environment, then planned, purposeful intervention aimed at individual and social change is indicated.

Social functioning is a match between the needs and abilities of the individual and the opportunities and demands of the environment.

When we use the term *social functioning,* we imply that there is a match between the needs and abilities of the individual and the opportunities and demands of the environment. Whenever a gap between needs and opportunities surfaces, social workers are uniquely equipped with the knowledge and skills to intervene. Enhancing social functioning is one of the primary functions of social work practice.

SOCIAL WORK FUNCTIONS

A component is functional to a system if it enhances the functioning of the system.

Function is defined as "the kind of action or activity proper to any person or thing; the purpose for which something is designed or exists."[9] In this sense social work is a component of the broader social structure; the wider society sanctions social work to perform certain tasks that will be functional, that is, that will contribute positively to the functioning of society.

A recent text summarized the purpose of social work in the following way:

The purpose of social work is to provide services directly to individuals, families, households, and groups to help them cope with unchangeable social problems, reduce or eliminate those problems that can be changed, or experience growth in those areas where enhancement of social functioning is desired. Of equal importance is the activity of the social worker to influence groups, organizations, communities, and even society to provide helpful social programs and create an environment that is conducive to satisfying and productive lives for all people.[10]

These two functions, often attributed to social work—promoting the personal and collective achievement of life potential and problem solving—are important but very general descriptions of social work functions. Pincus and Minahan have differentiated seven major functions of social workers that develop in more detail how these broad functions are met. They suggest that social work activities perform one or more of these social functions.

Coping capacity refers to the ability to use mental processes or behaviors to avoid or relieve pain.[12]

A resource system might be a mental health clinic, an employer, a welfare office, a landlord, etc.

Social control functions are discussed in Chapter 18.

1. Help people enhance and more effectively utilize their own problem-solving and coping capacities.

2. Establish initial linkages between people and resource systems.

3. Facilitate interaction and modify and build new relationships between people and societal resource systems.

4. Facilitate interaction and modify and build relationships between people within resource systems.

5. Contribute to the development and modification of social policy.

6. Dispense material resources.

7. Serve as agents of social control.[11]

Each of these social functions assigned to social work is pursued within a unique perspective, or frame of reference, that guides social work practice.

FRAME OF REFERENCE

In Chapter 1 we discussed how the different professions are each guided by a unique frame of reference.

The frame of reference refers to the guiding principles that provide the social work professional with a unique approach to problem analysis and intervention. These guiding principles are:

1. The private troubles of people in social situations are related to the public issues which bear on them.[13]

2. General systems theory will guide the problem analysis.[14]

3. People will be seen in interaction with their environmental resource system.[15]

The next three sections examine these principles in detail.

Each time a social worker begins a problem assessment, she will be guided by these principles. However, there is considerable variance in the emphasis placed on the cause of the problem and therefore the particular intervention chosen to solve the problem. Some social workers see past personal experience and individual characteristics as the major variables that determine how people function in their present situation. They will assess problems very differently from the social worker who emphasizes the importance of structural and institutional barriers to adequate functioning. Both types of practitioner will draw from a broad knowledge base, but their difference in perspective will lead to different interventions. These differences will affect problem definition, identified goals, the structure of the worker–client relationship, and the tasks and activities to be undertaken.

To illustrate the differences, we can look at two different approaches to a problem in marital conflict. One social worker, operating from a more individually oriented view, might work with the family to improve communication patterns. Another social worker may see inherent problems with the expectations individuals have of the institution of marriage. This social worker will help the couple analyze the marriage itself: What needs can realistically be met in the relationship? How can more reasonable goals be set by both individuals? It may be functional for society to assign a wide variety of tasks to the family; however, some of these are unrealistic for many couples. Such couples need to learn realistic expectations. In this approach, even though the social worker is working with individuals, the locus of the problem is in the expectations society has placed on the married couple, which led them to experience marital problems. In the first approach, the worker assumed that marriage as defined by society is not problematic—the problem was in the way the individuals related to each other.

This example illustrates the first guiding principle—the relationship between private troubles and public issues. There is a long history of debate within the profession on whether to focus on private troubles or public issues.

PRIVATE TROUBLES AND PUBLIC ISSUES

C. Wright Mills suggested the private troubles/public issues dichotomy.[16] He identified *troubles* as those difficulties occurring within the character of the individual and within the range of immediate relations with others. He saw as *issues* those difficulties that go beyond the individual and reflect society as a whole and the ways its various institutions interact and overlap.

Historically, social work has been concerned with difficulties people have within their social situations.[17] Whether we view these difficulties as private troubles or public issues changes depending on the dominant ideology, the stage of knowledge development, and the resources available.

Ideology is the values held by the most powerful group in a society. Chapter 4 discusses the impact of ideology on practice.

Unemployment, for example, represents both a private trouble and a public issue. To the individual and her family, day-to-day problems (inadequacies in food, shelter, transportation, and health care) add to the psychological stress of unemployment. The pressure to provide, combined with little or no opportunity to do so, may lead to emotional difficulties within individuals as well as strained relationships within the family. As long as few individuals are unemployed, unemployment is a private trouble. When societal resources are available to solve the problem of joblessness, the intervention is logically limited to solving personal problems.

However, unemployment may be a public issue too, particularly when the private sector does not provide enough jobs to support the work force. Our present economic system functions properly only when approximately 7 percent of the work force is unemployed. But when 7 percent of the popu-

Is elderly poverty a private trouble or a public issue?

Social integration refers to the process by which individuals come to value their membership in a society and to feel responsible for abiding by its rules.

lation has no means of support, unemployment becomes a public issue—not only because individual families are suffering but also because the entire system is jeopardized by the alienation and frustration of the unemployed. Complex public issues such as unemployment require a societal response. The fabric of social integration essential to social functioning can break down unless the government or some sector of society responds to needs not being met in the marketplace.

During the Great Depression of the 1930s, society responded to this problem by making the federal government an employer. Public programs such as the Works Progress Administration (WPA) employed people to build roads, dams, bridges, and schools. During the 1960s, programs such as AD-VOCAP provided employment for many poor people. ADVOCAP was a locally administered program of the federal War on Poverty that was particularly involved in finding jobs for the poor. ADVOCAP still exists but has only a small percentage of its original funding. Today, government's response to unemployment is to provide incentives to the private sector to create jobs.

When confronted with an unemployed client, the social worker deals directly with the individual's problem but is severely limited by how society has defined the problem and what solutions are available.

Divorce is another difficulty traditionally perceived as a private trouble. But as the divorce rate rises, divorce too is increasingly perceived as a public issue. One of the structural responses we have seen to the problem of divorce is a changing approach to the collection of child support. Divorced parents traditionally had to collect support on their own or petition the court to force the absent parent to contribute. Recently, a number of states have taken on the task of collecting the support, thereby decreasing the number of families not receiving the ordered payments. This is a major change in family policy, based on the changing perception of divorce as a social as well as an individual problem.

Social workers need to be particularly sensitive to the structural causes of problems suffered by oppressed people. When problems are caused by racism, poverty, and prejudice, we can do a great deal of harm by attributing the problem to the individual. Lum suggests that many of the problems that bring minorities to social agencies are systemic problems.[18] Blacks, for instance, are disproportionately unemployed and underemployed. This situation can lead to personal as well as economic problems. The relatively high level of depression among black men is likely related to the greater stress they experience. Recognizing the systemic link to the individual problem is crucial. The depression of black men provides an excellent example of the need to attend to both the public issues and private troubles. Even though it may have a systemic base, the individual depression must be treated.

For social workers, these private trouble/public issue questions are a basic ingredient in all problem assessments. Societal and personal values will also influence the assessment process. A social worker's personal frame of reference will influence whether he sees unemployment as a predictable outcome of a capitalistic society or as a personal problem that can be solved only by changing the individual. Social work is the profession designated by society to deal with these problems by balancing societal and individual needs. Whether the emphasis in the assessment is placed on the individual or on structural causes, neither component can be ignored. In the next section we describe how understanding systems theory can help a social worker make complex assessment and intervention decisions.

GENERAL SYSTEMS THEORY

General systems theory provides a way of analyzing, understanding, and explaining the complex interactions of a system. A system is any unit we wish to analyze—physical, biological, or social. All systems exist within a context that affects them and that they, in turn, affect. A system is both a part and a whole.[19] A family, a neighborhood, and a public welfare department are all systems that social workers will experience. Each of these systems consists of interdependent and interacting parts, together creating a whole greater than the sum of the individual parts. We say systems are *symbiotic* when a change in one part of the system creates changes in the other parts.

To understand the concept of the whole being greater than the sum of the parts and the idea of symbiosis, you might consider your experiences in solving problems. If five people each come up with independent solutions to a difficult organizational problem, they are unlikely to produce either the quality or the quantity of solutions they might have if they had worked together. Hence, the sum of the group's ideas is greater than the sum of all the individuals' solutions. To illustrate the concept of symbiosis, if that same group of five people meets for three weeks and in the fourth week one of the members drops out, roles and tasks within the group will change in response.

Boundaries and Equilibrium

Systems theory provides a clear perspective on the reciprocal influence of primary and secondary reference groups. In other words, it helps us understand the effect individuals, families, groups, and the environment have on one another. Systems theory prods us to take a different view of the individual. People are seen both as individual physical systems and as elements in a larger social system.

Systems theory stresses the importance of boundaries. Since the systems are limitless, it is necessary to determine some limits for what will be considered in assessment and intervention. One variable that determines the boundaries for intervention is the social worker's individual perspective. Although systems theory inclines a person to consider interaction among all systems, it does not preclude emphasizing one system over another, nor does it determine what systems must be included.

We can use the family system as an example of a boundary-maintaining unit. The boundaries must be stable enough to endure, yet partially open to allow interaction with the educational, occupational, and neighborhood systems. When we say that systems must be dynamic and flexible, yet stable enough to endure, we are referring to the idea of maintaining *equilibrium*. A family system must maintain equilibrium to survive. Each time economic or social problems cause stress, new behavior and adaptations must be acquired. Desertion by the family breadwinner may disturb the equilibrium. Equilibrium returns as the roles and functions filled by the absent provider are assumed by remaining family members or outside agencies. Temporary disequilibrium is common enough to be seen as part of the human condition.[20]

When a system maintains equilibrium it remains in balance.

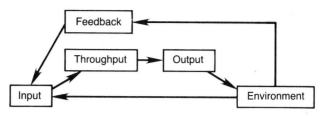

FIGURE 2–1

Feedback

Feedback is another element of systems theory. Systems must receive both positive and negative feedback; accurate feedback gives both warnings and reassurance. Open social systems maintain themselves by a constant flow of energy and information. At its simplest, an open system maintains itself by adapting to changes, moving and growing in harmony with the exchanges and interrelationships of its environment. Systems function in generally predictable ways. The flow chart in Figure 2–1 shows how systems process the energy and information needed to carry out their tasks. To illustrate this interaction, we can look at a child care center. The most important "input" is the children who will attend the center. In addition, there will be staff, physical surroundings, and investors, to name just some of the input variables. The "throughput" is the care the children receive at the center. The "output" will be contented, well-tended children, parents who can function at work, and some profit for the owners. The center's environment will include licensing agencies, neighbors, parents, and funding sources. Each component in this environment will provide feedback to the center. The licensing agency will have input into requirements for original licensing and will then provide ongoing feedback about how the center is fulfilling those requirements. If the feedback mechanisms are adequate, problems will be handled at an early stage and equilibrium will be maintained. If the center does not receive negative feedback or fails to respond, functioning could be disrupted by loss of the operating license. The center also needs to receive feedback from parents to assure a client base. Each significant part of the environment must provide feedback to the center to keep it functioning effectively.

A system such as a day care center works in the loop process. It monitors itself and gains information about changes within and without and in its relationships to other systems in the environment. If the response to the system's activities is positive, growth results. Negative responses encourage change in the system. Feedback modifies the system so it can continue to take in and use the energy needed to move toward its goal.

Throughout the entire process the system must remain in relative balance with itself and other systems in the environment. Since a change in one part of the system in time produces changes in other parts, the better the feedback system the more constant the equilibrium. If a system is too rigid, it may fail to respond to needed changes; if too unstable, chaos may result.

Characteristics of Open Systems

Chapter 10 presents a systems analysis of organizational structure. Bureaucracy is analyzed in some detail.

Open systems have unique structural, behavioral, and functional characteristics. To understand a system we must understand these characteristics. By structural characteristics we mean boundaries, hierarchy, and centralization. We have already discussed the concept of boundaries and their importance. By *hierarchy* we mean the way the system is organized.

If you look at different social service agencies, you might find one that is organized on a bureaucratic model, with each level within the organization clearly identified as administrative, supervisory, or direct practice. In such an agency the direct practice workers would have little or no contact with the administrative staff. Their input would be strictly through their supervisor. In another agency the director might have an open door policy, where any staff member can have direct input to the administrator.

You can also see this characteristic in families. In one family communication from child to parent is always filtered through the other parent. In some families it is unusual for the children to make requests directly to the father; the mother brings requests to the father. In other families the mother is the breadwinner and the father is the primary parent and conduit for family communication. Other families may be structured on wide-open lines of communication. What is seen as good-natured humor between son and father in one family may be treated as insolence in another family.

By *centralization* we are referring to the way a system makes its decisions. Decision-making structures can vary in agencies and families in much the same way that hierarchy does. One agency may have a management team to make decisions; another may have an autocratic director who does not allow significant input into decision making. Some families allow children a great deal of input into goal setting and even financial decisions, while other families limit these decisions strictly to the parents or even just one parent.

Functional Characteristics

Functional characteristics include the communication processes, the division of labor, and adaptive mechanisms. The difference between structural and functional characteristics is not always clear. Structural characteristics refer to the way the system is organized; functional characteristics refer to the actions that maintain the system. For a family or agency to survive, there must be a communication system, some kind of division of labor, and adaptive mechanisms.

We can analyze the functional characteristics of a family faced with caring for a chronically impaired grandparent. Once this individual joins the family unit, the equilibrium of that family is threatened. The workload is considerably increased, freedom of movement on the part of family members is curtailed, and increased financial pressures are experienced. To maintain equilibrium, the communication system must be adequate to allow family members to discuss both their needs and their abilities to deal with this problem. The more efficient the communication system, the more effectively tasks (division of labor) can be assigned on an appropriate basis, and the more likely the family is to adapt positively to the added pressure. Part of the division of labor and adaptive mechanisms might be expanding the family boundaries to receive assistance from neighbors, the church, or social service or health agencies.

Systems in Social Work Practice

The National Resource Center on Family Based Services at the University of Iowa School of Social Work has relied heavily on systems theory to understand family functioning. They suggest that the principles we have presented as basic to systems theory are also basic to working with families. The principles they outline provide one example of how systems theory guides family practice.

The systems theory principles provide a framework in which to assess the problem of a serious juvenile offender. Once a child is arrested for a serious crime, the equilibrium of that family is threatened. The boundaries are redefined as the police, the courts, and the social service agency cross boundaries that are usually held sacred by the family. The goal of the family worker will be to restore balance by identifying and repairing breakdowns in the system's (family's) functioning.

GUIDING PRINCIPLES

A Systems Approach to Family Practice

- The members of a family make up a complex whole, which cannot be adequately understood by understanding its members individually.

- A change in one member of the system encourages all others in emotional contact with that person to make compensatory changes [symbiosis].

- A problem manifested through one family member is viewed as an aspect of a problem in the family system.

- Each family has certain rules which are self-regulating and peculiar to that family. As they develop and operate over time, these rules constitute the family history [structure].

- All systems exhibit an innate tendency toward homeostasis, i.e., systems seek a balanced state. No matter how dysfunctional that state, its equilibrium will resist intervention and change.[21]

Equifinality

A final concept of systems theory important to social work practice is *equifinality*. We have alluded to this concept when we talked about different perspectives leading to different assessments and interventions. Equifinality implies that there is more than one possible interpretation of the nature and cause of the problem and therefore more than one way to achieve the desired outcome. Let us apply the concept of equifinality to the problem of truancy.

Equifinality accounts for differing methods of social work practice.

One social worker may see truancy as a private trouble. After a thorough problem assessment, the worker decides that the problem lies within the teenager. Based on this assessment the worker could set up a behavior modification program. This intervention could lead to a significant decrease in truancy.

Another social worker might take a wider systems approach to the same teenager and decide that the problem lies in the family structure. This social worker might work with the family to improve communication and decision making, and this too might lead to a decrease in truancy. This is what we mean by equifinality—given the same problem, different diagnoses and interventions could be generated. The goal-oriented change process could produce the same results in spite of very different means to that end.

Where Is the Problem?

On another level, systems theory allows diverse goal identification. For example, in analyzing a case of child abuse, one social worker might begin by assuming that difficulties occur because of the way the particular family lives and works. Such an orientation that emphasizes an attempt to change the individual family's pattern is referred to as *systems improvement*.[22] Systems improvement implies that the design (the social structure) of the family system itself is adequate. The social worker's job is to ensure that the family system performs according to expectations. Here, improving the system means looking for the reasons the family has departed from established (and unquestioned) norms.

Systems improvement is related to private troubles.

A contrasting approach suggests that the family's difficulties result from a norm of family structure established by our society. This analysis of abusive parents begins with the assumption that a family's difficulties spring from the societal design of the family system.

The concept of system design is essential to an analysis based on public issues (structural problems).

This model is sometimes applied to black families. During slavery, black families were continually separated, with the father expected to serve only his master. Economic needs were met (however inadequately) by the slave master, not the father. Nurturing their children was impossible for most slave fathers. Others suggest that it was not slavery but industrialization or capitalism that broke down the structure of the black family.

Modern society, however, expects black fathers to nurture and support their families. Yet society is organized in a manner that makes adequate employment exceptionally difficult for black men and women. Such an analysis suggests that systems improvement will not be enough. At minimum, pieces of the system must be redesigned.

In summary, we can say that systems' characteristics and principles can provide social workers with tools of analysis needed for virtually all practice situations by providing a way to organize information about people, their problems, and the interactions taking place within their environments. Systems theory facilitates the understanding necessary for day-to-day social work. By accommodating conflicting approaches, systems theory also accommodates a broad and diverse political base. Until the profession develops a better understanding of the causes of social problems, their resolution is more likely if social workers do not limit inquiry and intervention to one system or theory. Using systems theory as a guiding principle increases our ability to see the complexity of the problem and prevents us from prematurely pinpointing the individual as the cause of the problem.

ENVIRONMENTAL RESOURCE SYSTEM INTERACTION

The target of social work intervention is the whole of social problems, rather than the rehabilitation of victims of social problems alone. Social workers promote the interaction between individuals and the environment for the betterment of both.[23] The importance of the environment to social work practice makes it our third guiding principle of the social work frame of reference.

Environment in social work practice includes all the variables affecting the problem: physical, social, cultural, and interpersonal. Mary Richmond, in the earliest books on social work, stressed the importance of the environment. In *What Is Social Casework* she suggested that caseworkers who have a clear picture of clients' relationships with friends and to work, recreation, neighborhood, community, and country can understand clients' problems better.[24]

The environment was of critical concern to settlement house workers such as Jane Addams, Florence Kelley, and Julia Lathrop, who worked diligently to improve sanitation and health conditions in urban areas. Bertha Capen Reynolds was committed to making the workplace more conducive to a higher quality of life.

The social environment consists of the values, norms, and beliefs that control social interaction and determine how the individual uses and responds to the physical environment. As social workers we are concerned with the adaptive fit between individuals and their environment. People are not merely passive recipients but rather actors in a dynamic and reciprocal relationship with their environment.

Social work practice may take the form of getting individuals to adapt to their environment when appropriate, or to alter their environment when feasible. For instance, once an elderly person has suffered a chronically impairing condition, it becomes necessary for that individual to adjust to reduced mobility. However, that individual can, either alone or with the aid of a social worker, attempt to make the immediate environment more conducive to a higher quality of life. This may involve something as simple as installing handrails or ramps in place of stairs.

While we place strong emphasis on the importance of the environment, we need to keep in mind the concept of boundaries. The environment of a given client can be very large and complex. The social worker needs to limit attention to the aspects of the environment that are relevant to the problem being solved.

Assessment of clients' environments will vary, depending upon their life situations, individual needs, strengths, resources, and opportunities. Hepworth and Larsen have classified basic environmental needs.[25] Drawing from their work, we can develop a list of factors to address.

As social workers we are particularly attuned to the need for social support systems. By this we mean:

1. Attachment to other human beings, which provides a sense of affection, meaning, self-worth, and love.
2. A feeling of integration or belonging, which comes from being part of a group with whom we share interests and values.
3. A feeling of being needed by others, which usually means the opportunity to nurture. This is particularly important for suicidal patients. One can go on in the face of considerable adversity if there is a feeling of having something to offer that someone else needs.
4. A sense that there are people to rely on for help and guidance in resolving problems.

Other basic needs in addition to social support include

1. Access to necessary health, legal, and spiritual care.
2. Access to child care for working parents.
3. Access to recreation activities.
4. Transportation to work, shop, vote, etc.
5. Adequate housing.
6. Adequate police and fire protection.
7. Adequate employment or other financial resources to provide economic security.
8. Opportunities for self-improvement.

The emphasis we have placed here on the environment is not different from what we discussed in systems theory. The environment is just one component of systems theory—but to social workers it is often the crucial component.

Having defined social work and identified the unique frame of reference for social work practice, we now look at the roles social workers assume in practice.

SOCIAL WORK ROLES

The sociological concept of role developed in an attempt to explain how people relate to one another. George Herbert Mead analyzed how the human self grows through social processes and relationships.[26] He stressed that it was not possible to understand people without understanding the social context in which they lived; it was within the social context that certain patterns of behavior were imposed and learned, that attitudes and relationships became fixed and consistent. Now referred to as socialization, the imposition of social patterns on behavior, this powerful process defines expectations in nearly every situation, personal and professional.[27] A role reflects a society's expectations of behavior, attitudes, and values for a particular status or position either acquired by birth or achieved later in life. Age and sex are important determinants of roles. Joseph Anderson defines roles as follows:

> Roles are defined in terms of role expectations. A role has certain privileges, obligations, responsibilities, and powers. When role incumbents put these obligations and responsibilities into effect, they are said to be performing their role. The expectations define what individuals should or should not do so long as they are the incumbent of a particular role.[28]

The mechanism by which socialization proceeds is meaningful interaction and identification with others. Over time identifiable patterns develop that illustrate how social roles involve consistent and reiterated patterns of conduct.[29]

Roles serve many functions in social work practice. Roles provide a comprehensive pattern for both behavior and attitudes and suggest particular strategies for dealing with recurring situations. Roles are defined as quite specific social entities even though they may be played out by any number of different individuals. Social role expectations provide a major means of identifying and placing people within their social context.

Professional roles have changed over time, as has the focus of social work practice. For example, "advocate" is now considered an important role for social workers in addressing certain problems. Prior to the "Great Society" of the 1960s this was not the case; social workers were unlikely to "speak for the client by presenting and arguing the client's cause . . . in . . . the effort to

The socialization process is presented in Chapter 9.

A role is a set of behaviors that are expected of a person in a given situation.

Role expectations are constant, while individual attributes of the person involved are variable.

win for the client."[30] The emphasis on human rights and civil liberties of the 1960s was reflected in this new social work practice role. Social work roles develop and are shaped and recast as the objectives of the profession, the mood of society, and the needs of clients shift.

Role definition is a flexible and fluid process that corresponds with the assignment the profession receives from society to deal with certain social problems and tasks. The individual social worker meets the challenge of these societal assignments through using abilities, skills, and knowledge in relationships with all those involved in the change system. These relationships may be collaborative or conflictual. Specific roles used most frequently in direct practice and stressed in professional education are commonly termed broker, enabler, teacher, mediator, and advocate.[31] Indirect practice incorporates these roles as well as additional roles such as planner, supervisor, policy developer or analyst, and administrator.

As the social worker becomes involved in the social work process the necessity of multiple roles becomes apparent. A frightened client seeking legal satisfaction in a child custody matter may need the social worker to be supportive, encouraging, calm, and reassuring. In dealing with the court, that same social worker may need to take on an adversarial or advocate role to help protect the client's right to make choices and be treated with respect.

Broker

In this role the social worker "serves as a linkage between the client and other community resources."[32] Acting as a broker requires a broad knowledge of the specific community and the operating procedures of the agencies, organizations, or services that may be needed. Like a real estate agent or stock broker, the social worker attempts to make connections and make things happen in an attempt to assist the client in achieving goals. Because parts of the social service system are complex and unresponsive, some people will not be able to navigate the process successfully. While assisting clients to find needed resources may not carry the prestige of doing psychotherapy, it is frequently the most important service a social worker can provide. Some examples of brokering might include finding a shelter for a battered woman, helping someone negotiate the paperwork process to receive public assistance, or helping a family find respite care for a chronically impaired person.

The broker role may also include "case management" of a client's situation.

Advocate

Advocacy is a concept borrowed from the legal profession, but it has taken on unique characteristics in social work. The legal advocate and the social work advocate roles are not equivalent. The legal advocate must be guided by the client's wishes. The social work advocate must be guided by the client's

The advocate role assumes very direct efforts on the part of the social worker.

wishes but limited by the best interests of society.[33] As an advocate the social worker becomes the speaker for the client, presenting and arguing the client's cause when necessary. In this partisan representation of the client the goal is to win. The client system, of whatever size, may not in fact be directly involved. For instance, social workers may work with attorneys to bring a class action suit to benefit clients. They may also lobby legislators on behalf of their client. The key to using this role is a firm and clear contract with the client. The terms and limits of the advocacy effort must be explicit and clearly understood.

Enabler

See the case study at the end of this chapter for a look at the social worker as enabler.

Rogerian theory is discussed in Chapter 11.

Enabler is the role most frequently associated with the social work profession. An enabler is one who assists clients to find strengths and resources within themselves to produce whatever changes may be needed or to accomplish the goals desired.[34] The social worker as enabler has the responsibility to facilitate change in a given situation by offering encouragement, support, and reassurance. This role incorporates many assumptions of Rogerian theory and is frequently utilized in dealing with individual problems. In this role the social worker enables the client to change or achieve the desired goal by concentrating on the client's own strengths and abilities and helping the client to apply them to the specific problem situation. The client is primarily responsible and the "responsibility of the worker is to facilitate or enable the client's accomplishment of a defined change."[35] Whether the source of the problem is identified as the individual or the environment, the worker helps the client find the inner strength to alter her own behavior or, if possible, the environment.

Teacher

One technique used by the social worker as teacher is role-playing, or behavioral rehearsal. Chapter 11 describes behavioral techniques.

The teaching role is similar to the enabling role, since it is directed toward strengthening the client's ability to effect change in the problem situation. The teaching role involves introducing additional information and resources into the situation. Education has long been seen in our society as a way of improving social position; it can also be a way for a client to learn how to overcome a difficult situation. Teaching can involve skills such as communication or parent effectiveness training; it can involve teaching clients and client groups how to become politically effective. Numerous situations can be improved by teaching clients new knowledge and skills.

Mediator

The social worker in the role of mediator will use techniques to try to bring about a convergence of the perceived values of both parties to the conflict, help each party recognize the legitimacy of the others' interests, assist the parties in identifying their common interests in a successful outcome, avoid a situation in which issues of winning and losing are paramount, break the conflict down to separate issues, and help parties identify that they have more at stake in continuing a relationship than the issue of the specific conflict.[36]

As a mediator, the social worker acts to reconcile differences and to intervene between conflicting parties in order to promote reconciliation, settlement, or compromise. Conflict may occur in many arenas in which social work is involved; it might be a dispute between natural parents and foster parents, between parents and children, between teachers and parents, or between separated husbands and wives (divorce mediation is a recently developed specialty within social work). Whatever the arena, the social worker strives to resolve disputes.

SUMMARY

This chapter has presented various definitions of social work practice commonly found in the literature. In each of these definitions we found consensus that the goal of social work is to strengthen people's ability to cope with the tasks and problems they face in life and to promote improvements in the environment. We further stressed the importance of the goal of social work by discussing the functions of the profession.

The second portion of this chapter identified the unique perspective or frame of reference that guides social work practice. We pointed out that whatever specific model of practice or theories about individuals, groups, and families a social worker uses, all social workers will be guided by three principles:

1. an understanding of the relationship between private troubles and public issues
2. a systemic approach to problem assessment and intervention
3. an understanding of the interface of the individual and the environmental resource system

Among the many important concepts of systems theory, we discussed the concept of equifinality, which suggests that there is more than one method to achieve an outcome. This concept is particularly important because we will be introducing you to a variety of methods and models of practice. Our goal is to provide you with what is known about social work practice and at the same time to encourage you to see the unexplored potential of the field. Social work is a young and developing field in which there is considerable room for individuals to contribute to the expanding knowledge base.

In the final section of this chapter we discussed social work roles—the specific set of behaviors expected of social work practitioners.

This chapter has covered some of the most basic elements of social work. It should prepare you to understand why generalist practice fits with the social work frame of reference, to recognize the importance of personal and professional values and how they are shaped by the dominant ideology, to appreciate the roles of the professional association, to recognize the evolution of practice through history, to motivate you to obtain the social work knowledge base, and to examine the various fields of social work practice.

Once again, a case study illustrates the concepts discussed in this chapter. The case study was chosen to show that social work is a process that follows certain steps. Although the steps overlap considerably and the flow is not always straightforward, there must be a guiding framework to follow, which we call the problem-solving or social work process.

The case study is an example of indirect practice, as the social worker is developing a program and resources rather than providing individual service. The function of the social worker is program development that will help the impaired elderly make more effective use of their own problem-solving capacities to cope with chronic illness.

Chronic illness in this scenario is seen as a public issue. It is part of the normal aging process, and the community is seen as the appropriate level of intervention. The private troubles of many families may also be alleviated by this program. Social workers in direct practice make referrals to such programs.

A systems approach is a prerequisite to success. There is already a network providing services to the elderly. People must see this program as important, potentially effective, and able to fill a gap in the present service delivery system. Boundaries of other agencies must be recognized or resistance will sabotage this program. Feedback must be continuous to keep receiving the necessary input of referrals and resources.

The program must maintain an open systems approach. Referrals depend on clear communication of program goals. Other professionals need to know whom to refer to the program. Environmental resources are a key component of program success. Many of the impairing conditions of the chronically impaired elderly cannot be changed, but the environment can be made more responsive to their frailties.

CASE STUDY
Generalist Practice in a Community Setting

The social worker was contacted by the director of the community retirement center to provide program planning consultation. The director felt that the equipment and facilities of his nursing home could and should be made available to chronically impaired in the community who could use some of the services but did not require twenty-four hour care. Since a new program in the community might disrupt interorganizational relationships as its domain developed, the director felt it was important to develop this project with community involvement and commitment. Successful implementation of the program required community support. One way to increase community support was to include the professionals in the aging network in program development. The vehicle to facilitate this ground floor involvement was a needs assessment of the elderly in the community. The contract between the program director and the social worker was to conduct a needs assessment that accurately reflected the community need and was conducive to program development. Practice principles are evident throughout this case.

PROBLEM IDENTIFICATION

Unnecessary institutionalization of the elderly is expensive and may disrupt social relationships vital to the well-being of older persons. It also involves excessive expenditures for construction of facilities, personal maintenance, and staff support. Unnecessary institutionalization also leads to extensive depletion of personal, family, or public funds. Even more important, natural helping systems are disrupted and the emotional health of the individual is adversely affected. The overwhelming preference of the elderly to maintain independent living arrangements, combined with the high cost of nursing homes, makes it imperative to develop programs with the potential of increasing the time the elderly can remain in the community.

GOAL IDENTIFICATION AND SOLUTION SEARCH

The goal of this project was to identify what circumstances force older people to enter long-term institutions prematurely and to develop community commitment to a creative and cost effective alternative to institutionalization. While any one agency can develop a specific program designed to meet the community care objective, it seemed clear that true dependency prevention must be a community project. With this in mind the social worker attempted to discover a solution to the problem. To do so she needed to

1. determine whether a significant number of older persons in the community could remain independent if given restorative, preventive, and/or educational services;

2. determine what services were presently available to avoid duplication and battles over turf;

3. explore the willingness of existing agencies to cooperate in a coordinated effort to promote independence in the older population;

4. explore available knowledge in this subject area.

   In this case available knowledge included the literature, expertise of service providers in the aging network, and three "experts" on aging—three active senior citizens in the community. All agreed that the first step in the intervention plan needed to be a thorough assessment of the need.

DEVELOPMENT OF THE INTERVENTION PLAN

The model of needs assessment was designed to exploit the process to insure implementation of the program developed. An effective needs assessment would play an important role in helping communities face decisions in the distribution of resources, reveal both the extent and severity of need, reveal segments of a population inadvertently missed in the normal course of service delivery, and provide community support and acceptance of programs subsequently developed. Underlying this approach to needs assessment was the assumption that it was one step in the more complex planning process. When viewed in the context of program planning, needs assessment must blend citizen and consumer participation with professional judgment in a manner that stimulates the subsequent steps of coordination and integration of existing community services. The people who judge the results have to be involved in the development of the program—particularly in identifying which needs have the highest priority.

IMPLEMENTATION OF THE INTERVENTION PLAN

Five major steps were essential to successful program implementation: (1) securing a commitment from the community to use the needs assessment data, (2) developing a planning board to include potential clients, professionals, and community representatives, (3) identifying potential funding sources,

(4) selecting the assessment technique most appropriate to the population being assessed and most likely to provide the information required by the funding source, and (5) analyzing the many different types and sources of information simultaneously. Discussion of each of these steps will further clarify the social work process.

Step One: Securing a Commitment to Use the Data

This project began with a very specific purpose. However, if the data collected were of interest only to the program being developed it would have limited importance. In trying to determine broader community needs and priorities, a great deal of data was gathered: 266 different pieces of information from each individual. The advantage of such an exhaustive study was that the individual being interviewed sensed a concern about himself as a whole person instead of just an old person. An obvious disadvantage was the time it took to conduct the interview and the exhaustion of the party interviewed, although the interview technique was structured to prevent fatigue. Further, only data that agencies would actually use were collected. The specific techniques used to secure the commitment of the community were: (1) to set up a coordinating committee that would also serve as a planning board (all agencies that could potentially use the data generated were invited to have a participant on this committee); (2) to have those committee members determine which questions would be useful to their agency (as well as which questions could increase the general body of knowledge pertaining to the elderly); (3) to allow the coordinating committee a chance to respond to three different versions of the questionnaire to confirm that their questions had been included; (4) to allow coordinating committee members to be instrumental in identifying the study population; (5) to forward all requests for service to the county Coordinator of Older Adult Services, who then channeled the requests to the appropriate agency, and (6) to guarantee that participants would receive a copy of the report generated.

Step Two: Developing a Planning Board

Developing a planning board was based on the premise that any community program needs the endorsement of community members and professionals. Even though funding may be provided by an outside source, clients, staff, and physical resources come from the community. Positive evaluation by the community of the sponsoring agency and the programs is necessary, and the proper time to begin getting this endorsement is at the outset. Contributions from planning board members included expertise in program planning, community organization, financial support, public relations, and program knowledge. As community members came to share ownership in the ideas generating the program, they began to take on additional tasks. For example, sometimes in the course of an interview a serious individual need would be identified. Since the interviewers were not in a position to respond to these needs, board members took on the responsibility of finding ways to respond whenever possible. The board was committed to assuring that the needs assessment did not lead to unfulfilled expectations. While not every identified need was met, the existence of the planning board greatly increased the responsiveness.

Step Three: Identifying Funding Sources

The major purpose of the needs assessment was to support the need for a community alternative to institutionalization programs. Therefore, data were needed that could meet the requirements of funding sources and local agencies. This guided the structure of the questionnaire developed.

Step Four: Selecting Assessment Techniques

Discussion with the elderly and the visiting nurses revealed that the elderly would be very threatened by random selection. The decision was made to use a "snowball" sample, with professionals and the older citizens on the planning board identifying potential respondents. These board members would then contact the proposed respondents to reassure them that the questionnaire and the interviewer were nonthreatening. Once initial participants were interviewed, they were asked to refer friends and neighbors to us. This approach paid off because organizers were able to reach many frail elderly who would not have consented to a personal visit or phone call without this prior contact. Semistructured questions were asked by social work students especially trained in interview techniques.

Another method of data collection used was the Nominal Group Technique (NGT) — a structured group exercise to elicit in-depth responses from seven to nine people to a specific question.[37] The Delphi Technique was also used. This has the same purpose as the NGT, but is done anonymously. Individuals are asked to give written responses to a specific question. It is useful for people who cannot come together face to face. Students interested in planning could benefit by familiarity with these techniques.

Step Five: Analyzing and Synthesizing Data

Given the three different types of data collected, synthesis and evaluation were necessary. This evaluation phase addressed the quality of the data collected, but even more important to the program planning process, it documented a need for the proposed program. The program developed because evidence of established need convinced a funding source to support it, professionals to make referrals, and clients to enter the program. This intervention was just one phase of an extensive program planning process.

NOTES

1. Woody Allen, *Getting Even* (New York: Random House, 1966).
2. B. R. Sheafor, C. R. Horejsi, and G. A. Horejsi, *Techniques and Guidelines for Social Work Practice* (Newton, Mass.: Allyn and Bacon, 1988), 11.
3. H. Specht, *New Directions for Social Work Practice* (Englewood Cliffs, N.J.: Prentice-Hall, 1988), 47–48.
4. H. Bartlett, *The Common Base of Social Work Practice* (New York: NASW, 1970), 84–127.
5. Werner Boehm, "The Nature of Social Work," *Social Work* 3, 2 (April 1958): 18.
6. National Association of Social Workers, Standards for Social Service Manpower (Washington, D.C.: NASW, 1973), 4–5.
7. Allan Pincus and Anne Minahan, *Social Work Practice: Model and Method* (Itasca, Ill.: Peacock, 1973), xii.
8. Betty Baer and Ron Federico, *Educating the Baccalaureate Social Worker* (Cambridge, Mass.: Ballinger, 1978), 68.
9. *Random House Dictionary,* s.v. "function."
10. Sheafor et al. *Techniques and Guidelines,* 12.
11. Pincus and Minahan, *Social Work Practice,* 15.
12. S. Dixon, *Working with People in Crisis: Theory and Practice,* 2nd ed. (Columbus, Ohio: Merrill, 1987), 37.
13. Pincus and Minahan, *Social Work Practice,* 13.
14. John P. Van Gigch, *Applied General Systems Theory* (New York: Harper and Row, 1978), 4; Robert Berger and Ronald Federico, *Human Behavior: A Social Work Perspective* (New York: Longman, 1982), 40.
15. Carel Germain, *Social Work Practice: People and Environments. An Ecological Perspective* (New York: Columbia University Press, 1979).
16. C. Wright Mills, *The Sociological Imagination* (New York: Oxford University Press, 1959), 8.
17. Pincus and Minahan, *Social Work Practice,* 105.
18. D. Lum, *Social Work Practice and People of Color* (Monterey, Calif.: Brooks/Cole, 1986), 3.
19. Ludwig von Bertalanffy, *General System Theory Yearbook for the Society for General Systems Research,* ed. L. von Bertalanffy, Fol. 1 (Bedford, Mass.: Society for

General Systems Research, 1956), 11; and *General Systems Theory* (New York: Braziller, 1968).

20. Dixon, *Working with People in Crisis,* 8.

21. From *Placement Prevention and Family Reunification: A Handbook for the Family-Centered Service Practitioner.* Prepared by the National Resource Center on Family Based Services, School of Social Work (Iowa City, Iowa: University of Iowa, 1984), 6.

22. Van Gigch, *Applied General Systems Theory,* 4.

23. R. J. Parsons, S. H. Hernandez, and J. D. Jorgensen, "Integrated Practice: A Framework for Problem Solving," *Social Work* 33, 5 (September–October 1988): 417–421.

24. M. Richmond, *What Is Social Casework* (New York: Russell Sage Foundation, 1922), 132.

25. D. Hepworth and J. Larsen, *Direct Social Work Practice: Theory and Skills,* 2nd ed. (Chicago: Dorsey, 1986), 215–220.

26. George Herbert Mead, *Mind, Self and Society* (Chicago: University of Chicago Press, 1934).

27. Peter Berger and Brigitte Berger, *Sociology: A Biographical Approach* (New York: Basic Books, 1972), 55.

28. Joseph Anderson, *Social Work Methods and Processes* (Belmont, Calif.: Wadsworth, 1981), 112.

29. Berger and Berger, *Sociology,* 53.

30. Beulah Compton and Burt Galaway, *Social Work Processes,* rev. ed. (Homewood, Ill.: Dorsey Press, 1979), 342.

31. Ibid., 338.

32. Ibid., 339.

33. Ibid., 362.

34. Ibid., 340.

35. Ibid.

36. Ibid., 342.

37. Andre Delbecq, A. H. Van de Ven, and D. H. Gustafson, *Group Techniques for Program Planning* (Glenview, Ill.: Foresman, 1975).

Chapter

3

The Generalist Model

Professionals are paid for doing, for operationalizing, and not simply speculating on the nature of life. Their stock in trade is technique and society holds them responsible for their ability to perform their work with skills not available to the ordinary citizen. How-to-do-it is the bread and butter of the lawyer, the doctor, the engineer—and the social worker.[1]

A model is by definition an abstraction created to explain, analyze, and develop the reality it represents. Model cars, model airplanes, model homes, model cities, and mathematical models all represent desired outcomes in the "real" world. A model can be either abstract or specific. Whenever you develop a model, the amount of agreement about that model will depend on how specific the model is: the more specific, the more disagreement and discussion it is capable of generating. The model of social work we are presenting is intended to be somewhat abstract and yet provide enough detail for you to understand, question, and contrast with other models of practice you will find in the literature or experience in your field placements.

WHAT MAKES A MODEL GOOD?

There are certain characteristics you should look for when comparing models of social work practice. In Chapters 1 and 2 we stressed the importance of analyzing problems at the interface of individual and environment; therefore, the model of practice you choose must, first of all, provide ways of dealing with all the significant people involved in a practice situation, not just the identified client.

The second attribute to consider is whether the model of practice accounts for the physical and social environment that impinges on the problem situation. Sometimes it may seem easier to adopt a model that concentrates on individual functioning and thereby limits the intervention to working with

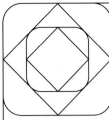

DIAGNOSTIC QUESTIONS

Models of Social Work Practice

1. Does the model direct me to look at all people involved in the situation, or does it assume the problem lies within the identified client?
2. Does the model account for the environmental factors that impinge upon the problem situation?
3. Does the model provide an understanding of how the people involved are affected by their environment and how they can affect the environment?
4. Using this model of practice, will I know where to start?
5. Who has used this model? With which groups? With what results?
6. Are there measurable outcomes using this model of intervention?
7. Using this model, will I be engaging in social work practice or will I be emulating another profession?

that individual. That type of model might be appropriate for psychologists or psychiatrists but would not prepare you for social work practice.

Third, in addition to taking account of the environment, the model must provide a way of understanding and affecting the interactions between and among the people and the environments of concern. Fourth, it must provide a starting point for the social work practitioner to begin the necessary work. Fifth, it must be consistent with both the definition of practice and the frame of reference used for practice. Sixth, to the extent possible, it should be based on proven methods and provide a means for evaluating the success of the intervention.

The accompanying box contains the diagnostic questions we have developed to summarize the characteristics we believe are necessary for a model of social work practice.

Chapter 2 discusses the use of systems theory to understand the environment.

You may want to review the definitions and frame of reference presented in Chapter 2.

WHY THE GENERALIST MODEL?

In the early development of social work knowledge, there was a tendency to develop methodology based on the number of people being served at any one time. Social workers who dealt with individuals were trained in the casework method. Those who worked with small groups or families specialized in group work. Administrators, social planners, and community workers were trained in a methodology known as community organization.

The three traditional models of social work were casework, group work, and community organization.

This approach to practice led to problems, because social work intervention tended to be based on the expertise of the worker rather than the needs of the problem situation. This has been referred to as the "law of the instrument" principle or "specialization by solution."[2] In addition to letting the expertise of the practitioner define the area of intervention, there was also a tendency for social workers to work only with victims of the social problems, rather than trying to change the social situation.

Casework, group work, and community organization have all been severely criticized on the grounds that they fragment problems and services needed to bring about a solution and lead social workers to respond with what they know best rather than what is most appropriate. These approaches also tend to underestimate the interrelatedness of contemporary life.

Traditional methodologies did not adequately address the complexity of practice.

As early as 1966, Helen Harris Perlman, a scholar involved in developing principles of practice for the caseworker, suggested that

> maybe the way to go about identifying social work practice activities is not within the traditional boundaries of casework, group work, and community work at all, but *across lines* by asking ourselves what kinds of problems call for what kinds of services and actions [emphasis added].[3]

In 1973 Pincus and Minahan wrote *Social Work Practice: Model and Method*, presenting their model of generalist practice.

In the early 1970s, Pincus and Minahan developed this idea further, conceptualizing a model of practice guided by the developing body of general systems theory. Their model of practice moved the emphasis away from seeing the identified client as the target of intervention. They suggested that in each practice situation the social worker must analyze the relationships among *all* the people involved in the problem situation. In addition, they broadened the analysis by requiring the social worker to identify who will benefit from the work to be done, who has provided the sanction for that work, who needs to be changed or influenced, and who needs to be counseled to achieve the desired outcomes.[4]

The social work process is a specific set of operations that takes place in each intervention.

Rather than a methodology based on the size of the client group, Pincus and Minahan developed a social work process that takes place in practice regardless of the problem or size of the system. This process was illustrated in a community setting in the case study in Chapter 2; the case study at the end of this chapter illustrates the social work process in working with an individual. Pincus and Minahan laid the groundwork for organizing practice around the particular problem or situation of concern. This makes sense because social workers only become involved when people are experiencing stress or problems.

A current model of generalist practice, integrated practice, reinforces and clarifies the importance of seeing the gestalt or wholeness of the social problem. In the words of Parsons et al., "In integrated practice, the target of social work intervention is the whole of social problems, rather than the rehabilitation of victims of social problems alone."[5] And Heus and Pincus observe, "Generalists will need to guide and engineer the problem definition and means of solution, as well as the development and management of community resources for mutual problem solving."[6]

Problems can be viewed from several perspectives: What type of problem is it? Who "owns" the problem? Where is the problem located? The generalist model forces the social worker to deal with the problem in all its complexity, assuming that this is the only effective way to solve the problem.

In addition to understanding the problem, the social worker must understand other parts of the system. The social worker herself is part of a system. The agency she works for, her job description, the sanction she has received from the community, her knowledge base, and the social work frame of reference and code of ethics are just a few aspects of the social work system that will be relevant to this case.

The *client system* is made up of the person or people who ask for help and those who will benefit by the intervention. There must be some type of contract between the client and the social worker to activate the "official" client system. This contract is sometimes a formal agreement but is frequently a consensus to work on specific goals. Depending upon the complexity of the problem, the specificity of the terms of the contract can vary. In addition to the specific contract with the client, there is the unwritten contract that the social worker will abide by the profession's code of ethics, which provides some protection for the client.

Much has been written in the social work literature about the involuntary client. Working with this population requires very specific knowledge and skills. (Chapter 18 discusses working with involuntary clients.) At this point we simply note that at least at the outset, the identified client may not have entered into a voluntary contractual agreement with the social worker.

By *target system* we are referring to all those people, policies, and organizations that must change if the intervention is to be successful. The concept of the target system is very helpful in keeping the social worker from assuming that the client is the automatic target of change. Once the problem has been thoroughly analyzed and the significant actors and environmental

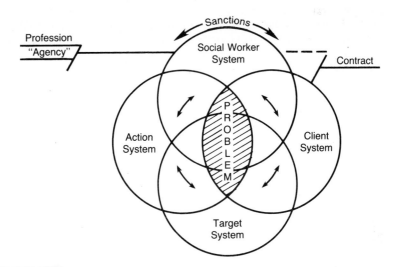

FIGURE 3–1

contingencies identified, the client is frequently part of the action system, rather than the target of change.

The *action system* is all the people and resources that can be used to influence the target system to change. These concepts parallel those developed by Pincus and Minahan in 1973.[7] This problem-focus model is illustrated in Figure 3–1. To make these concepts clearer, we can apply them to a brief case study.

CASE STUDY
Integrated Generalist Casework

Jane, age 35, mother of five school-age children, has been referred to the self-support unit because Aid to Families with Dependent Children (AFDC)[1] requires all parents with school-age children to register for work placement to retain eligibility for AFDC.

A generalist social worker will not start from the assumption that lack of motivation is the reason Jane has not found employment.[2] The presenting problem may be lack of income or employment for Jane, but the impediments to gainful employment may be varied. To address this problem successfully, the social worker and Jane may need to deal with a number of other problems first.

The social worker will first be aware of the constraints of the agency in which he is employed.[3] How the agency is organized can be a resource or a detriment to Jane in finding work. The agency may even become a target of change.

Although Jane is the identified client, her goal may not be the same as the goal identified by the agency.[4] In order to enter into a contract for service, the social worker will need to engage Jane in the process. If Jane is an involuntary client, there are times when agency mandates will require that she cooperate. However, an effective social worker can usually arrive at this contract through consensus and possibly co-optation, rather than conflict. Research and practice knowledge tell the social worker that most individuals prefer to work if the opportunity is available and the person feels capable of performing the work.

More than likely, the AFDC mother of five children is suffering from a lack of resources and self-esteem which makes the pursuit of employment very threatening to her. A thorough assessment of the situation may show that transportation, child care, and lack of job skills are the real impediments, rather than lack of motivation.[5] The generalist social worker will help Jane develop the resources (action system) and teach her how to use them. Intervention will be targeted at all points on the continuum affecting the problem. Jane will be offered services that build trust, educate, create a sense of power and competence, and encourage a sense of self-esteem.

Support groups might be created to provide ongoing support and decrease the sense of isolation. The generalist model moves the worker away from providing service that translates need into deficiency, places the deficiency onto the client, and then separates that deficiency into a specialized area of service such as counseling.[6] The object of effective generalist practice is to see Jane not only employed but an active participant in shaping her environment. In addition to solving her immediate problem, the social worker will have left her with skills to solve future problems.

---

[1] AFDC is a program that provides financial assistance to low income families when a parent is absent or unable to work.

[2] Generalist practice helps avoid "blaming the victim."

[3] The social work system itself must be analyzed and understood as it relates to the individual case.

[4] The client system must be understood in terms of who is asking for service and who can benefit.

[5] The social worker must identify the action system – the people and resources that can bring about the desired change.

[6] The appropriate target of change cannot be identified until the systematic analysis is complete.

In presenting the generalist model of practice, we have made some implicit assumptions about the relationship between the social worker and the client. Since the professional relationship is an important component of practice, we want to devote some discussion specifically to the subject.

THE SOCIAL WORK RELATIONSHIP

The most basic characteristic of humanity is that we live our lives within relationships to other people. From its earliest beginnings social work has recognized the importance of human interaction and attempted to employ the concept of relationship in a conscious and deliberate way for the benefit of the people served.[9]

A social worker "must keep physically, emotionally, and intellectually prepared to use self as a positive instrument of change."[8]

A professional relationship is formed for a purpose; when that purpose is accomplished the relationship ends. These relationships involve self-discipline, self-knowledge, and congruent use of self by the social worker, as well as knowledge of the people with whom the relationship is formed.

Social workers form many relationships in their work. In the course of serving just one client, a social worker may have contact with a landlord, teacher, employer, doctor, politician, police, program administrators, neighbors, community groups, or other professionals. Within these contacts, the social work relationship has common elements that relate to the nature of the task to be accomplished.

The importance of the social work relationship has led to numerous discussions and publications about exactly what the key components of the social work relationship are. The most common variables identified are concern for others, commitment, acceptance, positive regard, empathy, authority, genuineness, congruence, and goal orientation.

Empathy is taking on the perspective of the other person.

Concern for others is probably the most common motivation for entering the profession. Students often express dissatisfaction with the conditions surrounding some group's existence: the poor, the disabled, the elderly, or some minority group. Social work offers an opportunity to enter a profession with the potential to change these conditions. *Commitment* to this goal involves spending four to six years of your life preparing to enter the profession. Commitment is tested throughout your professional career as you keep working for change, sometimes under very trying conditions.

Acceptance and *positive regard* communicate the social worker's respect, concern, and interest for the well-being of the client. As a new social worker you may struggle with this aspect of the relationship when you work with clients who have engaged in socially reprehensible behavior. Knowledge and experience, guided by strong supervision, will help you understand that acceptance and positive regard apply only to the person and not to the behavior. Acceptance and positive regard become easier as you experience helping such people change their behavior. As you come to know your clients and understand the environment they must survive in, accepting the individual is a natural outcome—understanding breeds acceptance.

Empathy is not the same as sympathy. As human beings, we frequently feel sympathy for the predicament of the client. This is not necessarily conducive to implementing change. Empathy, in contrast to sympathy, is an intellectual exercise of the skill of understanding the viewpoint of another person. Rather than feeling anger at the spouse abuser, we understand the fear and anger of the battered wife. Rather than feel sorry for delinquents from dysfunctional homes, we need to understand how they justify their behavior by blaming their parents. No matter how sorry we might feel for that individual, our sympathy will only reinforce the behaviors that contributed to their presenting problems. As we understand their thinking, we can help them change their behavior.

Authority is an important aspect of the professional relationship. As a beginning social worker you may be dismayed that clients who are older and more educated actually accept you as an authority who can help solve their problem. Two important components of this characteristic are (1) the sanction you have been given by the community to perform these tasks and (2) the professional knowledge, values, and skills you bring to the situation.

Authority is power based on community sanction and professional knowledge.

Community sanction gives us access to the client. But only our own abilities maintain that authority in the relationship. Authority is not the same as control, although authority by its very nature conveys some control.

Genuineness is the social worker's involvement in the profession because of a sincere caring for people. Like any other field, social work includes people who "stumbled into" the profession through lack of direction rather than fundamental commitment.

Congruence is the extent to which the social worker's response reflects an understanding of how the client views the problem. This is closely related to both genuineness and empathy. It is unlikely that you will get a client to participate in the change process until they feel there is some degree of agreement, or congruence, in how you each define the problem.

Goal orientation is the final key element. Throughout this book we define social work as a goal-oriented change process. The professional relationship must reflect this view. In fact, the goal itself limits how long the relationship will continue. Since it is a professional relationship, it will end once the goal has been achieved. In some instances it will end if the client determines she no longer wants to pursue the identified goal.

Since social workers tend to be very caring people, many have difficulty letting go of the relationship. A case in point involved a probation and parole worker who did a presentence investigation on a woman convicted of infanticide. Two years later the worker was still visiting the woman and continuing what she saw as a therapeutic relationship long after there was any sanction for her services. Whose needs were being met—the social worker's or the client's? Goal orientation keeps the professional relationship focused on the purpose of the relationship.

The Importance of the Relationship

The importance of the relationship to successful practice has been documented in the research. What are the key components of this relationship? To date, empathy, nonpossessive warmth, and genuineness have been identified as being related to successful outcomes.[10] It is not easy to identify and convey to new students what makes clients trust some social workers with their most intimate and even shocking concerns and then moves them to change when previously the clients were immobilized. Social work techniques are much more clearly conceptualized and easier to teach than social work relationships. Relationships are a large part of what many refer to as the art of social work.

A common thread in the literature on social work relationships is that the key to understanding the nature of a relationship in social work practice is the purpose for which that relationship is developed. This purpose, linked directly to the assessment and definition of a specific problem and the desired goals, determines not only the parameters of the relationship itself but also the specific interventive roles assumed by the social worker. It is from the analysis of the work actually done by social workers that the nature of the helping relationship and the professional roles and behaviors employed within the relationship have been identified.

THE PROBLEM-SOLVING PROCESS

The problem-solving process has been broken down into phases or steps. We first identify those steps, discuss how to accomplish each step most effectively, and finally present a case study illustrating the steps.

> Social workers guide the process, not the client.

1. Problem identification: client and social worker agree on a definition of the problem.

2. Goal identification: the social worker and the client reach a goal consensus—the desired outcome of the intervention. *GOAL HAS TO BE ACHIEVABLE*

3. Solution search: the social worker uses professional analytical skills and information from other systems to determine what resistances to change are impeding the desired outcome.

   DON'T HAVE TO KNOW THIS FOR THE TEST

4. Development of intervention plan: the social worker develops an intervention plan to overcome the resistance.

5. Implementation of intervention plan: the client and the social worker agree on specific actions to be undertaken by each to implement the intervention plan.

6. Monitoring the plan.

7. Evaluation and termination: the social worker and the client jointly evaluate the effectiveness of the intervention in solving the problem.

Step 1: Problem Identification

The first step, problem identification, is the phase at which the social worker and the client agree on what the problem is and what needs to be changed. Devore and Schlesinger have identified the skills that facilitate the problem identification process: (1) stage setting, (2) tuning in, and (3) attending.[11]

Stage setting is the purposive use of space to enhance comfort and communication. This includes such basic conditions as privacy, enough physical space to maintain a comfortable distance, and physically comfortable settings. These needs, especially privacy, vary considerably among clients.

Tuning in implies getting in touch with feelings expressed and unexpressed by the client. The tuning in process begins even before meeting the client, when you draw from your bank of basic knowledge of human behavior, of the specific issue at hand, and of the ethnic reality of the individual involved. Dixon has recognized the importance of ethnicity but also warns against making unwarranted assumptions about any client before the first meeting.[12]

As an example of tuning in, we might consider the case of a disruptive sixteen-year-old Navajo girl who has just been admitted to public school after four years at a school run by the Bureau of Indian Affairs. Among the issues one should consider in tuning in is the possibility that some of the problems might be the result of poor education at the Indian school. If the child is now living in her own family, the social worker might consider "reentry" problems; if she is in a foster home, we might expect certain behavior problems from the dynamics of parent–foster child relations. Other factors to consider are the ethnic makeup of the classroom and the community, the learning capabilities of the girl, and the presence or absence of significant support systems.

Attending skills help you pay attention to cognitive, emotional, verbal, and affective cues. Body language and appropriate dress give significant messages. You must also be cognizant of differential ethnic responses. For example, Asians and some American Indians are uncomfortable with eye contact. Some working class people are more comfortable with professionals who remain relatively formal.

Accurate assessment must precede intervention.

These are just some of the skills that will help you and your client come to an agreement about what the problem is and what changes the client wants to achieve. Depending on the variables unique to each situation, this agreement comes about in various ways and takes various forms. This step is most clearly reflected when a client desires services, knows what problems he would like to work on, and can clearly identify what kinds of help he needs. However, this is not the typical initial contact for a social worker. Frequently social workers make the initial contact based on a referral from another agency. The client may or may not see the situation as problematic. If the client does not desire to work on the identified problem, we refer to him as a potential client until the social worker determines that services are not needed or desired and that discontinuing service efforts will not endanger anyone. If the social work process is to proceed, there must be consensus on the definition of the problem.

Step 2: Goal Identification/Contracting

The contract is a consensus between worker and client about what the problem is, what action to take, and what goal to achieve.

Once you have completed step one, you enter the contract phase. In this stage the client and social worker jointly identify a desirable outcome. For instance, a social worker working with a teenager in conflict with her parents over social activities may be asked to mediate with the parents to gain more privileges for the child. The social worker cannot agree to work for this goal unless in his professional assessment such an intervention would be in the client's best interest.

Contracting guards against the professional imposing her own goals on the client and helps give focus to the treatment. In spite of the potential benefits of contracting, it can be detrimental to practice if the worker is not sensitive to the client's perception of the process. The principle of contracting is good when it promotes client autonomy and self-determination. As a technique for rapid engagement of clients in the helping process, there is a danger that class and ethnic perceptions will not be given proper attention.[13]

Good Tracks suggests that contracting in this manner will be ineffective in the American Indian community, where only time and offering of concrete services will build the trust necessary for a professional relationship.[14] In contrast, Asian-Americans are likely to feel more comfortable if their expectations are acknowledged clearly in the early stage of the relationship.

Step 3: Solution Search

The third step, a search for solutions, calls upon the social worker to draw upon research findings and theoretical knowledge about individual behavior and the social environment, community resources, organizational structure, policy and procedures, and systems to assess why the problem behavior is occurring, what components of the environment support the negative behavior, and what changes need to take place. Frequently the social worker must deal with resistance at this stage. Resistance may come from the client, relevant agencies, the schools, the community, or even the client's family.

We call this stage "solution search" to indicate that there are specific criteria that help us select the best intervention—the one that has the greatest probability of succeeding with a particular client and a particular problem. The social workers who are most effective in practice have the skills to evaluate their own intervention and to draw appropriately on the findings of others. The success of this stage is more probable if the social worker is well grounded in the empirical findings from practice.

Step 4: Development of the Intervention Plan

The social worker moves into development of an intervention plan based on the solution search. Ideally, the client and social worker develop this plan together. The plan must reflect the reality of what change is feasible and what resources are available. The plan will clearly state the problem to be addressed, the method of addressing the problem, ongoing indicators of whether the intervention is working, an end point for the intervention, and a means of evaluating the intervention.

Step 5: Implementation

The fifth step is implementation of the intervention plan. The client and the social worker must agree on specific actions each will take to implement the plan. The social worker must understand what the client needs and expects from him and the agency. The client needs to understand the expectations she must fulfill. It is very important that the social worker set up evaluation criteria at the outset to measure whether the intervention is successful. This outcome measure provides accountability to the agency and the client and should also be a learning tool for the social worker. This step helps build the empirical base for practice.

Step 6: Monitoring the Plan

Effective social workers continually assess what skills they are using and how successful they are in using those skills. As they become aware of their own strengths and weaknesses, they understand when to refer a client to someone more effective and in what areas they can be resources to their colleagues.

The social worker must evaluate the intervention plan at each step, determining whether each of the activities the client and the social worker are engaging in is functional to the agreed-upon goal, how long the contract remains in force, and whether the intervention plan can be improved.

Step 7: Evaluation and Termination

Successful termination requires adequate preparation.

The final step in the social work process is termination. Since it is a professional relationship, it ends when the goal is met, when the client and social worker agree the goal is not feasible, or when the client no longer desires services. At times professional relationships end because a client moves or the social worker changes jobs, retires, or becomes ill. When terminations can be anticipated, they should be planned.

Hepworth and Larsen identify tasks necessary to successful termination:

1. determining the appropriate time to terminate
2. resolving the feelings of loss typical of separation
3. identifying what has been accomplished (evaluation), and
4. setting up a plan to maintain gains achieved.[15]

This fourth task often requires the social worker to help the client identify sources for support that had been provided by the worker. It is important that the client not view termination as rejection.

Although we have presented the social work process as an orderly procession through each step, actual practice is not so simple. The social work process is fluid, with the social worker going back and forth between the steps as necessary. Practice takes place in a dynamic, ever-changing environment. Social workers are constantly redefining the problem and renegotiating the contract as conditions change. Problems change and new solutions become available, causing significant changes in the plan originally developed.

We are not suggesting that the process can be ignored, however. Understanding the process helps you understand what conditions are necessary to implement the plan effectively. It provides a constant checklist to keep you aware of the process.

In Chapter 2, the case study of generalist practice used a community organization model. Now we will illustrate generalist practice with a casework example. This case study was chosen to illustrate the social work process, professional roles, functions, relationships, and the importance of ethnic sensitivity. The goal is to show the importance of social work knowledge to effective intervention.

SUMMARY

In this chapter we presented a model of practice that has been widely adopted in the field. We believe the generalist model of practice is the desirable model because it is consistent with the social work frame of reference, problem focused rather than individually focused, and provides clear direction to the practitioner in assessment, intervention, and evaluation.

In presenting the generalist model, we addressed the four systems relevant to effective practice: the social worker system, the client system, the target system, and the action system.

The importance of the social work relationship was addressed, as well as an attempt to delineate the important components of that relationship. We recognized that the social work relationship is as much art as skill and is difficult to teach new students.

Finally, we addressed the social work process—the actual steps the social worker follows in practice. While recognizing the fluidity of the process, you should understand and follow the process. At each stage we made some suggestions that should help you increase the effectiveness of that stage.

We now present a case study of generalist practice. The client in this study is a teenage American Indian experiencing adjustment problems. This case study illustrates the process and some of the specific knowledge necessary for effective social work practice.

CASE STUDY
Generalist Casework Practice

Sharon Whitethunder, a sixteen-year-old Native American of the Winnebago Tribe, was referred to Children's Services because she was not attending school. Sharon is in her junior year in high school. Until this year, Sharon had been a B+ student and had caused no behavior problems. Although she is concerned about Sharon's absenteeism, the school counselor is even more concerned that Sharon is considering dropping out of school. The counselor feels Sharon is experiencing personal problems that are affecting both her motivation and the quality of her work. Sharon states she does not have a problem. She knows her attitude and goals have changed but does not see why anyone should care. Sharon appears angry but does not have a focus for her anger. While Sharon's behavior is not really disruptive, the school counselor feels Sharon needs someone to help her work out personal problems.

SOCIAL HISTORY

Sharon Whitethunder is an attractive, healthy Native American with above average intelligence. Her mother and father lived in a common law marriage that produced five children. They presently live in different midwestern states. Neither of the parents works steadily and each of them indulges quite heavily and frequently in alcohol. The children see their parents only at Indian powwows. Ranging in age from nine to sixteen, the children have lived with the maternal grandmother for the last eight years. The grandmother is in her late seventies. Although she is very loving, neither her temperament nor her health is conducive to supervision of children. As a result, Sharon has assumed many of the parental functions for her younger siblings. The grandmother receives Aid to Families with Dependent Children (AFDC) as a nonlegally responsible relative and is quite satisfied with the amount she receives. Mrs. Crow (the grandmother) was married for forty-five years to the chief of the Winnebago tribe. She continues to be strongly committed to preserving Indian ways. She is not very happy that the social service department recently forced her to move into the city. She was much happier in her home on the cranberry marsh, where she could cook in the ground and live among her people. Although she now has a ten-room house, the family lives in three rooms. Mrs. Crow feels it is all right for the children to attend the white school but does not like some of the ideas they are taught. She would much rather they attend Indian school, but none is available in the state. Mrs. Crow and her family are descendants of Indians who were brought from South Dakota to harvest cranberries. The cranberry growers built small homes for the harvesters to live in, but when cranberry harvesting became mechanized, some of the Indians stayed on in homes that the owners, however, no longer maintained. Because her home had no indoor plumbing or central heat, the social services department decided the home was unfit for the children. Although her family has lived in the Midwest for three generations, Mrs. Crow still feels her home is in South Dakota. It is very important to Mrs. Crow that she and her descendants return to South Dakota for certain religious holidays; all her family participate in the rituals at these celebrations.

INITIAL CONTRACT

Since Sharon was a minor, contact was made with both Sharon and her grandmother. It was clear that Sharon had a deep love for her grandmother, but that some of her grandmother's ideas were causing conflict within her. In the initial contact Sharon talked about her plans for the future. She wanted to become a medical technician, but her grandmother felt she had already gone to school long enough. During this first visit Mrs. Crow made frequent references to the "Indian way." It soon became apparent that Sharon was torn between the two very different cultures in which she has been raised. Part of her related to her friends at school, who were planning their futures in the working world; the other part of her related to Grandma, who wanted Sharon to stay close by and take care of her and the children. With Grandma's reluctant permission, it was agreed that Sharon would continue to meet with the social worker. While the grandmother did not view

Sharon's behavior as a problem, she understood that the children must attend school or her right to custody might be questioned. Mrs. Crow had a basic fear of the social services department and was inclined to cooperate out of fear that she might lose the children. In spite of her agreement to the initial contract, however, she resisted Sharon being seen by the social worker; she frequently had Sharon do tasks for her when she was supposed to meet with the social worker. The social worker made frequent calls on Mrs. Crow to reassure her and gain her cooperation.

PROBLEM ASSESSMENT

The problem was not difficult to assess. Here was a sixteen-year-old girl caught between two cultures and three generations. At times Sharon wanted to break with her Indian culture and pursue a career. But when she would begin to work on this goal, she would experience guilt over her grandmother's reaction. As the professional relationship progressed, it became clear that neither consensus nor co-optation was going to be effective in changing the grandmother's attitude. If Sharon was to pursue her own goals, it would entail conflict with her grandmother's wishes and her entire value system.

SOLUTION SEARCH

The social worker initially engaged in a Rogerian-based enabling intervention to provide support for Sharon. The social worker felt it was not her role to direct Sharon but rather to provide a supportive, empathetic relationship that would enable Sharon to make the decision that was right for her. In addition it seemed clear that Mrs. Crow would be the target of change. By working slowly and in a nonthreatening manner, the social worker hoped that Mrs. Crow would come to appreciate and value Sharon's decisions. However, changing Mrs. Crow's attitudes proved to be impossible. Mrs. Crow had already managed to "hang onto" three of her own children. These children all lived in the same city as Mrs. Crow and spent most of their waking hours, and probably their sleeping hours, at her home. None was employed. Some had held part-time jobs, but all three were receiving AFDC. Mrs. Crow liked her children and grandchildren to be accessible and free to travel to powwows both in and out of state. Here

At an American Indian Center a worker takes time to listen to a young girl's concerns.

was a very closed family system that seemed to operate in a manner personally satisfying to most of the family members; problems arose only when a member wanted to leave the nest. Sharon's mother had created a precedent for breaking with this pattern when she left the family; it seemed reasonable to assume that her departure had also been traumatic.

Sharon needed help first to make the decision about her future. Which was more important to her: to maintain her strong family ties or to pursue a future of her own? Although it was clear she would have to make a choice, it was not predictable how long the alienation from her grandmother would last if Sharon went against her wishes.

INTERVENTION PLAN

Since Sharon's conflict was cultural, neither Rogerian nor behavioral nor psychoanalytic theory seemed adequate to solve her problem. After working with Sharon over a frustrating and unhappy three months, the social worker realized that an action system had to be developed to aid and support Sharon in this life crisis. Since Sharon's mother, Angeline, had succeeded in breaking with her family, she was identified as a potential action system for Sharon. Sharon had difficulty viewing her mother in this role, as she had never experienced a mother-daughter relationship with her; in fact, Sharon did not feel her mother would want to be bothered with her. After a good deal of hesitation Sharon agreed to let the social worker contact her mother. Even though Angeline lived more than 300 miles away, she was very concerned and seemed to understand clearly what Sharon was experiencing; she gave up her apartment in Chicago and came home to stay. Sharon and Angeline developed a strong friendship resembling a peer relationship more than a parent-child relationship. Sharon seemed much happier and began attending school regularly; still, Sharon had not decided what to do about her future.

EVALUATION PHASE

On a short-term basis, the intervention was apparently successful. Her mother having been engaged in her problem, Sharon seemed happier. Her school attendance and performance improved. But just as the social worker was preparing to terminate the relationship with an offer of continued service on request, Sharon informed her that she was quitting school and moving to Chicago with her mother.

RENEGOTIATION OF CONTRACT

The story does not end there. Sharon went to live with her mother for one month. The living conditions she endured, however, furnished her with the personal resolve to improve her own lot in life; Sharon returned with a strong commitment to pursue her education. The social worker suggested the possibility of foster care, and Sharon accepted this option. After living in the foster home for two months Sharon decided that she preferred to live with her grandmother and that she could do that without giving up her own goals. The social worker met with Sharon once a month for the next three months. Sharon was doing well in school and Mrs. Crow was not interfering with her school atten-

dance. The professional relationship was then terminated.

COMMENT

In the case of Sharon Whitethunder the social worker applied many levels of knowledge. Her theory of practice was a generalist one. In addition, she needed to understand how Native American families are different from mainstream families. One important difference is that, as a group, Native Americans reject the dominant values of acquisitiveness and competitiveness. Then, too, she had to deal with the grandmother's attitude toward appointments and time in general. In most instances she was careful to make appointments and not to drop in unannounced, although the family did not mind if she did drop in. The family kept appointments if there was nothing else to do. They did not have a telephone, and they did not believe in changing their plans or informing the worker of conflicting commitments. The social worker at first hesitated to drop in casually because she felt she was invading the family's privacy. However, after working with a number of Indian families in the area, she realized their homes were much more open to visitors than the homes of white families; it was not unusual to observe friends dropping in unannounced. Having material possessions, getting ahead, or making an impression are not part of their value system. Family and sharing are two dominant values.

The social worker had to know the law as well. If she had not been familiar with the custody laws, she might have attempted to stop the mother from taking Sharon to Chicago. Had she taken this approach, she would have found that she did not have the legal grounds to follow through, and she probably would have alienated both the mother and Sharon.

Family structure in this group of Native Americans was also different from that associated with middle-class white Americans. A large percentage of the Indian children in the community were cared for by their maternal grandmothers. This practice has been passed down for generations; the grandmother's own mother had cared for her children. This was a source of conflict between some families and their social workers, since the social workers felt it was the mother's responsibility to care for the children.

American Indians still tend to be more oriented to the collective than to the individual. When a social worker doesn't understand this commitment, she can cause problems for her client. To encourage Sharon to pursue her goals without recognizing her loyalty to the collective would have caused further trauma, rather than growth.

NOTES

1. William Schwartz, "Private Troubles and Public Issues: One Job or Two?" Lindeman Memorial Lecture (New York, National Conference on Social Welfare, 28 May 1969).
2. R. J. Parsons, S. H. Hernandez, and J. D. Jorgensen, "Integrated Practice: A Framework for Problem Solving," *Social Work* 33, 5 (September–October 1988): 417–421.
3. Helen Harris Perlman, "Social Work Methods: A Review of the Past Decade," *Social Work* 10, 4 (1965): 94–95.
4. Alan Pincus and Anne Minahan, *Social Work Practice: Model and Method* (Itasca, Ill.: Peacock, 1973), 11 ns. Also see Carol Meyer, *Social Work Practice*, 2nd ed. (New York: Free Press, 1976), and Howard Goldstein, *Social Work Practice: A Unitary Approach* (Columbia, S.C.: University of South Carolina Press, 1973); Peter Leonard, "Towards a Paradigm for Radical Practice," in *Radical Social Work*, ed. Brake and Bailey (New York: Pantheon Books, 1975); and Jeffrey Galper, *Social Work Practice: A Radical Perspective* (Englewood Cliffs, N.J.: Prentice-Hall, 1980), 11.
5. Parsons et al., "Integrated Practice," 418.
6. M. Heus and A. Pincus, *The Creative Generalist* (Barneveld, Wis.: Micamar, 1986).
7. Pincus and Minahan, *Social Work Practice*, 53–68.
8. B. Sheafor, C. Horejsi, and G. Horejsi, *Techniques and Guidelines for Social Work Practice* (Newton, Mass.: Allyn and Bacon, 1988), 55.
9. Beulah Compton and Burt Galaway, *Social Work Processes*, rev. ed. (Homewood, Ill.: Dorsey Press, 1979), 159.
10. J. Fischer, *Effective Casework Practice: An Eclectic Approach* (New York: McGraw-Hill, 1978), 191.
11. W. Devore and E. Schlesinger, *Ethnic-Sensitive Social Work Practice*, 2nd ed. (Columbus, Ohio: Merrill, 1987), 184.
12. S. Dixon, *Working with People in Crisis: Theory and Practice*, 2nd ed. (Columbus, Ohio: Merrill, 1987).
13. Devore and Schlesinger, *Ethnic-Sensitive Social Work Practice*, 202.
14. J. Good Tracks, "Native American Noninterference," *Social Work* 18, 1: 30–35.
15. D. Hepworth and J. Larsen, *Direct Social Work Practice: Theory and Skills*, 2nd ed. (Chicago: Dorsey, 1986), 578.

PART

II

THE PROFESSION OF SOCIAL WORK

In Part I we analyzed social work practice by comparing it to other human service professions, discussing its unique frame of reference and presenting a model of social work practice. In Part II we analyze the values that guide the profession and the effect of societal values on the profession, and we begin to discuss how these values affect practice.

In Chapter 4 we discuss three areas of values for social workers: values as they relate to the professional–client relationship, to our view of society, and to a commitment to professional practice. The first value area is a concrete, personalized set of values that has led us to the profession of social work and continues to affect our direct practice with clients. The second area relates more to our view of society. As we discuss ideologies, these value sets are more clearly identified. We use the liberal, conservative, and radical typology to discuss societal value sets. The third area of values — commitment to professional practice — is discussed in Chapter 5, where we present the attributes of the profession. In this chapter we suggest that professional practice means being familiar with and using the social work knowledge base, being committed to the service ideal, and limiting our practice to our own area of competence.

Finally, we look at the professional associations that have been developed to guide and direct professional practice. The National Association of Social Workers has delineated levels of practice and competencies appropriate for each level. The Council on Social Work Education is the accrediting body for colleges and universities that train social workers. Important professional issues such as vendorship and licensing are discussed.

Part II is designed to provide you with basic knowledge about the structure of the profession and its guiding values. Although knowledge is important, it cannot lead to professional social work practice by itself. Values are critical. To assure ethical practice, organizational structures have been put into place. Within the profession there is continuing debate about the appropriateness of goals such as licensing and vendorship; our discussion will give you a beginning understanding of these issues.

In Part II we display the tremendous choice and potential for people entering the field. Since social work is a young profession, it continues to be characterized by conflict and debate that keep it a vibrant and responsive field.

Chapter

Social Work Values and Ideology

It does make a difference in human existence whether the highest value is moral excellence or the possession of wealth; whether value standards are strictly applied or whether a general permissiveness is the order of the day; or whether the stress is placed upon human beings as the supreme value or upon profit and economic utility. What men regard as worthy of their best efforts, individually and collectively, determines the value pattern of their times and gives meaning and relevance to their general world view.[1]

S ocial work practice is shaped by ideology and values. Values are powerful guides to action that can be tracked through the day-to-day practice of a social worker. Values are our beliefs about people, human nature, and what we see as "good." An ideology is the value system of a group; the belief system of any group will be tied to its political and economic self-interest.[2]

An ideology is the integrated aims, assertions, and theories constituting a politico-social program.

Analyzing our assumptions about what constitutes "good" is important, but the value set of the wider society has a much more powerful effect on how social work is practiced. By comparing the prevalent ideologies and how their views of the individual and society vary, it is possible to understand both how these value systems shape the political and economic structures of a society and our own value systems.

In this chapter we discuss social work values identified by the profession and analyze what they mean to social work practice. We then discuss ideology, that is, how the values held by larger society impinge on social work practice.

SOCIAL WORK VALUES

The National Association of Social Workers has identified the following values as guides to social work practice:

Commitment to the primary importance of the individual in society.

Respect for the confidentiality of relationships with clients.

Commitment to social change to meet socially recognized needs.

Willingness to keep personal feelings and needs separate from professional relationships.

Willingness to transmit knowledge and skills to others.

Respect and appreciation for individual and group differences.

Commitment to developing clients' ability to help themselves.

Willingness to persist in efforts on behalf of clients despite frustration.

Commitment to social justice and the economic, physical, and mental well-being of all in society.

Commitment to a high standard of personal and professional conduct.[3]

The social work values address three distinct areas: the professional–client relationship, social worker's view of society, and our commitment to professionalism.

Professional—Client Relationship

Attitude toward the client affects the relationship.

The professional relationship requires respect for human dignity, free will, and confidentiality. The commitment to the primary importance of the individual means that all individuals are equally important regardless of race, social class, sex, or past behavior. Social work has the commitment to recognize the good in what may appear on the surface to be despicable characters. Belief in the inherent good present in people guides social workers in enabling destructive individuals to become productive and constructive members of society. This commitment is reflected in respect and appreciation for individual and group differences and willingness to persist in efforts on behalf of clients.

Diversity is highly valued by social workers.

Client self-determination is a key social work value.

The commitment to helping clients help themselves originates in our recognition of and respect for the individual's self-determination and free will. We neither accept nor condone behavior of our clients when it is detrimental. In many instances it is the social worker who is charged with the responsibility to confront and work to change this behavior. Respect for the individual does not extend to respecting the individual's behavior.

Priviledged communication is only legally protected in states with licensing of social workers.

Confidentiality is essential so that the client knows that innermost thoughts, insecurities, and behaviors will be held in confidence. However, this confidence cannot be extended when a client's behavior is likely to harm either self or others. Privileged communication is a legal term. In some states with social work licensing, information received by the social worker in the professional role cannot be used as testimony against the client.

SOCIAL WORKERS' VIEW OF SOCIETY

Social work values foster a belief in redistribution of resources in our society.

The second area of values relates to the social worker's view of society. As a profession and as individual social workers, we have a commitment to make society more responsive to the needs of the less fortunate. All social workers

Jane Addams (1860-1935), founder of Hull House and winner of the Nobel Peace Prize in 1931, helped define social work as a profession of social reform and social action.

must have a commitment to social and economic justice as well as the physical and psychological well-being of society. This is a very broad-based value that can lead to diverse views on how the goal can be achieved. Some social workers view income redistribution programs (Aid to Families with Dependent Children, Supplemental Security Insurance, Food Stamps) as the most important means of achieving social and economic justice. Others believe that guaranteed employment would be the best method. Still others believe that economic and social justice is not possible under the present economic structure.

See Chapter 13 for an explanation of these financial assistance programs.

Professional Commitment

The third broad area of social work values relates to the profession. This value system addresses the fact that social workers are involved in a professional, not a personal, relationship. The only need the professional can bring to the relationship is the need to implement a successful plan of treatment. Personal needs are not to be met in the professional relationship; in particular, sexual relationships between social worker and client are never con-

Misuse of the professional relationship has caused the enactment of new legislation to protect the clients.

doned. Chapter 3 presented an extensive discussion of the social work relationship.

The other area of values related to professional conduct requires that social workers have knowledge and skill. They must constantly strive to improve their knowledge base and share with other professionals experience or knowledge that can contribute to the development of the profession.

Each of these value domains is profoundly related to the ideology of the wider society. While social work values remain consistent over time, our ability to maximize these values alters with societal changes.

Professional social workers have an obligation to contribute to the knowledge base of the profession.

IDEOLOGY

Extremely radical or conservative practitioners will experience dissonance in social work practice.

The ideology most prevalent at any point in history will be reflected in social welfare policy, which in turn sets the parameters of social work practice. Practitioners adopting a value system that is very far to one extreme or the other will have a more difficult time in practice. However, as we will see when we study the history of social work in Part III, sometimes the demands of extreme or fringe groups make progressive reforms more palatable. In other words, sometimes policymakers are willing to grant certain funds or programs as a compromise against more radical reforms. Some historians believe that the Social Security Act was passed largely because socialistic movements were becoming more powerful. Passing the Social Security Act diluted some of their support.

Social workers must be aware that much of what we believe is fact is actually socially constructed belief.

It is important to understand ideology because it shapes our social construction of reality. What may be presented as an objective description of reality is actually a justification for the social priorities or interests of certain powerful groups. Ideologies may be instruments of group interest; they may also justify and rationalize inequality and group power.[4] The same ideology cannot serve the interests of both the working class and the owners of production.[5]

We can understand this idea more clearly if we look at what has happened to labor unions over the last forty years. Throughout modern history, organized labor has been the major institution pressing the interests of the working and lower middle classes. This representation has gone far beyond the demand for higher wages. It has extended to participation in the formulation of government policies concerning taxation, the allocation or redistribution of wealth and income, health care, education, occupational safety, employment, and vocational training.

In advanced Western democracies, there is a direct correlation between government domestic spending and the strength of the trade union movement. In the United States, the trade union movement has lost a great deal of its power over the last decade; this same period saw a major decrease in domestic spending. No other major organization cuts across racial and ethnic lines to defend progressive distributional policies of taxation and spending.[6]

During the 1950s and 1960s, organized labor had a cooperative alliance with big business. As the United States lost its competitive edge in the marketplace, big business moved into an adversarial position, blaming the unions for loss of competitiveness, productivity, and quality, ultimately (they claimed) leading to less employment.

First the Reagan administration, and now the Bush administration, has convinced large portions of the working class that tax policies that are a sure winner for the wealthy will also be in their best interest — despite historical evidence that tax cuts for the wealthy do *not* produce the type of investment society needs most or "trickle down" to enhance the general welfare. In other words, political leaders have defined a social reality for the working class that neither reflects historical reality nor protects its group interest.

To move beyond value-laden assumptions, it is necessary to understand the preconceptions on which such assumptions are based. As social workers we need a thorough understanding of the fundamental assumptions that underlie policy and practice. Every policymaker, practitioner, researcher, and author is guided by an ideology. Whether or not individuals are conscious of their own ideology, it affects their actions. How these individuals answer certain basic questions helps explain the different types of policy we have, the different models of practice, the different findings from similar research, and the different types of social work texts.

The basic but often unstated questions are:

1. What preconceptions does this individual hold about people? What does the person believe motivates individuals? What controls do individuals require? What is this person's view of human potential and how it can be maximized?

2. What does the individual believe is the appropriate role for the state to play in the welfare of citizens? (State in this sense means the totality of government: the federal, state, and local levels.) What role does the person think the state presently plays? In other words, how is the state involved in social welfare, and how should it be involved?

3. What assumptions does the individual make about the economic system? Who benefits, and how are the benefits distributed?

4. What assumptions does the person make about the political system? Who has power? How is that power mobilized?

5. What is the individual's vision of an "ideal" political system? An "ideal" economic system? What type of society should we strive for?

These questions provide the tools to look past the social construction of reality to the value base defining the reality. For such an analytical tool to be useful, it must be simple and understandable. Having identified the questions to ask, we need to group the answers in meaningful value sets. This grouping

A *typology* is a simplification of a complex set of characteristics. The most common typology in the social work literature is liberal, conservative, and radical.

The institution of social welfare is society's response to meeting human needs.

Residual has become synonymous with conservative, liberal with institutional.

Fair play combines the liberal and conservative perspectives. Fair shares reflects the radical perspective.

As you read about each perspective, fill in the blanks in the chart on page 82.

Capitalism requires modifications.

is known as developing a typology. The typology we will use comprises the conservative, liberal, and radical perspectives. However, we cannot understand the relationship of ideology to practice without understanding the relationship of practice to the social welfare institution.

THE SOCIAL WELFARE INSTITUTION

In American society, the institution of social welfare is a formal system that supplements informal systems such as family, friends, and church, to bring societal resources to bear on meeting human needs. It encompasses social welfare policy and laws, the social service delivery system, and the human service professions.

An early typology developed by Wilensky and Lebeaux addressed two attitudes toward social welfare—the residual and the institutional.[7] The *residual* approach sees welfare as temporary and minimal. The *institutional* approach views welfare as an ongoing primary institution. These terms are common in social work literature. The institutional conception of social welfare was expanded by writers such as Romanyshyn and Kahn to include a developmental approach.[8] More recent authors such as Gordon and Galper have incorporated the residual, institutional, and developmental conceptions into the conservative and liberal perspectives and have added the radical perspective.[9] Another thought-provoking schema, the fair shares vs. fair play, has been developed by Ryan.[10]

The typology we have adopted for this book is the conservative, liberal, and radical, since these terms are the most inclusive and the most common in the literature. Before applying this typology we must clearly define our terms, because not everyone uses these terms in the same way. Any time we use a typology, we lose some of the richness of the data and introduce the potential for oversimplification.

In spite of its imperfections, this typology can increase your understanding of the assumptions shaping the social work profession. This is not a new typology, but rather a clarification of the concepts in the literature.

Since the liberal perspective is closely associated with mainstream social work practice, we begin the analysis with discussion of first the liberal and then the conservative perspective. At that point we move to an analysis of mainstream social work literature, which reflects a generally liberal perspective with some overlay of conservative principles. Finally, we analyze the radical perspective.

The Liberal Perspective

From a liberal perspective, the present economic system is basically a benevolent one, and the reason that most Americans enjoy a high standard of living. Liberals see social problems as a natural dysfunction of industrialization. Merton and Nisbet typify this approach in their widely used text *Con-*

temporary Social Problems. They assume our economic and political structure is good because it has produced an

Industrialization created affluence.

> imposing command of physical resources, high standards of private consumption, effective maintenance of public order and security, freedom from the uncertainties of life that plagued our ancestors, and relatively high levels of humanitarianism.[11]

But in addition to these advantages, industrialization has also led to social problems.

> There are also, of course, squalid slums . . . sudden eruptions of violence and bigotry . . . people for whom the struggle for food and shelter remains obsessing and precarious. Thus,we are not free of social problems, and some of them seem to grow almost in direct proportion to our affluence.[12]

Welfare is a legitimate function of government.

If one accepts Merton and Nisbet's implication that along with the high standard of living come certain social problems, then social welfare becomes a legitimate function of the government and industrialized society. This analysis suggests that the state's involvement in social welfare is consistent with the liberal conception, as defined by Wilensky and Lebeaux:

The welfare system mitigates the dysfunctions of capitalism.

> Social welfare becomes accepted as a proper legitimate function of modern industrial society in helping individuals achieve self-fulfillment. The complexity of modern life is recognized. The inability of the individual to provide fully for himself or to meet all his needs in family and work settings is considered a "normal" condition; and the helping agencies achieve "regular" institutional status.[13]

Competitiveness is necessary for productivity.

Liberals assume that the basic values of capitalism (individualism, acquisitiveness, and competitiveness) automatically serve the best interests of society. However, preserving freedom does not necessitate preserving every feature of capitalism. Liberals wish to modify capitalism, to intervene in the process, and to minimize the number of people not benefiting from the system, but not to fundamentally change the economic system itself. The welfare state evolves from the altruistic, progressive forces innate in human beings. The social welfare institution is a basically desirable way to meet human needs and organize society to respond to the problems of industrialization and urbanization.[14]

Though liberals are committed to decreasing inequality, they also fear that true equality would decrease productivity and efficiency. People must be motivated by want or need to be productive. Recognizing the potential dysfunctions of a system based on acquisitiveness and individualism, liberals see government as the proper instrument for correcting the deficiencies of the marketplace as long as the availability of workers is not threatened.[15] The developmental view (within the liberal perspective) assumes that it is desirable for a society to set up a social welfare institution simply to make living better and to fulfill human development — not only to solve a problem.[16] Liberalism is also committed to civil liberties. Liberals believe that the abridgment of civil rights is a much greater threat to society than the crimes possibly prevented by the reckless pursuit of law and order. Liberals vigorously oppose preventive lockup of potential criminals and involuntary commitment of mental patients, for instance.

Civil rights are even more important than public safety.

An example may clarify concepts developed thus far. In 1981, NATO voted to ban the sale of certain infant formulae to underdeveloped countries, in response to evidence presented by the World Health Organization that these formulae had been instrumental in causing the malnutrition and death of many children.[17] The United States cast the lone dissenting vote on this boycott. Consistent with the free market perspective of the Reagan Administration, the United States delegate suggested that this ban interfered unnecessarily with free trade. The conservative view holds that if the product is not good, people will not buy it. The liberal perspective asserts that the advertising techniques used in these underdeveloped countries corrupted the mechanisms of the marketplace. Theoretically, the institutional or liberal perspective assumes that it is appropriate for government to protect the people from misleading advertising; in fact this assumption did lead to at least two trials of companies producing the baby formula.[18] The developmental approach finds it acceptable and desirable for the government to intervene and stop the inappropriate sale of baby formula simply for the good of society, in spite of the loss of profit to the private sector. The developmental approach assumes that a society makes decisions based on what will increase the quality of life; it does not assume that this is the same as increasing profit. Developmentalists see the provision of such protection as a proper role of government.

Some authors suggest that anyone desiring to become acquainted with social work should start with the mainstream perspective, then explore the "tributaries."[19] The mainstream in this case is the liberal perspective of social work, with which we began our analysis. The reason for examining the tributaries (the conservative and radical views) is to increase understanding of the mainstream. A consensus view of practice may be easier to understand, but it is not accurate. The realities of practice require a more comprehensive view of the societal values shaping practice. With that goal in mind, we move to an explanation of the conservative perspective.

The Conservative Perspective

A recent study of what Americans think about inequality found that "for the vast majority of Americans in all racial, gender, and age groups, there exists a dominant ideology that is remarkably stable over time and espouses widespread availability of economic opportunity."[20] It follows from this ideology that if people are poor, it is justly based on their individual efforts. Further, people believe that inequality is functional because it encourages individuals to work.

The dominant ideology identified in this study is consistent with conservative principles. This study found that liberalism, which predominates in the social work profession, is not well integrated with the dominant ideology of the wider society.

Unrestrained capitalism is good for society.

The basic assumption of the conservative perspective is that free enterprise (the market system, capitalism) is good. The more capitalism is allowed to develop uninhibited by government, the better off everyone will be. Conservatives believe strongly in private property—welfare confiscates property from one person or group and gives it to another. Welfare has the effect of subordinating the individual to the state and destroying individual initiative. Senator Barry Goldwater, a long-time spokesperson for the conservative ideology, suggests that welfare transforms the individual from a "dignified, industrious, self-reliant spiritual being into a dependent animal."[21] While conservatives like Goldwater would not go so far as Herbert Spencer and the Social Darwinists, who suggested the poor be allowed to starve, they would limit welfare to private, voluntary charity. Private charity is acceptable because it arises from the generosity of the donor, rather than the right of the receiver.

Welfare harms the individual.

This view was reflected during the presidential election campaign in 1988, when candidate George Bush referred to private charity as "a thousand points of light," implying that individual charity brightens society, while public welfare does not.

Conservatives stress the unlimited potential and free will of every human being; the individual is capable of overcoming economic and personal problems. In short, the conservative perspective suggests that the causes of social problems are located in the moral character of the individual; the economic system (capitalism) is blameless. The only appropriate role of government is as a protector from aggressors, whether those aggressors be countries infringing on territorial sovereignty or individuals infringing on the property rights of owners. Since all societies need rules, government must provide a means to modify the rules, mediate differences in interpretation, and enforce compliance. Government is necessary because of human imperfections.

Social problems are caused by individuals, not by the economic system.

Property rights take precedence over civil rights.

Conservatives believe government should stay out of the welfare business and leave private enterprise to operate with minimal restraint, but many conservatives have attempted to legislate what some consider personal decisions affecting women and children. Two recent examples are the push by some conservatives (notably Jerry Falwell and his Moral Majority) to mandate prayer in the schools and to limit abortion. Liberals claim that conservatives are less concerned about protection of civil liberties and strive to promote their own version of the common good.

Vice President Bush illustrated this view when he denigrated the American Civil Liberties Union, an organization that has fought to protect civil liberties, during the campaign. Vice President Bush implied that the ACLU was a destructive, even subversive, organization. He even implied that membership in the ACLU made Governor Dukakis unfit for the presidency.

The Heritage Foundation is a conservative "think tank" that has been highly regarded by the Reagan and Bush administrations.

The Heritage Foundation has suggested ending protection of individual privacy. They want the F.B.I. to be able to conduct break-ins and investigate political groups only *suspected* of criminal activity or intent. They clearly state that civil liberties are secondary to the requirements of national security and internal civil order. Their report argues that serious surveillance of dissident groups requires "such standard intelligence techniques as wiretapping, mail monitoring, informants and at least occasional illegal entries." Some of the groups they urge should be under closer surveillance include "anti-defense and anti-nuclear" lobbies, the Communist Party U.S.A., New Left groups, and the Ku Klux Klan.[22]

Conservative social workers reinforce much of the modern apparatus of social control. They support work requirements for welfare recipients, severely limited welfare benefits, and harsh punishment for criminals. They assume that families should take care of their own and that jobs are available for those willing to work. Welfare should be a temporary substitute for a job, and benefits should carry the stigma of the "dole."

Being "on the dole" is historically a very negative term.

The 1980s were governed by the assumptions underlying the conservative perspective. "Reaganomics," for example, was replete with conservative assumptions. *Wealth and Poverty,* distributed by President Reagan's budget director to employees in the Office of Management and Budget, presents as fact (social reality) conservative assumptions about individuals, the state, and the economic system.[23] Profit and economic utility take precedence over economic security in the conservative world view. Maximization of human potential is predicated on competition, rather than cooperation. This move toward conservatism did not bode well for social workers committed to income redistribution, social change, and client empowerment.

As this ideology permeates our social programs there is renewed emphasis on social control and individually oriented treatment modalities. That is why a significant portion of many state budgets is going toward prison construction and, in spite of rhetoric about controlling drug distribution, scarce funds are allocated to individually oriented treatment programs. Further, Medicare guidelines for third party payment require 3000 hours of training under a psychiatrist or a clinical social worker. This clearly limits social work intervention: if the service is to be reimbursed, the problem *must* be treated as an individual problem. Treatment must also be provided in an institution or professional office—home visits (always an essential component of social work practice)—are not reimbursable.

Ecological social work emphasizes the importance of the environment in individual problems.

While the conservative perspective is not very conducive to ecological social work practice, understanding the values underlying this perspective will help you understand current policies and political influences on practice.

The Social Work Perspective

The assumptions underlying the liberal perspective are generally assumptions that structure the majority of social work literature and practice. Ephross and Reisch surveyed the most widely used introductory social work texts and found that none adopted a conservative or radical stance; all clustered within the liberal perspective.[24] Ephross and Reisch identify the following clusters:

- Left—"which relates most directly to public issues and views social work as fundamentally related to social change"[25] (similar to Kahn's developmental view);[26]
- Centrist—"which acknowledges clearly the connections between social work clients and societal forces and events, but does not deal with the need for political, social, and economic changes;"[27] and
- Right—"which views societal forces as part of the field within which individuals and families exist but stresses this connection largely for the purpose of understanding how to work better with individuals and families (It avoids questions about social change.)."[28]

Ephross and Reisch's findings support the theorists who imply that liberalism and conservatism are best seen as being on a continuum. In spite of real differences, the consistencies appear greater than the discrepancies in their study. These authors analyze the social work literature using the basic questions underlying the typology we are using in this book.

1. What assumptions does the book contain about the political and economic structure of society?
2. What assumptions does the book contain about the nature of social class and social class relationships?
3. What assumptions does the book contain about the nature of social change?

In addition, general implications for a definition of social work practice are noted for each book.[29]

However, the authors do not answer the very question they have identified as important: How are class interests and political-economic structure related?

Since Ephross and Reisch studied only influential texts, their findings reflect the most widely held perspectives in current social work education. Their article provides considerable evidence that the liberal perspective permeates the literature assigned to social work students. Mendelsohn's observation that as social work became more committed to professionalism it became more important to define an area of expertise at least partly explains the lack of critical analysis.

The new professionals certainly recognized that social problems were more than manifestations of individual malaise. Social problems were rather manifestations of the social, economic, and political system. The question became whether to work to correct the system or to work with the victims of the

Social work practice is shaped by the belief systems of individual workers. These social workers are protesting at a Mother's Day March for Peace.

system. The professional field opted to work with the victims primarily, and both the quality and the content of professional social work training were influenced by this decision.[29]

Although analysis shows "the system's" contribution to social problems, society funds social work, and since social work depends on public funds

the profession of social work must reflect the prevailing values, assumptions, and attitudes of the social system. As a consequence, the practice of social work is basically concerned with helping the victim rather than alleviating the causes of the problems.[30]

The state of the art in social work practice is limited by the reality that social workers are agents of society, and practice is basically designed to change or assist victims rather than remove the societal causes of their problems.

The Radical Perspective

The most critical analysis of both social work and social welfare has come from members of the profession who identify themselves as radical practitioners. Although radicals too come in many varieties, one assumption they

all hold in common is that the present economic system does not operate in
the interest of the common person. Radicals believe that the economic system benefits the ruling class and the state and is designed to maintain the
privileges of the ruling class. Webber describes the state in the following
manner:

**Capitalism is the cause
of social problems.**

> The state is a product and manifestation of the irreconcilability of class contra-
> dictions. The state arises where, when, and to the extent that class contradic-
> tions cannot be reconciled. And, conversely, the existence of the state is an
> organ of class rule, an organ for the oppression of one class by another; it is
> the creation of "order" which legalizes and perpetuates the classes.[31]

Piven and Cloward view the social welfare system and particularly the
relief system as an important component in maintaining class privilege. In *Regulating the Poor* they cite historical evidence to support the following position:

**Welfare controls (not
helps) the poor.**

> The key to understanding of relief-giving is in the functions it serves for the
> larger economic and political order, for relief is a secondary and supportive in-
> stitution. Historical evidence suggests that relief arrangements are initiated or
> expanded during the occasional outbreaks of civil disorder produced by mass
> unemployment and are then abolished or contracted when political stability
> is restored. We shall argue that expansive relief policies are designed to mute
> civil disorder and restrictive ones to reinforce work norms.[32]

In their more recent book, *The New Class War,* Piven and Cloward suggest
that relief has become embedded in a general structure of income support
programs for such a wide range of constituencies that subsistence programs
have been replaced by a variety of permanent income-maintenance entitlements. A fundamental change has taken place in our society—"working people who once looked to the marketplace as the arena for action on their economic grievances and aspirations now look more often to the state."[33]

Webber's analysis of the role of the welfare institution, consistent with
the earlier Piven and Cloward thesis, suggests that capitalists gain the most
from welfare programs. In addition to the grants businesses receive, every
welfare penny goes immediately into the hands of landlords, supermarkets,
and utility companies.

**The wealthy benefit
most from welfare pro-
grams.**

> It is common knowledge that programs involving money transfers to "low in-
> come" families and individuals are at levels far below need—even by the
> state's own determination of poverty lines. Moreover the welfare services are
> granted as privileges, that are paid for by the ordinary working people who
> bear the burden of taxation, and they are withdrawn or cut back depending on
> the fluctuating needs and dictates of capital.[34]

In addition to differing with liberals and conservatives on their view of
the state, radicals see individuals and their relation to one another in a different light. Whereas liberals and conservatives believe that true equality
would be detrimental to motivation and productivity, radicals believe human
beings achieve their full potential when they produce without being com-

**Individuals are moti-
vated by commitment,
not competitiveness.**

pelled by the physical necessity of selling themselves as a commodity. Radicals suggest it is in the best interest of society and the individual that everyone be allowed and required to contribute to society. Galper expresses this idea succinctly: "In every society it takes the efforts of the majority of us, working with our hands and minds to produce the goods and services on which the physical maintenance of life depends. Making society work is a collective effort."[35]

Competition and private property distort humanity.

The radical view implies that capitalism, based on possessiveness and competition, distorts the best impulses of human beings. The present economic system is irrational, since it produces for profit rather than social need, requires inequality and exploitation, distorts the value and meaning of human life, and contains inherently anti-democratic features.[36]

Workers should have political and economic power.

Workers should share in production decisions.

Visions of an ideal economic system vary among radical theorists. One proposal for restructuring the economic system is contained in the Carnoy and Shearer work *Economic Democracy*. The two fundamental reforms they suggest for the United States today are the shift of investment control from corporate domination to the public, and the reconstruction of economic decision making through democratic and worker/consumer controlled production.[37] Carnoy and Shearer argue for structural reforms in the American economy that would make periodic fights to preserve welfare benefits unnecessary. These structural reforms would be based on American ideals of individual freedom and rights. People would have to be convinced that the prescribed reforms would result in a more, not less, humanistic society, an extension of democracy, and an increase in material well-being. But political democracy remains a myth until people can construct an economic democracy that allows the common person power to make economic decisions—not just earn wages. Until that power is wrested from the few and returned to the many, political democracy remains an illusion.

In summary, the radicals see people as basically good and willing to contribute to society when provided the opportunity. Individual productivity and potential is maximized by removing want and insecurity. The welfare state is a limited attempt by government to ameliorate the most blatant injustices of capitalistic development. Corporations that require increased government services for defense cause budget deficits. Military buildup is necessary so that corporations can expand abroad, and welfare services at home are necessary to control and pacify the unemployed when the economy does not provide enough domestic jobs to maintain civil order.[38]

Government provides socialism for the rich, capitalism for the poor.

Radicals suggest the nature and application of welfare programs have worked to maintain the continuity of corporate capitalist development under politically difficult conditions. While welfare does improve the relative income position of the poor, it does so in a way that reinforces their low status and forces them to feel vulnerable to changes in the economy.[39]

Gwen Gilbert criticizes the profession on a practical level for facilitating the oppression caused by our present economic arrangement. She sees this problem as so pervasive that the basic content of social work education would have to be changed to prepare students to work for human liberation, rather than oppression. Educational requirements necessary for nonoppressive (radical) practice include

1. appropriate knowledge for analysis of the economic, political, and social structures that perpetrate oppression,
2. appropriate concepts for understanding the devastating impact of these structures on the lives of the oppressed; and
3. direction for the formulation and use of new and diverse strategies for change in response to the resultant goals of survival, liberation, and being.[40]

She also points out that nonoppressive practitioners must have a knowledge of self (value clarification), and particularly of how their behavior contributes to oppression or liberation. Gilbert's critique of social work practice underscores the dilemma of social work as identified by Mendelsohn— "Who pays for the service?" Certainly few who choose to enter the field of social work want to support oppression. While the difficulty of practicing liberating social work in traditional settings is obvious, there are social workers

Radical practice is liberating practice.

who have found radical, liberating practice possible. But by and large, social workers have been limited by skill and resources to helping clients cope and adjust to difficult situations, and have not been able to make the far-reaching societal changes necessary for the liberating practice Gilbert desires.

To make the comparison between the liberal and radical perspectives clearer, we draw on a recent analysis of feminist social work.[41] The authors define socialist feminism similarly to what we have defined as the radical social work perspective. Therefore, we use Nes and Iadicola's socialist perspective to illustrate radical assumptions. The liberal and socialist perspectives both address the issues we have defined as key components of ideology. Excerpting from their analysis, we can make the comparisons shown in Table 4–1.

Nes and Iadicola's work is not limited to identifying the perspectives. They take this knowledge to the application stage and suggest how the analysis translates into practice at each stage of the social work process. While the conceptualization is the work of these authors, we again translate their work into our own typologies in Table 4–2.

These tables illustrate the concepts we have developed in the typologies. We have not included the conservative perspective in this comparison because the goals of feminism are in conflict with the goals and assumptions of conservatism. Feminism is in part an attempt to overcome the discrimination inherent in the conservative perspective.

Ideologies: A Summary

The values and ideologies that shape social work are complex. But however enumerated or elaborated, those values do not exist in a vacuum. Values exist within a large and diverse societal context, and the profession makes a

TABLE 4–1
Comparison of Liberal and Radical Perspectives

Subject	Liberal Perspective	Radical Perspective
Nature of social order	Free market system is the foundation of economic and political freedom. However, system needs "fine tuning."	Modes of production and reproduction are basis of social order and power.
View of the "good" society	Welfare state capitalism; equal opportunity to compete and maximize potential	Democratic socialism— elimination of class, patriarchy, and all other forms of oppression.
Strategies to achieve good society	Political organizing; Legal reform; Affirmative Action	Organize oppressed groups; build coalitions; overthrow patriarchy, class, and all forms of oppression.

Based on work done by J. Nes and P. Iadicola, "Toward a Definition of Feminist Social Work," Social Work 34, 1 (January 1989), 2–21.

selection from the premises available that it can support and build upon. Recognizing that the liberal perspective is the primary perspective, an understanding of the conservative and radical ideologies explains some of the directions in which the profession is pulled. Social work is in the uncomfortable position of being criticized from both sides. Radicals criticize the profession for facilitating oppression; conservatives criticize the same actions for creating dependencies. While some educators suggest that it is desirable to have students master the liberal perspective of social work before exploring the alternates, we advocate educating students for practice by providing a broader analytic framework. To provide one perspective on practice, although a common approach in social work education, does not prepare students for the dissonance they will experience as they encounter attacks on their chosen profession. By considering three very different perspectives on social work practice, students will increase their capacity to withstand the demoralizing effects of destructive criticism and to experience professional growth from constructive criticism. It may also help students to understand the conflicting values they may experience.

SELF-AWARENESS RELATED TO PRACTICE

Self-awareness is one of the profession's major tools. "Self-awareness is the ability to recognize when the judgmental, noncaring self interferes with the ability to reach out, to explore, to help others mobilize their coping

TABLE 4–2
Social Work Practice Within the Liberal and Radical Models

Social Work Process	Liberal Perspective	Radical Perspective
Problem Identification	Identify individual deficits and problems in the opportunity structure, especially those rooted in sexism.	Identify impact of institutional processes and belief systems; examine personality attributes that are the outcome of systems of domination.
Assessment	Assess degree and manifestation of individual deficits; blockages in opportunity structure; interplay between individual deficits and opportunity structure; and availability of institutional supports.	Assess primary and secondary relationships in terms of domination; assess impact of class, race, and general socioeconomic condition on the client; examine issues of alienation, self-fulfillment, and locus of control.
Intervention	Traditional theories; advocacy to ensure against discrimination based on sex.	Consciousness raising; support, self-help, and advocacy groups; coalition building; empowerment; encourage political action.
Goals	Correct individual deficits; open up opportunity structure; establish support groups; promote client fulfillment; validate choices.	Create individual and collective awareness that personal problems have their roots in oppression; mobilize political resources to promote change; create alternative communities for women.

capacities."[42] Self-awareness involves the skill of recognizing the client's strengths and weaknesses and how these characteristics affect your own motivation and ability to provide service.

As long as values remain abstractions, practice tends to be harmonious. Exactly how these values are put into day-to-day practice, however, can be a source of considerable disagreement among professionals, as well as between practitioners and the communities they represent and serve.

Identifying personal values and being self-aware are important parts of developing plans and specific actions in work situations. Social work is an ongoing translation of abstract principles into specific activities, and

In Part V, "Fields of Practice," we illustrate how values become translated in different settings.

understanding differences in value applications from person to person is essential.

Value differences are the source of strong disagreements and very different choices about specific activities to be undertaken. Frequently, when there is marked disagreement on how to proceed, it is brushed off as a mere difference of opinion. If values are as compelling as we assert, then it is a disservice to pass off lightly issues that may require resolution if the work being done is to succeed. Socialization of students into the norms, values, and culture of the profession is an integral part of professional education. Value clarification should be at the heart of professional education.

The process of value clarification develops understanding of what is happening, so that people can work together to accomplish specific goals even though there may be a difference in values. We hope that the comparison of ideologies we have presented will help you make an informed choice about entering the profession and help you understand the people you work with, both clients and coworkers.

If the liberal perspective most closely frames your reality, you will experience little or no difficulty in accepting social work values. The code of ethics, the major texts, the professional culture, and social work methodology are all consistent with a liberal ideology. Your sense of frustration will come from the larger society, which does not fully subscribe to the same degree of liberalism.

If you hold conservative values, there will be some areas in social work practice that accord with your value base; however, some of the populations with whom you work will not fit into your concept of "deserving." The literature and practice in the field will probably create value conflicts for you. You need to analyze the NASW Code of Ethics closely to make certain the profession's ideology does not conflict with your sense of morality.

If you agree with the radical perspective, you will be sensitive to the oppressive as well as the beneficial aspects of social programs, and will probably find agency or program restrictions problematic. Since it is unlikely that you will have access to better programs, it is especially important that you follow the rules necessary to assure that clients receive the benefits that are available. Some radicals argue that since the present services only protect the status quo, radical social workers should not work within these settings. Should you hold this view, it would be important for you to work in an alternative setting. While the present benefit programs have obvious shortcomings, they are frequently the only means clients have to meet basic needs. Unless you have an alternative way to meet clients' needs, you should not deprive the poor of resources in an attempt to promote a revolution to bring about equality.

When radicals are willing to work within the present structure of the service delivery system, they can make important contributions to both policy and professional practice. A radical critique of our present system keeps in the forefront the structural causes of social problems and the potentially oppressive features of treatment programs and social welfare policies.

IDEOLOGY, POLICY, AND PRACTICE

The importance of ideology is best illustrated by its effect on policy and therefore practice. Two examples show how ideological perspectives affect analysis, policy, and practice in interventions with drug abuse and delinquency.

A Practical Example: Drug Abuse

Liberal.   From a liberal perspective, drug abuse is the result of social disor-
ganization and addiction is a physical or mental disease. A combination of
social (such as workplace alienation, family dislocation, marital problems),
psychological, and biological elements cause the disease. Although the disease may be an individual problem, the individual is not responsible for the
social conditions that may have contributed heavily to the disease and should
not be punished. Identifying drug abuse as a disease is one way liberals attempt to remove the stigma from drug addiction. Narcotics Anonymous is a
treatment program that makes the same assumption. Consistent with this assumption, intervention is individually oriented: it attempts to make the individual "well." Since liberals are attuned to the social causes of drug addiction,
they see it as appropriate that society should assume responsibility for both
treatment and prevention programs.

Conservative.   From the conservative perspective, drug abuse becomes a
problem when it threatens existing institutions. Individuals have the right to
take medication (in whatever dosage) prescribed by a physician as long as
that medication increases their ability to meet role expectations. When people
take drugs to the extent that they cannot function appropriately, then drug
usage becomes a problem. Drug users are weak or inadequate in their ability
to face reality or cope with everyday life. The conservative response to drug
overuse is punishment. Punishment for upper class abusers may be limited
to stigmatization, if they have the financial ability to compensate for potential
role deficiencies without threatening the status quo. Members of the lower
class tend to be channelled into the correctional system.

  Until drug usage interferes with social roles, it is not a problem. Whatever the social class, drug abuse is an individual problem or crime, to be dealt
with by negative sanctions. Since the problem lies within the individual, intervention can only be helpful at an individual level. This intervention generally aims to control the individual through punishment.

Radical.   Radical analysts see drug usage as an important component in
controlling oppressed groups. They suggest a clear contradiction in the policies of a government that impedes importation and distribution of "illegal"
drugs at the same time it promotes the legal use of similar drugs. Radicals
raise the broadest spectrum of issues under the question of "drug abuse."

Feminists, for example, are concerned about overprescription of drugs to control women. Recent reports claim that 45 percent of American women take mood-altering drugs; only half as many men receive such prescriptions.[43] Traditionally, women have been portrayed as hypochondriacs whose pains are a manifestation of emotionalism, rather than illness or justifiable dissatisfaction. One woman who had undergone psychiatric hospitalization for "psychosomatic" stomach pains subsequently died of cancer; another died of a brain tumor while being treated for psychosomatic head and neck pain.*

Another example of pharmacological social control is the sedation or medication of highly active children. One pediatrician remarked, "If a mother can't handle the kids, we just have to medicate them."* In reality, such medication is frequently prescribed at the request of schools rather than at the mother's.

Radicals contend that our social response to drug abuse merely protects the status quo, and that the definition of abuse itself is politically motivated. If a substance is used by a professional to control an individual who may upset the status quo, it is not abuse. This supply channel (the licensed professional) is also open to people who can afford to be addicted to legal drugs, as long as their behavior is not disruptive. Drug use becomes "abusive" or criminal when lower class individuals go outside of the law to obtain relatively the same effects the wealthy purchase legally.

Is drug abuse a crime, an illness, or a choice? Varying attitudes lead to diverse answers to this basic value question.

Frustration with society's inability to stem the illegal drug trade has led both liberals and conservatives to discuss a radical approach to the problem: legalization of drugs.

The market theory would suggest that drug laws — not drugs — cause the most damage to society. If drugs were legal, the black market would evaporate. If the profit were removed from drug trafficking, it would cease to exist. The very discussion of legalizing drugs underscores how ineffective societal control mechanisms have been in this area. It has been predicted that legalization would save the government $8 million a year in police, court, and prison costs, as well as generating billions in tax revenues.[44]

This seemingly radical argument has moved into the mainstream. In May, 1988, the mayors of Washington, Baltimore, and Minneapolis, along with several members of Congress, called for congressional hearings to consider legalization.[45] The issue raises in-depth discussion of values held about the individual and society. How do we protect society from the individual? How do we protect the individual from society? Whose interests will be served, and at what costs?

---

* These examples were taken from the author's practice experience.

A Second Example: Juvenile Delinquency

Liberal.   The liberal perspective suggests a complex relationship between the individual and society. Although crime is considered irrational behavior, social problems usually push the individual toward the irrationality of crime. The problem is with the system as well as the individual. Liberals have considerable faith in rehabilitation programs, and believe that if society would put enough value (and money) into studying the problem, the causes of delinquency could be understood and the problem solved. Liberals stress the cause of the problem as social, rather than individual.

Conservative.   The conservative perspective has a less complex view of delinquency. The individual (not the system) is diseased, with little or no hope of rehabilitation. All delinquents should be punished, regardless of mitigating social conditions. Since delinquency is a threat to society, delinquents should be removed from society. The greatest hope for decreasing delinquency lies in increasing the severity and length of punishment. Intervention in delinquency is defined as more police and equipment, longer sentences, and, to extreme conservatives, preventive lock-up. This perspective is reflected in the "law and order" or "get tough on crime" mentality.

Liberals and conservatives agree on a number of points: both view the social order as rational and the violators as irrational; both feel the individual needs to change, either through punishment or treatment; and both see urban crime as the most threatening because it is the most violent.

Radical.   Radicals suggest that understanding juvenile delinquency requires understanding that crime is rooted in the structure of American political and economic institutions. Society emphasizes urban crime because it is lower class crime that threatens the property of the upper class. The purpose of the justice system or the state is to protect the ruling class. The very act of determining a certain behavior is criminal is structured by ruling class interest. Any act can become criminal by fixing a penal sanction to it and processing it through the judicial machinery. For example, certain acts have been viewed as criminal at different times and in different societies — possession of marijuana, heroin addiction, abortion, poverty.

Radicals see juvenile delinquency as a rational response to the goals of a capitalistic society. Capitalistic societies value acquisitiveness and competitiveness. If lower class juveniles cannot achieve financial success legally, they will create opportunities to achieve success illegally. In actuality, it may be *more* rational for many juveniles to take the illegal route than it would be to delude themselves that they can "make it" legally.

A radical framework makes intervention difficult, since radicals believe the insecurity and competitiveness required by capitalism cause crime. Therefore, the solution—removal of the inequality and racism necessary to capitalism—would be to change the fundamental economic structure. Realistically, the radical perspective does not contribute immediately applicable intervention techniques to decrease crime, but it does make a persuasive argument for understanding criminal behavior as a rational act. Radicals refuse to blame social workers for high recidivism rates. The social workers are scapegoats for an ineffective system that ignores the structural causes of juvenile delinquency.

In contrast to the liberal and conservative views, radicals suggest that crime is rational in a capitalistic society, and that the judicial machinery protects the ruling class and controls the lower class. It is not more of the present array of social services juvenile delinquents need, but rather the opportunity to participate in and benefit more equitably from society.

A critical analysis of a problem such as juvenile delinquency can be disconcerting. Historically, society has experienced cycles of punishment (conservative perspective) and treatment (liberal perspective). In spite of the different approaches, the incidence of delinquency remains relatively stable—at intolerable levels. The radical perspective, which suggests that the answer to juvenile delinquency is a basic restructuring of societal values and the economic system, is unlikely to be tested. Neither individual social workers nor the profession is prepared to take on such a monumental task.

The kinds of social work interventions we undertake are determined by our value system, rather than by empirically supported knowledge of the cause and effect of juvenile delinquency. If the conservative attitude toward delinquency prevails, the intervention will be swift, harsh, and certain punishment. Liberals will continue to fight for development of prevention and treatment programs. Radicals will work to overcome the oppression that they see as the cause of juvenile delinquency. No one knows how to cure the problem, but many will work to eliminate it, guided by their own personal and professional values.

SUMMARY

Based upon what you have learned in this chapter, fill in the blanks of the chart in Figure 4–1. Once you have completed this task, pick a social problem (other than delinquency or drug abuse) and identify for each perspective:

1. What is the locus of the problem (individual or society)?
2. How is that problem related to industrialization or capitalism?
3. What is the state doing about the problem? What should it do?
4. What has been the outcome of programs to date?

FIGURE 4–1

Fill in the blanks, following the definitions of the conservative, liberal, and radical perspectives given in this chapter.

	Assumptions About Individuals	View of the Present Economic System	Present Role of the State	Normative Role of the State	Cause of Social Problems	Outcome of Present Services or Programs
Conservative						
Liberal						
Radical						
Issues:	a. Inherently good or evil/potential b. What motivates human beings?	a. Who benefits the most? b. How does it apply to society?	a. Whose interests are served? b. Who benefits from social welfare programs?	a. Whose interests should be served? b. Who should benefit from welfare programs?	a. Individual b. Social system c. Economic system d. Political system	a. Liberation of lower class b. Greater economic security c. Weakening of individual d. Oppression of lower class

NOTES

1. W. H. Werkmeister, *Historical Spectrum of Value Theories* (Lincoln, Neb.: Johnsen Publishing Co., 1970), 1:xii.
2. George T. Martin and M. N. Zald, *Social Welfare and Society* (New York: Columbia University Press, 1981).
3. Published 1982, National Association of Social Workers, Inc. Reprinted with permission, from *NASW Standards and the Classification of Social Work Practice,* Policy Statement 4, p. 18.
4. Jean Anyon, "Ideology and U.S. History Textbooks," *Harvard Educational Review* 49 (August 1979): 361–383.
5. Marlene Webber, "Abandoning Illusions: The State and Social Change," *Catalyst* 6 (1980): 41–66.
6. T. B. Edsall, *The New Politics of Inequality* (New York: Norton, 1984), 141–148.
7. H. L. Wilensky and C. N. Lebeaux, *Industrial Society and Social Welfare* (New York: Free Press, 1958), 138–147.

8. John M. Romanyshyn, *Social Welfare: Charity to Justice* (New York: Random House, 1971); Alfred J. Kahn, *Social Policy and Social Services* (New York: Random House, 1979).

9. David Gordon, *Problems in the Political Economy* (Lexington, Mass.: Heath, 1977); Jeffrey H. Galper, *The Politics of Social Services* (Englewood Cliffs, N.J.: Prentice-Hall, 1974).

10. William Ryan, *Equality* (New York: Pantheon, 1981).

11. Robert Merton and R. M. Nisbet, *Contemporary Social Problems* (New York: Harcourt, Brace and World, 1961), 3.

12. Ibid., 4.

13. Wilensky and Lebeaux, *Industrial Society,* 140.

14. Galper, *Politics of Social Services.*

15. Gordon, *Problems in the Political Economy.*

16. Ralph Dolgoff and Donald Feldstein, *Understanding Social Welfare* (New York: Harper, 1980).

17. Frances M. Lappe and J. Collins, *Food First: Beyond the Myth of Scarcity* (New York: Ballantine, 1979).

18. Ibid.

19. Armando Morales and Brad Sheafor, *Social Work: A Profession of Many Faces,* 2nd ed. (Boston: Allyn and Bacon, 1980).

20. J. R. Kluegel and E. R. Smith, *Beliefs About Inequality* (New York: Aldine, 1986).

21. Barry Goldwater, *Conscience of a Conservative* (New York: Manor Books, 1960).

22. *Milwaukee Journal,* 16 November 1980.

23. George Gilder, *Wealth and Poverty* (New York: Basic Books, 1981).

24. P. H. Ephross and M. Reisch, "The Ideology of Some Social Work Texts," *Social Service Review* 56 (June 1982): 273–291.

25. Ibid., 275.

26. See, for example, Romanyshyn, *Social Welfare;* Ruth R. Middleman and Gale Goldberg, *Social Service Delivery: A Structural Approach to Social Work Practice* (New York: Columbia University Press, 1974); David Macarov, *The Design of Social Welfare* (New York: Holt, Rinehart, and Winston, 1978); Allan R. Mendelsohn, *The Work of Social Work* (New York: New Viewpoints, 1980); Alfred Kahn, *Social Policy.*

27. Ephross and Reisch, 280. Examples of Centrist texts include Allen Pincus and Anne Minahan, *Social Work Practice: Model and Method* (Itasca, Ill.: Peacock, 1973); Carol Meyer, *Social Work Practice* (New York: Free Press, 1970); Frank Loewenberg, *Fundamentals of Social Work Intervention* (New York: Columbia University Press, 1977); Beulah Compton and Burt Galaway, *Social Work Processes* (Homewood, Ill.: Dorsey Press, 1975).

28. Ibid. Examples of Rightist texts include Walter Friedlander and Robert Apte, *Introduction to Social Welfare,* 4th ed. (Englewood Cliffs, N.J.: Prentice-Hall, 1974); Max Siporin, *Introduction to Social Work Practice* (New York: Macmillan, 1978); Howard Goldstein, *Social Work Practice: A Unitary Approach* (Columbia: University of South Carolina Press, 1973).

29. Allan R. Mendelsohn, *The Work of Social Work* (New York: New Viewpoints, 1980).

30. Lappe and Collins, *Food First.*

31. Webber, "Abandoning Illusions."

32. Frances F. Piven and Richard Cloward, *Regulating the Poor: The Functions of Public Relief* (New York: Pantheon Books, 1971).
33. Frances F. Piven and Richard Cloward, *The New Class War: Reagan's Attack on the Welfare State and Its Consequences* (New York: Pantheon Books, 1982).
34. Webber, "Abandoning Illusions."
35. Galper, *Politics of Social Services.*
36. Ibid.
37. Martin Carnoy and Derek Shearer, *Economic Democracy* (White Plains, New York: Sharpe, 1980).
38. Ibid.
39. Ibid.
40. Gwen Gilbert, "The Role of Social Work in Black Liberation," *The Black Scholar* 19 (December 1974): 16–23. Reprinted in Morales and Sheafor, *Social Work,* 2nd ed.
41. J. A. Nes and P. Iadicola, "Toward a Definition of Feminist Social Work," *Social Work* 34, 1(January 1989): 2–21.
42. W. Devore and E. G. Schlesinger, *Ethnic Sensitive Practice* (Columbus, Ohio: Merrill, 1987), 88.
43. Elinor Polansky, "Women and the Health Care System: Implications for Social Work Practice," in *Women's Issues and Social Work Practice,* ed. Elaine Norman and Arlene Mancuso (Itasca, Ill.: Peacock, 1980), 183–200.
44. *Milwaukee Journal,* 22 May 1988.
45. Ibid.

Chapter

5

Attributes and Professional Associations

The social work profession's right to act—its authority—is not based on moral assumptions but is earned by the value-based knowledge and skill garnered in practice and focused in a particular area of expertise that is recognized and sanctioned by the wider community.[1]

This chapter addresses what it means to be a member of a profession and what a profession is. We then look at some of the major associations that shape the social work profession.

PROFESSIONALIZATION

Throughout history there has been debate within and outside the profession about whether social work is a profession, a subprofession, or a paraprofession. There have always been factions within the profession that saw increased professionalization serving the best interests of the client and the profession. The benefits to social workers would include increased pay, prestige, and community support, more financial support for research, a higher caliber of people entering the profession, and third party payments.

Clients would benefit from increased professionalization because they would have increased protection against unqualified practitioners and a higher quality of service. This would be achieved through more effective mechanisms for sanctioning unethical or incompetent social workers. Clients would also benefit by the protection of confidential privilege. A final indirect benefit for clients would be an increase in the profession's power base: the public would be more likely to accept its advocacy for progressive change if social work acquired more status.

Confidential privilege assures clients that the information they provide in the professional relationship cannot be used in court.

Objections to increased professionalization include charges that increased educational requirements would discriminate against the educationally deprived; that licensing and continuing education requirements would be burdensome; that licensing protects professionals, not clients; and the concern that as professionalization increases, so does the price of services, ultimately leading to a decrease of services to the poor.

During the 1980s there was increasing interest in professional status as social workers attempted to obtain reimbursement for their services from health insurance and other third party vendors. Vendorship was listed as the highest priority goal of the 1984 National Association of Social Workers Delegate Assembly in the area of professional standards, and was the primary agenda item for lobbying Congress during the 1985–86 program year.[2] Vendorship status means that social workers would have to be recognized by insurance companies as autonomous providers of service who could therefore receive payment for their services. This is of primary concern to clinical social workers.

In 1975 the National Federation of Societies for Clinical Social Work hired its first lobbyist to advocate for the interests of clinical social workers and their patients in federal legislation and health care policy. The lobbyist's first project was an assessment of the status of clinical social work in comparison with other mental health disciplines. They found that clinical social work was ten years behind psychology in the struggle for parity with psychiatry, reflecting a similar time lag in obtaining uniform state licensing. The absence of uniform state licensing was seen as a major obstacle to participation for clinical social workers in the three largest federally funded health care programs — Medicare/Medicaid, CHAMPUS (Civilian Health and Medical Programs of the Uniformed Services) and FEHBA (Federal Employees Health Benefits Program).

Today, even though only 35 states license social workers, both psychologists and clinical social workers are covered by CHAMPUS and FEHBA; Medicare is still controlled by the physician monopoly.[3]

Since licensing is a major issue within the profession, it is important to put it in perspective. Licensing signifies that a group has met the three prerequisites of a profession: a cognitive or intellectual component, a service orientation, and a monopoly on certain services.[4]

Cognitive or Intellectual Component

Professional expertise must be grounded in a body of theory that is relatively abstract, systematic, and communicable. The knowledge base must be constantly tested, clarified and restructured. Mastery of this body of knowledge requires advanced education that is carefully designed and intellectually demanding.

Part IV identifies the major components of the social work knowledge base.

The social work knowledge base includes an understanding of human behavior and the social environment that incorporates knowledge of human growth, development, and social functioning and an understanding of the interrelationships between people. This theoretical body encompasses concepts of how human systems develop, change, and malfunction, and how interrelationships between systems are formed and continue to operate.[5] Related to this general knowledge base is an understanding of general political, social, and economic systems, plus the systems unique to social work practice.

In addition to the more general theories of humanity, social workers must acquire a practice theory base. Practice theory is a statement of the nature of the principles and processes of the profession and of the responsibilities assumed by the practitioner. This incorporates professional norms and values. In other words, social workers must learn to use their theoretical knowledge in a manner consistent with the methods and values of the profession.[6]

Finally, social workers seek mastery of theories of practice—the specific operational procedures and skills of the social work profession. Some currently popular theories of practice include the eclectic model, the generalist model, the life model, and the task-centered model.[7] The more traditional theories of practice are based on casework, group work, and community organization models.

The profession's strong commitment to theory-based practice is reflected in its code of ethics. The code directs social workers to become and remain proficient in professional practice and the performance of professional functions. It requires that social workers accept responsibility for employment only on the basis of existing competence or the intention to acquire the necessary competence. It prohibits social workers from misrepresenting professional qualifications, education, experience, or affiliations.

In addition, the code encourages social workers to engage in scholarship and research to expand the knowledge base, while at the same time protecting research participants from unwarranted physical or mental discomfort, distress, harm, danger or deprivation. The profession's approach to theory development is expansive. The complexity of problems social workers confront is not amenable to explanation by a single body of theory. We draw particularly from the disciplines of biology, psychology, and sociology to develop our knowledge base and to increase our effectiveness in providing services.

Mandate for Service

Our commitment to service directs us to provide the best possible service to every client, regardless of the client's problem or social status. This requires putting the client's needs ahead of our own, should there be a conflict. Social work traditionally has been the primary profession serving the most socially and financially oppressed groups in our society. Until recently, private practitioners have been the exception. Today, private practice appears to be one of the fastest growing arenas for social work. Approximately 30 percent of all NASW members engage in at least part-time private practice.[8] There is some concern that this movement to private practice detracts from our commitment to the most oppressed groups. Some suggest, however, that private

The National Conference on Social Welfare (NCSW), which began as the National Conference of Charities and Corrections in 1873, was the major annual forum for the discussion of national issues affecting social work.

practice is an effective method of providing access to social work services to clients who previously have been excluded.[9]

Private practitioners are not limiting themselves to psychotherapy with middle and upper class clients. In Hawaii, there is a private practice that specializes in child protective services; in Maryland, private practitioners are developing a network of services for the frail elderly; in Michigan, private practitioners provide employee assistance services; and in Southern California they provide adult protective services.[10] There is evidence that social workers are being required to develop alternative structures to provide the same services we have traditionally provided in public agencies.

The NASW Code of Ethics statement, "The social worker should regard as primary the service obligation of the social work profession," reflects the degree of commitment the profession has to society and to service. Primacy of service to the client is also reflected in the code's mandate to "serve clients with devotion, loyalty, determination, and the maximum application of professional skill and competence."

Finally, the code charges social workers with promoting the general welfare of society in addition to the individual good. Social workers "act to prevent and eliminate discrimination against any person or group on the basis of race, color, sex, sexual orientation, age, religion, national origin, marital status, political belief, mental or physical handicap, or any other preference or personal characteristic, condition, or status." They "act to ensure that all persons have access to the resources, services, and opportunities" they need.

As social workers, we strive to expand choice and opportunity with special regard for disadvantaged or oppressed groups and persons and to promote conditions that encourage respect for the diversity of cultures that constitute American society. Sometimes this requires us to advocate policy change and legislation to improve social conditions and to promote social justice. The code clearly reflects our dual mandate to solve private troubles and to address public issues. One of the debates surrounding how we can do this more effectively concerns the importance of social work licensing. Licensing only takes place when a group has a monopoly on certain areas of knowledge and skills.

Monopolistic Component of Professionalism

When a profession attains a monopoly, it provides services no other profession is allowed to provide, controls the mechanisms for recruitment and education, accredits professional schools, sets requirements for licensing and regulation, and evaluates and censures unprofessional behavior.

Licensing is the ultimate sanction of the monopoly by the community. By 1987 thirty-five states had some form of social work licensing. In 1989 social workers in seven states actively organized to lobby for vendorship; those in two more began planning their campaign initiatives, and those in Missouri, Wisconsin and New Jersey sought licensure or upgrading of licensure.[11]

Licensing is the strongest form of legal regulation. Its purpose is to ensure that individual practitioners have achieved the required educational status and are capable of practicing with at least a minimum level of competence. Applicants must pay a fee for a license; they face legal action if they practice unethically or without a license. Licensing protects both the job title and the professional activities.

In states that have passed social work licensing, it has not been problematic to grant exclusiveness of title; rather, problems have emerged as states try to determine what activities should be limited to those individuals holding a social work license. Social workers are trained to do many tasks that are beneficial to society; few would want to limit others from performing these socially constructive tasks. States that have licensing tend to grant a monopoly on the use of the title, enforce credential requirements, require examination of knowledge and skills upon entry into the profession, and impose some kind of continuing education requirement. These states affirm that granting licensure privileges to the social work profession is important for the protection of clients; no state would allow licensure merely to protect a professional monopoly.

Some states have both licensing and vendorship.

It is important to point out that while licensure and vendorship are closely related, licensure does not ensure vendorship status. Some states that do not have licensure do have vendorship status for some social workers. Illinois, for instance, has both licensing and vendorship. The Illinois insurance code states:

> Each insured that is covered for mental, emotional, or nervous disorders or conditions shall be free to select the physician licensed to practice medicine in all its branches, licensed clinical psychologist, or licensed clinical social worker of his choice to treat such disorders and the insurer shall pay the covered charges.[12]

Some states have vendorship but not licensing.

In contrast, Wisconsin does not have licensing of social workers, but does have limited vendorship. Wisconsin's Administrative Code states that to be eligible to provide psychotherapy services as an employee of a board-operated or hospital outpatient psychotherapy facility, a social worker must: (1) have a master's degree in social work from a graduate school of social work accredited by the Council on Social Work Education, with course work emphasis in case work or clinical social work, and (2) be listed in or eligible to be listed in either the National Association of Social Workers Register of Clinical Social Workers or the National Registry of Health Care Providers in Clinical Social Work.[13] Wisconsin allows a wide variety of master's degreed individuals to be certified for third party payment. The one requirement is that they work under the supervision of a certified psychiatrist or psychologist for two years. Wisconsin is clearly limiting its reimbursement to traditional psychotherapeutic services.

Another means for protecting a monopoly is to have conditions attached to receiving public funds. An example of this is the requirement in Title XIX (Medicaid) that requires any nursing home receiving Medicaid funds to have a social worker involved in admitting, caring for, and planning for patients. This legislation specifically requires that the social worker have a degree from an accredited undergraduate program or be receiving supervision from a person with a master's degree in social work.

Professional Attributes: A Summary

Social work has a distinct knowledge base, much of which continues to be based on practice knowledge, rather than empirically based. This is the result of the complexity of the behaviors and problems we face and our commitment not to adopt a single model or theory prematurely.

The service component continues to be the primary reason for the existence of the profession. Social work does not have a monopoly on services, but we are beginning to garner some of the benefits such as vendorship that are usually limited to licensed professions. Licensing is clearly the primary goal of the social work professional association.

PROFESSIONAL ASSOCIATIONS

National Association of Social Workers

The National Association of Social Workers (NASW) is the largest organization of professional social workers in the world. Its 120,000 members are in 55 chapters throughout the United States and in the Virgin Islands, Puerto Rico, and Europe.

According to its bylaws the association has a threefold responsibility: (1) to promote activities appropriate to strengthening and unifying the profession as a whole, (2) to promote sound and continuous development of the various areas of social work practice that meet human need, and (3) to promote efforts in behalf of human well-being by methods of social action.[14]

NASW's primary functions include promoting professional development, establishing professional standards of social work practice, advancing sound social policies, and extending membership.

For the 1990s NASW has established major priorities in five crucial areas: (1) securing adequate public and private financing for human services, (2) gaining public recognition and legal regulation for the social work profession, (3) combatting discrimination, (4) promoting political and legislative activity, and (5) continuing education.[15]

There are three classes of membership in the association: regular, associate, and student. Regular membership is open to all persons holding either a master's or bachelor's degree in social work from an accredited program. Associate membership is primarily for those employed in the field who do not have a social work degree. Student membership is limited to full or part-time students in an accredited graduate or undergraduate social work degree program.

An important unit within NASW is the Academy of Certified Social Workers. MSWs and PhDs may become members of the academy by completing two years of employment supervised by an academy-certified social worker, passing an exam, submitting professional references, completing an interview, and paying dues. The goal of the academy is to protect clients from abuse and incompetence on the part of inadequately prepared practitioners. Many agencies specify membership in the ACSW as a condition of employment.

Policing Practice.   The Committee on Inquiry has the responsibility of hearing and determining complaints filed in accordance with policy approved by the Delegate Assembly and of making recommendations to the Board of Directors for the improvement of complaint procedures.

When an ethics complaint is filed against a social worker, the local chapter Committee on Inquiry provides the initial response. The national Committee on Inquiry is an appellate body for parties contesting the decisions of chapter committees on inquiry. If appellants are still not satisfied, they can appeal to the NASW Board of Directors. If a violation of the NASW code is found, a number of

The American Association of Social Workers (AASW), the National Association of School Social Workers (NASSW), and the American Association of Schools of Social Work (AASSW) are all examples of specialized professional organizations in social work. In the 1950s they set up booths at the National Conference on Social Welfare to inform social workers about the different organizations.

sanctions may be imposed. The chapter may privately censure the member, deliver a written reprimand, or authorize supervision of the member's practice. Only the national level can suspend membership.

Between 1979 and 1985 292 cases were filed against social workers. Seduction of clients, abuse of confidentiality, mishandling of fees, and dereliction of responsibilities to colleagues and employers were among the grievances filed.[16] Sadly, a number of the people who forfeited their NASW affiliation because of sexual misconduct continue to practice and are beyond the reach of any restraining sanctions. Perhaps when a social work licensure system exists in all 50 states, effective controls over ethics violators will exist.[17]

For the present, adherence to appropriate behavior depends on socialization to professionally responsible conduct. The major portion of that socialization takes place in the educational system and is the province of the Council on Social Work Education.

Council on Social Work Education

CSWE is the official accrediting body for schools of social work. The council sets educational requirements that must be met for accreditation. The most recent curriculum policy statement became effective in 1984. Indirectly the council has considerable impact upon students, because it dictates general requirements for coursework and field experiences. The accreditation process is designed to ensure that students receive the necessary preparation. Most states that have social work licensing require that applicants' degrees be from an accredited program.

National Federation of Societies for Clinical Social Work

On July 24, 1971, the National Federation of Societies for Clinical Social Work (NFSCSW) was formed in Houston, Texas. Among numerous subgroups within the profession, NFSCSW has clearly come to the forefront in lobbying for licensure, vendorship, and credentialing. The NFSCSW has established training standards for practice by clinical social workers specializing in psychoanalysis and psychoanalytic psychotherapy and works actively to protect the right of clinical social workers to practice this specialty.

The NFSCSW offers a Board Certified Diplomate in Clinical Social Work. Diplomate status is the highest credential for independent clinical social work practitioners. Eligibility requirements to be examined for diplomate status are as follows:

1. a graduate social work degree from an accredited program
2. a minimum of two courses in personality theory, one of which included material on psychopathology, the other, on normal growth and development; and four clinical methods courses in practice with individuals, couples, families, and groups, or three clinical methods courses and one additional course in personality theory
3. at least one year in direct clinical social work practice with individuals, couples, families, or groups while in graduate school OR one year postgraduate supervised direct clinical social work practice in a structured teaching environment. This supervision may not be counted toward the two years of postgraduate supervised clinical social work practice experience or toward the five years of postgraduate degree for clinical social work practice.
4. not less than 7500 hours of direct client contact extending over not less than five years, with not less than 3000 of these hours within the past ten years
5. a minimum of 3000 hours of supervised postgraduate practice with individuals, couples, or groups obtained in not less than two years. At least 1500 hours of this practice experience must be supervised by a clinical social worker. Only 1500 hours of the required 3000 hours of supervised practice can be supervised by a mental health professional of another discipline (a clinical psychologist or board certified psychiatrist).
6. licensure in states that regulate social work

The NFSCSW represents individually oriented psychotherapists who have significant power in setting credentials for professionals and criteria for

TABLE 5–1
Levels of Social Work Practice

Practice Level	Description of Level	Preparation for Practice
1. Basic Professional	Practice requiring professional practice skills, theoretical knowledge, and values that are not normally obtainable in day-to-day experience but that are obtainable through formal professional social work education. Formal social work education is distinguished from experiential learning by being based on conceptual and theoretical knowledge of personal and social interaction and by training in the disciplined use of self in relationship with clients.	Requires a baccalaureate degree (BSW) from a social work program accredited by the Council on Social Work Education (CSWE).
2. Specialized Professional	Practice requiring the specific and demonstrated mastery of therapeutic technique in at least one knowledge and skill method, as well as a general knowledge of human personality as influenced by social factors, and the disciplined use of self in treatment relationships with individuals or groups, or a broad conceptual knowledge of research, administration, or planning methods and social problems.	Requires a master's degree (MSW) from a social work program accredited by the CSWE.

Source: Copyright 1981, National Association of Social Workers, Inc. Reprinted with permission from **NASW Standards for the Classification of Social Work Practice** *(Washington, D.C.: The Association, September 1981), p. 9.*

services that will be reimbursed. We have presented so much detail about this group because of its potential to influence the future of the profession. Social work practice has always been circumscribed by the kinds of services that society is willing to finance. There is legitimate concern that the profession shaped by the NFSCSW would not include commitment to public issues now embraced by social workers.

Black Social Workers Association

One group likely to be concerned about the direction set by NFSCSW is the Black Social Workers Association. It was formed at the 1968 National Con-

TABLE 5–1
continued

Practice Level	Description of Level	Preparation for Practice
3. Independent Professional	Achievement of practice based on the appropriate special training, developed and demonstrated under professional supervision, which is sufficient to ensure the dependable, regular use of professional skills in independent or autonomous practice. A minimum of two years is required for this experiential learning and demonstration period following the master of social work program. This level applies both to solo or autonomous practice as an independent practitioner or consultant and to practice within an organization where the social worker has primary responsibility for representing the profession or for the training or administration of professional staff.	Requires an accredited MSW and at least two years of post-master's experience under appropriate professional supervision.
4. Advanced Professional	Practice that carries major social and organizational responsibility for professional development, analysis, research, or policy implementation, or is achieved by personal professional growth demonstrated through advanced conceptual contributions to professional knowledge.	Requires proficiency in special theoretical, practice, administration, or policy or the ability to conduct advanced research studies in social welfare; usually demonstrated through a doctoral degree in social work or a closely related social science discipline.

The Black Social Workers Association was founded thirteen years after the formation of NASW.

ference on Social Welfare in San Francisco. Although many reasons prompted its formation, the growing importance of the black power movement was a principal cause. The failure of integration, an increased emphasis on black professionals, and a growing sense of racial solidarity were also important. Black social workers believed there was a need for more direct action to bring about meaningful change.[18]

The charter of the Black Social Workers Association stressed key issues.

1. The ethnic composition of the NASW board and its planning, executive, and nominating committees was disproportionate to that of the conference.

2. White racism was the major mental health problem facing the nation.
3. The BSWA should lend its full support to the National Welfare Rights Organization.
4. The BSWA should commit itself to reconstructing systems relevant to the needs of blacks through whatever means necessary.[19]

Association of Black Social Workers

The Philadelphia Alliance of Black Social Workers held the first annual National Conference of the Association of Black Social Workers (ABSW) in 1969. The ABSW currently has over twenty chapters in the U.S. and is established as a national nonprofit organization.[20]

Since its formation the ABSW has initiated many activities to promote better understanding of the black community within the profession. It has helped develop the Black Coalition for Welfare Rights and given technical assistance to several other black organizations. The ABSW has also improved the image of the social worker in the black community. Finally, the ABSW has stimulated black and white social workers to examine their sensitivity to the black experience and how it relates to the field of social welfare.

Professional Associations: A Summary

The NASW is the primary professional organization of social workers. The Council on Social Work Education is the accrediting body for the profession. We have presented background on NASW and CSWE because of their primary positions within the profession. We also discussed the NFSCSW to show what can be accomplished in the political arena with commitment and financial support. We suggested that this group may be leading social work in general toward a conservative, individually oriented model of practice. The black social work associations are not as strong either financially or organizationally. Their emphasis continues to be on public issues; their goal is to lead the profession toward social rather than individually oriented change.

There are many interest groups within NASW, such as Christian social workers, rural social workers, gerontological social workers, the gay and lesbian task force, clinical social workers, and black social workers, to name just a few.

CASE STUDY
Illustrative Practice Competencies for the
Basic Professional Social Worker (BSW)

KNOWLEDGE

- Basic and general knowledge of human behavior, social systems and social institutions.
- Awareness of social problem areas—their cause and impact on individuals, families, and communities, and the appropriate resources and methods involved in dealing with them.
- Knowledge of basic theories and methods of case work or group work.
- Working knowledge of at least one specific method of intervention or treatment.
- Working knowledge of basic research techniques and sources of specialized professional knowledge.
- Specific knowledge of social planning and community organization methods.

RESPONSIBILITY

- Functions under direct and regularly provided professional supervision.
- Is instructed in specific details of tasks, assuming a general knowledge of professional methods, functions, and objectives.
- Casework or other professional judgments must be renewed to confirm decisions that affect clients in complex situations.
- Acts professionally on one's judgment within an assigned scope of practice.
- Determines client's or community's needs for service within one's practice area. Initiates or terminates one's own or another's services.
- Supervises others in services they are qualified to provide.
- Is advised of administrative or consultative supervision. Requires regular direct supervision for learning specialized practice.

SKILL

- Ability to relate in positive or appropriate relationships under adverse conditions.
- Ability to recognize primary behavioral dysfunction of individuals and groups.
- Ability to make a basic social assessment and service plan.
- Awareness of community resources relevant to identified needs.
- Ability to relate as a professional participant in an agency program.
- Ability to carry out basic techniques of social research.
- Ability to conduct or participate in methods of community organization and planning.
- Ability to conduct a comprehensive social study or treatment plan within a given service.
- Ability to initiate and develop community group programs within given standards.

SITUATIONAL COMPLEXITY

- Routine service or tasks whose goal is easily achievable.
- Single function of limited difficulty.
- Clear expectation of clients.
- Clients with noncompetitive interests when resources are available.
- Temporary, uninvolved helping relationship.
- Identified emotional and social needs with only limited or potential resources.
- Some degree of unconscious motivation.
- Service goals are achievable.

SOCIAL CONSEQUENCES

- Minor potential effect, the impact being limited to one or a small number of clients.

- Potential errors or shortcomings limited in scope.
- Benefits significant, but not essential to health or life.
- Service or program involves a significant social problem.

CLIENT VULNERABILITY

- Minimal risk to persons or groups.
- Potential risks temporary or correctable.
- Client or groups with a clear and valid expectation of service.
- Actions closely or regularly supervised or evaluated.
- Actions or decisions governing a client's situation subject to prior approval.
- Actions or activities have no significant impact on costs.
- Significant health or emotional need or risk of injury involved.
- Service or treatment errors not readily corrected or ameliorated.
- Clear identifiable impact on the client or community.
- Administration and planning of a program have a minor impact on costs.

SOCIAL FUNCTION

- To provide information on rights, benefits, and services.
- To obtain social and personal information or data within specified limits of ethics and confidentiality.
- To advise the public or clients of social expectations and requirements in a constructive, helping relationship.
- To develop data or other research information for the analysis or study of social problems.
- To deal with negative or mildly hostile persons or groups on behalf of society.
- To enable clients or persons seeking aid to understand, accept, or use help in relation to a social problem.
- To interpret and build trust among resident individuals or groups in services designed to provide help.
- To enable individuals or groups to involve themselves in socially constructive activities or changes in conduct.
- To work with hostile persons or groups to achieve or improve understanding or cooperation.

National Association of Social Workers, 1981. Reprinted with permission from *NASW Standards for the Classification of Social Work Practice* (Washington, D.C.: The Association, September 1981), 20–21.

CASE STUDY
Illustrative Practice Competencies for the Independent Professional Social Worker (MSW plus experience)

KNOWLEDGE

- Sufficient expert knowledge to teach or communicate social work practice and theory to professionals in other disciplines or in an interdisciplinary service.
- A thorough knowledge of at least one method of professional practice and specialized knowledge of others.

RESPONSIBILITY

- Acts professionally on his or her judgment.
- Determines clients' or the community's need for service within one's own practice area. Initiates or terminates one's own or another's services.
- Requires instruction only in highly complex, new or specialized methods or procedures of treatment, research, planning, or other mode of work.

- Obtains professional supervision on a consultative basis, as needed.

SKILL

- Ability to conduct a psychotherapy of a highly complex or demanding nature.
- Ability to conduct differential diagnoses of individuals or groups, involving complex and unconscious factors.
- Ability to administer an autonomous social work, health or mental health program of limited scope or one of major scope within a larger organization.
- Ability to take full professional responsibility in a multidisciplinary setting or for general community development or services.

SITUATIONAL COMPLEXITY

- Severe conflicts between persons or groups served.
- Multiple causative factors — major lack of resources.
- Clear evidence of unconscious needs that restrict the ability of a client to change.
- Highly complex emotional and social goals of service.

SOCIAL CONSEQUENCES

- Actions with the potential for a major or long-lasting impact.
- Activities that provide the basis for reviewing, studying, or developing a policy.

CLIENT VULNERABILITY

- Administration, planning, or research involve moderate costs or risks.
- Actions involve the potential for a risk to mental stability.
- Inability of clients or groups to identify their own needs.

SOCIAL FUNCTION

- To negotiate and mediate among deeply opposed persons or groups to achieve socially sanctioned objective.
- To conduct broad-scale research studies that deal with specific social or community issues.
- To provide treatment to overcome major problems involving social dysfunctions, behavior, or severe risk to others.

National Association of Social Workers, 1981. Reprinted with permission from *NASW Standards for the Classification of Social Work Practice* (Washington, D.C.: The Association, September 1981), 23.

 ## CASE STUDY
Illustrative Practice Competencies for the Specialized
Professional Social Worker (MSW)

KNOWLEDGE

- Knowledge of personality theory, interpersonal communications, social group relations, or community organization theory.
- A working knowledge of several methods of interpersonal helping or treatment. Knowledge of at least one psychotherapeutic technique.

- A broad and beginning specialized knowledge of at least one such knowledge area.
- Knowledge of the theory and techniques of professional and personnel supervision and organizational administration.
- Basic knowledge of the administration of social programs.

● Knowledge of the appropriate techniques and methods of research or planning.

RESPONSIBILITY

● Normally functions under periodic or consultative supervision. Requires learning for specialized practice.

● Is advised of administrative requirements and expected to adhere to them adequately.

● Requires instruction only in highly complex, specialized, or new methods or procedures.

● Directs or administers a program staffed by professional social workers and other personnel.

● Reviews work of subordinate professional workers. Assigns and evaluates social work activities.

SKILL

● Ability to establish constructive relationships with resistant clients by overcoming strong initial resistance or dealing with conflict-laden or complex situations.

● Ability to design and conduct research.

● Ability to provide psychotherapeutic treatment under supervision.

● Ability to administer a social service program of limited scope within a larger setting.

● Ability to determine differential treatment needs.

● Ability to provide professional social work training or supervision.

● Ability to represent the discipline of professional social work within an interdisciplinary program.

● Ability to develop and conduct a treatment-therapy program or service without direct supervision.

● Ability to provide a specialized treatment or method of service.

SITUATIONAL COMPLEXITY

● Involves two or more clients with divergent interests.

● Multiple service functions with responsibility for coordination of services or personnel.

● Goals present major difficulties.

● Clients who are emotionally confused or have conflicting social needs.

● Resources not readily available.

SOCIAL CONSEQUENCES

● Activity requires interdisciplinary coordination.

● Actions have a serious but temporary impact and involve more than one client.

● Service or program involves a significant social problem.

CLIENT VULNERABILITY

● Actions involve the potential for a long-lasting but not life-threatening condition or a risk to mental stability.

● Ability of client or groups to identify needs is severely limited.

SOCIAL FUNCTION

● To overcome strong resistance to participation or use of socially required assistance or conduct involving the protection of others.

● To achieve socially desirable changes in conduct involving significant emotional and mental growth and change.

● To achieve long-lasting or broad-scale change toward socially desired objectives.

National Association of Social Workers, 1981. Reprinted with permission from *NASW Standards for the Classification of Social Work Practice* (Washington, D.C.: The Association, September 1981), 22.

LEVELS OF PRACTICE

One task of NASW is to define the professional domain and the parameters of social work practice. In 1979 NASW set up a task force to classify levels of practice. The task force examined four areas to differentiate requirements at the four practice levels: knowledge required by the position, degree of autonomy in practice, type and complexity of skill required, and complexity of problems faced by clientele. Table 5–1 summarizes the different practice levels designated by NASW (see pp. 94–95).

It is clear from these standards that associate degrees or years of experience do not qualify one for membership in the professional organization. In reality these standards represent a desired professional norm rather than an accurate description of who is practicing social work. The NASW competency standards for each level of practice are on pp. 97–100.

Entry Level: Non-Degreed

For most of our professional history, the majority of workers in public welfare agencies who were identified as social workers or caseworkers had little or no professional education in preparation for their position. Most of these people held the title of social worker but were ineligible for membership in the professional association.

The 1960s saw considerable development of human service careers sponsored by programs such as the Manpower Development Training Act. This legislation encouraged hiring of indigenous workers. Technical schools have responded by developing associate degrees for human service workers. NASW, however, does not recognize this as a professional degree. Limiting yourself to this level of education will seriously curtail professional career advancement.

States differ on entry level requirements. While the normal route to social work positions is increasingly through a professional school, many people are still entering social work without a degree. In 1987, 120,000 social workers were members of NASW. This figure represents fewer than one third of the people employed in social work positions.

A person with an Associate of Arts degree is not considered to be a professional social worker.

Bachelor of Social Work

The first level of professional social work practice has been at the bachelor's level since 1970.

Before 1970 NASW admitted only MSWs to full membership in the professional organization. In 1970 they admitted to full membership persons with a BA or BSW from a CSWE-accredited school. This move clearly made the association more representative of the reality of the profession; it also provided increased impetus for undergraduate education. Before 1970 students received no immediate benefit from pursuing a social work degree instead of another social science degree, even if they planned to pursue a career in social work. By admitting BSWs to membership and increasing undergraduate professional requirements the profession moved toward deprofessionalization. The CSWE now requires BSW programs to provide a liberal arts education along with approved courses in social welfare institutions and policies, human behavior and the social environment, practice, research and field experience.

Task differentiation among social service aides, BSWs and MSWs is unsettled. Who may do what is ambiguous and not legally defined. The social service classification plan developed by NASW in 1973 outlined appropriate tasks for social workers with bachelor's degrees. They are qualified to

> Provide supportive casework services,
> Conduct workshops to promote and interpret programs or services,
> Organize local community groups and coordinate combined efforts of groups regarding social problems,
> Consult with other agencies on problems of cases served in common; coordinate services between agencies in helping multi-problem families,
> Conduct basic data-gathering or statistical analysis of data on social problems,
> Develop information to assist legislators and other decisionmakers to understand problems and community needs,
> Serve as an advocate of clients whose needs are not being met by available programs or by a specific agency,
> Work with groups to assist them in defining needs or interests and in deciding upon a course of action, and
> Administer units of program within an overall structure.[21]

Master of Social Work

The MSW is the premier degree of social work practice. From 1940 until 1970, and in spite of resistance from undergraduate programs, it was the only recognized level of professional practice. Since the 1970 decision to recognize BSWs as professionals, debate and confusion over how to differentiate the degrees has reigned. At one point it seemed that the difference between BSWs and MSWs would be the difference between the generalist and the specialist. In 1976 the House of Delegates of CSWE approved a policy stating: "Graduate degree programs in social work shall consist of advanced specialized education that requires and is built upon the core of social work knowledge, skills, and attitudes, and content in basic supporting disciplines."[22] NASW Standards (1973) suggested that MSWs should be prepared to

> provide therapeutic intervention under supervision,
> organize a community coalition to work on broad-scale problems,
> provide a social work component within a multidisciplinary setting,
> conduct group therapy sessions within a clinic setting,
> develop and conduct research involving basic statistical techniques,
> work on program planning for a major public agency providing social services,
> teach on a social work faculty,
> administer a social service program,
> serve as a team leader in a service unit, and
> work in a program planning section of a social service agency.[23]

The tasks identified for MSWs and BSWs are similar. No task on the MSW roster, other than teaching on a social work faculty, is not done regularly by BSWs or even by social service aides. The debate over differentiation of practice levels will no doubt continue for some time. Instead of clarifying differences between BSWs and MSWs, the report of the 1979 task force was even less specific.

Doctorates

Doctoral education in social work officially began at Bryn Mawr College in 1920. The purpose of doctoral education has been consistent throughout its seventy year history. The core objectives were outlined by the Advisory Committee on Advanced Education (CSWE) in 1964.

> Core objectives for all doctoral programs are to equip the student for continuing scholarship and to prepare him for leadership in advancing the profession and its practice. Specifically, the doctoral program is designed to enable the student to extract, organize, extend, test, communicate or apply knowledge to achieve the purpose of social work in society.[24]

As the CSWE report suggests, doctoral education is geared primarily to preparing educators and researchers; current programs put little emphasis on training administrators. There is some sentiment in NASW that there should also be a practice doctorate; some people feel this could be a DSW rather than a PhD. While this may become the practice in the future, at the present time there is little difference between the DSW and the PhD.

Some professional schools offer a DSW (doctorate in social work) while others offer a PhD in social work or social welfare.

Levels of Practice: A Summary

Identifying distinguishing characteristics of each level of practice continues to present difficulties for the profession. Throughout its history NASW has had task forces working on this problem. While the classifications are by no means fully developed or mutually exclusive, the most recent (1981) differentiation by competencies has been presented. These classifications illustrate both the diversity and the potential of social work practice.

In Chapter 3 we discussed how different ideologies affect practice. The professional values, attributes, and associations largely represent the mainstream of the profession. While it would be too cumbersome to present the complete radical and conservative critiques of these issues, you can gain a sense of the conflicting pressures on the profession by comparing the Radical Code of Ethics and the National Association of Christian Social Workers' Statement of Objectives and Faith against the NASW Code of Ethics.

CASE STUDY
The NASW Code of Ethics

This code is intended to serve as a guide to the everyday conduct of members of the social work profession and as a basis for the adjudication of issues in ethics when the conduct of social workers is alleged to deviate from the standards expressed or implied in this code. It represents standards of ethical behavior for social workers in professional relationships with those served, with colleagues, with employers, with other individuals and professions, and with the community and society as a whole. It also embodies standards of ethical behavior governing individual conduct to the extent that such conduct is associated with an individual's status and identity as a social worker.

This code is based on the fundamental values of the social work profession that include the worth, dignity, and uniqueness of all persons as well as their rights and opportunities. It is also based on the nature of social work, which fosters conditions that promote these values.

In subscribing to and abiding by this code, the social worker is expected to view ethical responsibility in as inclusive a context as each situation demands and within which ethical judgment is required. The social worker is expected to take into consideration all the principles in this code that have a bearing upon any situation in which ethical judgment is to be exercised and professional intervention or conduct is planned. The course of action that the social worker chooses is expected to be consistent with the spirit as well as the letter of this code.

In itself, this code does not represent a set of rules that will prescribe all the behaviors of social workers in all the complexities of professional life. Rather, it offers general principles to guide conduct, and the judicious appraisal of conduct, in situations that have ethical implications. It provides the basis for making judgments about ethical actions before and after they occur. Frequently, the particular situation determines the ethical principles that apply and the manner of their application. In such cases, not only the particular ethical principles are taken into immediate consideration, but also the entire code and its spirit. Specific applications of ethical principles must be judged within the context in which they are being considered. Ethical behavior in a given situation must satisfy not only the judgment of the individual social worker, but also the judgment of an unbiased jury of professional peers.

This code should not be used as an instrument to deprive any social worker of the opportunity or freedom to practice with complete professional integrity; nor should any disciplinary action be taken on the basis of this code without maximum provision for safeguarding the rights of the social worker affected.

The ethical behavior of social workers results not from edict, but from a personal commitment of the individual. This code is offered to affirm the will and zeal of all social workers to be ethical and to act ethically in all that they do as social workers.

The following codified ethical principles should guide social workers in the various levels of responsibility in which they function professionally. These principles also serve as a basis for the adjudication by the National Association of Social Workers of issues in ethics.

In subscribing to this code, social workers are required to cooperate in its implementation and abide by any disciplinary rulings based on it. They should also take adequate measures to discourage, prevent, expose, and correct the unethical conduct of colleagues. Finally, social workers should be equally ready to defend and assist colleagues unjustly charged with unethical conduct.

I. The Social Worker's Conduct and Comportment as a Social Worker

A. Propriety—The social worker should maintain high standards of personal conduct in the capacity or identity as social worker.
   1. The private conduct of the social worker is a personal matter to the same degree as is any other person's, except when such conduct compromises the fulfillment of professional responsibilities.
   2. The social worker should not participate in, condone, or be associated with dishonesty, fraud, deceit, or misrepresentation.
   3. The social worker should distinguish clearly between statements and actions made as a private individual and as a representative of the social work profession or an organization or group.

B. Competence and Professional Development—The social worker should strive to become and remain proficient in professional practice and the performance of professional functions.
   1. The social worker should accept responsibility or employment only on the basis of existing competence or the intention to acquire the necessary competence.
   2. The social worker should not misrepresent professional qualifications, education, experience, or affiliations.

C. Service—The social worker should regard as primary the service obligation of the social work profession.

1. The social worker should retain ultimate responsibility for the quality and extent of the service that individual assumes, assigns, or performs.
2. The social worker should act to prevent practices that are inhumane or discriminatory against any person or group of persons.

D. Integrity — The social worker should act in accordance with the highest standards of professional integrity and impartiality.
1. The social worker should be alert to and resist the influences and pressures that interfere with the exercise of professional discretion and impartial judgment required for the performance of professional functions.
2. The social worker should not exploit professional relationships for personal gain.

E. Scholarship and Research — The social worker engaged in study and research should be guided by the conventions of scholarly inquiry.
1. The social worker engaged in research should consider carefully its possible consequences for human beings.
2. The social worker engaged in research should ascertain that the consent of participants in the research is voluntary and informed, without any implied deprivation or penalty for refusal to participate, and with due regard for participants' privacy and dignity.
3. The social worker engaged in research should protect participants from unwarranted physical or mental discomfort, distress, harm, danger, or deprivation.
4. The social worker who engages in the evaluation of services or cases should discuss them only for professional purposes and only with persons directly and professionally concerned with them.
5. Information obtained about participants in research should be treated as confidential.
6. The social worker should take credit only for work actually done in connection with scholarly and research endeavors and credit contributions made by others.

II. The Social Worker's Ethical Responsibility to Clients

F. Primacy of Clients' Interests — The social worker's primary responsibility is to clients.
1. The social worker should serve clients with devotion, loyalty, determination, and the maximum application of professional skill and competence.
2. The social worker should not exploit relationships with clients for personal advantage, or solicit the clients of one's agency for private practice.
3. The social worker should not practice, condone, facilitate or collaborate with any form of discrimination on the basis of race, color, sex, sexual orientation, age, religion, national origin, marital status, political belief, mental or physical handicap, or any other preference or personal characteristic, condition or status.
4. The social worker should avoid relationships or commitments that conflict with the interest of clients.
5. The social worker should under no circumstances engage in sexual activities with clients.
6. The social worker should provide clients with accurate and complete information regarding the extent and nature of the services available to them.
7. The social worker should apprise clients of their risks, rights, opportunities, and obligations associated with social service to them.
8. The social worker should seek advice and counsel of colleagues and supervisors whenever such consultation is in the best interest of clients.
9. The social worker should terminate service to clients, and professional relationships with them, when such service and relationships are no longer required or no longer serve the clients' needs or interests.

10. The social worker should withdraw services precipitously only under unusual circumstances, giving careful consideration to all factors in the situation and taking care to minimize possible adverse effects.

11. The social worker who anticipates the termination or interruption of service to clients should notify clients promptly and seek the transfer, referral, or continuation of service in relation to the clients' needs and preferences.

G. Rights and Prerogatives of Clients—The social worker should make every effort to foster maximum self-determination on the part of clients.

1. When the social worker must act on behalf of a client who has been adjudged legally incompetent, the social worker should safeguard the interests and rights of that client.

2. When another individual has been legally authorized to act in behalf of a client, the social worker should deal with that person always with the client's best interest in mind.

3. The social worker should not engage in any action that violates or diminishes the civil or legal rights of clients.

H. Confidentiality and Privacy—The social worker should respect the privacy of clients and hold in confidence all information obtained in the course of professional service.

1. The social worker should share with others confidences revealed by clients, without their consent, only for compelling professional reasons.

2. The social worker should inform clients fully about the limits of confidentiality in a given situation, the purposes for which information is obtained, and how it may be used.

3. The social worker should afford clients reasonable access to any official social work records concerning them.

4. When providing clients with access to records, the social worker should exercise due care to protect the confidences of others contained in those records.

5. The social worker should obtain informed consent of clients before taping, recording, or permitting third party observation of their activities.

I. Fees—When setting fees, the social worker should ensure that they are fair, reasonable, considerate and commensurate with the service performed and with due regard of the clients' ability to pay.

1. The social worker should not divide a fee or accept or give anything of value for receiving or making a referral.

III. The Social Worker's Ethical Responsibility to Colleagues

J. Respect, Fairness, and Courtesy—The social worker should treat colleagues with respect, courtesy, fairness, and good faith.

1. The social worker should cooperate with colleagues to promote professional interests and concerns.

2. The social worker should respect confidences shared by colleagues in the course of their professional relationships and transactions.

3. The social worker should create and maintain conditions of practice that facilitate ethical and competent professional performance by colleagues.

4. The social worker should treat with respect, and represent accurately and fairly, the qualifications, views, and findings of colleagues and use appropriate channels to express judgments on these matters.

5. The social worker who replaces or is replaced by a colleague in professional practice should act with consideration for the interest, character, and reputation of that colleague.

6. The social worker should not exploit a dispute between a colleague and employers to obtain a position or otherwise advance the social worker's interest.

7. The social worker should seek arbitration or mediation when conflicts with colleagues require resolution for compelling professional reasons.

8. The social worker should extend to colleagues of other professions the same respect and cooperation that is extended to social work colleagues.
9. The social worker who serves as an employer, supervisor, or mentor to colleagues should make orderly and explicit arrangements regarding the conditions of their continuing professional relationship.
10. The social worker who has the responsibility for employing and evaluating the performance of other staff members should fulfill such responsibility in a fair, considerate, and equitable manner, on the basis of clearly enunciated criteria.
11. The social worker who has the responsibility for evaluating the performance of employees, supervisees, or students should share evaluations with them.

K. Dealing with Colleagues' Clients—The social worker has the responsibility to relate to the clients of colleagues with full professional consideration.
1. The social worker should not solicit the clients of colleagues.
2. The social worker should not assume professional responsibility for the clients of another agency or a colleague without appropriate communication with that agency or colleague.
3. The social worker who serves the clients of colleagues, during a temporary absence or emergency, should serve those clients with the same consideration as that afforded any client.

IV. The Social Worker's Ethical Responsibility to Employers and Employing Organizations.

L. Commitment to Employing Organization—The social worker should adhere to commitments made to the employing organization.
1. The social worker should work to improve the employing agency's policies and procedures, and the efficiency and effectiveness of its services.

2. The social worker should not accept employment or arrange student field placements in an organization which is currently under public sanction by NASW for violating personnel standards or imposing limitations on or penalties for professional actions on behalf of clients.
3. The social worker should act to prevent and eliminate discrimination in the employing organization's work assignments and in its employment policies and practices.
4. The social worker should use with scrupulous regard, and only for the purpose for which they are intended, the resources of the employing organization.

V. The Social Worker's Ethical Responsibility to the Social Work Profession

M. Maintaining the Integrity of the Profession—The social worker should uphold and advance the values, ethics, knowledge, and mission of the profession.
1. The social worker should protect and enhance the dignity and integrity of the profession and should be responsible and vigorous in discussion and criticism of the profession.
2. The social worker should take action through appropriate channels against unethical conduct by any other member of the profession.
3. The social worker should act to prevent the unauthorized and unqualified practice of social work.
4. The social worker should make no misrepresentation in advertising as to qualifications, competence, service, or results to be achieved.

N. Community Service—The social worker should assist the profession in making social services available to the general public.
1. The social worker should contribute time and professional expertise to activities that promote respect for the utility, the integrity, and the competence of the social work profession.
2. The social worker should support the formulation, development, enactment

and implementation of social policies of concern to the profession.

O. Development of Knowledge—The social worker should take responsibility for identifying, developing, and fully utilizing knowledge for professional practice.

1. The social worker should base practice upon recognized knowledge relevant to social work.
2. The social worker should critically examine, and keep current with, emerging knowledge relevant to social work.
3. The social worker should contribute to the knowledge base of social work and share research knowledge and practice wisdom with colleagues.

VI. The Social Worker's Ethical Responsibility to Society

P. Promoting the General Welfare—The social worker should promote the general welfare of society.

1. The social worker should act to prevent and eliminate discrimination against any person or group on the basis of race, color, sex, sexual orientation, age, religion, national origin, marital status, political belief, mental or physical handicap, or any other preference or personal characteristic, condition, or status.
2. The social worker should act to ensure that all persons have access to the resources, services, and opportunities which they require.
3. The social worker should act to expand choice and opportunity for all persons, with special regard for disadvantaged or oppressed groups and persons.
4. The social worker should promote conditions that encourage respect for the diversity of cultures which constitute American society.
5. The social worker should provide appropriate professional services in public emergencies.
6. The social worker should advocate changes in policy and legislation to improve social conditions and to promote social justice.

7. The social worker should encourage informed participation by the public in shaping social policies and institutions.

SUMMARY OF MAJOR PRINCIPLES

I. The Social Worker's Conduct and Comportment as a Social Worker

A. Propriety. The social worker should maintain high standards of personal conduct in the capacity or identity as social worker.
B. Competence and Professional Development. The social worker should strive to become and remain proficient in professional practice and the performance of professional functions.
C. Service. The social worker should regard as primary the service obligation of the social work profession.
D. Integrity. The social worker should act in accordance with the highest standards of professional integrity.
E. Scholarship and Research. The social worker engaged in study and research should be guided by the conventions of scholarly inquiry.

II. The Social Worker's Ethical Responsibility to Clients

F. Primacy of Clients' Interests. The social worker's primary responsibility is to clients.
G. Rights and Prerogatives of Clients. The social worker should make every effort to foster maximum self-determination on the part of clients.
H. Confidentiality and Privacy. The social worker should respect the privacy of clients and hold in confidence all information obtained in the course of professional service.
I. Fees. When setting fees, the social worker should ensure that they are fair, reasonable, considerate, and commensurate with the service performed and with due regard for the clients' ability to pay.

III. The Social Worker's Ethical Responsibility to Colleagues

J. Respect, Fairness, and Courtesy. The social worker should treat colleagues with respect, courtesy, fairness, and good faith.

K. Dealing with Colleagues' Clients. The social worker has the responsibility to relate to the clients of colleagues with full professional consideration.

IV. The Social Worker's Ethical Responsibility to Employers and Employing Organizations

L. Commitments to Employing Organizations. The social worker should adhere to commitments made to the employing organizations.

V. The Social Worker's Ethical Responsibility to the Social Work Profession

M. Maintaining the Integrity of the Profession. The social worker should uphold and advance the values, ethics, knowledge, and mission of the profession.

N. Community Service. The social worker should assist the profession in making social services available to the general public.

O. Development of Knowledge. The social worker should take responsibility for identifying, developing, and fully utilizing knowledge for professional practice.

VI. The Social Worker's Ethical Responsibility to Society

P. Promoting the General Welfare. The social worker should promote the general welfare of society.

CASE STUDY
A Code of Ethics for Radical Social Service Workers

Jeffrey Galper

Radical social workers have developed their own code of ethics in an attempt to counterbalance what they see as a conservative bias in the NASW code. In the following excerpt Galper takes each item from the code of ethics and suggests how it might be revised for more humanistic service. Just as the NASW code encapsulates the analysis and goals of conventional practice, this version reflects the analysis and goals of radical social workers.

1. I regard as my primary obligation the welfare of all human kind.

     The existing Code suggests that the social welfare worker regards as a primary obligation the welfare of the individual or group served. The limiting and destructive nature of the individualistic and pluralistic strategies that follow from this obligation have been documented.... The well-being of any one of us is inseparable from the well-being of all of us, and this awareness must be reflected in radical practice.

2. I will work toward the development of a society that is committed to the dictum, "From each ac-

cording to his or her ability, to each according to his or her need."

     The existing Code is concerned with nondiscrimination, in the civil libertarian sense, and commits the worker to serving all persons without bias. We have described the limitations inherent in the notion of equality of opportunity, which this plank reflects, and have suggested that our focus must be on outcomes as well as processes.

3. I will struggle for the realization of a society in which my personal interests and my personal actions are consistent with my interests and actions as a worker.

     At present, the Code suggests that personal interests be subordinated to professional responsibility and that statements and actions as a professional be kept apart from statements and actions as a private person. The personal fragmentation and politically conservative implications of this arrangement [have] received attention elsewhere.... Our work and our lives must become increasingly integrated.

4. I will consider myself accountable to all who join in the struggle for social change and will consider them accountable to me for the quality and extent of the work we perform and the society we create.

The current Code commits the worker to be responsible to himself or herself for this work. The need for collective accountability and struggle, however, is paramount. While personal standards are always desirable, we must add to them the critical collective concern.

5. I will work to achieve the kind of world in which all people can be free and open with one another in all matters.

The existing Code's commitment is to respect the privacy of all persons served. Without suggesting that one violate the trust of others, the emphasis on privacy must be counteracted inasmuch as our society is adept at using privacy to control us by keeping us apart. Openness is critical to the development of a society organized around positive mutual commitments.

6. I will use information gained from my work to facilitate humanistic, revolutionary change in the society.

The Code's commitment to the responsible use of information gained in professional work on the one hand implies a desirable concern for integrity. On the other hand, it suggests commitment to professional practice above a commitment to radical social change. This is not acceptable in radical practice.

7. I will treat the findings, views, and actions of colleagues with the respect due them. This respect is conditioned by their demonstrated concern for revolutionary values and radical social change.

This plank in the old Code argues for respect of colleagues per se. No commitment can be made to professional colleagues that is not in the context of a commitment to larger social values. Inasmuch as they do not have such a commitment, their findings, views, and actions must be rejected and challenged, though their humanity must always be acknowledged.

8. I will use all the knowledge and skill available to me in bringing about a radically transformed society.

The old Code's concern is that practice be conducted within the recognized knowledge and competence of the profession. This does not facilitate the kind of total engagement and total use of all resources which is required in the struggle for radical change.

9. I recognize my responsibility to add my ideas and findings to our society's knowledge and practice.

The existing Code's concern for adding such ideas and findings to social welfare knowledge and practice is worthy but limiting. Social work is a vehicle and servant. It is neither the temple nor the master.

10. I accept my responsibility to help protect the community against unethical practice by any individuals or organizations in the society.

The present Code asks for protection against such practices in the social welfare field. This is not enough. Our commitment is to struggle against the destructive elements of the whole.

11. I commit myself to use myself fully in the struggle for revolutionary change.

The existing Code urges readiness to provide services in public emergencies. Our society, at this time, is experiencing an emergency in an ongoing way. There is no more appropriate time for us to engage. Earthquakes, floods, and fires are minor happenings compared to the daily destruction wreaked by our institutions in the normal course of events.

12. I support the principle that all persons can and must contribute to the realization of a humanized society.

The old Code stresses the need for professional education for professional practice. Inasmuch as radical work is concerned with the fundamental reorganization of our society, all persons are potentially equally qualified and engaged students and participants.

13. I accept responsibility for working toward the creation and maintenance of conditions in society that enable all people to live by this Code.

The present Code's stress on enabling social workers in agencies to live by that Code is isolating and limiting in view of the tasks before us.

14. I contribute my knowledge, skills, and support to the accomplishment of a humanistic, democratic, communal socialist society.

The Code's suggestion that we contribute knowledge, skills, and support to programs of human welfare is desirable but limited. We must be clear about our goals and courageous in putting the notion of a radically altered society on the agenda.

It seems likely that, for any one of us, if there is a will, there is not necessarily a way. Acting collectively, however, the possibilities of what we can create are very exciting. While radicals are more given to manifestos than codes of ethics, we need to find ways to think together about how we can proceed. If this Code . . . serve[s] any useful political purpose, it will be to facilitate that thinking.

Jeffrey Galper, *The Politics of Social Services,* © 1975, pp. 224–227. Reprinted by permission of Prentice-Hall, Inc., Englewood Cliffs, New Jersey.

CASE STUDY
NACSW Statement of Objectives and Faith

The National Association of Christian Social Workers began at a series of annual conferences at Wheaton College in the 1950s. Originally incorporated as the Evangelical Social Work Conference and later renamed, the NACSW has expressed concern that

> our social structure has tended to place increasing responsibility for the general welfare in the hands of government. Social work concern and activity, in spite of its firm roots in a Christian world view, has become displaced from its foundation, and reflects a humanistic value system and understanding of humanity. This creates areas of tension for Christians who desire to act on the social concern by entering the social work profession.[25]

Membership in this association is open to persons who support its objectives, accept its Statement of Christian Faith, identify with its Statement of Social Work Practice, and pay the annual dues.

I. Objectives of NACSW

   A. To provide Christians in social work with opportunities for fellowship, personal growth, education, and a corporate witness to, and influence on, the world.

   B. To promote a Christian world view in social work and social welfare expressed through social agencies, local churches, educational institutions, and national organizations.

   C. To encourage awareness within the Christian community of contemporary human need and of the social work profession as an avenue for ministering to this need.

II. Statement of Christian Faith

   A. We believe that the Bible is the inspired and infallible Word of God, and that it is the authoritative basis for what we believe and how we live.

   B. We believe that there is one God, eternally existent in three persons: Father, Son, and Holy Spirit.

   C. We believe in the deity of our Lord Jesus Christ; His virgin birth; His fully human but sinless life; His ministry of reconciliation, and forgiveness; His vicarious and atoning death; His bodily resurrection; and His ascension to the Father.

   D. We believe that for the Salvation of lost and sinful humanity, regeneration by the Holy Spirit is essential.

   E. We believe in the present ministry of the Holy Spirit by whose indwelling Christians are enabled to live godly lives individually and corporately.

F. We believe in the spiritual unity of all believers in our Lord Jesus Christ, who together provide a caring community and a corporate witness to faith in Him.

G. We believe in the interdependence of all humanity and the necessity of commitment to the total well-being of all people.

H. We believe in Christ's present Lordship over all areas of our lives including, but not limited to, our involvement in social, economic, and political systems.

I. We believe in the personal return of our Lord Jesus Christ to the earth, in power and judgment.

III. Statement of Social Work Practice

A. We recognize a dynamic relationship between our life in Christ and our professional activities.

B. We are committed to working toward actualizing each person's total well-being and to eliminating oppression and violence.

C. We acknowledge that we are not to be motivated by earthly power, wealth, or security.

D. We encourage and support the highest standards of social work education, practice, and ethics for individuals and agencies.

One can identify many potential problems for NACSW professionals working within an organization that operates largely on public funding, which requires a separation of church and state. There is also some question of separating their own religious beliefs from the interests of their clients. How would Jews, agnostics, or Christians whose beliefs differ from the social worker's be served by members of this group?

SUMMARY

Professionalization of social work has had a shifting course over the last twenty years. During the Nixon administration the government launched a direct attack on the profession. John Ehrlichman, infamous for his role in the Watergate scandal, openly asserted that it was time for social workers to find "honest" work. Social work was caught in the crossfire between the Left, which criticized its conservatism, and the Nixon administration, which branded it as radical. In the 1980s Reagan's advisers in *Mandate for Leadership* called for more training for professional social workers because the liberal arts majors who supposedly dominated the profession were too radical.[26] These contradictory responses reflect the conflicting assumptions about the social work profession. One conservative president (Nixon) saw increased professionalization as a radical threat; another conservative president (Reagan) saw increased professionalization as a conservative influence.

The debate about the desirability of social work becoming more professionalized is complex. If social workers pursue increased professionalization, it is certain that educational requirements will become more demanding, regulation will be more strictly enforced, money for research will be more readily available, salaries will increase, and more prestige will attach to the field. Should the profession move toward deprofessionalization, educational requirements will be relaxed, less money will be spent on licensing, and workers already employed in related fields will have greater access to the profession; the profession's consequent growth will enhance the political influence of social workers as a group.

This chapter has presented the general attributes of social work as a profession—the cognitive, collective, and monopolistic components. The cognitive component includes three kinds of theory: general theory, practice theory, and the various theories of practice. The social work mandate for service (collective component) includes service to individuals, society, and the profession. The monopolistic component addresses the regulatory mechanisms as well as the domain protection afforded to a recognized profession. These characteristics are consistent with the NASW's Code of Ethics.

NOTES

1. P. Saxton, "Vendorship for Social Work: Observations on the Maturation of the Profession," *Social Work* 33, 3 (May—June 1988): 198.
2. "NASW Program Goals, 1985–87," *NASW News* 29 (October 1984): 8.
3. K. Adams, "The Evolution of Clinical Social Work: A Lobbyist's View," *Progress Report.* National Federation of Societies for Clinical Social Work, Inc., Winter 1989.
4. E. Greenwood, "Attributes of a Profession Revisited," in *The Emergence of Social Welfare and Social Work,* 2nd ed., ed. N. Gilbert and H. Specht (Itasca, Ill.: Peacock, 1981).
5. B. Compton and B. Galaway, *Social Work Processes* (Homewood, Ill.: Dorsey Press, 1979), 49.
6. Ibid., 41.
7. For detailed discussion of each model, see J. Fischer, *Effective Casework Practice* (New York: McGraw-Hill, 1978) (eclectic); A. Pincus and A. Minahan, *Social Work Practice: Model and Method* (Itasca, Ill.: Peacock, 1973) (generalist); C. Germain, "The Ecological Perspective in Casework Practice," *Social Casework* 54, 6 (June 1973): 223–230 (life model); and W. Reid and L. Epstein, *Task-Centered Practice* (New York: Columbia University Press, 1977) (task-centered).
8. Westat, Inc., "A Study of Attitudes of NASW Members . . . ," unpublished report (September 1984), quoted in Saxton, "Vendorship," 290.
9. Saxton, "Vendorship."
10. D. Harris, Presidential Address, NASW Conference on Clinical Social Work, San Francisco, September 1986.
11. *Progress Report,* NFSCSW, Winter 1989.
12. Illinois State Statutes, Chapter 73, Section 370c.
13. Wisconsin Administrative Code, Rules of the Wisconsin Title XIX Program, Health and Social Services Chapters HSS 101–108, April 30, 1988.
14. NASW Bylaws.
15. Ibid.
16. A. Berliner, "Misconduct in Social Work Practice," *Social Work* (January 1989): 69–72.
17. Ibid.
18. Charles Sanders, "Growth of the Association of Black Social Workers," *Social Casework* 52, 5 (May 1970): 278–279.
19. Ibid., 279.
20. Ibid.

21. *Standards for Social Service Manpower* (NASW, 1973).

22. Policy Statement on Social Work Practice and Education and Structure and Quality in Social Work Education. Adopted by the CSWE House of Delegates, March 1976.

23. *Standards for Social Service Manpower.*

24. Jeanette Regensburg, *Some Educational Patterns in Doctoral Programs in Schools of Social Work* (CSWE, 1966).

25. Pamphlet published by the National Association of Christian Social Workers.

26. Charles Heatherly, *Mandate for Leadership: Policy Management in a Conservative Administration* (The Heritage Foundation, 1979).

PART

III

HISTORICAL DEVELOPMENT OF SOCIAL WORK

Social work originated in late nineteenth-century England, where there was growing discontent with the kind of society that had been created by industrialization and by the political and economic practices of laissez-faire capitalism. The early ideas from which social work grew soon traveled to the United States. . . . Discontent within a society that was shaped by values and institutions of laissez-faire capitalism, a society whose industries and urban concentrations were destructive of many people, led to diverse ideas for change.[1]

Social work is a young profession tracing back only to the late 1800s. In its first century important social progress has been made in spite of occasional failures. Today social work continues to build on its strengths and learn from its errors. Our historical analysis of social work has three goals: to identify how tradition defines practice, to clarify the origins and consequences of our definition of deviance, and to recognize the limitations of our understanding of human behavior. We hope this brief discussion will help students recognize what activities are functional and dysfunctional to current social work goals, encourage them to guard against becoming oppressors of "deviants," make them aware of the current limitations of knowledge, and give them a personal resolve to expand the limits of that knowledge.

Analyzing history and how past practice reflected past times helps clarify how present practice reflects the present time. It introduces important questions. How much of what social workers presently do is dictated by tradition? How much "traditional" practice should be eliminated or modified? What new methods need to be developed to address our present times? Do present methods of intervention reflect current need? Do social workers respond to need or do they respond with the methods they know best, regardless of their applicability to the problem? To what degree does reimbursement policy of third party payees dictate practice?

A primary mandate social workers have from society is to deal with deviants—individuals who do not behave according to societal norms or do

117

not accept the dominant values of society. In 1926 the Milford Conference Report stated:

> Social casework deals with the human being whose capacity to organize his own normal social activities may be impaired by one or more deviations from accepted standards of normal social life.[2]

If society had no poor, mentally ill, delinquents, or criminals there would be no social work profession. Social workers espouse maximizing human potential, but society would not support a profession for that purpose alone. People who are "different" must be kept from disrupting the functioning of society.

Political, Social, and Environmental Constraints

The earliest forms of organized mutual assistance have advanced through the years from diverse and unrefined methodologies to the unifying paradigm of generalist practice and from loosely knit professional groupings to a single national professional organization. As the profession developed, however, its goals and structure have always been shaped by current political, economic, and social conditions. The effect of the environment is reflected in the development of mainstream professional practice but is exemplified even more clearly in the black community's effort to meet human needs.

The history of the United States is a history of maltreatment of the black, the Mexican American, and the Native American populations. Individual citizens and social institutions have contributed to this injustice, and social work is no exception. From its earliest beginnings social work participated in the segregationist policies of the broader society. There were white settlement houses and "colored" settlement houses; white women's clubs and "colored" women's clubs; white fraternities and "colored" fraternities. Our history has made it clear that if blacks wanted to receive relief or aid of any kind they had to look to themselves.

The Axinn and Levin text *Social Welfare: A History of the American Response to Need* illustrates this tendency. In their historical analysis, veterans and blacks represent the two extremes of American attitudes about the worthy and unworthy poor.[3] Veterans were given special consideration for social welfare benefits because they had served in the armed forces. For minorities a different picture emerges. Blacks, in particular, have suffered the dual difficulties of class and color, racial discrimination and poverty. On the whole it can be said that social work has responded historically to the needs of poor Americans of European descent.[4]

An Ideological Framework for Social Work History

An historical perspective on social work can broaden your understanding of how ideology affects practice. Theories about poverty and deviance are not formed in a vacuum. Nor is the effect of these theories neutral.

History shows how theories about poverty evolved from specific economic, social, and political environments; it illuminates the different assumptions, values, and goals implied by various theories; it illustrates how these theories have been used by different individuals, organizations, and classes to promote their economic, social, and political interests; and it shows the influence of the past on contemporary theories and policies. In contrast, the typical study of social work history assumes a benign social and political environment and identifies the Charity Organization Society as the precursor of casework, the settlement house and recreation movements as the progenitors of group work, and the civil rights movement, Saul Alinsky, and the United Way as the inspirations for community organization theory and practice.

The Evolution of Practice

While social work has been shaped by many historical forces, certain movements have more directly affected the philosophy and skills of social work practice. The Charity Organization Society and the settlement movement are two that have been widely discussed in the social work literature. These movements reflect both the liberal and conservative strains in our history. Less frequently discussed are the contributions of the radical theorists (for example, the abolitionists, radical feminists, or unemployed councils) who represent earlier political-economic approaches to alleviating social problems. While they were not social workers, they do reflect the philosophical base of radical social workers today. It is important to recognize the importance of "fringe" elements; their programs for social justice may not have won acceptance in their time, but their presence made less radical social work movements more acceptable.

Part III addresses the major sources of social work ideology and practice by outlining historically (Chapter 6) the assumptions about the cause of individual and social problems, the founding social welfare movements, early strategies, and subsequent methods that have evolved. The context for the evolution of professional practice is set with the presentation of the earliest forms of governmental response to social problems, beginning with England's Statute of Laborers in 1349. Study of early American responses shows strong traces of English influence. As the United States became increasingly industrialized, the societal response to social problems became more formalized and professionalized (Chapter 7). From these formal responses, social work emerged as a profession, beginning in the late nineteenth century. The roots of professional practice are examined in significant social movements and the historical development of methodology (Chapter 8).

The "proper" role of women is presented as a powerful influence on the profession of social work. Finally, parallel developments in service provision to minorities are presented. The history of black social work identifies an area where traditional methods of social work have failed. Black movements illustrate the larger society's response to minorities, since blacks have historically been excluded from both the profession and the service delivery system. Part III illustrates how values and ideologies have cut across the different sizes and types of client groups and interventions. Throughout history there have been liberals, conservatives, and radicals who have used casework, group work, and community organization skills for problem-solving.

Notes

1. Gerald Handel, *Social Welfare in Western Society* (New York: Random House, 1982), 210.
2. The Milford Conference, *Social Casework Generic and Specific: A Report of the Milford Conference* (Washington, D.C.: Reprinted by the National Association of Social Workers, 1974), 17.
3. June Axinn and Herman Levin, *Social Welfare: A History of the American Response to Need,* 2nd ed. (New York: Harper and Row, 1982).
4. Toby Ferrell, *Why Not Us? Blacks and Social Welfare* (Unpublished monograph, 1982).

Chapter

6

History of Poor Relief

The goals of social welfare programs for the poor derive from the goals of the larger society for itself and from the view that society holds of itself and of its various members. In turn, decisions about who is needy and how the needy are to be helped bear upon economic development, political organization, social stability, and family integrity. . . . Because social welfare goals touch a core of ideologies, they tend to polarize Americans.[1]

Knowing the history of poor relief is essential to understanding social work practice and social welfare policy today. Poverty has existed throughout recorded history. The response to poverty has been guided by a humanitarian influence but has been limited by the needs of the economic system.

THE MIDDLE AGES IN EUROPE

Prior to the fourteenth century, poverty in the Middle Ages (400 A.D. to 1500 A.D.) was treated quite differently than it is today. Religious motivation was the paramount incentive to relieving the suffering of the poor. A concern for "thy neighbor and thyself" pervaded religious teaching. Christians were admonished to "Do unto others as you would have them do unto you," and "Give, and it shall be given unto you . . . For with the same measure that ye mete withal it shall be measured to you again."[2] The Church was the administrator of poor relief, and church canonists turned to biblical text as their guide to poor law construction. The culture respected the individual regardless of material possessions; in medieval poor law, the poor had a right to assistance and the better off had a duty to provide it. The only test of eligibility for assistance was evidence of need. Moreover, "In case of doubt it is better to do too much than to do nothing at all."[3]

> The earliest social welfare institution was the Church.

Not only did the Church assert the dignity of the individual, but also the economic system (feudalism) provided a subsistence to most of the

121

population. Most people lived a rural life. People vulnerable to economic insecurity and attack surrendered their freedom and land to more powerful men. They exchanged a portion of what they produced for protection of the lord of the manor. In exchange these serfs received protection and gained the right to stay on the land.[4] The laborers exchanged their freedom for economic security.

The End of Feudalism

By the end of the fourteenth century feudalism was ending and a wage system was taking over. Laborers had increased freedom and decreased economic security. People made the most of their new freedom by travelling about seeking higher wages; their new mobility threatened the landowners who had previously dominated society. The new merchant class replaced the landowners in power and prestige. Still Christianity continued to influence the beliefs of the people. The merchant class was concerned with justifying its accumulated wealth in the eyes of God. Merchants strove to achieve the best of both worlds: maximum accumulation of wealth in this world, and salvation in the hereafter. Through private charity merchants felt they could atone for the injustices that crept into their business dealings. One method of distributing charity adopted by the merchants was the funeral dole: when a merchant died his estate would distribute money and food to the poor. But doling out money at funerals contributed to the vagrancy problem in England. To combat this problem, merchants often left orders to distribute money only to the industrious poor, "not to those who were astute enough to stop working in order to live by the indiscriminate almsgiving that went on at funerals."[5]

THE STATUTE OF LABORERS

In the fourteenth century the landowners faced new threats. Merchants were usurping the power and privilege of the propertied class. Laborers were increasingly moving about and demanding higher wages. As long as labor was plentiful, landowners had to be concerned only about looting. But between 1315 and 1321 England suffered a great famine; fewer laborers were available, and those who could work demanded higher wages. The problem became even more acute when the bubonic plague struck in 1348. England lost one-third of its population. During the last half of the fourteenth century workers could demand high wages and good working conditions; employers had to compete for labor. This was the first true taste of freedom for workers and competition for landowners. To regain their power the landowners had to decrease the power of labor.

England lost nearly one-third of its population to the plague within two years.

It was under these circumstances that the Statute of Laborers was adopted. This statute was an attempt by the English landowners to assure a sufficient supply of agricultural workers at low wages. One paragraph has special significance.

King Edward III issued the Statute of Laborers in 1349.

Because that many valiant beggars, as long as they may live of begging, do refuse to labor, giving themselves to idleness and vice, and sometime to theft, and other abominations; none upon the said pain of imprisonment, shall under the color of pity or alms, give anything to such, which may labor, or presume to favor them towards their desires, so that thereby they may be compelled to labor for their necessary living.[6]

This law set up certain conditions for laborers. A maximum wage was set; landowners no longer had to compete for labor since they were allowed to pay only a certain wage and could be punished for paying more. The Statute of Laborers also permitted landowners to choose their workers; the laborer's choice was not considered. In addition to setting these harsh conditions upon work, the law also provided penalties for begging or almsgiving. Whoever was inclined to provide assistance to a poor worker would be punished.

ENGLISH POOR LAWS IN THE AGE OF CAPITALISM

Controlling Vagrancy and Begging

Until the 16th century begging had been the societal response to poverty. Not only the poor, but also mendicant friars and university students lived by begging. As England progressed from feudalism to mercantilism to capitalism, labor statutes became progressively harsher. Begging, an acceptable and even honorable occupation for certain groups in the Middle Ages, became a crime. The first mention of special treatment for the "impotent to serve" was in 1388; these people were to have lesser punishment for begging, but they had to stay in their own communities. The Statute of Laborers in 1495 provided that beggars would spend three days and nights in stocks, but pregnant women and the extremely ill would be punished less severely. In 1504 persons over sixty and the ill were added to the group receiving lesser punishment.[7]

During this period we first see the distinction between the worthy and the unworthy poor.

The fifteenth century was relatively prosperous. While laborers lived poorly by present standards, they had the bare necessities of life, and relief was largely unnecessary. As the fifteenth century drew to a close, however, poverty began to increase. One reason for the growing impoverishment of workers was sheep raising. Sheep raising required many fewer workers and much more land than crops. The problem became so great that in 1534 Henry VIII tried to limit the number of sheep per estate to two thousand.[8]

The movement from serfdom to freedom created a whole new set of problems. Under feudalism life was stable; war and famine were the only major threats to the serfs' livelihood. As capitalism grew, individual freedom increased at the price of economic security. As England moved into industrialization, poverty became the concern of government. Once the economic system no longer provided security to individuals, the government was left to provide some means to assure security. Industrial society has since been baffled by the problem of how to provide people with the equivalent protection against sickness, old age, and unemployment — security that feudalism had provided, however inadequately.

Mercantilism changed the economic structure of society, and begging and private philanthropy were no longer able to handle the problems of poverty. The Statute of Laborers in 1531 was the first assumption of government responsibility for the care of the destitute. The introduction to the statute made it clear that idleness was a vice to be punished, but it also recognized the necessity of helping those genuinely in need. The statute decreed that mayors, justices of the peace, and other local officials

While the Statute of 1531 established public responsibility for the poor, it also threatened to punish them severely for begging.

1. Shall make diligent search and inquiry of all aged poor and impotent persons which live or of necessity be compelled to live by alms of the charity of the people.
2. Shall have power [to assign impotent persons limits within which they may beg] and to give in commandment to every such aged and impotent beggar that none of them shall beg without the limit to them so appointed.
3. Shall also register and write the names of every such impotent beggar in a bill or roll indented.
4. Shall make and deliver to every such impotent person by them enabled to beg, a letter containing the name of such impotent person, and witnessing that he is authorized to beg, and the limit within which he is appointed to beg.[9]

The major points of the statute were that beggars had to be registered and given a letter of authorization and a territory to beg in, parish constables were to search out invalids, and able-bodied beggars were to be punished more harshly. These may seem to be no provisions at all, but actually they represent the beginning of the assumption by government of the care of persons in economic distress. In setting up eligibility requirements and certifying beggars, England had made important movement toward public administration of relief. However, even authorized begging was not adequate to provide for the poor. Therefore, the Statutes of 1536 provided a more comprehensive system of relief and harsher punishment for the able-bodied. Some elements of the Statute were as follows:

1. All and every person or persons being whipped or sent unto their countries in form aforesaid, at the end of every ten miles shall repair unto the constable of any parish, being directly in his way towards the county and place whereunto he is so appointed, and upon sight of his letters given unto him at the time of his whipping . . . every of the said constables and others the King's subjects shall and may furnish him with competent meat, drink, and lodging for one night only or for one meal, and so he shall continue his daily journey of ten miles until such time as he shall come unto the hundred and place whereunto he is assigned to go.
2. Any of the aforesaid ruffelers, sturdy vagabonds, and valiant beggars . . . upon due examination and proof of the continuance of his said loitering, wandering and idleness, or vagabondage, shall eftsoon not only [be] whipped again . . . but also shall have the upper part of the gristle of-

his right ear clean cut off . . . [if] having the upper part of the right ear cut off, as is aforesaid . . . and . . . found guilty . . . of continual loitering and idleness, then every such sturdy vagabond and valiant beggar . . . shall have judgment to suffer pains and execution of death as a felon and as enemies of the Commonwealth.

3. [The justice and other officers] shall have authority . . . to take . . . children under the age of fourteen years and above the age of five years, in begging or idleness, and to appoint them to masters of husbandry or other crafts or labors to be taught, by the which they may get their living when they shall come of age.[10]

Parish relief was similar to contemporary local county relief for the poor.

This statute set out the nature of the provision, the method of administration, the government's responsibility for collecting contributions, and the administrative structure for relief. The parish became the unit of administration; for the first time a paid staff administered relief.

The Poor Laws of 1601

Except for a trend toward exceeding harshness in 1547 (when beggars were to be branded with a *V*, and if caught a second time, branded with an *S* and enslaved forever), new laws followed the spirit of the 1531 and 1536 statutes. An economic depression in 1594 precipitated a famine and bread riots that led to a revision of the statutes; the Poor Law of 1601, Elizabeth 43, was actually such a revision. These new statutes are important because for the first time the total act was rewritten. Further, these laws were to stand with only minor changes until 1662.

Many of our current welfare practices are direct descendants of the English Poor Laws.

The patterns that developed between 1531 and 1601 are still embodied in contemporary social welfare policy.

1. Relief is to be locally administered and financed. Both the General Revenue Sharing Act of 1972 in the Nixon era and the State Federalism concept in the Reagan administration reflect this attitude. It is unlikely that the Bush administration will change this policy direction.

2. The administrator is to be a public official.

3. The unemployed are categorized; both treatment and benefit are to be related to the individual's relationship to the work force. No able-bodied person is to benefit by the relief system. Handicapped and elderly people who cannot work—the "worthy" poor—should be given help.

4. Families are to be responsible for themselves. With the Poor Laws grandparents were responsible for their children and grandchildren; adult children were responsible for their children and their parents. Present welfare policy states that parents are responsible for their minor children but are not financially responsible for their parents. Some states are presently considering a system whereby adult children would have to contribute to the care of their parents if they required nursing home care.

5. Children were to be given apprenticeships or training to ensure they would be productive members of society. This principle is less obvious currently because modern society prepares children for the workplace in educational settings rather than through apprenticeships; nonetheless, modern policy continues to reflect the importance of preparing poor children for the marketplace through the educational system. Wisconsin, for example, reduces the AFDC grant if eligible children are excessively truant.

Even though the Poor Laws set up the mechanism whereby relief was a legal right, the majority of relief funds still came from private charity. For two generations after the passage of Elizabeth 43, only about 7 percent of the relief came from public funds. Even so it is significant that, after two centuries of attempting to control the poor through repression, England recognized a positive obligation to the destitute.

The 1662 Law of Settlement and Removal

The Law of Settlement and Removal decreed that the overseer could remove from the parish anyone who he thought might become needy. This was determined by whether the person paid more than 10 pounds per year rent. There was a belief that many indigents were moving from local parishes to the more urban parishes where the assistance was more liberal. This law

This law is similar to this country's residency requirements.

represented a return to serfdom: an individual belonged in the parish of birth. The law permitted repression: not only were individuals forced to work for whoever wanted them, but also at whatever price the employer named. In addition to these horrendous conditions, local authorities were empowered to force laborers back to their original place of residence. The law also provided a means of conveying the poor back to their parish of settlement. To further ensure available labor when needed, a provision was made for "certificates of settlement" to be given if workers were needed in a certain area. The certificate of settlement allowed the laborers to go to the parish where they were needed during harvest and ensured that their parish of settlement would take them back when they were no longer needed. This law was a significant victory of the landowners over laborers. In 1795 the law was amended so that persons could not be removed unless they asked for assistance.

In the United States, similar residency requirements remained in effect until April 21, 1969, when in *Shapiro v. Thompson,* the Supreme Court declared that considering residency a requirement for granting public assistance was unconstitutional. The federal government is presently considering allowing some states to reduce public assistance payments in counties that border on lower-paying states. This is a reflection of the concern that families will migrate for higher welfare payments as well as of the attitude that states are each responsible for their own.

WORKHOUSES: INDOOR RELIEF

At the same time that Parliament was passing punitive laws such as the Law of Settlement and Removal, a countermovement in England suggested that poverty could best be relieved by making all citizens, including children, productive. Andrew Yarranton was a proponent of this approach to poverty. Following a trip to Germany he wrote a report describing Germany's workhouses and suggesting that England could be more competitive commercially if it adopted this system. Yarranton's report (published in 1677) stated that

Welfare provided to people in their own homes is outdoor relief. Institutional care and workhouses are examples of indoor relief.

> In all these parts there is no beggar, nor no occasion to beg; and in all towns there are schools for little girls, from six years old and upwards, to teach them to spin, and so to bring their tender fingers by degrees to spin very fine, which being young are thereby easily fitted by degrees to spin very fine, which being young are thereby easily fitted for that use. Whereas people overgrown in age cannot so well feel the thread. Their wheels go all by the foot, made to go with much ease, whereby the action or motion is very easy and delightful. And in all towns there are schools according to the bigness, or multitude of the poor children.

One of the major concerns of social work has been the proper care of children. These children were playing in an early settlement house.

I will show you the way, method, rule, and order how they are governed. First, there is a large room, and in the middle thereof a little box like a
pulpit. Secondly, there are benches built around the room as they are in our
playhouses; upon the benches sit about two hundred children spinning, and
in the box in the middle of the room sits the grand mistress with a long white
wand in her hand. If she observes any of them idle, she reaches them a tap;
but if that will not do, she rings a bell which by a little cord is fixed to a box,
and out comes a woman; she then points to the offender, and she is taken
away into another room and chastised. And all this is done without one word
speaking. And I believe this way of ordering the young women in Germany
is one great cause that the German women have so little of the twit twat. And
I am sure it would be well were it so in England.[11]

Yarranton's was an example of a positive, optimistic view of how the
poor could serve society and lend strength to the nation. Cynical, punitive
proponents of workhouses, however, overshadowed Yarranton and his
ideas. In 1722 the workhouse law was passed. Proponents of the workhouse
argued that institutional care (indoor relief) would be less expensive than caring for people in their own homes (outdoor relief). Their plan was to make
workhouses so horrible that people would go hungry rather than enter the
workhouse.

Workhouses were usually managed by whoever would do it for the
least amount of money. Since managers were paid according to the number
of people they served, it was in their personal interest to spend as little as
possible on the poor. Within ten years of the passage of the workhouse law
(1722), over one hundred workhouses had been established in the London
area. Workhouses were run like prisons, even though people housed in them
had not broken the law. Children suffered tremendously.

Death rates of workhouse children under one year old were as high as
82 percent. In one workhouse only three of nineteen babies survived; in another not a single child survived; a third workhouse record showed only
seven out of one hundred children survived over a three year period.[12] As the
conditions and the cost of the workhouse became known, policies swung
back toward outdoor relief.

**All poor people were
placed together in
workhouses without
medical help and often
in unsanitary condi-
tions.**

**Charles Dickens wrote
about life in a work-
house in *Oliver Twist*,
published in 1837.**

THE SPEENHAMLAND ACT: A RETURN
TO OUTDOOR RELIEF

By 1795 industry was becoming mechanized. Factories and power machines
were replacing cottage industries and handwork. The commons were being
enclosed for sheep farming; the poor were no longer able to engage in
subsistence farming on common land. Prices were increasing; wages were
decreasing; riots and looting were occurring. Rather than raising wages so that
laborers could meet the cost of living, the Justices of Berkshire, meeting at
Speenhamland, proposed to use relief to make up the difference between what

The allowance given to supplement the wages based on the bread scale is similar to guaranteeing a minimum wage based on the cost of living.

families earned and what they needed to subsist. This allowance was known as the *bread scale:* when a gallon loaf sold for 1 shilling, the parish supplemented a family's pay up to three shillings. Speenhamland had four methods through which the able-bodied were aided without entering the workhouse. The most widely used was the allowance in support of wages, or bread scale. The Roundsmen system was similar; the allowance was used for people who were already working and the Roundsmen system was for the unemployed. A report based on the Roundsmen plan (written in 1795) stated,

> In the winter and at other times, when a man is out of work he applies to the overseer, who sends him from house to house, to get employ: the house-keeper who employs him, is obliged to give him victuals, and 6d a day; and the parish adds 4d (total 10d a day) for the support of his family; persons working in this manner are called roundsmen, from their going around the village or township for employ.[13]

The third method used was the labor rate; landowners were responsible for the unemployed. The parish would determine wages and then distribute the unemployed among the employers, who were required to provide employment or pay the difference in increased taxes. This system led to the displacement of workers already employed. The fourth and most infrequently used method of providing outdoor relief was employing poor laborers on public projects.

The effects of Speenhamland were disastrous for everyone. Wages went down, people on relief increased, laborers' initiative and hope were destroyed, landowners had no incentive to pay decent wages, the laborers' standard of living fell. A movement back to the workhouse ensued.

INFLUENTIAL THINKERS

Count Rumsford: The German Response to Poverty

The doctrine of less eligibility means making relief less than what a person could earn if work were available.

At about the same time, Count Rumsford (an American by birth) was charged with clearing Munich of beggars. Instead of attempting to make people happy through virtue, his system proposed making people virtuous through happiness. The way to clear Munich of beggars was to adopt effective measures for maintaining and supporting the poor. He did not believe workhouses should be odious; in fact, he thought that work and relief should be provided in homes when possible. Under Count Rumsford's guidance, Munich developed the most thorough and comprehensive relief program of its time. Rumsford's system included not only relief, but also employment, aid to children, child placement, nurseries, and educational programs. Although it too reflected a doctrine of less eligibility, it did not make relief punitive.[14]

Thomas Chalmers: Casework Methodology

Reverend Thomas
Chalmers organized a
system of private giving
to the poor.

One other small-scale operation developed at this time did not have immediate widespread effect, but reappeared fifty years later in the charity organization society movement. Reverend Thomas Chalmers (1780–1847), a minister of the Church of Scotland, objected to using church and public funds for relief. He thought the laity rather than the clergy should serve as almoners. Chalmers trained members of his parish to visit families and make a thorough study of their situations. Drawn from the wealthy families of the parish, these deacons used personal influence, attention, advice, civility, and good will (all enhanced by their elevated social status) to alleviate suffering in the parish. Chalmers raised all the money for his parish from collections, and he was such an excellent speaker that people traveled many miles to hear him speak. He agreed to make no more referrals to the workhouse if he could keep the funds he raised in his own parish — St. John's, the poorest parish in Glasgow. He believed each parish should take care of its own. Thomas Chalmers was at St. John's from 1819 to 1823. His success was largely attributable to his own fundraising abilities, rather than the casework methodology that he developed.

Adam Smith: The Harmony of Economic Self-Interest

Adam Smith proposed
a gradual elimination
of government involve-
ment in poor relief.

Adam Smith (1723–1790), widely recognized as the father of modern economics, also had considerable impact on poor law thinking. He was an optimist, perhaps because his writings predate the misery that the Industrial Revolution would bring to England. In his model, the best of all possible economic systems would result if each person were free to act in his or her own self-interest. Smith believed that competition, not regulation, would limit the power of businessmen. He assumed that there was a harmony of interests among all economic classes. *The Wealth of Nations* (1776) favored high wages to spur industriousness, population growth, savings, large markets, and a division of labor. Smith believed that the difference between the classes was based on nurture, not nature. His was an optimistic vision of all classes ascending together on the road to prosperity.[15]

Thomas Malthus: Poverty and Overpopulation

Malthus proposed an
argument that we hear
today: the poor will
keep having children
to receive more wel-
fare.

This happy view was to be overridden by the negative view of the poor prevalent in the work of Thomas Malthus (1766–1834). Malthus was an ordained minister who brought bad tidings to the poor. His *Essay on Population* (1798) set forth the law of population: if unchecked, population tends to outstrip the food supply. If there is no moral restraint to curb population growth, then famine, misery, pestilence, or war will do the job. The poor had only themselves to blame for their misery; poverty was the natural punishment for overbreeding. The poor should not be given relief since it would only encourage them to have more children; high wages would have similar consequences. Malthus saw poverty as useful and inevitable; it disciplined the poor, who would not work without the threat of starvation. His arguments justified low wages and terrible working conditions. The upper class movement to abolish relief gained strength from Malthus's argument. The Poor Laws of 1834 embodied the Malthusian approach to poverty.[16]

POOR LAW REFORM OF 1834

In 1832 a Royal Commission for Inquiring into the Administration and Practical Operation of the Poor Law was appointed to reform the Poor Law and to stop outdoor relief. This commission produced a 13,000-page study biased against the reliefer (pauper) and full of praise for the indigent independent laborer. Subjective reporting permeated this document, exemplified by this quotation.

> In the pauper's habitation you will find a strained show of misery and wretchedness; and those little articles of furniture which might, by the least exertion imaginable, wear an appearance of comfort, are turned, as it were intentionally, the ugliest side outward; the children are dirty, and appear to be under no control; the clothes of both parents and children in nine cases out of ten, are ragged, but evidently are so for the lack of the least attempt to make them otherwise; for I have very rarely found the clothes of a pauper with a patch put on or a seam made upon them since new; their mode of living, in all cases that I have known (except and always making the distinction between the determined pauper and the infirm and deserving poor, which cases are but comparatively few) is most improvident. Whatever provisions I have found, on visiting their habitations, have been of the best quality; and my inquiries among the tradesmen, as butchers, chandler's shopkeepers, etc., have all been answered with—"They will not have anything but the best."
>
> In the habitation of the laboring man who receives no parish relief, you will find (I have done so), even in the poorest, an appearance of comfort; the articles of furniture, few and humble though they may be, have their best side seen, are arranged in something like order, and so as to produce the best appearance of which they are capable. The children appear under parental control; are sent to school (if of that age); their clothes you will find patched and taken care of, so as to make them wear as long a time as possible; there is a sense of moral feeling and moral dignity easily discerned; they purchase such food, and at such seasons, and in such quantities, as the most economical would approve of.[17]

Rather than "burden" people with the whole report, the commissioners selectively reported findings. Their report implied that most recipients were able-bodied and that administration of relief was lax; its purpose was to eliminate outdoor relief. The commissioners also stressed less eligibility; paupers should not live better than the poorest workers. The report stated that

> it is shown that in proportion as the condition of any pauper class is elevated above the condition of independent labourers, the condition of the independent class is depressed; their industry is impaired, their employment becomes

unsteady, and its remuneration in wages is diminished. Such persons, therefore, are under the strongest inducements to quit the less eligible class of
labourers and enter the more eligible class of paupers.[18]

This report led back to the policy of making the workhouse the only
source of relief and making the conditions of the workhouse so bad that no
one would want to enter. The Poor Law of 1834 instituted a number of policy
changes: outdoor relief was to be abolished, relief was to be supervised nationally, the poor were to be classified as worthy or unworthy and placed in
separate portions of the workhouse, and less eligibility was to prevail. Workhouses were like penal institutions; England officially declared poverty a
crime.

COLONIAL AMERICA 1647–1776

Very different economic, social, and political conditions prevailed in colonial
America. England had to deal with unemployed masses; America needed every possible laborer. Unemployment was not a problem, but sickness, disability, and widowhood resulting from the difficult living conditions engendered considerable need for relief. Colonial Americans did not immediately
distinguish between classes of poor—all problems were seen as economic
problems. Rothman cites the example of the lunatic.[19]

Lunatics came to public attention not because they were afflicted with
delusions or fears, but because they suffered from poverty. In this spirit a
Massachusetts law (frequently copied elsewhere) established that "when and
so often as it shall happen any person to be naturally wanting of understanding, so as to be uncapable to provide for him or herself," then the town, in
the absence of relatives and personal property, was to provide for their
relief.[20] No one was willing to support the rogue or vagabond. This was not
a great problem because everyone knew the people of the community, and
there was strong community pressure to be productive.

Why then did a country with such different concerns adopt the English
Poor Laws? Some suggest that colonial Americans had a strong sense of
locality—citizens felt a duty to take care of their own. Others point to the fact
that no private charity was organized to respond to problems of poverty, so
a public institution was compelled to address those problems. Finally, every
laborer was needed, and the Poor Laws set up a mechanism to force everyone to work.

The Puritan Ethic

The Puritans believed poverty and idleness were sins.

Calvinism and the Puritan ethic were also influential in the development of
colonial poor law. Social status was a manifestation of predestined grace.
This outlook justified a decrease in community ownership and an increase in

private property. Poverty was seen as part of God's design; it allowed suffering and benevolence. The wealthy were stewards of God and had a duty to protect God's wealth. While poverty was part of the natural design and public relief was necessary, it was not to be forgotten that the poor were morally flawed and should not be pampered.

Families

Colonial families were to provide for themselves; each member was to be a productive and contributing member of society. Public well-being came before individual or family well-being. If a family was not able to raise children in a manner appropriate to this end, the children were placed with a family that could. One state tested the fitness of a family by whether or not children knew the alphabet at the age of six. If they did not, they were placed with another family to receive a decent Christian education. Families that were not financially successful were dangerous, economically and morally. Children were bound out to be educated in honest and profitable trades and to learn the principles of religion and law. It was important to protect children from the contagion of parental failures. Adult poor were also farmed out to the lowest bidder. As the colonies became more populous, workhouses were built to administer proper punishment and put the poor to work.[21]

Crime

The colonial attitude toward crime reflected a belief in predestination. The identification of disorder with sin made it difficult for lawmakers to distinguish between major and minor infractions. Both were testimony to natural depravity and the power of the devil—sure signs that the offender was destined to be a public menace and a (literally) damned sinner. This attitude underlay the heavyhandedness of the 18th century code that set capital punishment as the sanction for crimes as different as murder, arson, and horse stealing. Even a child's disrespect for parents prefigured a life of crime and damnation. A passage from the writings of Reverend Benjamin Wadsworth reflects this belief.

All types of crime merited harsh punishment.

> When children are disobedient to parents, God is often provoked to leave them to those sins which bring them to the greatest shame and misery . . . when persons have been brought to die at the gallow, how often have they confessed that disobedience to parents led them to those crimes?[22]

The standard theory of crime was that the family had failed to train its charges to their social and religious obligations and had left their depraved nature unchecked. Sin demanded retribution; whippings or harsh physical punishment would not rehabilitate, but terrorize the guilty into good behavior.

THE REVOLUTION TO THE CIVIL WAR

The early federal period witnessed many changes in the treatment of social problems, particularly poverty, mental and physical illness, and crime. Poverty continued to be seen as an individual aberration rather than a social problem. Relatives were legally responsible for family members; relief was viewed as unnecessary. Local communities were the most important source of political decisions; state governments were distant, consisting of a group of legislators who met for two weeks every two years. Families and neighborhoods were self-sufficient. As industrialization progressed, state government became more significant and local government less so. Still, it was up to the overseer to ensure that no one shirked his or her responsibility to work.

> The overseer was a local official responsible for administering the poor law.

Farming Out

Methods of dealing with the poor varied from town to town. Some towns farmed out their poor; the overseer had to hire someone to take care of the poor person. Orphans and children whose parents were on relief were bound out to proper families. Some adults were auctioned off to the lowest bidder, and a few were sent out on the Roundsmen system. Prevalent liberal economic theory suggested that what was spent for the poor decreased the amount available for capitalists and productive people. Poverty and relief were problems to study.

> The individual rights of someone who was poor were not considered during the federal period.

The Study of Poverty

In 1818 the New York Society for the Prevention of Pauperism set up a study to find the causes of poverty. This study found that ignorance, idleness, intemperance, want of economy, imprudent and hasty marriages, lotteries, pawn brokers, houses of prostitution, and the generosity of charitable organizations were all causes of poverty.[23] In response to those findings, the society developed a plan whereby "friendly visitors" would advise families to save their money and encourage them to be productive. This plan was never really implemented.

> The Quincy Report (1821) and the Yates Report (1824) led to growth in the establishment of almshouses and workhouses for the poor.

In 1821 a committee in Massachusetts led by Josiah Quincy found that outdoor relief was both expensive and injurious to morals. Quincy and his committee had studied homes where the children had been bound out and adults had been farmed out or auctioned. They found that the poor were treated with barbarity and neglect, the education and morals of the pauper children were almost wholly neglected, inadequate provision was made for employment, and little attention was given to the disbursement of public funds. According to the committee the almshouse was the only answer to these many shortcomings of outdoor relief. A few years later the Yates Report concluded that workhouses would not only benefit children morally but would also help the economic system.

Prison: Punishment and Rehabilitation

Until 1790 jails were for the poor and detainment of prisoners, not punishment. Punishment until that time generally meant time in the stocks, whipping, flogging, branding, mutilation, and hanging. Cesar Beccaria's *Essays on Crime and Punishment* (1764) introduced the utilitarian approach to punishing crime. Beccaria argued that crime should be clearly defined, laws should be codified to allow defense, and punishment should fit the crime and be based not on vengeance, but on instilling good citizenship. This approach based imprisonment on the offense committed and put prisoners to constructive tasks.

The Quakers led the move for prisons as rehabilitative units. Inmates in Quaker prisons were not to associate with each other; they needed solitude to reflect on their evil ways. Prisoners could read the Bible, but should not engage in any other activity. The goal of imprisonment was redemption.

Crime was then perceived as an exercise of free will, not predestination. The environment could be a source of temptation or inspiration. Constructive punishment could lead to a decrease in criminal behavior. Juveniles were placed in separate institutions called houses of refuge or schools for industry. Some juvenile inmates were lawbreakers; some were just poor. Discipline was harsh, and didactic moralizing was an important part of the programs in these houses and schools.

Health Care

The first half of the 19th century was a time for great breakthroughs in medicine. Bleeding, blistering, and purging had been the most common treatments for illness. Studies done in Paris showed that this type of treatment was actually detrimental to the health of the patients. Hospitals had traditionally been a form of poor relief. Infirmaries in almshouses became hospitals. American doctors were dependent on European medicine for many advances that were made; the United States did not allow medical students to work on cadavers. Illness too had been seen as a moral fault under the principle of predestination. Now physicians were beginning to understand biological components of illness.[24]

In 1794 Bellevue Hospital in New York began as part of an almshouse.

Mental Health and Moral Treatment

Treatment of mental illness advanced at the same time. Once perceived as demonic possession, mental illness was now sometimes associated with physical causes. Bleeding and blistering or the tranquilizer chair became popular treatments. Patients in straitjackets sat in the tranquilizer chair and were spun about until they became calm. In colonial America the insane had almost always been kept at home in a cellar or shed, usually behind locked bars; now doctors began setting up private madhouses that began to prescribe "moral" treatment. Moral treatment was based on the theory that the brain was susceptible and malleable. Physical illness as well as the environment could affect the brain. The physician was to discover the source of the difficulty and correct it. Treatment usually involved separation from home or other pathological circumstances. Such was the origin of asylums.

Asylums provided the potential for a carefully controlled environment and restoration of patients' balance. But only the rich could afford moral treatment. Patients who could afford the treatments responded favorably; a certain Dr. Todd cured twenty-one of twenty-three patients in one asylum. In the 1840s there were nineteen asylums, but only seven or eight good ones. There were over 17,457 reported cases of bizarre insanity. One in seven patients was under medical supervision; the rest were in attics, almshouses, and jails.[25]

Dorothea Dix: The Spread of Moral Treatment

Dorothea Lynde Dix, despite poor physical health, spent her entire life lobbying for reforms in treatment of the insane.

Dorothea Dix (1802–1887) was an important force in the mental health movement. Dix taught Sunday school in East Cambridge Jail, where she observed lunatics in unheated cells. She began visiting other places where the mentally ill were kept, compiling case-by-case records of the misery and abuse she observed. She was responsible for founding or enlarging thirty-two mental hospitals in the U.S. and abroad. Dorothea Dix was very impressed with moral treatment and tried to make it widely available.[26]

Her program for the mentally ill contained three points: patients should receive humane care instead of neglect, isolation, and cruelty; special state institutions should receive financial aid because individuals, local governments, and private charity could not afford to run the institutions; and patients should receive medical care based on the moral treatment model. In 1848 Dorothea Dix asked Congress to designate five million acres for mental institutions. Congress doubled the amount of land and passed the legislation. President Pierce vetoed the bill because he said the welfare domain belonged to the states, not the federal government.

Charles Brace: The Child Saving Movement

Charles Loring Brace not only developed the idea of foster care but also helped to establish schools, lodging houses, summer camps, and shelters for vagrant children.

Children in the almshouses did not receive the care they needed. Almshouses tended to be undemocratic and anti-family; submission and obedience were stressed, and children were not allowed to develop as individuals. There were just too many children, and public education was taking away apprenticeship opportunities. One response to this problem was introduced by Charles Loring Brace (1826–1890). Brace was the director of the Children's Aid Society in New York City. He wrote *The Dangerous Class of New York,* describing his work with the poor children of New York City. Brace believed that the answer to poverty for children was foster care on Western farms that needed laborers. The only real resistance he got to his idea was from the Catholic Church, which was afraid he might be placing Catholic children in Protestant homes. Between 1853 and 1864 his agency placed 4,614 children on farms.[27] Brace's work has been featured in a public television special entitled "Orphan Train."

One of the earliest forms of day care was the kindergarten classes that were held in settlements such as this class at Hartley House.

AFTERMATH OF THE CIVIL WAR

Following the Civil War, the North and South developed differently and experienced different problems. The North experienced rapid economic growth, but even though the United States had become a leading manufacturer, poverty continued to grow. There was increased polarization of economic classes; while some owners pursued wealth ruthlessly, workers and farmers lived precariously. The North suffered a serious unemployment problem from 1873–79, and labor unions lost much of their strength because of a large reserve labor force.

The Freedmen's Bureau, established by Congress in 1865, provided transportation, distributed medical supplies, and helped establish schools, hospitals, and orphanages.

The South had to deal with devastated land, transportation systems, and financial institutions. The rural areas were particularly impoverished. Black codes that limited the property rights of ex-slaves and forbade them to work as artisans and mechanics were enacted to control blacks. Blacks could work only in limited areas. Any unemployed black was subject to lease to farmers, and former owners had first chance to bid. The Freedmen's Bureau was the first federal welfare agency; it was housed in the War Department and was the major source of public welfare in the South. The bureau dealt with transient blacks and abandoned property. White townspeople opposed these programs and wanted blacks to work under former conditions; jobs created by the government interfered with this. General Otis Howard, the director of the bureau, was responsible for seeing that black educational institutions such as Howard, Fisk, and Hampton Universities were built. Personnel problems within the agency and political pressures from without led to its demise after just seven years (1872).[28]

SUMMARY

Understanding the development of social welfare policy prior to the 20th century sets the stage for a better understanding of the development of the social work profession. History illustrates how social work practice and social welfare policy have been shaped by the dominant values of the time. Today social welfare policy reflects the assumptions of the Statute of Laborers more closely than the religious motivation of the Middle Ages. With industrialization workers lost economic security and became dependent on the economic cycle. The social welfare institution provided members of society with some sense of order in a rapidly changing economic system. Lack of security was partially compensated by the welfare system in a manner that did not threaten the economic system. When cheap labor was needed, the social welfare system ensured its availability; when there was a surplus of labor, the social welfare system provided minimal subsistence for the unemployed. British and American poor laws have tended to respond to the needs of the economic system; religion and philosophy too have supported the social welfare institution as a stabilizing element in the economy.

Today we see social welfare as an instrument of the economic system in postindustrial society. As laborer positions paying upwards of $15 per hour are eliminated, new jobs programs are developed by government. The manifest function of these programs is to find employment for displaced workers. The latent function is to ease workers into lower-paying jobs and decreased affluence with minimal interruption to society or the economic cycle.

Before the Civil War professionalization began to creep into the social services: jails were designed to redeem the sinner, mental health institutions were beginning to treat the insane, and children were being placed in foster care. The tragedy of the Civil War changed the complexion of the social welfare system. North and South were faced with different economic and social problems. The major problems in the North were related to immigration, industrialization, and urbanization. The Charity Organization Societies and settlement houses were designed to respond to these problems. It is here in particular that one can discern the beginning of the social work profession. Since the worst poverty in the South was suffered by blacks, there was not the same societal concern about these problems. Blacks were left on their own to deal with their problems, and black responses often paralleled white services. Blacks, however, were generally limited to self-help groups that did not have the luxury of developing training schools for professionals and were limited to providing survival mechanisms to an impoverished, oppressed people who did not have the sponsorship of the wealthy.

These historical underpinnings of welfare illustrate the great diversity of responses a society can choose in dealing with poverty and other social problems. Differences in ideology and economic interests led England and Germany to different societal responses. Differences in economic base and racial make-up led to the development of different welfare systems in the North and the South. Obtaining a perspective on past societal choices provides insight for present choices. It also introduces the question of how much a profession can impact on society and how much society dictates the limits of professional practice.

NOTES

1. June Axinn and Herman Levin, *Social Welfare: A History of American Response to Need,* 2nd ed. (New York: Harper and Row, 1982), 1.
2. Blanche Coll, *Perspectives in Public Welfare: A History* (Washington, D.C.: U.S. Printing Office), 2.
3. Brian Tierney, *Medieval Poor Law: A Sketch of Canonical Theory and Its Applications in England* (Berkeley and Los Angeles: University of California Press, 1959), 65; cited in Coll, *Perspectives,* 3.
4. Gerald Handel, *Social Welfare in Western Society* (New York: Random House, 1982), 51.
5. Ibid., 59.
6. 23 Edward III, The Statute of Laborers, 1349. For a more complete survey of early poor laws, see Karl de Schweinitz, *England's Road to Social Security* (London: University of Pennsylvania Press, 1947).
7. De Schweinitz, *England's Road,* 8.
8. Coll, *Perspectives.*
9. 22 Henry VIII, c. 12, An Act Concerning Punishment of Beggars and Vagabonds, 1531.
10. 27 Henry VIII, c. 25, 1536.
11. Andrew Yarranton, *England's Improvement by Sea and Land to Outdo the Dutch without Fighting, to Pay Debts without Moneys, to set at Work All the Poor of England with the Growth of Our Own Lands,* London, 1677, 46–47.
12. Beulah Compton, *Introduction to Social Welfare and Social Work: Structure, Function, and Process* (Homewood, Ill.: Dorsey, 1980), 158.
13. Sir Frederic Morton Eden, *The State of the Poor: Or, An History of the Labouring Classes in England, From the Conquest to the Present Period,* Vol. 2, (London, 1797), 384.
14. De Schweinitz, *England's Road,* 91.
15. Helen Ginsberg, *Poverty, Economics, and Society* (Washington, D.C.: University Press of America, 1981), 20.
16. Ibid., 30.
17. *The Report from His Majesty's Commissioners for Inquiring into the Administration and Practical Operation of the Poor Laws, Published by Authority,* 1834, 88–89.

18. Sidney Webb and Beatrice Webb, *English Local Government: English Poor Law History, Part I* (New York: Longman, Green, 1927), 417–418; cited in Coll, *Perspectives, 61–62.*

19. David Rothman, *Discovery of the Asylum* (Boston: Little, Brown, 1971), 4.

20. Ibid.

21. Axinn and Levin, *Social Welfare.*

22. Rothman, *Discovery,* 16.

23. Walter Trattner, *From Poor Law to Welfare State* (New York: Free Press, 1979), 50.

24. James Lieby, *A History of Social Welfare and Social Work in the U.S.* (New York: Columbia University Press, 1978).

25. Ibid.

26. Ibid.

27. Trattner, *From Poor Law,* 93–111.

28. Axinn and Levin, *Social Welfare.*

Chapter

7

Societies, Settlements, and Social Justice

Professional social work in the United States developed from an imperfect union between the late-nineteenth century "scientific charity" movement, with its emphasis on friendly visiting and individual case diagnosis on the one hand, and the slightly younger social settlement movement, with its strong orientation toward social reform and social survey on the other. Leaders of the scientific charity movement sought to coordinate centrally all charity resources in a city, and volunteer "friendly visitors" investigated applications for assistance to determine how much aid they needed and the kind of help required. . . . In the early twentieth century, the social settlements not only provided clubs and classes for neighborhood residents, but collected descriptive and statistical data regarding neighborhood social conditions which they then utilized to agitate for social reform.[1]

During the late 1800s the problems associated with the industrial revolution brought about a need for massive delivery of services. People of all races flocked to the cities looking for work. As industrialization and urbanization increased, so did unemployment.

Without denying that the settlement and charity organization movements deserve primary recognition for the development of professional practice, this chapter seeks to illustrate the many different movements that have contributed to the present shape of practice. The unifying professional organization (National Association of Social Work—NASW) has been in existence only since 1955. Before the chartering of the NASW numerous professional groups identified themselves with titles such as the American Association of Group Workers, American Association of Hospital Social Workers, American Association of School Social Workers, and the American Association of Psychiatric Social Workers.

Analysis of the conservative, liberal, and radical heritage of professional practice will be presented. Presentation of the underlying philosophies is designed to clarify the connections between each of the ideologies and the practice that has subsequently developed.

INDUSTRIALIZATION: DIFFERENT RACES, DIFFERENT RESPONSES

Charity Organization Societies and the Settlement House Movement

The Charity Organization Society, the settlement house movement, and the less familiar social justice movements provide contrasting images of ideology shaping practice. Even though the Charity Organization Society (COS) and the settlement house movement developed at the same time in the United States, their analysis and response to social problems differed sharply. The COS's "Four Pillar" approach of investigation, registration, cooperation, and coordination contrasted sharply with the settlement movement's "Three Rs": residence, research, and reform. As these terms suggest, the COS stressed personal fault, and the settlement workers stressed social and economic conditions as the prime cause of hunger and poverty. To the COS the problem was pauperism; to the settlement movement the problem was poverty. Because settlement workers assigned so much weight to the social causes of poverty, they believed an effective solution would be social rather than individual.

The first American Charity Organization Society opened in Buffalo in 1877.

The first settlement house, the Neighborhood Guild, opened in 1866 in New York.

Both movements believed that the rich and poor would have to come together to deal with the problem. COS workers did "friendly visiting" to set an example and uplift the spirits of the poor. In the settlement movement the rich actually moved to the slum areas and tried to bring culture and education to the neighborhoods.

In the early stages of development neither movement had much appreciation for the other. Settlement workers criticized COS workers for their limited view of poverty. COS workers criticized the settlements as being too sentimental and unscientific. As the movements matured the distinctions and suspicions decreased and mutual projects were undertaken. For instance, a juvenile court project in Cook County was conceived by settlement workers, who directed the project but depended upon the casework skills of the COS workers to make it a success.[2]

Data collection was important to both movements. COS workers investigated applicants for assistance to determine how much aid they needed and the kind of help required. Settlement workers collected descriptive and statistical data about social conditions and used these data to agitate for social reform.[3]

The most important characteristic shared by the white settlement and charity movements was a belief in the basic economic and political structure. On the other hand, there were social reformers and revolutionaries of all races who believed that the social structure precluded equality. Instead of seeing society as open to all races and sexes, they suggested that societal institutions ensured continued inequality. These men and women fought for social, political, and economic equality by pursuing a fundamental redistribution of power to overcome structured inequality. Since these reformers believed that inequality was structured into society, they believed that societal transformation was necessary to overcome it.

National League of Women Voters
Dinner Conference
April 28 1932   Book Cadillac Hotel
D...   Michigan

Historically, women have organized to be better informed and to be able to inform others about issues affecting women. The League of Women Voters is an example of a conservative organization that sees women's issues as part of larger societal problems.

Although these groups are not frequently viewed as an integral piece of social work heritage, their work has significantly affected social work practice and they might be considered forerunners of present day radical practitioners. The groups mentioned in the analysis are radical feminists, abolitionists, councils of the unemployed, black labor councils, and the rank and file movement. (The National Welfare Rights Organization and the Black Panther Party are discussed in Chapter 8.)

Black Organizations

The response of white Americans to the problems of industrialization can be learned by reading any United States history book, but little has been written about how blacks approached those problems. What became of the millions of blacks newly freed from slavery? How were they to live with no money and no land? The Freedmen's Bureau, a federal program that lasted six years and provided education and jobs for poor southern whites and blacks, was a temporary answer. Ultimately the only solution for blacks was self-help.[4] Blacks had to rely on each other to survive.

The black self-help groups frequently organized into mutual benefit societies that provided for ill members and took care of burial and survivors when a member died. These societies included the Black Masons, the Knights of Pythias, Good Samaritan Societies, Free African Society, and the Brown Fellowship Society. By 1850 almost half the adult black population belonged to a mutual benefit society.[5]

After the Civil War the prevalence and the severity of black needs increased. In response, cooperatives such as the Farmer's Improvement Society of Texas were formed. One purpose of these organizations was to form cooperative buying and selling groups in the Oakland, Texas area.[6] Cooperatives worked to improve the homes of rural and village blacks and improve farming methods. This was in addition to the usual benefits of the mutual relief societies such as sick and death benefits to members and their families.

CONSERVATIVE HERITAGE

Charity Organization Society

The charity organization society movement began in England in 1867 and is another example of an idea borrowed from England.

The charity organization society movement is clearly the best known and most powerful source of conservative ideology in the profession. The COS solution to poverty was to investigate and register the poor, and to cooperate and coordinate with other relief agencies. These methods would overcome pauperism. The COS movement discounted the economic and social contributions to poverty and saw it instead as a "disease resulting from personal defect and evil acts—laziness, deceitfulness, intemperance, improvidence, inefficiency, extravagance, and sexual vices."[7] Charity was a necessary evil that provided material resources for the poor when they really needed spiritual sustenance. No principle of practice ranked higher in importance than coordinating relief to make certain no one received too much material assistance; too much charity was detrimental to character. Friendly visiting was a substitute for alms;[8] the friendly visitor was to show the poor how to be thrifty, moral, and industrious.

Mary Richmond wrote about methods of working with the poor in _Social Diagnosis_ (1917).

Poverty was an evil which could only be overcome by the good influence of the rich. Even into the twentieth century mothers' pensions and allowances were fought earnestly and sometimes bitterly by COS leaders including Mary Richmond, director of the New York COS. Richmond believed that sound relief practices could not be achieved under governmental auspices.[9]

Josephine Shaw Lowell worked for reforms in the working hours of women and the conditions of almshouses and prisons. She also promoted women's suffrage.

Josephine Shaw Lowell (1843–1905), an earlier director of the New York COS, gave primary importance to virtue, character, and morality. She thought that charity must tend to raise the character and elevate the moral nature:

> The main instrument to be depended upon, to raise the standard of decency, cleanliness, providence and morality among them must be personal influence, which means that a constant and continued intercourse must be

kept up between those who have a high standard and those who have it not, and that the educated and happy and good are to give some of their time regularly and as a duty, year in and year out, to the ignorant, miserable and vicious.[10]

Friendly visitors were committed to relieving distressed women and children and encouraging industry among the poor. Intervention was based on the assumption that the locus of the problem was the individual, and the individual must be the target of change. The one recognized social cause of poverty was undue generosity of the relief agencies.

In the early days of charity organization societies, the paid administrators were men; women did the volunteer work, primarily friendly visiting with clients. As this service became formalized many tasks originally done by volunteers were taken over by professional paid staff.

The practical goal of charity organization workers was to make productive citizens of the poor. From this conservative heritage sprang individually oriented models of casework, group therapy, and the social planning model.

Theory and Method.   The COS movement was a response of the upper and middle classes to the social dislocations of the post-Civil War industrial city. Theirs was a scientific approach to poverty guided by social Darwinist assumptions. Contempt for the poor was at the heart of social Darwinism, which misapplied evolutionary concepts to human society.[11] The phrase *survival of the fittest* originated with Herbert Spencer (1820-1903), who actually drew his ideas from Thomas Malthus rather than Charles Darwin. In fact, Spencer wrote about social selection almost ten years before the publication of Darwin's *Origin of the Species* (1859). Spencer argued that the poor were unfit and society would be better off if they were eliminated; welfare could only interfere with natural selection and perpetuate the weak. Survival of the fittest was a rallying cry against the poor. It was used to oppose social legislation and justify indifference to the terrible living conditions of the poor.[12] Spencer hypothesized that if relief practices supported dependency and misfits, then doling out relief would weaken the human species. The only appropriate assistance was work or spiritual guidance; the only remedy for poverty was self-help. "Protecting the ill-favored in the struggle for existence would only permit them to multiply and this could lead to no other result than a disastrous weakening of the species."[13]

National Urban League

One of the major Negro organizations, the National Urban League, emerged from several philanthropic groups in 1911.

Paralleling the white COS movement in method and goals was the National Urban League, the most outstanding example of blacks working with whites to gain equality in the deliverance of social services. Springing from the Committee on Urban Conditions Among Negroes (founded in 1910), the National Urban League was formed on October 16, 1911 and became the first black national social service agency. Its stated purpose was

to carry on preventive and constructive social work among blacks, for improving their social and economic conditions in urban centers; to bring about coordination and cooperation between existing agencies working in interest of Negroes and to develop agencies where necessary; to secure and train Black social workers; to make studies in cities to carry out these objectives.[14]

During its early years the Urban League concentrated on what it termed scientific social work.[15] Its main focus was researching and collecting data to downplay the racial and class differences among people. It also searched for solutions to problems such as unstable families, poverty, and illiteracy.

One quality of the National Urban League missing in many black human service organizations is its ability to change and adapt to the needs of its constituents. For instance, during the World War I era the migration of blacks to the city and an increase in job availability prompted the Urban League to provide vocational training and guidance. After the war the Urban League was again called upon, this time to protect the rights of those same workers.[16] Once the war ended, the demand for workers decreased, and of course blacks were the most expendable.

While white America was experiencing the roaring twenties, blacks were singing the same old last-hired-first-fired blues. One reason was the inability of blacks to get into the white labor unions. In 1925 the National Urban League created its Department of Industrial Relations to improve its associations with the American Federation of Labor.[17] This department also studied the job market so it could direct blacks to locations where jobs were available. This tactic served to distribute black workers and helped alleviate overcrowding.

With the 1940s the objectives of the National Urban League took on a broader perspective. They moved to assume higher standards of social work technique, in fact suggesting that all of the League's departments and affiliates should be headed by social workers, sociologists, or somebody knowledgeable in matters of race relations.[18] The hunger, poverty, illiteracy, poor health, and lack of recreation blacks faced were all believed to be caused by segregation and discrimination based on white racism.[19]

So after thirty years of working with relatively conservative white groups the National Urban League came to a new assessment of the root of blacks' problems—white racism. It was then that the National Urban League became more than just a small-time labor organization and became a full-fledged civil rights group. Currently it possesses the largest annual budget of any black civil rights organization.

The National Urban League has put its money to good use. By 1975 it had a national skills bank with a centralized computer system containing information on job openings throughout the country. People can submit their qualifications to the skills bank and be matched to an appropriate job. A law enforcement and manpower project helps recruit black police in an attempt to combat police brutality. The League's "street academies" help dropouts finish high school. The list of projects and accomplishments goes on and on.

Throughout its history the Urban League has remained interracial in its makeup and social work-oriented in its objectives. It works to reform society,

Leaders in the Urban League met at the 78th Annual Forum of the National Conference on Social Welfare in Atlantic City in 1951.

but it views the problems that blacks face as stemming less from capitalism than from white racism within the capitalist framework that dispossesses blacks.

Social Feminists and Women's Clubs

The women active in the COS movement could be described as social feminists, since they reflected the "proper" role of women. Their duty was to expand women's family role to the wider society; they had no desire to interfere in the work of men. A charter of the Charitable Society of St. Louis reflects this view of women.

> Women would yield to men the care of government for which they are better qualified. . . . it is hoped that women may claim (without danger of neglecting the dearer sense of duty which lies at home) the more humble field of benevolence as their sphere of action.[20]

Sheila Rothman described this role as "virtuous womanhood."[21] The woman was to develop her social, intellectual, and moral power in the most perfect manner to become a better mother, wife, and social reformer. She was to obtain the appropriate scientific and practical training for her distinct profession as housekeeper, nurse of infants and the sick, educator of children, trainer of servants and minister of charities. In the role of the virtuous woman, a wife had the awesome responsibility for both home and society. She was even to tame her husband. A contemporary woman made this comment in 1886:

> Few women understand at the outset that in marrying, they have simply captured a wild animal . . . the taming of which is to be the life work of the woman who has taken him in charge. . . . The duty is imposed upon her by high heaven, to reduce all these grand, untamed life-forces to order . . . to make them subservient to the behests of her nature, and to those vast undying interests which to these two and to their posterity center in the home.[22]

Rothman suggests that women had the mandate to tame society as well. Another quotation from that period suggested that women

> use their power to purify and amend society. If a woman be herself pure and noble-hearted she will come into every circle as a person does into a heated room who carries with him the freshness of the woods.[23]

Black Women's Clubs

Black churches and settlement houses alone could not handle the enormous needs of black people. Near the turn of the century a new idea began to take hold in the black community. Women's clubs had started forming all over the country; denied entry into white clubs, black women formed their own. These clubs provided the same benefits to their members that benevolent societies and Mason-like organizations offered men. But in contrast to male organizations, women's clubs reached out to the community. The male organizations sought to maintain themselves first and foremost. The social orientation of the women's clubs was consistent with the proper role of women for that era: to tame society.

By 1903 there were seven black women's clubs in Chicago alone.[24] The primary source of social welfare services available to blacks during the early 1900s, these clubs sponsored kindergartens, nursery schools, day care centers, and orphanages for young children. They also operated homes for elderly people and supported various educational institutions with fundraising activities.[25] Black women engaged in the same activities as white social reformers of the Progressive Era, but the movements were separate. Once educational institutions were developed many women used the buildings for community organizing as well. Emma J. Wilson, Cornelia Bowen, Lucy Lainey, Charlotte Hawkins Brown, Nancy Burroughs, and Mary McLeod Bethune were among the most active organizers.[26] These women raised financial support for schools and community buildings and in turn used them as centers or meeting places to conduct their social action activities.

The women's clubs of this period offered a wide range of activities. For instance, the Tuskegee Women's Club, organized in 1895 by Mary Margaret Washington, gave advice on child care, home economics, gardening, and sewing—skills necessary for the housewife.[27] It also operated a missionary and a small library, and helped out at the local jail and nearest settlement house. It participated in women's suffrage and political activities as well.[28]

Ida B. Wells formed a different kind of club. Lynchings and rapes of blacks were at an all-time high in the late 1800s. Wells started a national anti-lynching crusade in 1892, and in 1893 the Ida B. Wells Club was formed.[29] Wells launched an all-out campaign to discourage lynching and rape. She spoke out against the abuse of black women and in defense of black womanhood; she worked to eliminate police brutality and discrimination.

The Medical Profession

The medical profession was a powerful influence circumscribing the role of women. In spite of their great virtue women were thought to be weak. Menstruation was considered not only an illness, but also temporary insanity. Women were instructed to take to bed for pregnancy and menstruation. By equating normal body functions with disease, the culture made even competent women unfit for extensive activity outside the home. Women were more virtuous, civilized, and moral, but always susceptible to physical and mental derangement. Vassar, the first women's college (founded in 1865), treated women more like patients than students.[30]

LIBERAL HERITAGE

The Settlement House Movement

The settlement philosophy was very different from the scientific philanthropy of the charity organization societies. The first settlement, Toynbee Hall in England, was organized by a group of university students and faculty attempting to practice Christian socialism in the London slums. The most well-known settlements in the United States were Hull House in Chicago, established by Jane Addams after visiting Toynbee Hall, and Henry Street Settlement in New York, established by Lillian Wald.

Toynbee Hall was founded in 1884; Hull House and the Henry Street settlement followed in 1889 and 1893 respectively.

The settlement houses embodied the neighborhood ideal — the desire to create a community among people living in the same area. Interdependence of social groups was important and necessary to cope with problems. Settlement workers believed that by helping individuals they actually helped the whole community.

Concepts underlying the movement were participation in small groups, a belief in the democratic ways of life and a two-way responsibility between the community and the individual. Settlement workers attempted to unite the scattered industrial and religious elements thrown together in the great cities; they did not confine their commitment to the poor but included the working class as well. They felt that by developing a truly democratic society, America could provide all people the means to develop fully and allow them to take their places as responsible members of the human race.

Black Settlement Houses. During this period the large-scale migration of blacks to the North increased the need for settlement houses to help blacks adjust to life in the city. The White Rose Industrial Association was just such a place. It was organized in 1895 to train black girls and women to be self-sufficient and to live "right."[31] This association also set up settlement houses and offered aid to travelers in Norfolk, Virginia, and New York City for girls coming up from the South. In Chicago, Celia Parker Wooley established the Frederick Douglass Center in 1904.[32] The Frederick Douglass Center had a workshop and clubroom for boys, and held classes in manual training and domestic service. By today's standards these services may seem minor or unimportant, but at the time those were the only jobs open to blacks and such training represented a valuable opportunity for the unemployed.

Theory and Method. The primary settlement methodology followed John Dewey's "learning by doing" model. Like Dewey, settlement workers believed in informality and starting where the group was. The first university group work course was taught in 1920 by Grace Coyle at Western Reserve University. Settlement workers were much slower than caseworkers to teach their methods in a university setting. The conflict between settlement workers and friendly visitors continued between group workers and caseworkers.

> Group work was the primary social work methodology used by settlement workers.

Group work practice by settlement house workers has been referred to as the "social reconstruction through political action" phase of welfare work. They were committed to a democratic and humane society, and their accomplishments reflect their goals. Participating in society was necessary for mental health and preservation of the democratic ideal.

Professional Education. While early settlement workers were not concerned with codifying their methods, academics (particularly Grace Coyle) eventually described and taught settlement methods.

> Grace Longwell Coyle (1892–1962) is credited with defining the method of group work.

The first theoretical work on group work method was written by Grace Coyle.[33] *Social Processes in Organizing Groups* appeared in 1930, ten years after Professor Coyle had taught the first group work methods course at the School of Applied Social Sciences of Western Reserve University in Cleveland. Like the settlement house workers, Coyle envisioned working with groups to encourage growth of responsibility to the larger society. Democracy was to be enhanced and enriched by "socially intelligent citizens."[34] Group workers were among the professionals who formed the National Association of Social Workers in 1955.

The Social Gospel. Settlement workers tended to be young, single women, the first generation of women who were college-educated. Despite their education, traditional male positions were not open to them. If they were to have meaningful careers, a new professional domain had to be developed.

One of the main goals of settlements such as Hartley House was to improve conditions for people living in the cities and to restore communication between the college-educated and the working class.

Women were marginal in the male-dominated public world of occupations. For them a professional qualification was a badge of competence, a symbol of their right to follow paid professional work. For men such work was merely a phase in life, not a career in itself. The identity of the male derived from his role as clergyman, or from his prospects in business or the major professions. Men from good social backgrounds who engaged in social work for any length of time tended to participate in an organizing or managing capacity. It was the women's settlements then which developed training for social work as a career.[35]

The tremendous suffering caused by heavy immigration, industrialization, and urbanization offered many women an opportunity to be socially useful. Then, too, settlement work was often attractive to these women because of their commitment to the "social gospel." The social gospel was an attempt by conscientious ministers and priests to get their congregations to address problems of the poor. They wanted to establish the kingdom of God on earth through social reform. Washington Gladden, a Yale divinity professor

warned that "unless the churches became thoroughly aroused by these issues and used their influence to promote fundamental reform, they would
cease to be religious bodies and degenerate into institutions for the preservation of meaningless rites and superstitions."[36] Women saw in settlement
work "a sense of mission to God and to mankind that had been aroused and
nurtured by the religion of their youth."[37] Instead of entering the ministry,
which was closed to women, they chose a life of service to the poor.

Educated Motherhood: The Role of Woman

The Progressive Era ushered in a new ideal for womanhood that Rothman
labels "educated motherhood."[38] A new attitude toward children suggested
that children needed more than affectionate care; they needed mothers with
sophisticated skills of management too. Educators suggested that mothers
mold their children; suddenly women needed great preparation for the mothering task. The kindergarten was a societal response to this new perception,
but settlement women also worked with individual mothers. Workers taught
cleanliness and instilled American values. Settlement house workers were
making home visits similar to those of the charity organization society ladies,
with several important differences. Settlement house women were helping
neighbors; they emphasized hygiene and child development instead of virtue,
temperance, and frugality.[39]

> The Progressive Era lasted from 1896 to 1916.

This service to the poor went far beyond the traditional boundaries. Settlement house workers developed playgrounds, improved housing, worked
for housing legislation, organized neighborhood protests against destructive
city regulation, helped immigrants negotiate with traditional agencies, and
were peripherally involved in helping rural Southern blacks adjust to the city.
Settlement house workers supported labor, fought against child labor, and
protested political corruption.

Black Churches

> Chapter 6 discussed the early role of the church as a provider of social welfare. Here again we see the importance of the church.

The black church also played a vital role in the relief of blacks. Released
from slavery, blacks were left with the clothes on their backs and their
religion. The church stood strong during this period of crisis. Besides
establishing missions and giving out various forms of relief, the church also
involved itself in labor disputes on behalf of its congregation. Reverend T.
W. Walker, for example, pastor of a black church in Birmingham, Alabama,
helped organize local black women into a union in 1884. Many worked as
maids in the homes of more prosperous whites; Reverend Walker showed
them they were not getting adequate pay for their work. When the women
approached their employers for better wages they were fired. Reverend
Walker then united his church in a blacklisting of the employers. Eventually
the women were rehired and received the requested wage increases.[40] Walker
also used his church to form a Christian Relief Society that aided blacks
throughout Birmingham.

Southern blacks were not the only ones in need of services during this period. Northern blacks suffered hardships too, and the black church was there to lend a helping hand. St. Mark's Episcopal Church in New York City, led by its pastor Dr. William H. Brooks, aided blacks in Harlem, Brooklyn, and the Bronx by establishing social service missions in their communities.[41]

These examples are just two illustrations of how the black church responded to the needs of blacks in the late 1800s. From being advocates for their congregations to providing social services to those in need, black churches were the most prevalent source of social welfare available to blacks from the end of Reconstruction to the 1890s.[42]

Black Council for National Defense

Women have always dominated the social service field, and black social welfare is no different from the mainstream in this regard. Because of segregation blacks were excluded from services available to whites; the burden of relief for blacks fell upon black women.[43] Organizations such as the Tuskegee Women's Club, the Atlanta Neighborhood Union, and the Council for National Defense provided vital services for the black population. Women such as Ida B. Wells and Mary Margaret Washington provided the leadership.

Blacks faced difficult years between Reconstruction and World War I. Those who did not benefit from reconstruction were left to fend for themselves; without the aid of black service organizations many would have perished. But the contributions of these groups did not stop with the black community. They also played a vital role in World War I. The Committee on Women's Defense Work of the Council for National Defense consisted mainly of black women.[44] It helped care for families of absent soldiers, gave comfort kits to the soldiers, helped conserve and enlarge the food supply, and formed canning clubs. The committee also brought attention to the high infant mortality rate in this country.[45] It discovered a need for better community health services. To correct these problems the council set up programs to weigh and measure infants and provide them with milk. In addition, the committee sought to improve recreational facilities available to youth and pushed for nurse's training for black women. Medical personnel for black people had always been woefully inadequate; the committee compiled and circulated a list of hospitals where black women could be trained.

The liberal value assumptions inherent in the settlement house movement are reflected in ecological casework, social action models of group work, and the grass roots approach to community organization.

The characteristics of the more liberal settlement house and related movements were very different from the characteristics of conservative organizations such as the charity organization societies. The settlement workers' emphasis was on social action. They had little concern for scientific theories of poverty or human behavior. They used informal methods—they worked with the community rather than for the community. The poor were suffering because of social conditions, and the way to relieve the suffering was to change those conditions. They also believed that if the opportunity existed, the poor would become contributing members of society. Basic to their belief was that democratic participation of all citizens was in the best interests of both the individual and society.

RADICAL HERITAGE

People of color, feminists, gays, and youth declared that mainstream social work was too white, too middle-class, too patriarchal, and too identified with the bourgeoisie to be relevant to their needs. They created alternative self-controlled agencies: the Black Panther breakfast program, feminist health collectives and shelters for battered women. . . . Most of these were not staffed by professional social workers, although social workers sympathetic to the particular agency's ideology were sometimes employed.[46]

Social Justice Movements

A classic text on radi-
cal social work practice
is Saul Alinsky's *Rev-
eille for Radicals*
(1946).

Both the liberal and conservative strains of social work have been highly visible and concentrated throughout history. Radical strains have been more diverse and less well organized. The visibility of radical practitioners has varied tremendously throughout the last century. Saul Alinsky, probably the most well known and articulate of radical theorists, identified what he saw as the goal of community organization—an apt summary of the goals of most radical groups.

We are concerned with how to create mass organizations to seize power and give it to the people; to realize the democratic dream of equality, justice, peace, cooperation, equal and full opportunities for education, full and useful employment, health, and the creation of those circumstances in which man can have the chance to live by the values that give meaning to life. We are talking about a mass power organization which will change the world into a place where all men and women walk erect, in the spirit of that credo of the Spanish Civil War, "Better to die on your feet than to live on your knees." This means revolution. . . . There are people who say that it is not revolution, but evolution, that brings about change—but evolution is simply the term used by non-participants to denote a particular sequence of revolutions as they synthesized into a specific major social change.[47]

Radical approaches to
casework, group work
and community organi-
zation are described in
Chapter 8.

Taking a leadership role in radical social justice movements has been outside the professional experience and training of most social workers. Not until the War on Poverty released money to train social workers in community organization did social workers begin to specialize in that field. Between 1960 and 1969 the community organization majors rose from 1.5 percent to 9 percent of the social work majors.[48]

Even though the number of community organization specialists has risen, few of these social workers would identify with a radical practice framework. And in fact not all radical practitioners choose to practice community organization; some are caseworkers and group workers. Radical practice can comprise major protest movements, organized action at a community level, or individual casework. Whatever the intervention, radicals view the redistribution of resources and power as the ultimate goal of social work practice. While radical strategies are varied and less clearly defined than those that have come out of the settlement and charity movements, history shows that social work has sometimes facilitated radical movements and sometimes been the target for change for these movements. While the rank and file movement is the only clearly social work movement, social justice movements in general are the third important contributors to social work practice. The history of social justice movements also underscores the degree to which societal attitudes toward women have shaped both social work practice and social policy.

Radical Feminists and Abolitionists

In contrast to the social feminists involved in the Charity Organization Societies and the social gospel adherents of the settlement movement, some groups, primarily of women, have perceived those reforms as inadequate to deal with the societal human oppression. They have been and continue to be committed to a redistribution of power in society.

The anti-slavery struggle is an important component of this history; a study of this struggle points out not only the oppression of slaves but also of women. Lucretia Mott and Esther Moore were influential members of the anti-slavery movement who helped organize the first anti-slavery convention in 1833. Shortly afterward, they were joined by the Grimké sisters, Sarah and Angelina, from South Carolina. Society became frightened at women's increasing power and influence. White churches, powerful societal institutions, attempted to crush that power and influence. The Orthodox Congregational Church, for example, the largest and most influential ecclesiastical body in Massachusetts, issued a pastoral letter in 1837 calling upon all "churches under their care to defend themselves by closing their doors against the abolitionists who had set aside the laws of God by welcoming women to their platforms and allowing them to speak in public."[49] This letter went on further to define the "proper role" for women.

It may be interesting to contrast this "proper role" for women with the ideal role presented earlier in the chapter.

We invite your attention to the dangers which at present seem to threaten the female character with wide spread and permanent injury. The appropriate duties and influence of woman are clearly stated in the New Testament. Those duties and that influence are unobtrusive and private, but the source of mighty power. When the mild, dependent, softening influence of woman under the sternness of man's opinions is fully exercised, society feels the effects of it in a thousand forms. The power of woman is her dependence, flowing from the consciousness of that weakness which God has given her for her protection, and which keeps her in those departments of life that form the character of individuals and of the nation. There are social influences which females use in promoting piety and the great objects of Christian benevolence which we cannot too highly commend. We appreciate the unostentatious prayers and effort of woman in advancing the cause of religion at home and abroad; in Sabbath schools; in leading religious inquirers to the pastors for instructions; and in all such associated effort as becomes the modesty of their sex; and earnestly hope that she may abound more and more in these labors of piety and love.[50]

This letter exemplifies how an institution believed to be sanctioned by God had sustained slavery of both women and blacks. Not only did women have no rights within the church, they did not even have civil rights in the early 19th century. They were chattels of men, legal minors until they married and civilly dead upon marriage. They were not allowed to attend college, do public speaking, or have legal custody of their children. Like the slaves, they had no part in making the laws that governed them.[51] The church and the state united to keep the Grimké sisters silent; they were banned from speaking by the church and by legal decree from the city of Charleston, S.C. They were informed that if they should return to Charleston, they would suffer mob violence from which the state could not protect them. Churchmen also effectively blocked the participation of Lucretia Mott and Esther Moore in the World Anti-Slavery Convention in London (1840). They argued that to admit a woman was to violate the ordinance of Almighty God.[52]

In 1848 Lucretia Mott and Elizabeth Cady Stanton called the first Equal Rights Convention in Seneca Falls, New York.[53] This was the official beginning of the suffrage struggle. It was seen as an extreme movement because it went against the socially defined roles of women. The fruition of these efforts came seventy years later when the Nineteenth Amendment was passed and women's suffrage became a reality. But women's suffrage started out as a radical movement demanding rights for women *and* blacks; the Nineteenth Amendment did not pass until a much more conservative contingent joined in the struggle. In fact, one argument for passing the amendment was that if blacks (even more lowly than women) could vote, then women must be given the vote too.

This example illustrates the point that often "women's issues" and "minority issues" compete with each other for attention as well as resources.

Unemployed Councils

More recent examples of organizing to redistribute power were the unemployed councils active during the depression. Groups of men out of work congregated at local relief offices and took over those offices until their demands were met. In Chicago, the Unemployed Council organized 5,000 men to march on relief headquarters demanding three meals a day, free medical attention, tobacco twice a week, the right to hold meetings, and the assurance of no discrimination against council members. They forced the city to rescind a 50 percent cut in relief funds.[54]

Black Labor Councils

Asa Philip Randolph is probably the most renowned black union organizer. He first came into national prominence as the leader of the Brotherhood of Sleeping Car Porters. Black railroad porters were denied entrance into the traditional white unions, so they were forced to form their own; they were not accepted as members of the American Federation of Labor until 1925.[55] Randolph gradually worked his way up through the ranks and attained a seat on the American Federation of Labor's Executive Board. Randolph was a constant agitator on issues concerning black labor in any form. It was this constant agitation that helped to produce Executive Order 8802, signed by President Franklin Roosevelt on June 6, 1941, banning discrimination in factories working on national defense contracts.[56] Many jobs opened up for blacks, but even this order was inadequate to deal with the problem of discrimination.

That same summer Randolph threatened to organize 50,000–100,000 blacks to march on Washington D.C. because of discriminatory labor practices. This threat prompted the formation of the Fair Employment Practices Commission (FEPC) to investigate these unfair dealings. The establishment of the FEPC was looked on as a great achievement at the time and might have had far-reaching effects, but it did not have the necessary power to punish the wrongdoers it found.[57] A. Philip Randolph was the foremost spokesman for black labor during this time. At a minimum, he forced America to sit up and take notice of blacks as a labor force and helped blacks recognize their latent power as a labor force.

But Randolph was not the first to attempt to organize the black labor force. Over sixty years before, in December 1869, Isaac Myers, a ship caulker, organized a Colored National Labor Convention in Washington.[58] Attended by clerks, ministers, and politicians for the most part, it focused on the economic problems blacks faced. The main resolutions brought from the convention were that workers should organize cooperative trade unions and that there should exist no conflict between labor and capital. This is a clear example of the fact that many years ago blacks recognized that self-help was their only recourse to achieving equality in the field of labor.

> The value of self-help organizations for blacks was emphasized earlier.

Rank and File Movement in Social Work

> The rank and file movement in social work was active in the 1930s and 1940s.

Between 1929 and 1942 a visible minority of social workers openly questioned the prevailing values of the American system. They disagreed with the reforms of the New Deal because they saw them as an evasion of the need for a planned society in which production decisions would be based on need, not profit. They argued that the economic programs of the New Deal helped big business and big agriculture, but not society as a whole.

This group managed to publish its own journal, *Social Work Today*. Its first issue stated the purpose of the journal: to meet "the need for a frank, critical analysis of basic social problems and their relation to social work." It promised to "promote an interest in the fundamental reorganization society must undergo to provide security for all" and to "support labor's struggle for a greater measure of control as the basic condition of reorganization."[59]

In retrospect, it is difficult to determine how much support the rank and file movement or *Social Work Today* had from the social work profession. A

Bertha Capen Reynolds believed that the philosophy of social work could not be separated from the philosophy and values of society as a whole.

number of prominent social workers including Bertha Capen Reynolds allowed their names to be used as contributing editors. Individual chapters of the American Association of Social Workers were supportive, but the national organizations chose to remain silent.

May 1942 saw the last issue of *Social Work Today*. The reason for its demise is not totally clear, but it was very likely related to the Nazi invasion of Russia. The journal had taken a strong stand that America should remain neutral during the war. Once the Nazi invasion took place, the position of the journal changed. Instead of advocating neutrality, editorials and articles emphasized how social work could contribute to the war effort. The editors of the journal, along with the rest of American society, decided basic structural change would have to wait for the coming of peace.[60] Not until 1978 did another radical social work journal *(Catalyst)* appear.

SUMMARY

This chapter has identified the organizational sources of the various ideological perspectives that shape social work practice. The conservative and liberal philosophies of the charity organization and settlement movements have always been the dominant influence on practice. Radical social justice movements have been less influential but a continuing presence.

The charity organization movement was introduced as the historical source of conservative practice. Just as conservative assumptions guided the friendly visitors of the 19th century, so do they guide some practitioners in the 1990s. The conservative point of view holds that the client is the locus of the problem and hence the target of change. The poor and unemployed suffer because of personal shortcomings. The role of government should be limited; government assistance should go to the private sector to help stimulate the economy and create jobs. Social workers should get the poor to accept dominant values and become productive citizens. While the conservative philosophy is not the philosophy of the social work profession, its prominence in the 1980s shaped federal policy in a way that severely limits practice even in the 1990s.

Liberals, like their forebears in the settlement house movement, view social problems as a predictable outcome of industrialization. Government is an integral mechanism designed to protect the poor and to control excesses of the market system. Liberal practitioners continue to seek increased opportunities for oppressed groups, increased control over corporations, and more liberal benefit programs. Liberals do not disregard individual weakness but are just as likely to see environmental causes of problems.

Radical philosophy has guided smaller groups of social workers who have worked for basic restructuring of the economic system. Radical philosophy has guided women, labor, and minorities in fighting for more equitable distribution of societal resources.

NOTES

1. Steven J. Diner, "Scholarship in the Quest for Social Welfare: A Fifty-Year History of the *Social Service Review*," *Social Service Review* 51, 1 (March 1977): 3.
2. Ibid.
3. Ibid.
4. Toby Ferrell, *Why Not Us? Blacks and Social Welfare* (Unpublished monograph, 1982).
5. William Henry Katz, *Eyewitness: The Negro in American History* (New York: Pitman, 1967), 355; Franklin E. Frazier, *The Negro in the U.S.* (Toronto: Macmillan, 1957), 368–369; Benjamin Quarles and Leslie H. Fishel, Jr., *The Black American: A Documentary History* (Glenview, Ill.: Scott, Foresman, 1976), 161.
6. August Meier, *Negro Thought in America, 1880–1915* (Ann Arbor: University of Michigan Press, 1969), 123.
7. "The First Annual Report of the Society for the Prevention of Pauperism in the City of New York" (1818), in June Axinn and Herman Levin, *Social Welfare: A History of American Response to Need*, 2nd ed. (New York: Harper and Row, 1982), 69.
8. Walter Trattner, *From Poor Law to the Welfare State* (New York: Free Press, 1974).
9. Ralph Pumphrey and Muriel Pumphrey, *The Heritage of American Social Work* (New York: Columbia University Press, 1961).
10. Josephine Shaw Lowell, *Public Relief and Private Charity* (New York: 1884), 111. Quoted in Sheila Rothman, *Woman's Proper Place* (New York: Basic Books, 1978), 74.
11. Helen Ginsberg, *Poverty, Economics, and Society* (Washington, D.C.: University Press of America, 1981), 89.
12. Ibid., 90.
13. Robert Bremner, *From the Depths* (New York: New York University Press, 1956).
14. Jesse Thomas Moore, Jr., *A Search for Equality: The National Urban League 1910–1961* (University Park, Penn.: Pennsylvania State University Press, 1981), 47.
15. Ibid., 55.
16. Ibid., 59.
17. Ibid., 66.
18. Ibid., 96.
19. Ibid.
20. Susan T. Vandiver, "A History of Women in Social Work," in Elaine Norman and Arlene Mancuso, *Women's Issues and Social Work Practice* (Itaska, Ill.: Peacock, 1980).
21. Sheila Rothman, *Woman's Proper Place* (New York: Basic Books, 1978).
22. Ibid.
23. Ibid.
24. Gerda Lerner, "Early Community Work of Black Club Women," *The Journal of Negro History* 59, 3 (August 1978): 161.
25. Ibid., 159.
26. Ibid.
27. Ibid.
28. Ibid., 160.
29. Ibid.
30. Rothman, *Woman's Proper Place.*

31. Meier, *Negro Thought*, 134.
32. Moore, *A Search for Equality*.
33. Grace Coyle, *Social Processes in Organizing Groups* (New York: Harper, 1930).
34. Gerald Handel, *Social Welfare in Western Society* (New York: Random House, 1982), 226.
35. Noel Parry, Michael Rustin, and Carole Satyamurti, *Social Work, Welfare, and the State* (Newbury Park, Cal.: Sage, 1982), 25.
36. Bremner, *From the Depths*.
37. Ibid.
38. Rothman, *Woman's Proper Place*.
39. Ibid.
40. Moore, *A Search for Equality*.
41. Ibid., 39.
42. Ferrell, *Why Not Us?*
43. Ibid.
44. William J. Breen, "Black Women and the Great War: Mobilization and Reform in the South," *The Journal of Southern History* 44, 3 (August 1978): 422, 435–436.
45. Ibid., 437.
46. Betty Reed Mandell, "Blurring Definitions of Social Services: Human Services vs. Social Work," *Catalyst* 4, 3 (1983): 5–21.
47. Saul Alinsky, *Rules for Radicals* (New York: Vintage, 1972), 3.
48. Rino Patti, *Social Welfare Administration* (Englewood Cliffs, N.J.: Prentice-Hall, 1983).
49. Matilda Joslyn Gage, *Woman, Church and State* (Watertown, Mass.: Persephone Press, 1980).
50. Ibid.
51. Ibid.
52. Ibid.
53. J. Wetzel, "Interaction of Feminism and Social Work in America," *Social Casework* 57, 4 (April 1976): 227–236.
54. Frances Fox Piven and Richard Cloward, *Poor People's Movements* (New York: Pantheon, 1977).
55. Katz, *Eyewitness*, 295.
56. Ibid., 434.
57. Ibid., 227.
58. Julius Jacobson, ed., *The Negro and the American Labor Movement* (Garden City, New York: Doubleday and Co., 1968), 28–30.
59. Jacob Fischer, "*Social Work Today*, 1934–42," *Catalyst* no. 5 (1980): 3–23.
60. Ibid.

Chapter

8

Ideology, Theory, and Methods

In order to understand social work as it is conceptualized and practiced contemporarily, it is necessary to have some idea of how it developed. This is a part of the "why" of social work; contemporary practice is what it is in part because of the way the profession has developed. It is the product of a heritage of responses to need and concern in other times and situations. . . . Because the development of a systematic knowledge base is one of the important aspects of a profession, an understanding of the development of the practice theory enhances one's understanding of contemporary social work practice and theory.[1]

In considering social work as a career, it is important for you to realize that there are a number of stereotypes about social workers that arise from our history and people's ignorance about the profession. One stereotype presents social workers as "do-gooders" guided by emotion rather than by knowledge, who sincerely desire to help their clients and are willing to work long hours to do so. Although their intentions are good, their effectiveness is limited because they appeal to common sense and invalidated practice wisdom in addressing the needs of their clients.

Another popular stereotype is that of "flaming liberals" who allow their ideals and values to dictate practice rather than their professional knowledge base. They are likely to pursue radical reforms that fail to take into account the consequences of their efforts at change. A third stereotype is the pseudopsychotherapist who hides a lack of knowledge behind the veil of whatever trendy psychosocial technique is in vogue, whether it be Freudian, behavioral, gestalt, or transactional analysis. Finally, there is the stereotype of people who go about initiating changes without knowing whether the interventions will be successful in resolving the problem confronting their clients.

HISTORICAL BASE OF STEREOTYPES

This list of stereotypes is not exhaustive. It is intended to sensitize you to a number of conceptions people hold about social workers. Some of these views are rooted in social work as it was practiced in the early 1900s. Others are based on conditions that ceased to exist after the onset of professionalization in social work. Without denying the historical base in the social movements of the 19th century, there is clearly a difference between the activities of the volunteers of the 19th century and the professional activities of the 20th century. It is important not to equate charity work and workers with social work and social workers or professional social work thinking with social agency thinking.[2]

Present Base of Knowledge

Theoreticians in social work are stressing what can be measured as effective rather than trying to explain the cause of the behavior.

Today knowledge claims in social work stress an empirical focus that emphasizes description rather than explanation. Professional claims to knowledge (which guides methodology) are based less on appeals to grand theories of human behavior and more on classifications and interventions that have been subjected to reliability and validity checks.

Reliability of an intervention is the degree to which the outcome is the same over repeated trials. Validity is the degree to which the outcome you measure corresponds with the intended outcome.

This chapter analyzes the development of professional knowledge and methodology, that is, how we got from the volunteer activities of the 1890s to the empirical practice of the 1990s. As we have done throughout this book, we stress the diversity of practice throughout history, rather than attempting to present a monolithic profession. We explain how the values and knowledge prevalent at any one time have affected the practice of social work.

DEVELOPMENT OF COMMON METHODOLOGY

Social work roots date back to the friendly helpers.

In the early 1900s, when the notion of friendly helpers was challenged as not being professional, charity workers appealed to science to help them answer their critics, achieve professional status, and improve on their reform efforts. This resulted in the conceptualization of social work as "scientific charity."[3]

When Mary Richmond codified the social casework method in 1917, her formulation identified practice as a "skilled process of giving help."[4] Social casework borrowed heavily from the professions of medicine and law in identifying its major themes of social diagnosis and social evidence. In many ways social work started out by helping people who "fell through the cracks" of the medical and legal systems. Richmond's formulation is generally regarded as the first authoritative statement in social work, which began the theoretical foundation of the profession. It established social work as the "science of social therapeutics."[5]

Social Diagnosis

Richmond devoted significant attention to clarifying the systematic or comprehensive mode of inquiry required of caseworkers in making social diagnoses. In fact, she considered the social diagnosis a pivotal part of the knowledge and skill that all caseworkers should have in common, whether they worked in child protective agencies or in charity organization societies. The purpose of the social diagnosis was to provide workers with knowledge of the client's whole problem. This approach was widely supported in psychiatry as well. Adolf Meyer advocated a holistic theory of psychiatry and the use of a comprehensive case history. Like the social diagnosis of Mary Richmond, Meyer's comprehensive case history required "knowledge from biology, physiology, psychology and sociology to understand human behavior."[6]

The focus of attention in the social diagnosis was the client's social difficulties. Richmond clarified this focus and its importance to social work in the following quote from *Social Diagnosis*.

> When a human being, whatever his economic status, develops some marked form of social difficulty and social need, what do we have to know about him and about his difficulty (or more often difficulties) before we can arrive at a way of meeting his needs? The problem may be one of childhood or old age, of sickness, of exploitation, or of wasted opportunity, but in so far as it concerns some one individual in his social relationships it is not alien to social work as here understood. The effort to get the essential facts bearing upon a man's social difficulties has commonly been called "an investigation," but the term here adopted as a substitute — *social diagnosis* — has the advantage that from the first step it fixes the mind of the case worker upon the end in view.[7] (emphasis added)

Although the social work profession recognized the need to obtain the essential facts relevant to a client's problem, they still encountered significant difficulties in evaluating the information gathered during their investigations. That is, they needed more knowledge to gauge the degree of importance assigned to the evidence they gathered from observing their clients' behavior. This problem is still a major issue confronting social work practice. Yet it has only been in the last twenty years that the profession has formulated the principles that are designed to guide them "in selecting from a group of unassorted observations and testimonies."[8] Today we see a great deal of emphasis on analyzing the reasoning processes used by workers in evaluating the clues obtained during the course of their investigations.

Social workers today still struggle to find concrete formulas to weigh social evidence.

Psychoanalysis: An Early Attempt to Develop Guidelines

When psychoanalytic principles began to dominate the field, many people felt psychoanalysis provided workers with a system for assigning weights to the facts observed during their investigations. Specifically, it directed workers to focus on emotional content and the relationship between the worker and the client. As Goldberg, Gibbons, and Sinclair have pointed out, the main emphasis in these psychoanalytic approaches to social work "was on the exploration of motives and of the early life experiences which were held to be responsible for the clients' current problems in living."[9]

Different theories of causation lead to different treatments.

Adlerian practitioners stressed client functioning, while Freudians stressed the unconscious.

Psychoanalysis seemed not only to explain the emotional difficulties of clients, but also to prescribe treatments that addressed different facts about the clients' motivations or life experiences. For instance, the views of Alfred Adler defined problems in terms of the persons' cognitive organization or life style rather than in terms of unconscious processes. As a consequence, Adler's approach advocated the use of life style investigations. The investigations focused on identifying the effects of life style convictions on client functioning. With the benefit of Adlerian theory, practitioners were able to pursue different objectives in their interventions with clients than with other approaches. In effect, the cause of problems became the major knowledge issue affecting practice, since it led to different views of client concerns and treatment interventions.

How Does a Profession Reconcile Diversity?

As this discussion of theory suggests, the social work profession tended to stress differences rather than commonalities of methodology. This question is at the heart of a profession—Are there principles that all social workers follow, or are individual social workers responsible for developing their own practice principles? Generic principles would be followed by all social workers regardless of field of practice or setting. At the Milford Conference the desirability of generic principles was first seriously debated. This group of distinguished social work educators suggested that

The Milford Conference was a national meeting of social workers held in 1929.

> the most significant contribution of social casework to society is . . . its increasing ability to deal with the human being's capacity for self-maintenance when it has become impaired by these and other deviations from accepted standards of normal social life.[10]

Although the conference originally aimed to identify generic skills, it ended up identifying a generic emphasis—client self-maintenance. Individual practitioners were to foster the client's maintenance through their own chosen methodology. In other words, rather than identifying what skills all social workers should have, the conference suggested that whatever skills the social worker decided to use should help the client become more selfsufficient.

The profession has still not identified either a single method or theory that all practitioners accept.

The National Association of Social Workers was formed in 1955.

The formation of a single professional organization provided a new impetus to look for commonalities in practice. After considerable debate, by the 1960s the problem-solving process seemed to emerge as a primary commonality for caseworkers, group workers, and community organizers.

The Problem-Solving Process: The Commonality?

Values influence how we assess problems.

Helen Harris Perlman stated, "The casework process is a problem-solving process in that it employs the orderly, systematic methods which are basic to any effective thinking and feeling toward action."[11] Helen Northern stressed the problem-solving theme in *Social Work With Groups*.[12] Community organization theorists like Murray Ross stressed the problem-solving process as an integral piece of community organization methods.[13]

However, the seminal work identifying the commonalities of casework, group work, and community organization was *Social Work Practice: Model and Method* by Allen Pincus and Anne Minahan.[14] The book's basic assumption is that a common core of concepts, skills, tasks, and activities is essential to the practice of social work, regardless of the many forms that social work practice may take. Pincus and Minahan called their approach the generalist model and explained that their model building was guided by their view of social work practice as a goal-oriented planned change process.

Following the work of Pincus and Minahan, many other educators adopted the planned change or problem-solving approach. The idea of problem-solving and planned change as the key commonalities in social work practice is now commonly accepted. Picard summarizes this idea by stating: "It is important to recognize that differences in philosophy do not change the process of planned change."[15] But while the process of planned change remains consistent across philosophies, clearly the target of the change and the goal of the social work intervention vary with the ideological basis of the social worker's assessment of the problem.

> One of the basic ideas of the problem-solving model is that all social living is, in fact, a problem-solving process.

Knowing the historical development of each method (casework, group work, and community organization) leads to an appreciation of the breadth of professional experience and expertise culminating in the generalist model and illustrates the effect of ideology on practice. An historical analysis exposes the richness of social work practice. Throughout the short history of the social work profession, liberal, radical, and conservative practitioners have worked with individuals, groups, and communities. Historically these professionals identified themselves as caseworkers, group workers, and community organizers.

CASEWORK

Historical Base of Conservative Casework

> Caseworkers were the first to pursue professional status. They continue to be the most dynamic and well-organized group within the profession.

Most early caseworkers were employed by the Charity Organization Society; as a group they were the first to pursue professionalism. The first summer school training program was conducted in 1898 at the New York School of Philanthropy. Mary Richmond, director of the New York COS and later the Philadelphia COS, organized the first training program and wrote the first social work text, *Social Diagnosis* (1917)—the first major presentation of the concepts underlying casework practice.

> The New York School of Philanthropy is now the Columbia University School of Social Work.

In spite of her close association with the COS, Mary Richmond also had a profound interest in the importance of the social environment to casework practice. In *What Is Social Casework* (1922) she clarified the importance of the environment.

> Social casework . . . in addition to its supplementary value in these other tasks, has a field all its own. That field is the development of personality through the conscious and comprehensive adjustment of social relationships, and within that field the worker is no more occupied with abnormalities of the

individual than in the environment, is no more able to neglect the one than the other. The distinctive approach of the caseworker, in fact, is back to the individual by way of his social environment, and wherever adjustment must be effected in this manner, individual by individual, instead of in the mass, there some form of social case work is and will continue to be needed. . . .

To state this in a more formal way is to arrive at my tentative definition: Social case work consists of those processes which develop personality through adjustments consciously effected, individual by individual, between men and their social environment.[16]

Yet Richmond's book was adopted by many who minimized the importance of the environment and concentrated on internal functioning. One reason this occurred was that her book was published when Freudian theory was quite popular. Since Richmond's book presented an atheoretical methodology, Freudianism quickly became the theoretical base for practice.[17] By combining the casework methodology of Mary Richmond and the psychoanalytic theory of Freud, caseworkers felt they were now truly professionals with a unique method and a theoretical base.

Confident they had attained professional status, the caseworkers invited Abraham Flexner, the leading authority on professional education, to address their national conference in 1915. Flexner startled the young profession by announcing that social casework was *not* a profession, since it did not have a unique method or theoretical base. Soon after, Mary Richmond codified social work methods in her book *Social Diagnosis* (1917). Richmond's book provided social work's modus operandi but did not delineate its theoretical base. The lack of a theoretical foundation for this book led many caseworkers to adopt the inherently conservative Freudian theory. Then too, the social and political events of the 1920s pressured caseworkers to become both more conservative and more concerned with professional status.

> Mary E. Richmond (1861–1928) published *Social Diagnosis* after over seventeen years of research and practice.

Economic Conditions and Social Work Practice.   The impact of economics on social work practice is considerable. In the late 1800s the United States suffered a severe economic depression. The societal response to this widespread suffering was a national effort at systemic change to combat poverty. The programs implemented at this time were so extensive that the period from 1896 to 1916 has been termed the Progressive Era. However, World War I overshadowed the social reform approaches to poverty as the entire country channeled its economic and social powers toward the war effort. The military victory of World War I was seen as an endorsement of the American economic system, and the business community was idolized. It was not fashionable to rally against the conditions of the workplace or the unemployment produced by shifts in the market; to do so invited questions about one's patriotism. Once again individual weakness was perceived as the cause of poverty; the functioning of the economic system was above question. Furthermore, many Americans were afraid about what was happening in Russia; the fear of Bolshevism made efforts to initiate social reform suspect. In re-

> When a large portion of society is suffering from poverty, policy-makers look at changes in the system rather than changes in individuals.

Charity Organization Society workers offered a conservative, scientific approach to investigating and helping the poor.

sponse to Russia's collectivism Americans strove for increased individualism. "The process of professionalization and abandonment of overt social reform activity was hastened not only by calls to serve one's country, during the World War I crisis, but also by the law and order oppression of the postwar era."[18]

In addition, the country was weary from war. Life was in turmoil: veterans suffered from shell-shock, families struggled to readjust, and women held important positions in the work force. People wanted a return to normal routine, veterans needed treatment and jobs, and women had to be returned to the home. Given these conditions, it is little wonder that caseworkers adopted Freudian theory—a theory that identified women as the weaker sex and explained social problems as unresolved complexes or inadequate development in the individual.

Mary Cromwell Jarrett (1876–1961) is given credit for the term "psychiatric social worker."

Psychoanalytic Casework.   In 1918 Mary Cromwell Jarrett organized the first formal training program for psychiatric social workers. Consistent with conservative principles, its purpose was to train social workers to help clients adjust to their social conditions. One target of change was working women who did not relinquish their positions in the work force. Freudian theory justified removing women from positions of power by identifying them as sexually deficient and biologically underdeveloped. Women were counseled to accept their inferior position and adjust to the status quo. Women who resisted were diagnosed as deviant and in need of adjustment-oriented casework.

Following the introduction of psychoanalytic principles in casework, the emphasis in the professional knowledge base shifted from identifying the common sources of information used in defining client problems (the approach taken by Mary Richmond) to that of understanding relevant explanatory theory. In fact, theoretical allegiances began to develop that created significant factions within the profession. The effects of these different allegiances will become clear when we discuss the theoretical developments of the 1940s and 1950s.

Historical Base of Liberal Casework

Some settlement workers also found casework methods helpful in helping immigrants fit into the American system. Adjustment counseling was necessary for some individuals, particularly immigrant women who had to adjust to the norms of a new country—norms that were constantly in flux. The casework method used by settlement workers closely resembles the ecological casework practiced today.

Ecological casework stresses the importance of the environment in social functioning.

Casework During the Great Depression. With the onset of the depression caseworkers again looked at the social causes of poverty. Casework did not disappear, but changed to a more liberal approach to problem assessment. The growing prevalence of poverty made it difficult to suggest that its cause was individual weakness. Determining eligibility (let alone worthiness) was almost impossible. Necessity and obvious suffering led caseworkers to assume that clients were honest in reporting need. Instead of providing psychiatric casework, caseworkers helped clients adjust to lower incomes. Caseworkers needed a working knowledge of housing conditions, rental rates, food costs, money management, and homemaker and health services.

Caseworkers turned from psychoanalysis to education and resource linkage. The environment was a critical component of the problem assessment. The caseworker helped the client manipulate that environment and use resources and what limited opportunities were available. The caseworker's goal was to help clients maintain themselves at an adequate level of functioning.

In 1935 Ellery Reed, director of the research department of the Cincinnati Community Chest, reflected this changed attitude toward the poor and unemployed. He expressed concern that "untrained" caseworkers would not understand what clients were suffering and would further clients' sense of defeat with patronizing sympathy or hard-boiled intolerance. Reed was concerned that thousands of persons without casework training were employed in community chest agencies. The most intolerant were those who had been recruited from the welfare rolls themselves.

Trained workers, although strongly in favor of work for clients when such can be found, at reasonable wages and under proper conditions, avoid using withdrawal of relief as a threat to club clients into accepting jobs which they sometimes resist as representing a further evidence of humiliation and failure-. . . the psychology of defeat is often changed by understanding the social causes of their unemployment.[19]

The 1940s: Reemergence of Conservative Trends

The 1940s brought a renewed emphasis on individual casework. The universities had become more involved in the education of caseworkers and new theories of human behavior and casework intervention were being developed. Leading theoreticians were adherents of the functional or diagnostic schools.

The diagnostic (or psychosocial) school of thought made a systematic effort to identify relevant psychosocial data, evaluate their significance, and appraise the problem and the means of change for the client. Although it emanated from a Freudian base, this practice took into account both external and internal problems of the individual.

> Caseworkers at that time were admonished not to dabble in the psychoanalyst's domain of the unconscious and to refrain from dealing directly with the forces of transference, resistance, and repression. Although sensitive to the potency of these hidden motives, workers assumed guardianship of the more conscious and cognitive realms of their clients' lives, thereby entering into their clients' world of daily experiences of coping, planning, and thinking.[20]

The ideas of Florence Hollis are presented in *Casework, A Psycho-Social Therapy,* published in 1964.

Florence Hollis, leading theorist of the diagnostic school, suggested that casework could operate on four different treatment levels: to modify the environment, to provide psychological support, to clarify (counseling), and to provide insight.[21] Adherents of the diagnostic school adapted the ego-psychology theories of Hartmann, Erikson, Horney, and Anna Freud to work with clients. Theorists such as Hartmann gave greater emphasis to the ego's conscious ability to master cognitive tasks than to the force of intrapsychic drives. Hamilton and Hollis present casework as a "corrective experience" that involves the client's positive identification with the worker and the modification of the client's repetitive dysfunctional habits of living.[22]

Jessie Taft (1882–1960), a social work educator and an authority on Rank, translated many of his works into English.

The functional approach was based on Otto Rank's will psychology. Will referred to the individual's ability to mobilize her- or himself toward a desired goal: "the deliberate use of time to arouse an awareness of motivation, the focus on the immediate present as the arena for mindful change, and the purposeful focus on the active processes occurring within the helping relationship."[23] Functional theory stressed the source of healing and helping power was part of the individual's innate power to grow and change. The "function" of the agency, rather than the client's need, became the pivotal problem in the helping process. Caseworkers were expected to know the helping process only as it related to their specific agency setting, such as foster care, public welfare, or prisons. They were not expected to be knowledgeable about helping in situations unrelated to their own professional settings. Treatment consisted of support and stimulation to use all of the client's available capacities for decision and action, but the client, not the professional, determined the final outcome.

Virginia Robinson and Jessie Taft were the primary theoreticians of the functional approach. In *A Changing Psychology in Social Casework* (1930), Robinson made the client the center of the process of helping, and made the client's choice of material from the past the caseworker's guide to what was important to the present.[24] It placed the dynamic of casework in the relationship between the client and the caseworker. Sharing with someone who had professional training made it possible for the client to see the problem more clearly and take hold of it with more courage and effectiveness.[25] Table 8–1 compares the diagnostic and the functional approaches to practice.

The 1940s were an important period for professional development, as lively and sometimes heated debate took place between these different schools of thought. The intellectual stimulation generated by the debate was conducive to the growth of professional knowledge. Bertha Capen Reynolds, opposing the prevailing point of view, suggested that contributions made by the psychodynamic and functional schools were complementary, not contradictory.[26] The penetrating diagnoses and the dynamic relationships of each stressed something essential, and each, without the other, could be carried to an absurdity. "If diagnosis means *seeing into* or *seeing through,* that is not possible without a relationship with the client which releases him to be himself, to explore his trouble freely because a helping person is there."[27] Reynolds also believed that professional relationships were enhanced by scientific training. Diagnosis effectively developed "weaves together the threads that both client and caseworker draw from life and work on together."[28] Subsequently Helen Harris Perlman's problem-solving approach attempted to achieve a measure of rapport between the diagnostic and functional methods.[29]

Virginia Robinson and Jessie Taft, lifelong companions, both taught at Pennsylvania School of Social Work in the 1940s and 1950s.

Charlotte Towle (1896–1966) was influenced by both the functional and diagnostic schools and tried to integrate their ideas in her writing and teaching at the University of Chicago.

The 1950s: The Age of Insecurity

The 1950s was an age of insecurity. An ever-present possibility of war and an economic system undergoing major changes contributed to a sense of uncertainty. A nationwide shift in the labor market occurred as increased specialization and routinization of work became the guiding principles of industry. With increased routinization, workers found less opportunity for creativity and less job satisfaction. Money became the single most important symbol of success and human relations were secondary. Political repressiveness also contributed to the lack of emphasis on poverty as a public issue. This was the heyday of McCarthyism and the witch-hunt—conformity was the byword. Working for social change or even calling attention to flaws in American society was dangerous. Critics of American society were labeled communists and sometimes blacklisted or even imprisoned.[30]

As an example, a classic social work text, Common Human Needs, was withdrawn by the Federal Security Agency that published it.

TABLE 8–1
Contrast of Diagnostic and Functional Models of Casework

	Diagnostic	**Functional**
Theory	Freudian, with an emphasis on the ego and its adaptive capacities.	Otto Rank's will psychology
Professional Role	Diagnostician and therapist; scientific objectivity	Helper
Client Role	Seen as ill and in need of treatment; may need protection from self or others.	Recipient of some specific service; sets own goals.
Developed by	Gordon Hamilton	Virginia Robinson and Jessie Taft
Method	Casework or group work. Treatment is a blend of processes directed toward modifying the person, his social or interpersonal environment, both person and environment, and the exchanges between them. The worker-client relationship is a major determinant of how much the client will be helped. In contrast to the specific social service of the functional school, the caseworker helps the client develop an understanding of the individual and his adaptive capacities. Relief of suffering can be obtained by the client's expressing fears, anxieties, and hostilities in the treatment interview.	Casework or group work. Casework is a method for engaging a client through a relationship process, essentially one-to-one, using a social service toward the individual's and the general social welfare.

Many people sought help for problems caused by financial pressures. But though these problems may have been caused by shifts in the labor market, they were treated as individual problems. Technique was stressed; a casework relationship that incorporated acceptance and self-determination was emphasized. Intake became a specialization. Emphasizing individual causes of poverty prompted some major methodological changes. Since individual problems engende red poverty, individual therapy was the supposed solution.

Casework was clearly
the dominant method
of the 1950s.

It was during the 1950s that caseworkers began to see behavior therapy as a valuable psychotherapeutic enterprise. B. F. Skinner, like Freud before him, provided a basis for believing that much of human behavior could be understood in terms of the individual.[31] Wolpe outlined techniques based on operant conditioning that were reportedly successful in dealing with neurotic behavior.[32] These techniques—assertiveness training, and systematic desensitization (as applied in the 50s) — basically ignored environmental influences on individual behavior.

After the sometimes divisive theoretical debates of the 1940s and early 1950s, the profession was once again concerned about formulating a common knowledge base, because the profession's identity was being eroded by a proliferation of specializations by method. However, this movement did not achieve immediate success because of the rigid commitments social workers had developed to their own theoretical approach. The upshot of this competition between theoretical schools was the emergence of an artificial separation between person and environment. Although most trained social workers recognized that it was impossible to isolate persons from their environment, their practice was typically limited to either the person or the social environment. This was in part because the available theories were not able to deal simultaneously with the person and the environment. In addition, most social workers restricted their conceptualization of clients' problems to their own preferred orientation, which emphasized explaining the *why* of problem concerns. These preferred orientations tended to be greatly influenced by prevalent ideologies.

> Intervention was often determined by the method of training rather than the client's problem.

Ideology and Social Work Practice.   If practitioners identified with psychological explanations of human behavior, their interventions tended to deal primarily with changing the individual. These practitioners rarely sought to change institutions or to modify the wider social conditions contributing to the problems of their clients. Their knowledge base focused on individual concerns. In fact, this situation stimulated many social reformers to question the legitimacy of using psychoanalytic or behavioral approaches within a profession such as social work.

In contrast, practice limited to sociological principles failed to address many of the pains suffered by clients while waiting for major institutional changes. Practitioners following sociological orientations focused most of their change efforts on modifying aspects in the society that contributed to the stresses and strains encountered by people in response to highly dysfunctional environments. These interventions did not address the immediate emotional and personal crises of the clients, since it was assumed that the dysfunctional responses of the clients were a symptom of underlying societal difficulties. Practitioners assumed that if the environment could be changed, this would in turn eliminate personal distress or emotional crises.

The 1960s: The Elimination of Poverty

The sociological/psychological debate in social work could be seen very clearly during the 1960s. The 1960s present a dramatic contrast between the different strains in the field of social work. Caseworkers, who were basically the power-holders in the profession, believed that with enough trained caseworkers poverty could be eliminated. Data from small pilot studies done in New York City supported their claims. Findings from these studies had been reflected in the 1956 Social Security Amendments and became the rationale for the 1962 service amendments to the Social Security Act, which provided considerable federal money for training and hiring social workers. Caseworkers basically accepted the premise that individual weakness caused poverty. If only the profession had adequate resources to train enough caseworkers, poverty would be eliminated. Since this analysis overlooked the social roots of poverty, casework became suspect because it could not deliver on its claim to "cure" poverty.

The outcome of these psychological vs. sociological debates was that the profession demanded that training programs expose social work students to both theoretical perspectives. In fact, the Council on Social Work Education's Curriculum Policy Statement of 1969 mandated that students be exposed to foundation knowledge relevant to both micro and macro practice. Micro practice involved interventions that were directed specifically to changes in individuals, families, or small groups, whereas macro practice involved any interventions that addressed organizational, community, or societal change. Furthermore, the 1969 policy statement recommended movement away from any single-theory approach to human behavior and from an exclusive focus on individual behavior.[33] To some extent, the position in this policy statement was in conflict with the work of the first Commission on Practice of the National Association of Social Workers. This commission devoted substantial attention to trying to eliminate the false dichotomy between person and environment that this policy statement indirectly supported. By mandating that students should be exposed to micro and macro theories, the CSWE was unintentionally sabotaging the efforts that the committee had previously made in trying to identify ideas and concepts that integrated persons and their environments.

The 1970s: The Push for Integrative Ideas and Concepts

In 1970, Harriet Bartlett published *The Common Base of Social Work Practice,* which analyzed trends within the profession. She devoted an entire chapter to identifying the barriers in social work thinking that impeded the growth and development of integrative modes of practice. She highlighted such barriers as the profession's rejection of the deductive approach and resistance to establishing frames of reference as key obstacles to be overcome. She also stressed the need to develop a common set of concepts that would allow all social workers to communicate with each other regardless of the setting in which they practiced. Without a set of concepts unique to social work, the profession's knowledge base was unlikely to advance. Bartlett suggested that *task* and *coping* were the appropriate integrative concepts for social work practice.

The deductive approach suggests general principles that apply to practice, rather than a case-by-case approach.

The Focus on Task and Coping in the Assessment Process.   In Bartlett's mind, the concepts of task and coping provided social workers with a means for conceptualizing human behavior across settings and fields of practice. The concept of task allowed workers to describe the "critical and demanding situations that confront people." That is, the common elements to any problem situation may be conceived of as the tasks or demands of the situation. Bartlett observed:

> Thinking about tasks leads to such questions as: What are the tasks presented to individuals and families in meeting the shock of serious illness, the attendant anxiety, and the permanent physical handicap that frequently results? What task faces the delinquent in prison if he is to move from the restricted prison environment toward a responsible role in community life?[34]

In order to answer these questions, she assumed that the worker would need to know the biological, psychological and social demands presented by each of these situations.

Besides having knowledge of the demands or expectations presented by problem situations, Bartlett also assumed that social workers need to assess the responses of their clients to problem situations. These responses represented what she referred to as coping. Coping was considered a central integrative concept because after workers identified key tasks, they also had to appreciate how clients were going to deal with these tasks. That is, any life task, regardless of its context, requires an adaptive or coping response. Therefore, all practitioners should acquire knowledge of the coping patterns associated with the common tasks confronting most individuals in everyday life.

In addition to having the knowledge of common life tasks and response patterns, Bartlett and her colleagues point out that social workers also need to know how people respond to non-normative events, such as having AIDS, losing a limb, moving into a racist neighborhood, or losing a home in a tornado. This knowledge of the relationship between coping patterns and the situations relevant to different fields of practice and agency work was referred to as specific knowledge.

Generic knowledge is that knowledge common and necessary to all professional social workers. *Specific knowledge* is common to all social workers within a certain field of practice or setting but not required of all social workers.

The concepts of task and coping clarify the forms of knowledge needed by social workers in order to understand and define the problems of their clients. Social workers must have knowledge of the general and the specific responses of people to problem situations. They also need to recognize which tasks are unique to certain problem situations.

For instance, if a family loses a child, each member of the family will face common as well as individual tasks. Indeed, the literature on loss indicates that fathers and mothers do experience different tasks in responding to the death of their child. Although they experience common biopsychosocial responses, they also confront different social demands that are often closely linked to gender-based factors. Mothers often grieve openly and immediately after the death of the child, which is not necessarily true of fathers. Fathers are expected to be the tower of strength who helps the mother through the emotional ordeal and keeps the family together. This repressed grief can cause psychological problems in the future. Similarly, a sibling in the family system may confront different demands from those of other family members. Some of these distinct demands may relate specifically to their level of cognitive or emotional development. For example, a six-year-old will have a different understanding of death from that of a fifteen-year-old or an adult. This important difference in cognitive development should contribute to coping responses from this child that are very different from those of an older sibling or a parent. Social workers should be aware of these differences and be prepared to evaluate the effect on individual and family functioning.

Focusing on tasks is one way for social workers to conceptualize the environmental demands encountered by individuals, families, and groups. With the benefit of this understanding, social workers could then "improve the balance between the people's coping efforts and the environmental demands."[35] In improving this balance, the focus was presumably not on the people's behavior, "but on the exchanges between them and their environment."[36] In essence, the assumption is that the integrative ideas of task and coping eliminated many of the previous difficulties associated with theoretical approaches to problem assessment that ignored the exchanges between persons and their environment.

In spite of the fact that the concepts of task and coping addressed the profession's stated focus on person and environment interactions, this focus remains an ideal rather than a reality in the eyes of some critics.

> Social workers presumably want to perceive person-interacting-with- environment as a whole, without an arbitrary division between person and environment. Thus far, that desired ideal has eluded social workers, just as it has eluded social scientists for whom it has also been a goal.[37]

Although the integrative concepts of task and coping stressed the fact that practitioners should understand the exchanges between persons and their environment, most of the change efforts of social workers rarely addressed the social conditions themselves. The problem of arbitrarily separating persons from their environment remains in spite of the emphasis the concepts *task* and *coping* place on evaluating the relationship between responses and environmental demands. Briar has argued that this is due in part to a lack of "conceptual terms to characterize the varieties of person-environment transactions."[38] Without such concepts, practitioners can still place undue emphasis on enhancing or changing the adaptive capacities of their clients rather than changing key environmental targets. Because of these problems, the profession once again sought refuge in theory: general systems theory and ecological systems theory.

The 1980s: Systems Theory—Panacea or Barrier?

Systems theory has become the most widely used theoretical orientation in the profession of social work. Its wide acceptance is due primarily to its opposition to a reductionist approach to problem assessment. Reductionism is a philosophical position that assumes that problems occurring at multiple levels can be reduced to a single level explanation or definition. An example of this philosophy is when physicians apply a biomedical model that falsely assumes that an illness can be defined and treated only at the physical level.

The psychosocial components of disease are discussed in Chapter 16.

Such an approach ignores the fact that an illness will always have psychological and social components.

"The psychological reactions of patient and family influence and are influenced by biophysical phenomena and affect the patient's illness behavior, clinical presentation, course and response to treatment."[39] Further, these responses make a significant contribution to the therapeutic relationship, and "to ignore the psychosocial domain is to don clinical blinders."[40]

In a similar vein, Auerswald compares the reductionist view of the specialist with a social worker operating from an ecological perspective.[41] With the specialist orientation, the person's problem is seen as belonging primarily to that person; the individual is sent to a specialist trained to deal with that kind of problem. The specialist, of course, sees the problem as an individual matter and does not look at how the person, the family, and the community relate; he or she is "often in the position of desperately trying to replace a fuse when the entire community power line has broken down."[42] In contrast, Auerswald suggests that if the individual's problem is seen from a systems perspective, it is much easier to determine in what life arenas the individual,

Anomie is normlessness or a lack or meaning and direction in life.

the family, or the group needs assistance to combat the anomie and dehumanizing character of our age. Pincus and Minahan reflect his idea when they suggest that the client and the target system may be very different individuals.[43]

As we have stressed throughout the historical section, the profession of social work has sought to remove its blinders and define problems in a fashion that does not ignore the contributions of social and biological factors to the coping responses of their clients. Since systems theory encourages individuals to focus on relationships among systems, it provides a useful framework for taking into account the biological and the social factors previously ignored by traditional casework practitioners. Although systems theory has been lauded as the solution to the person-environment dilemma, it has been observed that "the general and abstract nature of person-environment concepts and their lack of specificity as a guide to intervention limit the appeal of the ecological perspective to those currently engaged in direct practice."[44] Similarly, it has been noted that the concept of systems is too abstract to guide the analysis of practice that is concrete. Hudson and Harrison took an even more controversial position at the 1985 Practitioners as Evaluators of Direct Practice Conference in Seattle, Washington. They suggested that systems theory should be eliminated from the curriculum of schools of social work.

Concerns about the utility of systems perspectives are growing in the literature. Goldstein, for example, has pointed out in the *Handbook on Clinical Social Work* how difficult it is to operationalize key concepts in ecological or in general systems theories such as "interface." She states that "it may be conceptually useful, but efforts to apply it in practice lead one to feel as if one were working in the cracks or in between the chairs or in empty spaces."[45] That is, the concepts do not direct practitioners as to what behaviors are in need of change. Furthermore, they provide minimal guidance in identifying which of the concerns presented by a client are most susceptible to the interventive strategies of a social work professional. Concerns of this nature have directed some scholars in social work to advocate an eclectic approach.

The questioning of systems theory is consistent with the conservative ideology prevalent today.

The Emergence of Eclecticism

Fischer's *Effective Casework Practice: An Eclectic Approach* rejected the idea that practice should be guided by a single theory or treatment modality. Fischer's approach to practice assumed that practice should be guided by "a careful review of empirical research."[46] He also assumed that practitioners needed to evaluate theory and research critically since they would be "viewed as the two basic components of knowledge for practice."[47]

This approach to knowledge-guided practice gave as much priority to research methods as did Mary Richmond in her initial formulation of the casework method. However, Fischer stressed an analysis of both process and outcome.[48] Mary Richmond, on the other hand, was primarily concerned with evaluating what workers did regarding the information used in defining client problems.

Process is the study of what workers do. Outcome is how well they do it.

A critical point Fischer made in his book was that understanding how or why a problem came about does not necessarily provide information about how to change that problem. In his view, "an entirely different set of principles and procedures is necessary to provide guidelines for changing the problem."[49] He termed this form of knowledge *interventive knowledge.* Interventive knowledge focuses on the questions, "What can be done to modify this situation, and will it be effective?"

Interventive knowledge is intended to be used to prescribe principles and procedures for inducing change in behaviors and/or situations.

Fischer has not been alone in advocating a shift from causal/developmental knowledge to interventive knowledge. Task centered casework, as conceptualized by William Reid and Laura Epstein, has taken a similar emphasis. This approach to social work focuses on having clients identify tasks they wish to work on. As a consequence, the etiology or source of the problem plays less of a role in the solution to the problem, as is also true of Fischer's eclectic approach to practice. The planned change approach of Pincus and Minahan also de-emphasized causal/developmental approaches to problem assessment and problem change.

A similar approach has been advocated in psychiatry. Some of the difficulties of linking treatment with an etiological theory are

Freud's early feelings about schizophrenia excluded this disorder from psychoanalytic therapy.

(a) the cause of most mental disorder is unknown; (b) the treatment must then be consistent with the theory, which may determine what can and can-

A chronically depressed patient may recognize childhood deprivation as the cause of his depression, but this will not alter his many self-destructive behaviors.

Psychological approaches base diagnosis primarily on inferred psychological causes and mechanisms.

In the descriptive approach, a diagnosis is based on relatively objective phenomena, typically manifested in the form of signs, symptoms, and the natural history of the disorder.

The *DSM* III-R is discussed more thoroughly in Chapter 17.

not be treated; (c) a total commitment to any single etiological theory limits the therapist's range of interventions; (d) the goals of therapy often become the fulfillment of a theory rather than what the patient needs or desires; (e) even if a disorder's etiology is known, therapies addressing it are unlikely to rectify the patient's current disorder.[50]

As in social work, psychiatrists are beginning to question the "psychological" approaches to diagnosis and to the understanding of human behavior. In place of this approach, some psychiatrists are advocating a "descriptive" approach to diagnosis.

> The chief virtue of the psychological approach was that it indicated a disorder's cause, but since the etiologies of most mental disorders were unknown, psychiatry is moving away from the psychological tradition and returning to descriptive diagnosis.[51]

Indeed, both social work and psychiatry are professions that are attempting to develop empirically validated systems for classifying client problems and conditions. These empirical approaches have placed far less attention on either grand theories of human behavior or on etiological matters. In psychiatry, this formal assessment system is reflected in many of the principles underlying the *Diagnostic and Statistical Manual* (*DSM* III-R), which is the most widely used classification system in the field of mental health. The National Association of Social Workers is presently developing a descriptive system for assessing an individual's social functioning.

How Important Is Theory to Practice?

Values and ideology have always influenced which theories were popular.

When it was assumed that knowledge-guided practice was understood best as theory-guided practice, most practitioners subscribed to theories that supported their own values and views of human nature. Psychoanalysis has always been a major guiding force in practice. At times, social casework was considered almost synonymous with personality theory or causal/developmental theory.

Behavioral theory had received substantial support within the field of psychology long before it was considered appropriate for social work. Although behavioral principles were consistent with conservative principles, liberals tended to feel that this view of human nature did not fit with the values of the profession. These concerns decreased as cognition and choice were introduced into the behavioral equation. During the late 1960s and early 1970s significant attention was devoted to making behavioral principles relevant to social work practice.

As the notion of theory-guided practice began to be normalized within the profession, workers who dealt with larger-sized systems began to seek relevant social science theory to guide their practice activities. Sociology, social psychology and anthropology were the disciplines that provided the most relevant theory for macro practice. As the theory and practice in these areas progressed, separate educational sequences emerged that emphasized various "clusters of knowledge," such as role theory, community theory, and organization theory.[52] In fact, these sequences of theoretical content eventually led to the development of the alternative practice methods of group work and community organization.

Casework has always been the primary methodology of social work. Today there are still large groups of caseworkers who adhere to the position that practice must be guided by theory. However, the 1990s are likely to see more emphasis on pragmatism and empiricism than theory development. The direction casework takes in the next decade will have a decided effect on social work practice in general.

Although we have emphasized the mainstream (liberal and conservative) approaches to casework, we cannot leave this methodology without discussing casework from a radical perspective.

Casework: Radical Framework

Radical casework and therapy are recent social work phenomena with little history before the late 1960s. Traditional or psychoanalytic casework as generally practiced is politically conservative. Radical therapy, on the other hand, is more sensitive to the oppressive features of society. The goal of radical therapy is to help people recognize the injustices that may be causing or increasing their emotional distress. It raises clients' awareness that a competitive, consumption-oriented society shapes attitudes toward ourselves and those around us. Radical therapists encourage clients to understand how social institutions oppress them, rather than delving into their past and blaming their parents. The desired outcome of radical therapy is client empowerment that leads clients to oppose the forces oppressing them. Radical therapists would suggest that "therapy" is essential to dealing with internalized oppression, and only someone with specific liberating therapeutic techniques can reintegrate a meaningful sense of self and the world. Misuse of therapy can lead to increased alienation, rather than client empowerment.

Feminist therapy is one example of radical therapy. The literature on feminist therapy is vague about what a feminist therapist is and what she does. Walstedt defined a feminist psychotherapist as "someone who supports and understands the desire for female equality."[53] Silveira defined feminist therapy as "counseling which affirms women's liberation and proceeds without power differentials between the counselor and the counseled."[54] In an attempt to determine more specifically the nature and definition of feminist therapy, Thomas surveyed 135 therapists and interviewed 19 in some depth. She found that feminist therapy does not fit the traditional theoretical model; that is, a series of propositions and techniques, a model for problem assessment, and a training methodology, but instead is a part of a social movement or a belief system.[55]

Feminist social work
practice as defined
here is a good exam-
ple of radical social
work.

Belief systems identified in Thomas's research were consistent in many ways. Some prevalent views may be enumerated.

1. A rejection of the view that because of biological differences men and women serve different functions and engage in different social roles. Rather, a belief that different sex roles are the result of social conditioning and an institutionalized sexual class system.

2. Sex roles are oppressive to both men and women. There is particular emphasis on the psychological oppression of women, pointing to the damage suffered in regard to self-concept, identity formation, intellectual development and aspirations, and overall emotional well-being.

3. A strong emphasis on the potential of women and a belief that the woman knows what she wants and what is best for her.

4. A desire to free women of roles that prohibit them from realizing their goals.

5. A belief that the frame of reference for problem assessment must reach beyond traditional forms of assessment and address the psychological effects of the woman's social conditioning, sex roles, and secondary status.

6. An attempt to foster equality or mutuality in the relationship with the client. They view the traditional power imbalance between client and therapist as dysfunctional.

7. An emphasis on problem solving rather than emotive therapy.

8. A deliberate use of self—their values and experiences in conducting therapy.

9. A stress on increased independence. Therapy should not be a dependency producing interaction.

10. Therapy should include consciousness-raising.[56]

Thomas summarizes feminist therapy in a manner consistent with radical therapy. She suggests that unlike most therapy, feminist therapy does not merely alleviate stress but provides a way of life for the therapist and possibly the client as well.

Casework: A Summary

Casework, that is, work with individuals, takes on goals based on the ideology adopted by the practitioner. Caseworkers facilitate individual adjustment, link resources, or empower clients based on their philosophy of people and society.

Psychiatric casework was first practiced by charity organization society workers, and psychiatric caseworkers today tend to reflect assumptions similar to those underlying the charity organization movement. Ecological casework (under other names) was first practiced in the settlement houses; ecological (or systems-oriented) casework today operates on philosophical principles congruent with those of settlement workers. While radical case-work has only developed over the last twenty years, it is guided by principles consistent with radical social justice movements.

GROUP WORK

Group work—social work with more than one person—can also be practiced from a liberal, radical, or conservative perspective. The various forms of group work also spring from the philosophies inherent in the history of social work movements.

Conservative Forms

The theory and methods of the Charity Organization Society are presented in Chapter 7.

While the charity organization society movement is not usually seen as a source of group work practice, remedial group therapists tend to operate from assumptions common to conservative casework and the charity organization societies. Remedial group work emphasizes treating the behavior of the individual. The primary difference between psychiatric casework and remedial group work is the use of the group rather than the individual as a treatment tool. Remedial group work originally came into vogue with the child guidance movement. Psychiatrist Fritz Redl found that withdrawn or obstreperous children were not successful in the typical activity group. The social worker tried to develop the children's ability to relate to their peers and work cooperatively through specially designed therapy groups.

Robert Vinter wrote extensively on the process and knowledge necessary for group treatment. In Vinter's model the group leader was an eclectic therapist guided by social role theory, ego psychology, group dynamics, and more recently, systems theory. Vinter outlined several principles for social work practice.

Principles summarizing a problem-solving approach to group work are presented here.

1. Specific treatment goals must be established for each member of the client group.
2. The worker attempts to define group purposes so they are consistent with the several treatment goals established for the individual members.
3. The worker helps the group to develop the system of norms and values that is in accord with the worker's treatment goals.
4. The worker prestructures the content for group sessions based on the worker's knowledge of individuals expressed through his treatment goals as well as his knowledge of structural characteristics and processes that take place within the group.[57]

In this model the group leader uses a problem-solving approach and is in a professional position of clinical authority. While the authority must be accepted by the group, it is not fundamentally established by the group. The therapist does for the client as well as with the client. There is no assumption of group autonomy.[58]

The client is someone suffering from social maladaptation or deficiency. The clinician helps the individual achieve a more desirable state of social functioning. Individual treatment goals supersede group goals and the group leader selects group members.

Group work as a treatment modality first gained popularity in the 1940s, when a number of important theoretical advances were made. Guidelines were developed for diagnostic consideration of individuals' functioning in the group. Criteria were developed for forming effective groups. The foundation was set for clinical team participation. Finally, there was diagnostic utilization of groups where other treatment modalities co-exist. Group therapy guided by individualistic, conservative assumptions continues to be a prominent aspect of psychotherapy practice today.

Liberal Forms

The concepts underlying the settlement house movement are presented in Chapter 7.

While the settlement house movement furnished a more systems-oriented view to work with individuals, its major contribution was to the group work methodology. Vida Scudder summarized the methodology of the settlement movement: "It aims to bring to bear on the seemingly hopeless misery of our great cities that spiritual help, that uplifting life which comes through the power of a broad and organized effort."[59] Two types of group work—reciprocal and social goals models—have had their genesis in the settlement movement.

Reciprocal Group Work.   The reciprocal model aimed to help individuals by getting them more active in community decision making.[60] This move toward better citizenship benefited both individuals and society. Reciprocal group work seems to blend an ecological approach to casework with greater citizen participation in much the same way the settlement movement tried to train immigrants to citizenship and provide them the services they needed to meet larger goals—to make the immigrants a force for progressive change. With effective services immigrants would join the ranks as reformers.[61]

Current reciprocal group work has been conceptualized by William Schwartz as a mediating model of group work. This view supposes the individual and the group to be interdependent with each other and with society. The group leader is a mediator helping clients reach for what they need. The leader works with the client not only for the client; the leader himself has a deep investment in and an emotional commitment to the process. The group's goals relate to self-fulfillment as individuals and as a group. The process serves both the individual and society.

This model presupposes an organic, systemic relationship between individual and society. The group nourishes and mediates individual and societal functioning. Breakdown in this interdependency can be insignificant or critical. There is no a priori prescription or desired outcome—the ideal state is mutual aid. Field and social systems are the underlying theoretical base, with ideas

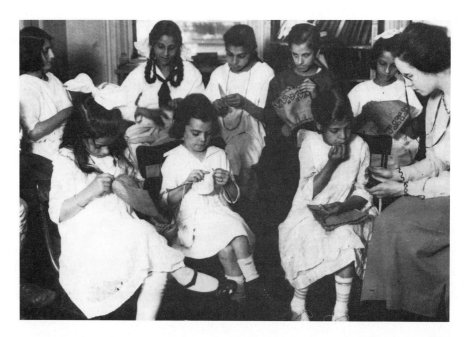

Some of the earliest forms of group work occurred in the settlement houses. This group of girls is learning to knit and sew.

from Adler, Fromm, and Sullivan carrying over into the assumptions that explain individual motivation and capacity for reaching out to collectives. Schwartz identified the tasks a reciprocal group worker must accomplish.

The primary tasks of the reciprocal group are presented here.

1. The task of searching out the common ground between the client's perception of his own need and the aspects of social demand with which he is faced.

2. The task of detecting and challenging the obstacles which obscure the common ground and frustrate the efforts of people to identify their own self-interest with that of their "significant others."

3. The task of contributing data—ideas, facts, and value-concepts—which are not available to the client and which may prove useful to him in attempting to cope with that part of social reality which is involved in the problems on which he is working.

4. The task of "lending a vision" to the client in which the worker both reveals himself as one whose own hopes and aspirations are strongly invested in the interaction between people and society and projects a deep feeling for that which represents individual well-being and the social good.

5. The task of defining the requirements and the limits of the situation in which the client-worker system is set. These rules and boundaries establish the context for the "working contract" which binds the client and the agency to each other and which creates the conditions under which both client and worker assume their respective functions.[62]

Three primary principles guide this model of group work: the leader helps the group to strengthen its goals through consideration of what it has in common with what group members are seeking; the leader interprets her role and defines a clear contract; and the leader protects the focus of the work. The reciprocal model requires honesty and forthrightness with no withholding of information. Therapy includes intensive individualizing and social focusing. This model of group work stresses individual mental health, and it assumes a unity between community participation and psychological functioning. Basically it is designed to help clients help themselves.

Social Goals Model.   The social goals model assumes that group work creates a broader base of knowledge and a skilled citizenry. The social worker is an "influence" person responsible for cultivating social consciousness in groups and also developing closer interpersonal relations. The leader is not to dictate a particular view, but does seek to inculcate a value of social responsibility. Theoreticians who have influenced this model are economic and political democracy theorists such as Dewey, Kilpatrick, and Lindeman. Relevant theories include opportunity theory, conflict, deprivation, and intergenerational alienation. This model also assumes a unity between social action and individual mental health.

Radical Forms

The radical group work framework can be compared to the radical casework perspective earlier in this chapter.

Radicals find group work methods particularly useful. Like radical caseworkers, group workers eliminate the authoritarian role of the therapist. While some individual therapy may be necessary, most radical therapy takes place in groups. Participants learn skills for helping one another. In addition to individual therapy, radicals involve clients in consciousness-raising groups, discussion groups, or classes which raise fundamental questions about the social system. In this setting the participant's power is maximized, and the authoritarian atmosphere is decreased.

Some radicals see group consciousness-raising as a major means of liberation. Leonard typifies this group in the following statement.

> Working with people . . . in an action system to achieve change will, for the radical social worker, be a major method by which critical consciousness can develop. The group is central to such work, for conscientization cannot be undertaken by one individual on his own. Group support helps to carry the tensions and anxieties which a developing critical consciousness and the liberating action that must follow are bound to create. . . . By working in group situations, the radical social worker has available a range of strategies which he shares with the group. The strategies of campaigns, collaboration, and confrontation are to be used by the action system in relation to the target of intervention, according to a careful political assessment of concrete situation.[63]

While traditional reciprocal group work strives to help people adjust and become active citizens, radical reciprocal group work strives to empower clients and encourage them to bring about social change. The social goals model differs primarily in terms of the targets of change. The traditional social goals model assumes the present system is good and with citizen participation the government will be responsive to the poor and powerless in society. The radical social goals model suggests that inequality is inherent in the social system and that people must change the system. The change itself entails a redistribution of political and economic power.

Group Work: A Summary

This brief study of the history of group work methods provides further evidence for the argument that the problem-solving process is consistent across models of social work practice. It has also been shown that the size of the group one chooses to intervene in is not related to one's ideological perspective. Conservatives, liberals, and radicals have all found group methods conducive to their professional goals.

COMMUNITY ORGANIZATION

The clearest ideological differences between traditional methods and radical methods is apparent in community organization. The earliest form of community organization dates back to the social planning techniques of the charity organization society. Methods similar to locality development were widely adopted by the settlement workers. Social action methods were used by abolitionists (1840s) and unemployed worker councils (1920s), but did not become part of social work methodology until the 1960s.

Methods used by abolitionists and unemployed worker councils are discussed in Chapter 7.

We begin discussion of community organization methods with the earliest form of community organization—social planning. Locality development models are briefly addressed, because their history is similar to the social goals model of group work. Finally, social action community organization is presented. Social action is the most frequently discussed and the least frequently used model of organizing.

Social Planning

This approach to community organization dates back to the charity organization society (COS) and is consistent with its ideology and methodology. A major goal of the COS was to bring rationality and control to relief giving. Administration as a specialization in social work has grown out of this approach to practice.

The social planning model is based on the premise that social change is a rational process. The community organizer or administrator identifies the social problem, its causes, and possible solutions. His professional roles may include data collector, analyst, program designer, implementor, and evaluator. The social planning model approaches community organization as a technical process to solve problems. The way to deal with social problems is

One of the earliest types of community action programs was organized sports activities for children after school.

through rational planning—deliberate, planned, and controlled change. Social planning requires expert planners with technical abilities.

The first community organizers to go through the educational system were groomed to manage organizations such as Red Feather, Community Chest, and United Way. The assumption underlying these programs has been that the social order is good and that deviations from this view are problematic. In the past and even today these organizations stress the desirability of private charity and giving only to the worthy poor. This ideological base is more consistent with the charity organization movement than either the settlement house or radical feminist ideology.

Community organization as a primary method of social work practice was not accepted by CSWE until 1962.

Rino Patti has summarized the history of administration in social work practice concisely.[64] His work illustrates the assumptions underlying administrative practice and its development in relationship to casework, the more prevalent social work method.

Patti suggests that social workers have been extensively involved in administration from the profession's beginnings. Since the first charity organization society was founded, social workers have been called upon to provide administrative leadership as well as policy planning and expertise for the social welfare sector. Some of our most luminous figures—Harry Hopkins, Julia Lathrop, and Grace Abbott, to name a few—have devoted much of their professional lives to developing and administering social programs. Patti identifies four periods (1900–1935, 1935–1960, 1960–1970, and 1970–1975) and analyzes developments in each period.

1900–1935. As social work entered the twentieth century, it comprised a loosely-knit network of volunteers, civic leaders, social reformers, labor organizers, paid workers, and agency administrators working in diverse settings and with diverse clientele. This network shared a commitment to improve the conditions of the poor and make the organization of charitable agencies more rational. There was no doubt within the profession that social casework was the preeminent methodology; administration received little attention. The consensus declared that administration was just an extension of the knowledge and skills of casework. The only training necessary for administration was training in social casework and experience as a caseworker.

Edith Abbott and Sophonisba Breckinridge (1866–1949), both of the Chicago School of Civics and Philanthropy, disagreed with this approach to administration. They argued that direct service practice was a necessary but insufficient preparation for administrative practice. They believed all caseworkers should prepare to eventually assume administrative and policy-making responsibilities. This debate reflects an ever-present tension in social work—the tension between those who believe the profession's purpose is to discover and try to eliminate the causes of social problems, and those who argue that the profession's most important task is to treat the victims of social ills.[65]

While Abbott and Breckinridge believed sound administration required a specific base of knowledge, professionals in general assumed knowledge of and competence in social casework was the foundation of all professional practice. Having acquired this foundation, all the caseworker needed was experience and familiarity with an agency to become an administrator.

Few schools offered courses in administration and those that did failed to give them very much institutional support. Research and scholarship did not fare much better. The professional literature of that period suggests that there was no national forum where the theory and practice of administration were discussed. A review of the literature suggests that the only concern about administrators was that they serve an apprenticeship in direct services and adopt the norms and values of the profession. Some suggest that this legacy continues to plague social work administration today.

1935–1960. The Depression had a tremendous effect on social work in general and social planning and administration in particular. Consistent with the COS philosophy that welfare should be under private auspices, what little administrative knowledge that had been developed addressed primarily the area of private voluntary services. The Social Security Act of 1935 stimulated an enormous demand for individuals to manage public social services. In spite of social work's lack of experience in public programs, government looked to it to help plan and administer the delivery of services. When federal grants were made available to train personnel to work in public agencies, schools reexamined their curricula to respond to the new demand. Rather than trying to develop new knowledge and skills necessary for effective administration, social work educators commonly tried to determine how exist-

---

Sidenotes (left margin):

Sophonisba Breckinridge offered the first course in public welfare administration in 1921 at the University of Chicago.

Schools of social work were slow to respond to the need for more social work administrators.

ing casework and group work skills could be applied to supervisory responsibilities in public agencies.

Mary Parker Follett articulated the philosophical foundations of administration.

Mary Parker Follett (1868–1933) was an exception to this approach.[66]
She wrote her first book on administration in 1924, but the field of management was too new to recognize her contributions. Follett was not fully appreciated until after her death in 1933. In 1940 many of her lectures were
collected in a volume entitled *Dynamic Administration.* Another volume of
her works appeared in 1949.

The 1940s was actually the point when social work began to see administration as a special area of practice. In 1950 a major study of social
work education criticized the profession for its failure to prepare social workers adequately for administrative positions.

Administration is seen today as one of the primary social work methods in schools of social work.

1960 to the Present.   The 1960s saw a tremendous expansion of the welfare bureaucracy, but without a concurrent expansion in the number of students majoring in administration. Perhaps the generally negative view of social institutions at that time prompted students to see their role as fighting
bureaucracies, not running them.

Fiscal scarcity in the 1970s had a profound effect on program managers
too. While administrators in the sixties advocated program expansion, administrators in the seventies assumed new burdens of diminishing funds and
increasing accountability. Social work was unprepared to provide professional managers to oversee either the expansion or the contraction of services. If this condition persists, the profession risks losing not only status and
jobs but also, even more important, the opportunity to espouse its traditional
values and objectives.

There has been some response to this danger. In 1976 the first social
work journal devoted specifically to administration was founded; as of 1982,
at least forty schools had specialized administration programs. Still, much remains to be done if social work is to continue to provide needed leadership
in public and private agencies.

The period from 1930 to 1960 saw the acceptance of administration as
a bona fide method of social work practice, though some educators still insisted it was secondary to casework and actively resisted it. In spite of this
resistance, there was widespread incorporation of introductory administration
content in social work education. The social planning practitioners of community organization had progressed from running charitable societies to running major governmental programs. The research and scholarship needed to
prepare these practitioners lagged considerably behind the need. Early practitioners could draw upon their knowledge of casework and group work, but
in the area they were required to practice (administration), they were limited
to practical wisdom developed through trial and error. Social welfare administration is likely to be a growing area in social work practice for some time
to come.

Locality Development

Locality development is similar in both philosophy and technique to the social goals model of group work. Both methodologies flow from practices established in the settlement house movement. Since settlement workers were more concerned with pragmatic intervention than in conceptualizing what they were doing, their methodology was not codified as early as casework's.

The roles that a social worker may use in locality development are presented in Chapter 2.

The goal of locality development is to improve social and economic conditions. Technological changes have produced an urban industrial society with social dislocation and alienation. In this model, dissatisfaction motivates change, and self-initiated change is believed to be more permanent than imposed change. This approach assumes that people want change and will work for change, and that pursuing change will lead to greater social integration. What the people of the community need is a facilitator who will give them confidence and know-how, increase their ability to solve problems, and help them achieve consensus and commitment. Involving the community in solving the problem is of paramount importance. The community knows best what it needs, and the change will be more permanent if the community works together to bring it about.

The community's capacity to change is related to the degree of integration and affected by apathy and prejudice as well as history and structure. The locality developer strives to overcome divisive and destructive tendencies among groups and to build common values and a consensus of community goals.

Specific examples of working with communities are given in Chapter 2.

The locality developer works primarily from a systems perspective. The community is essentially a social structural unit, a system in a system made of systems. As a social system the community tends toward stability—it tends to retain existing patterns of solving problems. Problems occur when established patterns become inadequate to deal with external change. The community organizer must assess three specific types of strain: faulty distribution of power, faulty patterns of energy or resource mobilization and use, and inadequate communication systems.

Given the community's conservative tendency, resistance tends to arise from four major sources: fear of the unknown or of inability to make the necessary change, reluctance to give up present conditions, existing patterns of relationships within systems and to other systems, and not knowing where to obtain assistance in making changes. The community organizer must address and overcome the client system's resistance to change and must overcome the divisive and destructive tendencies among groups to build common values and consensus.

Locality development methods were practiced extensively in the settlement house movement. During the 1950s, locality development began to be taught in social work methods. The community action programs sponsored by the War on Poverty adopted the assumptions of the locality development model (maximum feasible participation) and developed a considerable market for social workers with these skills. The 1980s clearly experienced a move away from these organizing principles and toward technical social planning.

The major assumptions underlying locality development are summarized by Rothman.

1. Community change can best be pursued through broad participation of a wide spectrum of people.
2. Planning should be done at the community level with the community setting the goals.
3. The emphasis is on process not outcome.[67]

Social Action

In stark contrast to the assumptions and tactics of social planning and locality development lies the social action approach. Saul Alinsky, Frances Fox Piven, Richard Cloward, and George Wiley are the best known social action theorists. Consistent with radical principles, each of these theorists has been significantly involved in the practice of social action principles.

Piven and Cloward analyze the conditions, potentials, and roles necessary for effective organizing.[68] First of all, they argue that leaders or organizers do not create social movements; rather, social movements rise in response to momentous change in the social order. This analysis assumes that the elite (or the ruling order) will not respond unless the lower class threatens the social order.

Piven and Cloward suggest that many community organization theorists overlook the fact that protest and the shape it takes are determined by the institutional structure. We are so taken with the myth of political pluralism that we do not even realize our political strategies are not freely chosen. We do not see the constraints inherent in the social structure. Another failure Piven and Cloward see in traditional community organization strategy is the inability to understand who protests. They suggest that, contrary to popular belief, it is not the most alienated or oppressed who protest but rather those whose lives are rooted in the institutional context—people who are integrated into a social group. The people most capable of protesting are those drawn together by work or some other common base and with some type of common target to strike. The potential gains of protest are also structurally limited; these authors suggest that any concessions the protesters might gain are only those consistent with the interests of dominant economic groups.

Yet in spite of the many limitations Piven and Cloward see in organizing the poor, they set lofty goals for the radical organizer. Traditional community organization goals aim to reform; radical community organization goals aim to procure a bigger piece of the pie for the lower class. Organizers are limited, but encouraged to enlarge the potential influence of the lower class however they can. In essence, then, the contributions of the radical community organizer are limited by social conditions; that is, community organizers cannot plan protests. They must wait for a protest to occur and then pursue strategies that escalate its momentum and impact.

Alinsky believed that in order for change to occur, conflict had to be generated.

Saul Alinsky (1909–1972), the father of radical methodology, would not have disagreed with the general principles developed by Piven and Cloward, but would have suggested that social action is possible and a redistribution of power and income can be attained through action at a community level. His strategies are outlined in *Rules for Radicals.*[69] Alinsky assumed that a disadvantaged group needs to be organized to receive its fair share from larger society, and that redistributing power and resources is accomplished by making changes in the formal policies of organizations or communities. Alinsky would suggest that the effectiveness of these strategies is proven by programs such as Model Cities and the Office of Economic Opportunity.

An explanation of private troubles and public issues is presented in Chapter 2.

Galper believes that opportunities for radical community organizers abound in everyday practice.[70] He suggests that their key task is to link immediate problems with longer-range agendas. (This is similar to the idea of linking private troubles and public issues.) Each worker assignment will then be seen in terms of long-run movement building on structural changes. Every project or work assignment then offers numerous opportunities for linkage with the broader political process.

The Black Panther Party for Self Defense

An excellent example of self-help in social welfare and social service delivery among blacks is the Black Panther Party. Founded in 1966 by Huey Pierce Newton and Bobby Seale, its full name is the Black Panther Party for Self Defense.[71] During their early years the Panthers used the gun as a temporary symbol to draw attention to themselves and show they were ready to defend themselves, but the role of the gun in Panther philosophy has been overemphasized. It temporarily established the Panthers in the black community as a group that could defend itself by any means necessary against police brutality and harassment.

Another early and temporary tactic was patrolling the police by riding around black neighborhoods armed with a gun, a law book, and a tape recorder. When they would come upon a black being arrested, they would supervise the proceedings and ensure that the matter was handled correctly. This practice caused many confrontations between Panthers and police, the result of which is well known.

The Black Panther Party (Self Defense was dropped in later years to better emphasize its political nature) has a plan upon which its programs and methods of service are based. Goals include

1. full employment of blacks,
2. the right to control politics of black community,
3. decent housing,

4. education that teaches black history,

5. exemption of blacks from military service,

6. release of all blacks in prison,

7. an end to police brutality,

8. trial by jury of peers, and

9. land, bread, housing, education, clothing, justice and peace.[72]

The Black Panther Party underwent a major change in its goals in the 1970s.

The Panthers alienated themselves from the black community during the late 1960s by becoming an elitist organization, forming coalitions with white radical groups, and emphasizing violence. But as they matured, they began to place more emphasis on local service delivery.

From 1972–1975 the Panthers underwent a vast reorganization and change of emphasis. Survival programs and more locally and community oriented services became the focus. The Oakland Community School, for example, was founded during this period and still operates today.[73] It handles 150 children of nursery and elementary school age. Members help the elderly shop and provide guard details to escort them to the bank to cash their Social Security checks. Free legal aid, free rat and roach control, dances, and martial arts training are some other programs.[74] To supplement the inadequate services of hospitals they also operate a volunteer medical research clinic.[75]

Along with the move back to the community, the Panthers also became politically active. Bobby Seale ran for Mayor of Oakland in 1973; although he did not win, he received over 47,000 votes (37 percent) and forced a run-off with the incumbent mayor. Another Black Panther, Elaine Brown, twice ran for city council, coming in second both times. She also served as a delegate for Jerry Brown at the Democratic convention in 1972.[76]

One facet of the Panthers' organization that did not change was the make-up of its membership. The Panthers began as a black organization and have remained one. One of the group's fundamental beliefs is that black people are primarily responsible for the work to be done in the black community. Self-determination must be a reality within the black community. Panthers believe that whites can help most effectively in their own communities.

During their history the Panthers have entered into alliances and coalitions with white organizations, but their membership has remained black. Upon returning to the black community, they received a warm reception simply because they were offering services the people needed and, just as important, they were bringing services to the people.

Even though evidence suggests that blacks are most effective when using self-help techniques, the dominant form of action taken by blacks has always been integrationist, as the longevity of organizations such as the National Association for the Advancement of Colored People and the National Urban League proves. Black separatist organizations have tended to come on the scene in a flourish and then die down in popularity.

National Welfare Rights Organization

One organization that attempted to take advantage of the 1960s wave of self-determination was the National Welfare Rights Organization (NWRO). The National Welfare Rights Organization banded (though loosely) racial groups into an organization demanding rights for poor people. Its membership reached as high as 75,000 families, grouped in 300 local chapters in 150 cities.[77]

The NWRO consisted primarily of welfare recipients and social workers.

Some of the NWRO's methods were not always well accepted by the public. Many felt that it was much too radical and prone to violence. But the NWRO wanted to grant full citizenship to the poor, and to make this point, members demonstrated, lobbied, negotiated, picketed, boycotted, and did almost anything they thought was necessary to achieve their goals.

The NWRO taught welfare recipients how to become more involved in changing public policy.

One of these goals was a guaranteed adequate income plan. The NWRO wanted every American citizen to be guaranteed a decent, livable income. Another goal was to enroll all eligible people on the welfare rolls. Many people were eligible to receive local, state, or federal assistance but either did not realize they were eligible or were kept from applying by a sense of pride.[78]

Because the NWRO was composed of hundreds of local grass roots organizations, the vast majority of its activities concerned local businesses and survival techniques. Concerned Parents for Adequate Welfare in Queens, New York, for instance, established a program for welfare recipients to get credit at Montgomery Ward.[79] Until then people on public assistance had been denied credit. They also pressured the Queens General Hospital because of its deficiencies in caring for the poor. Some of their daily activities included helping welfare recipients shop and find apartments. They provided babysitting, helped burned-out families find furniture, and went with clients to welfare hearings and court appearances.[80]

But radical demonstrations continued. During the late 1960s hundreds of people occupied welfare offices and refused to leave until more liberal benefits were given. At times they were successful.[81] In May of 1969 members of the National Welfare Rights Organization interrupted the meeting of the National Conference on Social Welfare and demanded $35,000 from the delegates to fund participation of the poor at the 1970 conference. They managed to collect $700 at the meeting, with a promise of the balance.[82]

Although their constant fight was for material gains, the National Welfare Rights Organization's greatest contribution was to put an end, if only temporarily, to the apathy among welfare recipients.[83] No longer did the poor feel guilty when receiving services or ashamed when cashing their checks at the supermarket; now they felt they had a right to a decent living. The National Welfare Rights Organization also put all responsibility for achievement and progress upon the people themselves. It was formed by the people to benefit the people. It operated with a shoestring budget, and it was people that kept it going, not politicians.

By the early 1970s the NWRO was no longer active.

Community Organization: A Summary

Community organization, social work, or problem-solving on a community level consists of a variety of techniques and goals. Just as casework and group work varied according to the practitioner's ideological perspective, so does community organization. The professional's view of the individual, the community, the state, and the economic system lead to diverse practical applications. Since the client system of the community organizer is by definition larger than that of casework or group work, it has the potential to make a greater impact on society. Community organization can either support the status quo or foster significant redistribution of resources.

SOCIAL WORK TODAY

The debate over intrapsychic or environmental intervention continues today. While the profession denotes the poor as the primary target population and the interface of the individual and environment as the unique area of professional expertise, this does not seem to be reflected by present day social work students. Rubin and Johnson studied the interests and aspirations of 257 students entering the direct practice program in eight master of social work programs. They found that most students saw the MSW as a route to becoming psychotherapists in private practice. These entering students claimed little commitment to social work's mission, dual focus, functions, or clientele.

> In particular, there is a pervasive impression that more and more of those entering the social work profession do so to work as psychotherapists in independent private practice—at the expense of those populations that need social workers in the public sector to help them obtain essential resources and acceptable living conditions.[84]

Social work educators have practical, theoretical, and philosophical concerns about the conservatism of today's MSW students. On a practical level, what becomes of a profession that concedes its unique domain and tries to compete with more established professions? Since practice is based on traditional social work roles and functions, which theory will guide this "new" profession? On a philosophical level, the concern is well stated by Rubin and Johnson: "Social work's commitment to equity, social responsibility, relatedness, and sacrifice should be a source of pride for practitioners and should not be dismissed on the road to the practice of psychotherapy."[85]

The seriousness of this concern was underlined by an editorial that appeared in the *Journal of Education for Social Work.* Hans Falck suggested that the paper by Rubin and Johnson "brings into focus a problem of which many of us have been intuitively aware for several years. That is, substantial numbers of students in schools of social work believe they are preparing for the private practice of psychotherapy."[86] Falck contended that psychotherapy has little to do with social work or its societal mandate. He argued that social work's logic, tradition, and history are based on a commitment to help the poor. Falck rejected as rationalization the argument that the poor will not receive psychotherapy if it is not available through private agencies.

Until social workers reject public financing of their professional education, Falck believes social workers must serve society since their education "was made possible by those they elect to serve *and by those they do not.*"

SUMMARY

This chapter has traced the evolution of professional methodology. The early 1900s marked the onset of professionalization of "helpers." Mary Richmond, Jane Addams, Grace Coyle, Vida Scudder, and the Abbott sisters are but a few of the individuals who contributed to professional practice by codifying its methods.

The prominence of the various methodologies has been closely linked with the prevailing ideology of the time. This remains true today, as witnessed by the concern of social work educators that the conservative ideology of present MSW students will lead to a loss of the dual focus of practice. If the profession responds to the conservative ideology of the day and deserts traditional roles, functions, and clientele, will these be taken over by the newly emerging human service profession?

History suggests some interesting answers. Perhaps social work will continue on its conservative trend as long as the national temper is conservative but will reverse itself when the national temper changes again; clearly this is what has occurred historically. On the other hand, social workers may not have a constituency to return to if new professions claim the domain they are now deserting. Not only has there been an upsurge in the training of generic human service workers, but the nursing profession too has taken an increasingly environmental approach to curing and preventing disease.

This review of history suggests both caution and optimism for the potential social worker. Historically the profession has accommodated liberal, conservative, and radical practitioners within its ranks. The danger is that the profession itself may be losing its focus and therefore its unique domain. The study of history provides a long-run perspective from which to view the pros and cons of these issues.

NOTES

1. Louise C. Johnson, *Social Work Practice: A Generalist Approach* (Boston: Allyn and Bacon, 1981).
2. Herman Levin, "Conservatism of Social Work," *Social Service Review* 56, 4 (December 1982): 607.
3. Carel Germain, "Casework and Science: A Historical Encounter," in R. W. Roberts and R. H. Nee, *Theories of Social Casework* (Chicago: University of Chicago Press, 1970).

4. C. W. LeCroy, J. B. Ashford, and W. W. Hudson, "Clinical Social Work: Fictions, Factions, and Future Directions," *The Urban and Social Change Review* 19 (1986): 8–13.

5. Harriet Bartlett, *The Common Base of Social Work Practice* (New York: NASW, 1970), 19.

6. R. K. Blashfield, *The Classification of Psychopathology: NeoKraepelian and Quantitative Approaches* (New York: Plenum Press, 1984), 16.

7. Mary Richmond, *Social Diagnosis* (New York: Russell Sage, 1917), 26.

8. Ibid., 38.

9. M. Goldberg, J. Gibbons, and I. Sinclair, *Problems, Tasks and Outcomes: The Evaluation of Task-Centered Casework in Three Settings* (London: George Allen & Unwin Ltd., 1985), 2.

10. *Social Casework Generic and Specific: A Report of the Milford Conference* (Washington, D.C.: National Association of Social Workers, 1974), Reprint.

11. Helen Harris Perlman, *Social Casework: A Problem-solving Process* (Chicago: University of Chicago Press, 1957), 3.

12. Helen Northern, *Social Work with Groups* (New York: Columbia, 1969).

13. Murray Ross, *Community Organization: Theory, Principles, and Practice* (New York: Harper, 1955).

14. Allen Pincus and Anne Minahan, *Social Work Practice: Model and Method* (Itasca, Ill.: Peacock, 1973).

15. Betty Picard, *An Introduction to Social Work: A Primer,* rev. ed. (Homewood, Ill.: Dorsey Press, 1979), 89.

16. Mary Richmond, *What Is Social Casework,* (New York: Russell Sage, 1922), 98–99.

17. Herman Borenzweig, "Social Work and Psychoanalytic Theory," *Social Work* 16, 1 (January 1971).

18. Levin, "Conservatism," 613.

19. Ellery Reed, "Efforts of Social Workers Toward Social Reorganization," *Social Forces* xiv (1935), 88.

20. Howard Goldstein, "Cognitive Approaches to Direct Practice," *Social Service Review* 56, 4 (December 1982): 546.

21. Florence Hollis, *Casework: A Psychosocial Approach* (New York: Random House, 1964).

22. Goldstein, "Cognitive Approaches," 546.

23. Ibid.

24. Virginia Robinson, *A Changing Psychology in Social Work* (Philadelphia: University of Philadelphia Press, 1930).

25. Bertha Capen Reynolds, *Social Work and Social Living* (New York: Citadel Press, 1951), 108.

26. Ibid.

27. Ibid.

28. Ibid.

29. Gordon Hamilton, *Theory and Practice of Social Casework* (New York: Columbia University Press, 1951).

30. Helen Ginsburg, *Poverty, Economics, and Society* (Washington, D.C.: University Press of America, 1981), 129.

31. B. F. Skinner, *Science and Human Behavior* (New York: Macmillan, 1953).

32. J. Wolpe, *Psychotherapy by Reciprocal Inhibition* (Stanford: Stanford University Press, 1958).

33. W. K. Brooks, "Human Behavior/Social Environment: Past and Present, Future or Folly?" *Journal of Social Work Education* 22 (1986): 18–23.
34. Bartlett, *The Common Base,* 96.
35. Ibid., 103.
36. Ibid., 104.
37. S. Briar, "Needed: A Simple Definition of Social Work," *Social Work* 26 (1981): 84.
38. Ibid.
39. B. Nurcombe and R. M. Gallager, *The Clinical Process in Psychiatry: Diagnosis and Management Planning* (London: Cambridge University Press, 1986).
40. Ibid., 305.
41. Edgar Auerswald, "Interdisciplinary versus Ecological Approach," *Family Process* 7 (September 1968): 202–215.
42. Ibid.
43. Pincus and Minahan, *Social Work Practice.*
44. H. Weissman, "Knowledge Base of Clinical Social Work," in *Handbook of Clinical Social Work,* ed. E. Rosenblatt and D. Waldvogel (San Francisco: Jossey-Bass, 1983), 2.
45. E. P. Goldstein, "The Knowledge Base of Clinical Social Work," in *Handbook,* ed. Rosenblatt and Waldvogel, 26–57.
46. H. L. Gochros, "Foreword," in J. Fischer, *Effective Casework Practice: An Eclectic Approach* (New York: McGraw-Hill, 1978), x.
47. J. Fischer, *Effective Casework Practice: An Eclectic Approach* (New York: McGraw-Hill, 1978), 3.
48. Ibid., 5.
49. Ibid., 53.
50. J. Maxmen, *Essential Psychopathology* (New York: Norton & Co., 1986), 7–8.
51. Ibid., 9–10.
52. Bartlett, *The Common Base,* 71.
53. Joyce Walstedt, *The Anatomy of Oppression* (Pittsburgh: Know, 1971).
54. Jeanette Silveira, *The Effects of Sexism on Thought* (Pittsburgh: Know, 1971).
55. Susan A. Thomas, "Theory and Practice in Feminist Therapy," *Social Work* 13 (November 1977): 447–454.
56. Ibid.
57. Robert Vinter, *The Essential Components of Social Group Work Practice* (Ann Arbor, Michigan: University of Michigan School of Social Work, 1955).
58. Catherine Papell and Beulah Roberts Rothman, "Social Group Work Models: Possession and Heritage," *Journal of Education for Social Work* no. 2 (Fall 1966): 66.
59. Vida Scudder, *On Journey* (New York: Dutton, 1937).
60. Vinter, *Essential Components.*
61. Ralph Pumphrey and Muriel Pumphrey, *The Heritage of American Social Work* (New York: Columbia University Press, 1961).
62. William Schwartz, "The Social Worker in the Group," *Social Welfare Forum* (1961): 155.
63. Peter Leonard, "Towards a Paradigm for Radical Practice," in *Radical Social Work,* ed. Roy Bailey and Mike Brake (New York: Pantheon, 1976), 60.
64. Rino Patti, *Social Welfare Administration* (Englewood Cliffs, N.J.: Prentice-Hall, 1983).

65. Stephen J. Diner, "Scholarship in the Quest for Social Welfare: A Fifty-Year History of the *Social Service Review*," *Social Service Review* 51, 1 (March 1977).
66. Myron Weiner, *Human Services Management* (Homewood, Ill.: Dorsey Press, 1982).
67. Fred Cox, John L. Erlich, Jack Rothman, and John E. Tropman, eds., *Strategies of Community Organization*, 3rd ed. (Itasca, Ill.: Peacock, 1979), 354–400.
68. Frances Fox Piven and Richard Cloward, *Poor People's Movements* (New York: Pantheon, 1977).
69. Saul Alinsky, *Rules for Radicals* (New York: Vintage, 1972).
70. Jeffrey Galper, *Radical Social Work* (Englewood Cliffs, N.J.: Prentice-Hall, 1980).
71. Thomas R. Frazier, ed., *Afro American History: Primary Sources* (New York: Harcourt, Brace, and World, 1970), 467.
72. Ibid., 468–70.
73. "The Odyssey of Huey Newton," *Time* 112 (13 November 1978): 38.
74. Peter Goldman and Gerald C. Lebenow, "Huey Newton Comes Home," *Newsweek* 90 (11 July 1977): 27.
75. Gwendolyn Evans, "The Panthers' Elaine Brown," *Ms.* 9, 8 (March 1976): 104–109.
76. Goldman and Lebenow, "Huey Newton," 7.
77. "Welfare Union Steps Up Its Demands," *U.S. News and World Report* 66 (23 June 1969): 36.
78. Carolyn P. DuBose, "Champion of Welfare Rights," *Ebony* 25, 6 (August 1970): 33.
79. Richard Rogin, "Now It's Welfare Lib," *New York Times Magazine* (27 September 1970): 76.
80. Ibid., 31.
81. *U.S. News*, "Welfare Union," 35.
82. Ibid., 36.
83. Dubose, "Champion," 33.
84. Allen Rubin and Peter J. Johnson, "Direct Practice Interests of Entering MSW Students," *Journal of Education for Social Work* 20, 2 (Spring 1984): 5.
85. Ibid.
86. Hans Falck, Editorial, *Journal of Education for Social Work* 20, 2 (Spring 1984).

PART

IV

THE SOCIAL WORK
KNOWLEDGE BASE

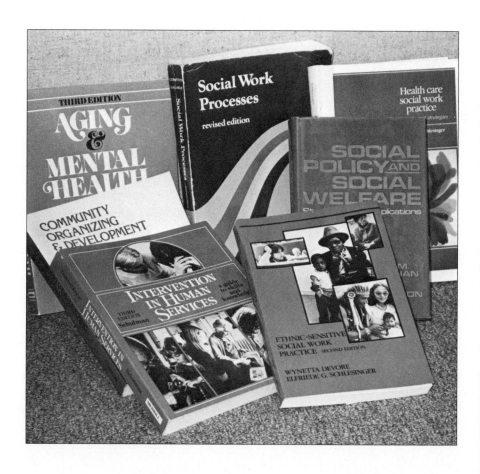

Without theory, practice becomes chaotic. . . . Theory gives meaning and clarity to what would otherwise be specific and isolated cases. On the other hand, without practice, theory becomes mere speculation. The realities of practice provide a check upon pure speculation . . . also, practice provides the problems which must be dealt with by any comprehensive theory.[1]

E very organization uses some kind of technology to accomplish its goals. At the Ford Motor Company the technology is tangible, because the process of assembling the elements results in a concrete product, an automobile. Automaking is characterized by a high degree of routinization; once the operational system is in place, the tasks become clear, the cause and effect relationships are clear, the process is repetitive, and the product is standardized. Technicians can be trained to know exactly what to do, since there is little or no variation in the problems they face accomplishing their task.

Professionals face a different kind of task. The professional's theoretical knowledge explains the technical knowledge and guides its application under different circumstances. Technicians apply technical knowledge repeatedly in identical or similar situations. Professionals do not simply apply rules; instead they learn to think in a particular way and to exercise judgment in specific situations guided by their general knowledge base. Not only must they master a knowledge base, but they must also use their intelligence and judgment — the hallmark of a profession. Rigid rules and details impede good professional practice. The professional person who masters technical information and knows concepts and theories but cannot make sound applications or good judgments is not effective.[2]

Part IV discusses the knowledge base of the profession, including sociological and psychological theories.

The knowledge base of social work practice contains three different levels of theory: general theory drawn from related disciplines such as psychology, sociology, anthropology, political science, and economics; practice theory (including knowledge of policy, services, programs, institutions, and the

Practice theories are presented in Chapter 3, and specific social work methods are reviewed in Chapter 8.

social worker's role in relationship to each of them[3]) that explains some of the ways social workers use knowledge in their day-to-day work; and specific social work methods, that is, theories of practice.

Louise Johnson describes the social work knowledge base as "eclectic, interdisciplinary, tentative at best, complex and often subjective."[4] Since the disciplines from which it draws its theoretical underpinnings have conflicting theories, the social work knowledge base is understandably tentative. Social work cannot develop an integrated theory base as long as it builds upon disciplines that offer contrasting models of human behavior.

Social work practice is filled with controversy regarding the relationship of theory and practice. Social work educators are committed to either theory-based or knowledge-guided practice. In core introductory courses students are often impressed with the importance of theory to practice. It is not unusual, however, for students' practicums to be guided by social workers who suggest they forget all the theory they learned in the classroom because it does not apply in practice. These practitioners suggest that the complexity and incongruity of theories are evidence of theory's irrelevance to practice, since it cannot determine what the the best course of action may be. It is true that while social work educators believe in the superiority of theoretically informed practice, they cannot always identify what this actually involves and how it might be achieved, let alone its practical outcome.[5]

This inability to articulate social work knowledge has been at least partially responsible for the anti-intellectual stance of many practitioners. Since social work is a purposeful activity, practitioners have to select, integrate, and use knowledge in the light of their functions, tasks, and the people and problems with which they work. In many cases practice has been forced to move beyond what has been articulated in theory; and practitioners have not been prone to create theory by clear and explicit articulation of what they do and why they do it. However, to argue that practice is and should be atheoretical is problematic. While knowledge is no guarantee of certainty, it does increase the frequency with which socially appropriate decisions will be made. No one can operate with a totally objective view. Everyone holds assumptions and beliefs about individuals; these assumptions and beliefs have practical consequences.

Scott Briar and Henry Miller contend that the choice for practitioners is not whether or not to have a theory, but what theoretical assumptions to hold. The atheoretical position amounts to a preference for implicit and hidden rather than explicit and self-conscious knowledge in social work. This preference protects practitioners from having practice evaluated on either political, ethical, or intellectual grounds. Since theories have implications for problem assessments and intervention decisions, an important step in improving practice is to understand how knowledge is used.[6]

Part of the demystification process in social work is related to the recognition of the different functions of knowledge to the profession. Knowledge in the liberal tradition is seen as a source of enlightenment; conscious calculation is believed to be superior to blind assumptions. This is the major traditional assumption about the contribution of social science knowledge to practice. Unfortunately that assumption has not always had fruitful consequences, since most of what has been taught and written has been relatively unhelpful for direct practice. If social science is to be useful to direct practice, it has the important mapping function of codifying, conceptualizing, and documenting the process and content of practice activity; it must make the implicit explicit.[7]

So far it has been suggested that social workers must take action on the basis of knowledge. But since social workers cannot conquer the total social science arena, what kind of knowledge is needed to support practice? Social workers need to understand **developmental, cognitive, affective**, and **interpersonal processes**; they must also know how personality functions and evolves in various situations. In addition, to practice effectively social workers must have more than a nodding acquaintance with **socioeconomic** and **demographic theories, fields of social policy, systems theory,** and **institutional organizations**.[8] Social workers must have a theory base that makes them aware that the structure of society and transactions with others are reflected in the self and the life structure of each individual. All human beings have their own particular world that presents them with opportunity, meaning, feeling, identity, and myths that they use and internalize selectively.[9]

The first chapter in this section, Chapter 9, addresses the context in which social work practice takes place. We look at social functioning specifically as it relates to social welfare and social work practice. The second, Chapter 10, analyzes social welfare organizations in terms of bureaucratic structures and interorganizational relationships. These two chapters identify important variables in the environmental context of social work practice.

Chapter 11 addresses the knowledge component that we refer to as biopsychosocial functioning. We add the biological and psychological components of social functioning, stressing the importance of each component and how they interact with each other.

Research is another integral component of the social work knowledge base that is discussed in Chapter 12. Familiarity with research findings directs us to the most effective interventions. Research also directs the social work process by evaluating whether our interventions are working and when we need to change our approach. Research knowledge is both a body of empirical findings and a method to enrich the social work process.

Chapter 13 analyzes how social policy sets the limits and potential for what social workers can accomplish. Understanding the nature of policies and becoming involved in decision making are potential sources of power for us and our clients. Social welfare policy determines how social workers will be involved in either making decisions or in implementing policies.

The final section, Chapter 14, discusses special populations and special issues. As social work professionals, we have identified unique groups and problems as practice priorities. Racism, homophobia, misogyny, and rejection of diversity are key problem areas. In this chapter we take an experiential approach to understanding the alienation experienced by people who are "different" in American society. We draw upon actual life experiences to convey what discrimination feels like to individuals experiencing it.

This sampling will give you a flavor of the complexity and importance of social work knowledge. Practice knowledge has cognitive, affective, and behavioral components. This section primarily concerns cognitive knowledge, although Chapter 14 emphasizes the affective components. The case studies identify some of the behavioral or interventive components of practice.

Notes

1. Ralph Tyler, "Distinctive Attributes of Education for the Professions," *Social Work* no. 33 (April 1952): 61.
2. James Gustafson, "Professions as 'Callings'," *Social Service Review* 56, 4 (December 1982): 505–515.
3. Pauline Hardiker and Mary Barker, *Theories of Practice in Social Work* (San Francisco: Academic Press, 1981), 1.
4. Louise Johnson, *Social Work Practice: A Generalist Approach* (Boston: Allyn and Bacon, 1983), 49–50.
5. J. Bailey, *Ideas and Intervention: Social Theory for Practice* (London: Routledge and Kegan Paul, 1980).
6. Scott Briar and Henry Miller, *Problems and Issues in Social Casework* (New York: Columbia University Press, 1971), 180.
7. Hardiker and Barker, *Theories of Practice,* 4.
8. Shirley Cooper, "Social Work: A Dissenting Profession," *Social Work* 22, 5 (September 1977): 363.
9. D. J. Levinson, *The Seasons of a Man's Life* (New York: Knopf, 1978), 1.

Chapter

9

Society and Social Work

One of the more obvious but important points to recognize is that understanding deviance involves studying both those who break the rules and those who make the rules.[1]

People have always strived to organize their existence. Every society needs to establish social order. Social welfare is one of the primary social institutions that create and maintain order in our society. *Social welfare* is the organized system of voluntary and governmental agencies that help individuals and groups attain satisfying standards of life and health and that seek to prevent, alleviate, or solve recognized social problems.

Social institutions include the political, economic and educational systems.

The institution of social welfare can be analyzed at a number of levels. First, we address how social welfare on an institutional level operates in relation to other societal institutions in maintaining social order. We do this by discussing the major social institutions and societal functions. We then look at how these abstract concepts we have defined as social functions translate into practice as individuals operate within the social institutions.

Social functions include production, distribution, consumption, social integration, social control, and others.

We use the example of women in the workplace to study how existing social structures and processes resist social change and how understanding these processes permits us to intervene effectively. Understanding social functioning guides us in helping women make the adjustment from homemaker to paid employee. Understanding the informal as well as the formal system improves the potential for women to move into nontraditional roles and facilitates their ability to bring their own strengths to these positions.

SOCIAL STRUCTURE

Many important components of social structure are not rules or laws but unwritten guides to behavior. Social order is dynamic; people are born into it. Social order exists because individuals are morally and psychologically de-

pendent upon it. Every individual needs the cooperation of other human beings, and in any group there must be order.

To maintain that order certain social functions must be met. Food and
other goods must be produced and distributed for consumption. This calls for
both a division of labor and the allocation of authority for decision making.
The more complex a society is, the more institutions must be designed to fill
these social functions and the more formalized the organization becomes.
Social workers need to understand how society meets each of the essential
social functions, what kinds of institutions have been developed to provide
these functions, and how social work and the social welfare institution fit into
the social structure.

In Chapter 4 we introduced the liberal, radical, and conservative ideologies as sets of beliefs about the individual and the society. In this chapter we
propose a less complex framework for analysis, which comprises the functionalist and conflict perspectives.

*The functionalist per-
spective is also known
as the order perspec-
tive.*

The functionalist perspective subsumes the conservative and liberal perspectives, which see the societal structure as basically sound, with only minor changes needed. In this view, societal systems operate to maintain order
and the status quo. All parts of every system are either functional or dysfunctional. The functional parts help maintain the system in a balanced state and
reinforce the status quo; dysfunctional components have either no effect or a
negative effect. In essence, existing structures are functional to societal order.

*The conflict perspec-
tive is also referred to
as the radical perspec-
tive.*

The conflict perspective posits that the present social systems exploit
the working classes and protect the existing hierarchical relations in society
for the ruling class. This view suggests that both social welfare and the social
work profession are functional only in protecting the powerful in this society.

SOCIAL INSTITUTIONS AND FUNCTIONS

As we mentioned, to survive a society must perform certain tasks that sociologists refer to as essential social functions. These include production, distribution, and consumption, socialization, social control, social integration, and
mutual support.[2] Societies must develop means to achieve these goals. *Institutions* are the patterns of relationships that develop to carry out the essential
social functions. The most visible and powerful institutions in our society are
the economic, political, religious, social welfare, educational, and familial.

Within each of these institutions there is a recurrent and consistent pattern of social relationships. There are certain things we have come to expect
of each of these institutions. The political institution, for example, has primary responsibility for social control. The family, the church, and the schools
are responsible for socialization and social integration. Historically, families
were able to fulfill many of these functions; with industrialization and urbanization this became more difficult. The mutual aid or social welfare system
has assumed some of the traditional family functions.

There is strong consensus in our society about the appropriate role of the political, economic, educational, and family systems. There is far less consensus on the role of the social welfare system. Some people believe that the social welfare system should merely be a backup system when the family or the marketplace fail. Others feel that the social welfare institution should be an ongoing, frontline means of providing for the well-being of society. Rather than tell you what the social welfare institution should be, we provide you with opposing views of how institutions meet essential social functions.

Production, Distribution, and Consumption

The production, distribution, and consumption of goods and services is the primary domain of the economic system. It is almost impossible for individuals or families to produce everything they need. Instead of each family producing for itself, we have a labor market in which individuals specialize by producing more than they need of one commodity in exchange for wages, which then allow them to purchase what they need. The way a society organizes to allow this exchange is referred to as the economic system.

Economic systems may be either capitalist, communist, socialist, or state capitalist.

Some of the questions you might ask yourself are: Do you believe that the present welfare system is harmful to the economic system, or does it actually help the economic system operate more effectively? Would a different kind of economic system produce a better or worse social welfare system? To help you analyze these questions we present two opposing views.

The Functionalist Perspective. In a capitalist system acquisitiveness and competitiveness are seen as functional and supportive to both the social and economic systems. The desire to have more purchasing power and be the best keeps people active in the labor force. High productivity in turn produces affluence. People who reject these values and refuse to work for a wage are not only dysfunctional, but ultimately decrease the standard of living for everyone.

This value system produces negative societal attitudes toward the elderly, the disabled, and people on welfare. Since the elderly and the disabled tend to be outside the paid work force, they are less valued and their benefits begrudged. Many middle-aged workers are very concerned that the high cost of social security payments and medical care may threaten their own future financial security. The debate about health care for "nonproductive" people becomes even more urgent as medical technology keeps more and more severely ill or brain-damaged people alive at great financial cost.

The functionalist perspective limits its analysis to production and usefulness. Functional analysis provides a rationale for evaluating and criticizing particular policies and structures within a consensual society whose basic values and structures are not disputed. Instead the debate is around the individuals who do not fit into the social order.

The Conflict Perspective.   Conflict theorists suggest that the economic institution itself is responsible for social problems. Further, they suggest that the role of the social welfare institution has been to preserve and protect the economic system, not to promote the welfare of individuals in the society. In this view, society's need for a healthy, docile, and expendable labor force is served by making benefits contingent upon the needs of the economic system. When workers are needed at low wages, benefit rates are lowered. In addition, the social welfare system does not actually provide economic security — it merely mitigates the most disastrous effects of poverty and exploitation that would occur if capitalism flourished unchecked.

Unemployment is the social problem most clearly connected to the economic system. There are two stages in the determination and distribution of income. First, a complex set of social, economic, and technical forces determines a given worker's total productivity, depending on skill and position. Then, the relative power of employer and employee determines the proportion of profit the worker receives in wages. The wages that workers receive are closely related to the power of the work group with which they are identified. In other words, power is more predictive of wages than is productivity.

Examples of the effect of power on wages can be seen with school teachers and nurses. Traditionally, these have been low-paid positions for a variety of reasons that probably include the fact that most nurses and teachers were women. As more men enter these fields, there is an increase in average wages for the profession. Perhaps even more significant is the fact that these professions have unionized. Both union membership and male cohorts have made these groups more powerful.

Owners are protected from paying high wages even when there is a labor shortage because relief programs assure a ready pool of labor. The unemployed can receive welfare benefits only as long as they are willing to accept whatever work is available, regardless of whether it pays a living wage for the individual or family.

In this country, it is popular to blame workers rather than executives of unprofitable corporations for layoffs or plant closings. In a typical radical indictment of this attitude, LeKachman notes, "Recent public policy focuses tax rewards upon the mismanagers of the private sector and benefit reduction and unemployment upon the casualties of their blunders."[3]

The Remaining Question.   The relationship between the social welfare institution and the economic system is extensive; it is less clear which segment of society is the primary beneficiary of the system. Is it more nearly accurate to say that the economic system makes possible the broad array of services designed to benefit the poor, or that the social welfare system operates in a manner that benefits the wealthy at great cost to the poor? Whom does the welfare system serve? Are the poor victims or beneficiaries of our welfare services?

Socialization

Socialization is the process through which individuals acquire the knowledge, skills, and values that enable them to participate effectively in society. Historically the family and the church were the primary institutions that fulfilled the socialization function. As society developed and more complex social skills and knowledge were required, new institutions developed or expanded to meet that function. Today educational institutions such as daycare centers, schools, and colleges are essential to the socialization function. Just as there are differing views on who benefits from the way the economic system is organized to meet the production, distribution, consumption function, there are differing views on how socialization is achieved. Since education is a primary agent of socialization, we illustrate the opposing views of the socialization process with an educational example. Understanding the concept of socialization is critical to our discussion of women in the work force at the end of this chapter.

The Functionalist Perspective.   The most widely accepted view of the educational system is that it has evolved to meet the needs of the economic system while providing opportunity and social mobility to the disadvantaged. The great equalizer in our society, education has been the vehicle for disadvantaged groups to achieve higher social status.

In the order perspective, then, the educational system is the means by which the underclass can achieve equality and social mobility. The purpose of the schools is to improve the productivity of the unskilled and the poor. Schools accomplish this by instilling values and teaching skills consistent with the needs of the economic system. If young people stay in school, study hard, and develop skills, they will be able to improve their social position. Poverty would not exist if the poor were properly educated. This view has led to social policies such as Title I, which provides money for education in areas with a high concentration of poor people. The assumptions of the order perspective derive from common views of the functioning of the marketplace.

1. Increased education will lead to increased economic productivity.
2. Testing done in the school system is a measure of the skills necessary for increased production.
3. The role of education is to decrease inequality.
4. Education is the key to social mobility.

The Conflict Perspective.   Rather than viewing education as the great equalizer, some view education as the great stabilizer of the present class system. Schools are not designed to help people rise in the social structure but to keep the poor in their place. Schools train young people to take their allotted positions in the inequality structure without contesting it.[4]

Socialization patterns differ between schools, based upon the social class of the students. The resources devoted to the children of those with commanding roles in the economy leave little financial support for the education of working class children. In poor working class schools the structure is very much like a factory—it places a high premium on obedience and punctuality and little value on creative work or individualized attention. Wealthier school districts can offer much greater opportunities—smaller classes, more electives, specialized teachers, independent work, and other skills required for adequate job performance in the upper levels of the occupational hierarchy.[5]

The Analytical Question.   The educational system is a primary tool of socialization, critical to the smooth functioning of society. It imparts knowledge, values, and skills. Do schools socialize students to strive for achievement and to make contributions to society in a way that is compatible with improving their own social status? Or do schools socialize students to take their predetermined place in the structure of inequality and to be satisfied with what they have?

Whether schools socialize for conformity or creativity, their impact is felt by all of society. Social workers often deal with people who have not been adequately socialized, who for various reasons have not accepted societal values or have failed to gain the knowledge and skill necessary for productive citizenry. A systems approach to practice suggests that the social worker needs to analyze both the system and the individual to see why socialization has not occurred.

The socialization process is of course much too complex to be attributed only to the schools. The values held by the people of a community, the types of social structures available, job opportunities, the legal system, and the police are just some of the means society has at its disposal to channel people into the roles it finds necessary for its maintenance.

Social Control

Social control over individuals can be accomplished by socialization or by sanctions. Social control is the means of ensuring that people conform to societal norms. To the degree that members of society are willing to restrict their own activities, laws are unnecessary. The more effective the socialization, integration, and mutual support functions are, the less visible and important the social control mechanisms are.

The Functionalist Perspective.   The political institution, particularly through its lawmaking and law enforcement function, is the primary institution of social control. Certain laws must be followed; if individuals do not abide by them, they will be punished. If the rules or laws are clear and fair, it will not be necessary to punish very often. A society that sets rules but does not have the ability to enforce them will not have control. The more frequently sanctions have to be imposed the more unhappy the people.

Chapter 18 provides an in-depth discussion of the function of punishment.

There is considerable debate about what types of sanctions are most functional. What is the effect of longer sentences or harsher punishment? What is the effect of more certain but shorter sentences? Can we combine punishment with some type of socialization to make it more effective? What about positive sanctions? People who feel they will be justly rewarded are unlikely to break rules. This may mean that they see themselves adequately fulfilling an appropriate role or that they will receive appropriate benefits for their efforts. Punishment is functional because it dissuades people from abandoning their assigned roles.

The Conflict Perspective. Socialization is the most powerful means of social control. Socialization does not control the alternatives available to the poor, women, and minorities, but rather controls the motivation to choose any but the traditional alternatives. Socialization is the presence in a society of consistent and controlling messages about the proper behavior for the individual.

Women have so thoroughly internalized the social definition of their role as servants to men as wives and caretakers of the next generation that no laws are necessary to enforce this choice. "Women reach this condition, the acceptance of their secondary roles as right and just, through the most insidious mechanism of social control yet devised—the socialization process."[6] The same process keeps the poor and minorities willing to do the most despised tasks for the lowest pay.

In this view, professionals—doctors, lawyers, social workers, and teachers—are primarily agents of social control.

The Control Dilemma. Many social workers find the notion of being agents of social control troubling. There is particular dissonance over issues of client self-determination and nondirectiveness. You might ask yourself whether social work would even exist if other social control mechanisms were really effective. The obvious places where social workers operate as agents of social control are prisons, welfare offices, and probation and parole offices. They serve this same function, however, in less obvious settings—therapy sessions, hospitals, and nursing homes. It is social control when the social worker intervenes to get a client to cooperate and adjust to institutional needs rather than continue to engage in disruptive behavior. Whether the social worker uses reward or punishment, it is still social control.

Social Integration

Chapter 11 discusses integration in terms of in-groups and out-groups.

Social integration is the process by which individuals come to value their membership in society and to feel responsible for abiding by its rules. Social integration is primarily a function of families, religion, the schools, and the market system. Chapter 15 discusses the importance of the family, especially as it relates to the social integration of antisocial children. Religion is one of the major integration institutions; the more integral religion is to one's life, the more likely one is to be a participating member of society. Religion gives one a sense of being part of a larger society. Without some kind of integrating mechanism such as family or community individuals become alienated from the society in which they live.

Since our society values individuals according to their contributions to the work force, employment is the crucial social integration variable. There are two opposing views of how employment is and should be related to social integration.

The Functionalist Perspective.   Some theorists suggest that the main goal of the welfare state has always been to integrate the disadvantaged into the mainstream of society.[7] Just giving the poor more income would not guarantee that they would aquire the skills and attitudes necessary to participate freely in American life. The disadvantaged do not need further economic resources but a more secure sense of order within themselves and their neighborhoods; their problem is more moral than economic. In fact, some people believe that the troubling behavior and economic conditions of disadvantaged people may be due to the social programs themselves, because they have created dependency. When people are given welfare they tend to drop out of active involvement in American life. To integrate the disadvantaged, society must obligate the disadvantaged to function as other people do. They can only be integrated as equals if the society is willing to require them to contribute.[8]

Even in the 1880s, people were concerned that welfare might create dependency.

The Conflict Perspective.   In this view social integration is a function of a capitalist society inherently related to its economic system. The regulation of individual behavior is intimately dependent on stable occupational arrangements. As long as people are fixed in their work roles, their activities and their future also seem fixed; they do what they think is right. These behaviors are shaped and reinforced by receiving a paycheck. When mass unemployment breaks that bond, people are cut off from the main institution by which they are regulated and controlled. Social integration in this sense is a superstructure that includes an elaborate group of beliefs or ritual behaviors that define what is right and wrong and why; what is possible and impossible; and the appropriate behaviors that follow from these beliefs.[9]

The Question of Integration.   Each perspective recognizes work as an important integrating mechanism. Each perceives work as important for both the individual and for society. However, there are many areas of disagreement. Should society provide jobs and force people to work when the market system cannot use the labor force profitably? Should the social welfare system provide unemployment benefits, minimal welfare payments, or social services to help the unemployed readjust, or should it use some combination of these methods? Under which conditions will society be the most integrated, or at least minimally alienated? The social problems created by widespread alienation can be more costly than relief programs. How can a society provide work opportunities for everyone under conditions that increase societal integration?

Mutual Aid

Mutual aid is as old as society itself. There is some evidence to suggest that in the animal kingdom, the species that survive are not necessarily the most powerful, but rather those most able to cooperate with one another.[10] It is not possible for humans to grow, develop, and make the most of their potential without support from other people. We need affection, approval, food, shelter, and clothing. We require exchanges of support, goods, and services.

This reality contradicts individualism, a value cherished by most Americans. If one were to believe a typical history text, we have all descended from rugged pioneers who were totally self-sufficient. The reality is very different. Life on the frontier was difficult; a community spirit was required for mere survival. In pioneer days communities banded together to hire a community doctor, to build homes, to gather crops, and to survive the hardships of bitterly cold winters.

As our society became increasingly complex, we have become increasingly interdependent. With each technological advance, the proportion of essential survival functions an individual can accomplish single-handedly decreases. Yet we continue to idealize the rugged individualist, to the detriment of the social welfare system. We do not have a comprehensive, well-planned social welfare system because we continue to believe that:

1. The best people are physically strong, psychologically independent, and able to flourish without help.
2. "Making it" is what counts.
3. Everything is possible if you try hard enough.
4. Money is the prime human motivator. Self-fulfillment as an end in itself is idealistic, or at least unrealistic.

These add up to the belief that those who fail to succeed are at least incompetent, and more likely, lazy or immoral. If one's life does not go well, there is no one to blame but oneself.[11]

The Functionalist Perspective.   The mutual aid function is appropriate to all private and public organizations that have a primary concern for both the well-being of the individual and society as a whole. Everyone's daily life is directly or indirectly dependent on and subsidized by government; everyone benefits from the support of governmental and nongovernmental social welfare.[12] This leads to a broader look at the relationship between our tax

The Amish survive as a group through community spirit.

system and the mutual aid or benefit system. It requires seeing the total governmental structure as being of benefit to all citizens and necessary to maintain social order. The federal structure is a necessity for the survival of democracy. Since everyone benefits from having this structure, everyone must share the responsibility for supporting it.

Senator Fritz Hollings, a contender for the Democratic presidential nomination in 1984, gave an example of how much people benefit from government and how easily they forget the source of the benefit.

> A veteran returning from Korea went to college on the GI Bill, bought his house with an FHA loan, saw his kids born in a VA hospital, started a business with an SBA loan, got electricity from the TVA and, later, water from an EPA project. His parents retired to a farm on Social Security, got electricity from REA, and soil testing from USDA. When the father became ill, the family was saved from financial ruin by Medicare, and a life was saved with a drug developed through NIH. His kids participated in the school lunch program, learned physics from teachers trained in an NSF program, and went to college

with guaranteed student loans. He drove to work on the interstate and moored his boat in a channel dredged by Army engineers. When floods hit, he took Amtrak to Washington to apply for disaster relief, and spent some time in the Smithsonian museums. Then one day he wrote his congressman an angry letter asking the government to get off his back and complaining about paying taxes for all those programs created for ungrateful people.[13]

The Conflict Perspective.   Even though many cultures value achievement, the United States is unusual in its victimization of "underachievers." We blame the victim for losing a sense of worth and strength. We then develop a profession such as social work to reintegrate the individual and rebuild a sense of worth. Victims of the economic system or other social problems often suffer a loss of confidence. If victims of a downturn in the economic cycle had the courage to reject the blame and fight for their economic security, government would more likely respond humanely to their problems. As long as social workers help them adjust rather than fight back, they are part of the problem.

Policy Questions.   How should the mutual aid system be financed? Who should pay? Who should benefit? Government confers tremendous benefits on all of us; without taxes there would be few schools, no roads, no garbage pickup. Is the mutual support function designed with the poor as beneficiaries?

SUMMARY

At the outset of this chapter we suggested that every society must meet the essential social functions. We discussed how the political, economic, religious, educational, and familial institutions have a relatively clear relationship to each of the essential social functions. The social welfare institution, on the other hand, does not generate the same consensus about its appropriate function. Diverse views of what the social welfare institution actually does and what it should do, and correspondingly diverse views of the state are related to diverse assumptions about people, their rights, and their responsibilities. The complexity of social work's relationship to the broader social structure suggests some reasons social work does not always receive support commensurate with the importance of the problems it must address.

As we discussed societal institutions, structures, and processes, you might have felt that this material is only relevant to administrators and policymakers, but not to those going into direct practice. For this reason, we have chosen to show how the concepts explained in this chapter contribute to the social work knowledge base.

To apply this knowledge we have chosen to show how these issues impact on women and their relationship to the work force. We show: (1) how social control mechanisms (societal and organizational) impact on women's

Correctional officers frequently counsel prison inmates.

ability to support themselves and their families; (2) how widely held beliefs and habits make career success for women more difficult to attain; and (3) how understanding this phenomenon leads to sound practice interventions.

This example should convince you of the importance of social structure to clients' individual functioning. Many of the concepts introduced in this case study will become even clearer as we discuss psychosocial functioning in Chapter 11.

The case study chosen might pertain either to a social worker who is helping a female correctional officer deal with stress or a prison administrator who wants to make career advancement a reality for women. Before beginning our case study, however, we review some of the political realities for women in the work place and social work's commitment to them.

From the earliest days of the Charity Organization Society, social work has been concerned with the poor and powerless. Originally the recipients of social work efforts were immigrants, unemployed men, and widows. It is only within the last twenty years that social work has recognized women as a substantial part of the poor and powerless, and further, that their poverty was rooted in the institutional structure of our society.

Elaine Norman and Arlene Mancuso identify three sources of discrimination against women:

1. the denial of equal access to the opportunity structure of the society;
2. the stigmatization of women by definitions of them as inferior to men and then the use of that stigma as an explanation and rationalization for the denial of equal access to the society's opportunity structure; and,

Although social work has been called a "woman's profession," female workers have not paid particular attention to the issues of women as clients.

3. the sense of helplessness in women created by this stigma, which translates into behaviors that suggest lack of confidence, ability, or capacity to effect changes in themselves or in the systems that oppress them.[14]

The historical patterns of inequity in education, employment, and salary have made women much more dependent on welfare than men. Women are six times more likely than men to be poor. Thirty-five percent of female-headed households are poor, while only six percent of male-headed households are poor.[15] Diana DiNitto and Thomas Dye identify eight reasons why women earn less than men.

1. Traditionally, many women have not been the major wage earners in the home.
2. The wages of working women have been considered as secondary to their husband's wages.
3. Women have been considered temporary employees who would leave their jobs to marry and have children.
4. Women's paid work has been considered as extracurricular activity to fill free time.
5. Women have had fewer opportunities for education that would lead to better-paying jobs.
6. Women have been forced to accept jobs that do not conflict with family schedules.
7. Career-oriented women have been thought of as selfish or neglectful of their families.
8. "Women's work"—cleaning, child rearing—are not wage-earning jobs.[16]

One professional career track that has become more accessible to women in the past decade is working in correctional institutions, which had been considered a male bastion for many years. Correctional institutions provide an excellent example of the unique pressures women experience as they move into roles which have been defined and held by men.

CASE STUDY
Women as Correctional Officers

Women have experienced less success than men as correctional officers (COs).[1] Several explanations have been offered as to why this is true. Some people suggest that women are unable to handle the stress and pressure associated with the role and are unwilling to compete with male officers for recognition and promotions. Such reasoning, known as "blaming the victim," justifies management's neglect of the careers of female officers. Here we examine variables related to success in the officer's role, and suggest contingencies under which women are likely to experience resistance, failure, and potentially, emotional transference with inmates.

---

[1] Women's failure has been explained as a combination of biology and psychology. Structural causes have been largely ignored.

NEW TECHNOLOGY/NEW PROBLEMS

The prison industry has undergone significant changes in technology over the last decade.[2] Structural changes have been incorporated to fulfill the safety, security, and biological needs of inmates, and COs are increasingly expected to contribute to the inmates' psychological growth. The technology has become more treatment oriented. These architectural and program changes have been concurrent with women entering the ranks of COs. Clearly, the movement to a human relations approach and the breaking down of employment barriers for women have had a positive effect on the prison environment. However, both of these advances have created a new set of management problems.

New technologies such as podular/direct supervision facilities can lead to emotional transference for officers.[3] The COs' loyalties can shift from organizational goals to over-identification with individual prisoner needs. As a society, we find many of our personal needs increasingly being met in the workplace, whereas they used to be met by family, church, and neighborhoods. Officers are told to "keep their personal life out of the institution." However, needs unmet by traditional support systems will frequently be met at the workplace. Therefore, managers must understand that these needs will either be met by competent management and peer camaraderie, or the CO will be susceptible to manipulation by inmates.

The social context of a prison presents unique difficulties for women officers. Women are more likely to be affected by emotional transference not because of inner traits, but because sensitive management and peer camaraderie are less likely to be available to women, at the same time that personal pressures are likely to be greater. Role theory and the socialization process provide a framework to understand why it is difficult for women to succeed in the role of CO.

ROLE THEORY AND THE SOCIALIZATION PROCESS

Socialization is the process through which individuals acquire the knowledge, skills, and values that enable them to participate effectively in the social interactions of the group. Social integration takes place primarily through social interaction with people who are significant for the individual. Research suggests that the best predictor of both job satisfaction and happiness for women is self-image and perceived support for her role.[17]

To understand the process of socialization is to see the development of self as a process, continuously created and recreated in each social situation one enters. New roles are taken up, expectations learned and identities assumed. While the CO position is conferred upon the woman by the hiring authority, her identity as a CO is socially bestowed, socially sustained, and socially transformed—it is bestowed in acts of social recognition.[4] Thus, a critical variable in the socialization of women into officer roles is not so much the woman's view of herself but the acts of social recognition (acceptance) demonstrated in the relevant social circle. COs tend to be cliquish; breaking into relevent networks usually places an unfair burden on women attempting to achieve success in officer positions—a burden not usually felt by men in equivalent positions. The person most easily accepted is not usually the most qualified, but rather the most like the predecessor or traditional officers. We are all more comfortable with people we feel are "just like us." Part of the selection (informal) process seems to be closely related to the maintenance of the status quo. Women have cracked the formal system but now have to break into the informal system. Male officers tend to see women as trespassers on their turf.

To become involved in a social role a person must develop relationships with other people in the social circle. Hence, the social circle itself is instrumental in achieving successful role performance. To facilitate the acquisition of the officer role for women, we need to change the social context. To understand the social circles surrounding female COs, some consideration must be given to the structure in which these positions exist.

PRISONS: THE CONTEXT

The prison system ranks right up there with the Jaycees and Elks Clubs in its determination to avoid in-

---

[2] Technology is the method by which the goods or services are produced.

[3] In podular facilities each unit or pod is self-contained.

[4] Women cannot function effectively until they are accepted by other officers.

filtration by women. As of June 30, 1984, only 11 percent of the custody/security staff in confinement facilities were women. Women constitute 8 percent of the custody/security staff in male facilities and 71 percent in female facilities.[18]

The role of the CO is very complex. An officer is the lowest-level employee, yet a manager. The CO is managed by a system of regulations and controls from above, but officers also manage the inmates who are in their charge. The CO is a low-status worker in interactions with the warden and other front-office personnel, but a higher-status manager in interaction with inmates. There is no real counterpart in the business or industrial world. Conflicting roles make the CO's job especially difficult to learn. They are responsible for keeping convicts peacefully confined, supervising prisoners who have no loyalty to the organization. Yet they have few incentives to offer the prisoners. They are to contribute to inmate rehabilitation by being nondirective and showing concern for personal problems, but they are also expected to act as police, protecting inmates from each other and fellow officers from inmates. Finally, they are to keep inmates busy at maintenance, housekeeping, and production tasks, to administer justice, and to ensure that escapes do not occur.

COs, especially in large maximum-security prisons, develop informal rules that govern their behavior. These rules are likely to deviate considerably from the formal rules of the organization. There is a widely held belief among COs that administration cannot be depended on to support custody staff. "They" do not understand what line staff experience in controlling inmates and therefore design policies that make the CO's job unnecessarily difficult. This attitude can cause COs to develop a "be loyal to the team" approach in which line staff protect each other from the administration. However, as the technology of the prison has changed, officers have less contact with each other and more with prisoners. Therefore, they become vulnerable to forming attachments with inmates.

This vulnerability is exacerbated for female officers because peer camaraderie is more difficult to obtain. To achieve this sense of being part of a group, the female officer must feel wanted by the group and must see the group as approachable. If she works in a male-only prison, 89 percent of her colleagues will be men. Many of these men may view women co-workers as unacceptable. Their feelings range from concern with how women will redefine the officer role to fear that women will not be able to back them up in an emergency. The female officer quickly receives the message that the reference (work) group she is trying to be a part of does not see her as valuable in terms of the work to be done. Further complications are engendered if experienced officers view her as a potential sex partner. This sets up a destructive cycle whereby she does not find the experienced people approachable and therefore socialization into the CO role does not take place.

Trust, liking, and respect are important components of approachability. Socialization into the role of CO requires the new recruit to approach and interact with other officers. For women, what should be a source of reassurance becomes a source of intimidation.

Much of peer camaraderie takes place through after hours socialization. Women quickly become aware that many decisions are made during "happy hour," not working hours. Men cement their working relationships in after hours sports activities. Basketball or baseball leagues, bowling teams, fishing or hunting trips, and just stopping for a drink allow male officers to develop trust and caring relationships. These activities are functional both for the officers and for the institution, but tend not to be available to the woman officer. Women are formally denied access to the organized activities and informally denied access to the after work gatherings. Even in the 1990s, wives tend to feel very differently about stopping for a drink with the boys than about stopping in mixed company. Women know that such behavior quickly becomes grist for the rumor mill, and that male officers are likely to misinterpret their behavior.

Everything we have said up to this point could in some instances be applied to either men or women. Clearly, there are men who do not fit into the traditional role set of COs and experience some of the same problems we have identified. Not all men are athletic or enjoy frequenting the local pub. However, there are additional complexities that women must face. In order to examine and clarify the conflicts of a woman successfully adapting to the CO role, we adopt a systems model to analyze the complexity of the multiple roles in which the woman finds herself.

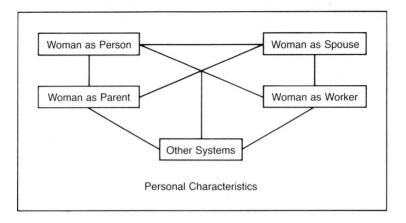

FIGURE 9–1
The Career Woman: A Systems Model (Quam-Macht)

A SYSTEMS MODEL

A system is defined as a complex of elements directly or indirectly related in a causal network, such that each component is related to some others in a more or less stable way within any particular period of time.[5] To fully understand the difficulties women experience, it is necessary to understand the intricacies of the ways in which women maintain a dynamic balance between the competing, conflicting, and cooperating parts of their personal life system. Analysis of these competing elements in a woman's life provides important interventive knowledge: (1) we can understand why women are more vulnerable to emotional transference, and (2) we can develop guidelines to identify where and when individual women may need additional support. This systems framework can be used in many different occupational settings.

There is always the danger that in learning more about the stresses women suffer, we will be providing the rationale for limiting women's opportunity. We believe that we have progressed to the point where we recognize women make an essential contribution to normalizing institutions and that their contributions are not the same as men's, but are equally valuable. Traditional officer roles have

been consistent with male roles; progressive institutions require the unique contributions of both male and female roles. This analysis addresses problems unique to women.

A basic premise of systems theory is that the whole is greater than the sum of its parts. Therefore, we want to look at the woman in her role as spouse, mother, person, and worker to see how each of these roles impacts on other elements in the system. For instance, lack of adequate child care can have a significant impact on all the other systems through marital strain, less than maximum performance on the job, job dissatisfaction, and feelings of inadequacy and guilt.

In Figure 9–1, four major systems of the career woman are presented (woman as person, as parent, as spouse, and as worker). Obviously, not all women are parents or spouses. In addition to these systems, there is a variety of other systems unique to each individual, such as woman as volunteer, as friend, as civic leader, or as daughter. There are also personal characteristics such as race, age, intelligence, and income, and environmental variables such as neighborhood and area of the country, all of which make up the life experience of the CO. While all of these variables affect the woman, we concentrate our discussion on the impact of the four major variables. This is an example of a general theory about women that we are using to make an application to women in a specific setting.

---

[5] A systems approach is an essential part of the social work frame of reference, as discussed in Chapter 3.

DIAGNOSTIC QUESTIONS

Woman as Person

1. Past socialization: What roles did her parents teach her would make her happy? What role models has she observed, and what attitudes and behaviors were reinforced, in her school, her neighborhood, and among friends? Is she feeling guilty about taking a "man's" job?

2. Learned coping patterns: What is her ability to handle stress, anxiety, and failure?

3. What are her goals and aspirations—her determination to pursue a career, her desire to have children?

4. Support networks: Are family and friends available to her? Do they provide support or discouragement?

5. Personal characteristics: What are her interpersonal skills, education, unique aptitudes?

6. Health: Premenstrual syndrome (P.M.S.), pregnancy, hysterectomy, and menopause can all affect a woman's vulnerability to transference.

Woman as Person

Research has consistently documented the second class position of women in all areas of society. This is evidenced dramatically in the field of corrections. Despite increased numbers of women entering the field and antidiscrimination legislation, women continue to earn less and advance more slowly in the field. Women make up 20 percent of the work force in correctional facilities, and almost one third of these women are in clerical positions. Only 17 percent of all administrative positions are filled by women.[19]

This inferior position of females is not a phenomenon confined to adulthood. Research with young girls has shown that they have lower levels of aspiration than boys and higher degrees of anxiety about the possibility of failure. So, in addition to entering a field that is dominated by male role models, the woman also brings with her early socialization patterns that tend to produce a negative self-concept. It should also be pointed out that few COs have more than a high school education and that they tend to come from families with very traditional gender role models.

Therefore, it is unlikely that female officers have received much support from either family or the educational system to pursue their nontraditional work role.

Although it is impossible to consider all facets of a woman's development as a person, the woman as person system would minimally include certain elements of which the social worker or manager should be cognizant, as shown in the diagnostic questions.

Woman as Spouse

Relationships create both strains and supports for the working woman. Husbands, live-in partners, and homosexual lovers all have a strong impact on a woman's ability to function maximally on the job. (However, research has been confined to married couples.) Research findings conflict on whether employment contributes to or disrupts marital adjustment. Some studies have found a positive relationship between women's employment and marital adjustment, while others have found that husbands of working wives express less happiness in their marriages. A husband's behavior and attitudes are critical to the success of a career woman. Some research indicates that women resolve conflicts by minimizing their own desires and conforming to their husband's expectations, while other research shows that the husband of a working woman is less likely to be

DIAGNOSTIC QUESTIONS

Woman as Spouse

1. How long has she been in this relationship?
2. Is she satisfied with the relationship?
3. What pressures does the relationship present?
4. Does she have support in the relationship?
5. What is the occupation of the spouse/lover? What income and job demands does it present?
6. What is her view of woman's role?
7. Does she have extended family involvement and expectations?
8. Does she share family responsibilities?
9. Does she have a friendship network with other couples?

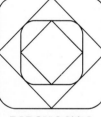

DIAGNOSTIC QUESTIONS

Woman as Worker

1. Has the proper role socialization taken place?
2. Is there flexibility that might be built into the position without compromising organizational needs?
3. Are there peer support groups that can support the officer's achievement goals?
4. Can the officer share personal problems with the supervisor without having it reflect negatively on job evaluations?
5. Is it clear to the officer that she is not to share her personal problems with inmates?
6. Is the officer becoming too protective of or "mothering" to certain inmates?
7. Has the officer identified a reference group with whom she feels she has personal and family problems in common?
8. Is the woman geographically mobile? This can have a great impact on her motivation, because upward mobility in corrections frequently requires willingness to relocate. Traditional families seldom move so that the woman can pursue employment opportunities.

concerned with power and more willing to share family roles equally with his wife. We would suggest that a husband's way of integrating family and work in his own life is crucial for the wife's career success.

The woman as spouse system directs you to be aware of more variables, as the diagnostic questions show.

Woman as Worker

Throughout this case study we have developed the premise that being a CO requires taking on unique roles. COs tend to be caught between the role of technician, which requires the individual to apply technical knowledge repeatedly in identical or similar situations, and that of professional, which re-

DIAGNOSTIC QUESTIONS

Woman as Parent

1. What are the number, age, and sex of children?
2. Are child care arrangements satisfactory?
3. How many parenting roles does the woman carry out? What is her attitude toward those roles?
4. Does she have available role models for her dual role?
5. Is she in contact with other mothers who are officers?
6. Does she have adequate parenting skills?
7. What are her feelings about societal expectations of a mother?
8. What kinds of pressure does she experience from supervisors and co-workers when she needs pregnancy leave or sick leave to care for her children?

quires a knowledge base, intelligence, and judgment. We have also pointed out how the work setting makes it more difficult for a woman to adopt the officer role. In the work setting she differs from her peers because she has a different socialization experience and does not have access to their peer support groups outside the work place. She also differs from many of the working women in her social status, who are more likely to be clerical workers. The diagnostic questions identify still more elements of particular significance.

Woman as Parent

The presence of children brings an additional dimension to a working woman's life. In fact, children are a major factor in determining whether or not a woman will work outside of the home. The necessity of placing children in alternative care situations can lead to role strain and guilt. For every study that shows that children learn independence when their mothers work, the working mother is likely to read an article that contends that children are harmed if their mothers work. The working mother who obtains satisfaction from her work and who has adequate arrangements to minimize strain in her dual role is likely to function maximally on the job.

The woman as parent system requires consideration of the elements shown in the diagnostic questions.

This systems framework will help you understand and analyze more completely the complexities that working women face. We have used the prison setting for our example, but the diagnostic questions can guide the problem assessment when you work with women in other employment settings.

Today assumptions about women's work being extracurricular activity have been widely challenged. Few women have the luxury of working simply for enjoyment. Most women work to support their children, either as a single parent or as an essential economic contributor to a two parent family. Although women frequently take temporary jobs, this tends not to be by choice. Most women want and need jobs in the primary labor force that provide a decent income, fringe benefits, and job security.

NOTES

1. C. Little, *Understanding Deviance and Control* (Itasca, Ill.: Peacock, 1983), 5.
2. N. Gilbert and H. Specht, *Dimensions of Social Welfare Policy* (Englewood Cliffs, N.J.: Prentice-Hall, 1974), 5.
3. R. Lekachman, Guest Editorial, *American Spectator* 15, 12 (December 1982): 1.
4. W. Ryan, *Equality* (New York: Pantheon, 1981), 122.
5. S. Bowles, "Unequal Education and the Social Division of Labor," *The Review of Radical Political Economics* 3, 4 (Fall–Winter 1971): 38–66.
6. J. Freeman, "The Building of the Gilded Cage," *The Second Wave: A Magazine of the New Feminism* 1, 1 (Spring 1971).
7. L. Mead, "Social Programs and Social Obligations," *The Public Interest* No. 69 (Fall 1981).
8. Ibid.
9. F. Piven and R. Cloward, *Regulating the Poor* (New York: Pantheon, 1971), 341–348.
10. P. Kropotkin, *Mutual Aid: A Factor of Evolution* (New York: Knopf, 1925), 293.
11. R. Dolgoff and D. Feldstein, *Understanding Social Welfare*, 2nd ed. (New York: Harper, 1984), 5–6.
12. B. Compton, *Introduction to Social Welfare and Social Work* (Homewood, Ill.: Dorsey Press, 1980), 14.
13. Quoted by George F. Will in *Newsweek* (20 December 1982): 92.
14. E. Norman and A. Mancuso, *Women's Issues and Social Work Practice* (Itasca, Ill.: Peacock, 1980), 3.
15. U.S. Bureau of the Census statistics cited in *The World Almanac and Book of Facts 1981* (New York: Newspaper Enterprise Association, 1981), 250.
16. D. DiNitto and T. Dye, *Social Welfare Politics and Public Policy* (Englewood Cliffs, N.J.: Prentice-Hall, 1983), 20.
17. M. Horner, "Fail: Bright Women," *Psychology Today* 3, 6 (1969).
18. Bureau of Justice Statistics, *1984 Census of State Adult Correctional Facilities*, Report NCJ-103957 (Washington, D.C.: Government Printing Office, April 1987), 7.
19. Ibid.

Chapter

10

Bureaucratic Structure and Social Welfare Organizations

One poignant message of the past decade, and perhaps decades before that, has been the power and pervasiveness of big organizations. To many of us they seem to dominate and control our lives.... If some control over organizations is to occur, then we first need to understand the hows and whys of organizational behavior.... But beyond the idea of simple protection is another reason why the study of organizations is essential: most of our major objectives are accomplished in the context of one or more organizations.[1]

In the preceding chapter we discussed the social structure and how the need for social order affects the social welfare system, social workers, and clients. In this chapter we look at the structure of the social welfare system. Bureaucracy is the structure most common to the system; bureaucratic structures provide both limits and opportunities for social workers. You can maximize these opportunities by learning how to be a good bureaucrat and a good colleague. Bureaucratic structures do not have to be inhumane. As individuals we all have the obligation to humanize our workplaces.

After discussing the intraorganizational structure of social services, we move on to interorganizational structure, that is, examination of the relationship between agencies. Clients are frequently caught in what they experience as a maze when they try to get needed services.

Clients often have to deal with a case manager to receive their financial assistance, a work development agency to find employment, social services and perhaps a day care center to find adequate care for their children, a vocational school, physicians, public health agencies, and perhaps others. All of these agencies may be providing services to the same family, sometimes even to one person. Social workers are often called upon to do case management, which means coordinating the needed services. Understanding interorganizational relationships is critical to the success of this role.

Finally, we present an unfortunate but true case of bureaucratic bungling that had dire consequences. Our goal in this chapter is once again to present knowledge that is essential to social work practice.

SOCIAL WORKERS AND BUREAUCRACY

Social workers learn to be enablers, facilitators, brokers, mediators, resource developers, and even teachers. One role they are seldom academically prepared for but will have to fill is that of bureaucrat. Social workers, particularly educators, resist the role of bureaucrat and fail to prepare students to fill this role effectively. When bureaucracy is discussed in the social work literature, it is usually in the context of conflict between professional and agency goals or the relationship of bureaucracy to professional burn-out.

This attitude toward bureaucracy and organizations in general creates a serious void in the preparation of social workers. Effective social work practice requires the ability to deal effectively and efficiently with organizational demands—a task as demanding as any of the other social work tasks. Pruger defines a skilled bureaucrat as a person who can manage the organizational environment in a manner that maximizes her ability to meet the requirements of the professional role.[2] In spite of what we might like to believe, formal organizations are necessary for a human service delivery system. Therefore, it is wise for social work students to acquire a theoretical and empirical basis for understanding organizational life.

BUREAUCRACY

Bureaucracy is more than a matter of structure. The quality and capabilities of the people who do the work are part of the equation. They can be more or less influential depending on how well the organizational environment is understood. Unfortunately, little serious effort has been given to the task of defining the needed expertise. . . . With good reasons many people distrust complex organizations, but to behave ineptly seems hardly more praiseworthy or useful. If social workers must be bureaucrats—and they must—they might as well be good ones.[3]

Just like societies, organizations must have order—a means of making actions within an organization predictable. Without organization, we have chaos. Different kinds of social organizations have different ways to keep order. The structure and control mechanism that works successfully in a family would not work well in a social welfare agency.

Within a social welfare agency, structure must provide for predictable unit activities and predictable relations within units. In other words, the intake worker needs to be able to predict how each unit will respond to the referrals it receives. The receiving unit also needs to know what the expectations are about how it will handle its referrals.

Max Weber was a German sociologist and political economist who first described the model of bureaucracy.

Max Weber (1864–1920), the intellectual father of bureaucracy, argued that the bureaucratic structure would survive all other forms because it was more efficient. There is some evidence of truth to this statement, particularly in the evolution of service delivery systems.[4] Although charismatic leaders may have been adequate in pre-industrial times, they could not provide adequate structure for the large organizations that evolved with industrialization. At the turn of the 19th century the great man theory had to be replaced by a system that could make operations more predictable and systematic. The bureaucratic structure was more efficient than systems based on custom or trust, and it often improved conditions for employees as well. Before the rise of bureaucracy managers had absolute power; workers had no recourse to other authority. As jobs became more complex, workers gained power and made demands. Rather than being a curse upon the work force, bureaucracy was a movement toward rationality and predictability; rules protected as well as guided workers. The essential characteristics of the ideal bureaucratic organization developed by Weber encompass six major components: (1) a specific division of labor, (2) hierarchy, (3) centralization, and (4) formalization; in addition, (5) employment constitutes a career, and (6) hiring and promotion are based on merit.

The great man theory held that organizations were best run by a strong, charismatic leader, rather than an administrative system.

Social workers frequently find themselves working in agencies with a visible bureaucratic structure. There is a clear division of labor among administrators, supervisors, social workers, income maintenance workers, and clerical staff. In some agencies the social workers themselves will specialize in protective services, older adults, or families, for example. The hierarchy is usually well defined and frequently discourages any exchange between the lower and upper levels without "going through channels." Social service agencies tend to be complex; formalization does not always simplify procedures. Writing in the 19th century, Weber visualized assembly line industries and less complex governmental agencies than today's social service agencies. Although Weber identified the importance of structure and the distribution of power in an organization, he was unable to address these variables in a manner that can guide the worker in the current multipurpose social service agencies.

To summarize, bureaucracy can be said to minimize or at least regulate the influence any one individual can have on an organization. It is also an important means by which individuals are made to conform to organizational needs. Structure is the setting in which power is exercised, decisions are made, and actions are carried out.

Even with its flaws bureaucracy has adapted and survived. Weber was correct: to date we have not developed a more efficient structure to replace it. Since this is the situation, social workers can benefit by becoming good bureaucrats. Robert Pruger's essay, "The Good Bureaucrat," offers social workers some concrete, constructive suggestions for combining effectiveness with survival in formal organization. In this section we draw heavily upon his work to help prepare good bureaucrats.

Many social service departments are housed in county courthouses.

Staying Power

The first requisite of a good bureaucrat is staying power. There is no way a social worker can achieve his goals if he does not stay in the agency long enough to bring his ideas to fruition. While it may give him a sense of power and righteousness to resign in protest, it also removes the power to make change. Though resignation may sometimes be in order, it should only be used when other avenues have been exhausted.

The social worker may fail to realize how much power and discretion she actually has. Some workers deal with the complexity and strain of their job by believing and acting as if there were no choice involved — only rules to follow. Formal organizations tend to tolerate this behavior, and so it is up to the individual to preserve and enlarge the discretionary aspects of the position. Complex organizations can provide workers with an excuse to become mere bureaucrats with little creativity or motivation to use the organization effectively to meet service goals.

Pruger provides a prescription for workers to preserve their options and expand their careers. The first step is to understand legitimate authority and organizational enforcement. On the most basic level, this suggests avoiding behavior that would lead to dismissal. Nearly every organization has a manual of published rules, laws, job descriptions, and work schedules. The statements define behaviors that are prescribed, permitted, and proscribed. Since these rules govern a variety of potential situations, they are by necessity general. Most dimensions of a social worker's job are beyond advance specification; it is not only undesirable but also impossible to tell social workers in advance what decisions they will have to face or what interventions will be most effective.

Organizations are also limited in their ability to observe an employee's behavior closely, because close supervision is costly. And even if an agency could afford intensive supervision, it would be unlikely to do so because of the potential demoralization of staff. The more professional the staff, the more negative the effect of inappropriately close supervision. Professionals are trained to use professional judgment and resent incursion into their domain of expertise. Since the limitation of surveillance on staff is a fact of organizational life, most workers do have choices and can make discretionary decisions. The good bureaucrat can make the most of his potential for achievement if he understands legitimate authority and how the organization can or is likely to enforce authority.

Conserving Energy

Pruger also suggests that the good bureaucrat will conserve energy. Two ways that workers waste energy are in feeling sorry for themselves for being overworked and underpaid, and by complaining about what they see as needless paperwork. Successful organizational members do not expect their actions to be constantly noted and rewarded but instead develop an internal reward system that provides reinforcement for the knowledge that the job was well done. The worker who disciplines her need to win recognition from higher officials increases her freedom to take initiative, promote ideas, and generally engage in creative behavior.

Indispensability

Two final suggestions from Pruger include making oneself indispensable to the agency and not yielding unnecessarily to the requirements of administrative convenience. Workers become indispensable when they have a skill or competence needed by the organization. This could be proposal writing, community organization, political acumen, budgeting, or any other skill essential to effective agency functioning. Related to these skills is the necessity to make certain the skill is used to fulfill the organizational mission and not just to benefit the organization. Particularly in times of fiscal constraint, agencies suffer from goal displacement—the survival needs of the agency tend to overwhelm and steal the efforts that should be expended toward the organization's mission. Robert Scott relates how this happened in a sheltered workshop for the blind. The workshop got caught up in turning a profit and started competing with private industry for the best blind workers when they were supposed to be helping the unemployed blind acquire skills to gain employment.[5]

FIGURE 10–1
Bureaucratic units usually have specifically assigned duties.

Director of Community Services

Services to Seniors	Chemical Dependency	Community Resources	Management And Planning	Mental Health	Mental Retardation	Family Services	Services to Handicapped
Adult Services	Detoxification	Day Care Licensing	Accounting	County Mental Health Center	Case Monitoring	Child Welfare	Volunteer Services
Home Management	Access Programs	Foster Care Recruiting and Licensing	Staff Training	Pilot City Mental Health Center	Case Management	Child Welfare Payments	Case Monitoring
Adult Protection	Outpatient Treatment	Adult and Child Placement	Computer Services	Prepetition Screening	Community Programs	Group Work	Decentralized Information and Referral
	Residential Treatment	Purchase of Service	Planning	Nursing Home/ Board and Care Consultation	Developmental Achievement Services	Court Unit	Indian Counseling
	Methadone and Antabuse	Centralized Verification for Day Care	Administrative Support	Contracted Outpatient Services		Purchased Social Services	Emergency Food and Shelter
	Chronic Case Management	Employability Services	Research & Evaluation	Residential Mental Health Services		Homemaker/ Chore	Representative Payee Coordination
			Systems Development	Day Treatment Programs		Day Care	Disability Assistance Appeals
			Word Processing	Circle F		Emergency Shelter	Services to the Handicapped
			Human Services Councils	Vocational Services			Borderline Retarded
							Physically Handicapped
							Hearing Impaired
							Visually Handicapped
							Adults in Need of Supportive Services

THE HUMAN ELEMENT IN BUREAUCRACIES

Thus far we have discussed characteristics found in formal organizations and offered some suggestions on how to be more effective working in a bureaucracy. This is a sound basis for the beginning social worker, but it is important to address at least briefly the human element in organizations and what decision makers need to know about dealing with workers. Social workers who become either supervisors or industrial social workers will need to study these questions in considerable depth. But every worker can contribute to making the work setting more supportive of individual growth. This brief discussion of human needs in the bureaucracy is meant to make students more effective and more empathetic co-workers in whatever setting they choose to use their skills.

The existential perspective suggests that one can only be happy in a job that one sees as being meaningful.

One of the most basic needs in a work setting is a need for meaning, a need addressed in psychology by theorists such as Frankl.[6] Since working, especially for professionals, encompasses so much of one's life, it would be difficult for a professional to have a sense of meaning in life without experiencing a sense of purpose or direction in the workplace. The degree to which one's professional work creates meaning for life is reflected in how frequently professional and personal relationships overlap. It is not unusual for doctors, lawyers, or social workers to prefer to socialize with other members of their profession. Much to the dismay of spouses, professional talk frequently permeates social gatherings. Though outsiders may be bored to tears, such shop talk reflects the degree to which an occupation or career gives meaning to life.

In Chapter 2 we discussed the concept of equifinality, that there is more than one way to achieve a goal.

People also desire a sense of conrol over life and particularly over work tasks. The need for control can be met by providing workers with options on how to achieve the outcomes expected by the agency. Allowing the workers to choose the method to be used can increase their sense of control. Even as co-workers we can reinforce an individual's sense of control by respecting and appreciating methods different from our own. Keeping things simple despite pressure to complicate matters also increases a sense of control. As we move deeper into the computer age, there is overwhelming pressure to gather marginal data that may be useful, because data can be easily stored and retrieved. To the social worker interested in dealing with human problems, unnecessary paper shuffling can decrease both the sense of control and the meaningfulness of work.

We all need to view ourselves as winners. A person labeled a loser begins to act like one. Too many administrators feel that people, especially bureaucrats, are lazy and will only produce if the system is designed to punish them for inactivity. One of the most well-grounded principles of behaviorism is that people are more likely to respond to positive reinforcement than to punishment. In spite of this many work settings concentrate on punishing errors and ignoring success. While Pruger is correct in suggesting that social workers should not waste energy feeling low because their accomplishments are not recognized, they may profitably spend time building their own reward mechanisms and providing reinforcement for co-workers.

PRACTICE PRINCIPLES

Bureaucracy

1. With all of its flaws, the bureaucratic structure has survived because it is the most functional structure for large organizations.
2. Recognize and use the power and discretion this structure allows.
3. Do not waste energy on what cannot be changed. Work hard for constructive change.
4. Develop the skills needed and appreciated by your agency.
5. Value the humanness of your co-workers.

Bureaucracy: A Summary

This discussion is meant to motivate you to study bureaucracy with the purpose of improving your practice. The practice principles summarize key points for social workers in bureaucratic agencies.

INTERORGANIZATIONAL STRUCTURE

It is important to examine formal organizations from another perspective—how they affect clients and client services. Understanding bureaucratic structures improves the professional's ability to increase the responsiveness of the service delivery system. Bureaucratic organizations present opportunities and obstacles for the professional, make possible a broad array of services for clients, and create considerable frustration for many clients. As professionals it is our obligation to decrease this frustration by making service organizations responsive to client needs.

Providing social services requires a service delivery system: a set of organizations that can obtain resources from the environment, transform those resources into programs and services, and deliver them to the client. Few people truly believe neighborhoods and churches can provide for the social and economic needs of our society. If we were to have a totally integrated service system, it would be sufficiently powerful to generate adequate resources and deliver them humanely and efficiently to all those in need.

Coordination of Human Services

Benson and others suggest several important attributes of a coordinated service delivery system.[7]

1. A coordinated system provides legally available services with minimal delay and red tape. Clients receive services to which they are legally entitled without undue waiting and stigmatization.

2. Services should not be denied because of inefficiency or rigidity of the service network. Interagency squabbles or lack of cooperation should not be reflected in client services.

3. Clients should get the full range of entitled services and expertise regardless of where they enter the network. For instance, if a woman enters the service network through a referral to protective services for leaving her children unattended, she should still receive child care services even if it requires going to another agency. This same woman may also need a different job; she should also be referred to job service for available employment. In a coordinated service delivery system, all of the necessary services would be made available regardless of which agency made the first contact.

4. Problems should be handled comprehensively and coherently. In addition to providing all the necessary services, services need to be delivered in a manner and sequence that the client understands.

Obstacles Clients May Face

Serious gaps in the delivery system do tend to occur, and some of the most needy go unaided. Service gaps tend to arise from four primary sources: lack of coordination, unclear program articulation, inflexibility of program requirements, and absence of needed services. Conditions necessary to overcome the gaps in service and to develop a coordinated network of services include a high degree of interaction between agencies, clear articulation of the services and boundaries of each program, and a certain degree of flexibility between agencies and programs. The service delivery system requires a high degree of interaction since a large portion of each agency's clientele is receiving services from at least one other agency. Variance in individual agency rules and requirements makes it difficult for the client to coordinate services between programs. Lack of coordination takes many forms. For example, a woman may find that her AFDC grant is reduced when she receives money from another agency such as the Division of Vocational Rehabilitation.

Clear program articulation is helpful for professionals who must work together but is even more critical for clients. What the agency does and does not do and who may receive its services must be clear. If the referring professional does not understand the receiving agency's program, inappropriate referrals are likely to take place. In addition, an inappropriate referral may put the client in the position of receiving incompatible and even contradictory services or at the very least, services that seem unrelated to the problem the client is trying to overcome. Poor articulation of programs puts an unfair burden on the client by making the client the principal link between agencies.

Flexibility is another key component of a coordinated delivery system. Flexibility can be lost by excessive formalization of relationships. Personnel need to have some adaptability and flexibility in making judgments. When workers must rely on an overly complex set of rules, they are more likely to lose sight of the client's unique problem. Inflexibility occurs when programs are available to meet the client's need, but clients are denied benefits due to eligibility requirements. This happens frequently when people are employed and a family member has expensive medical problems not covered by health insurance. To get the needed medical care, the family must forfeit its income.

Absence of services is a problem that varies considerably from one community to another. The rural elderly, for instance, are often unable to receive services because they lack transportation.

Obstacles Professionals May Face

Barriers to services occur on an individual level for the client, but practitioners also face barriers—organizational and professional. Aiken and others list some obstacles practitioners face in providing services.

1. Fragmentation of services
2. Inaccessibility of services
3. Lack of accountability of service agencies
4. Discontinuities of services
5. Dispersal of services
6. Wastefulness of resources
7. Ineffectiveness of services
8. Short term commitment of services[8]

No one wants to deal with difficult clients. Particularly in an age when accountability and efficiency are equated with processing numbers, there is little payoff personally or professionally for identifying and serving those most in need of services. In its most blatant form, this failure to serve the most needy has been called "creaming of clients." While few professionals would admit to supporting such practice, Paul Adams and Nancy McDonald illustrate how workers use professional rationalizations to "cool out" clients.[9] Instead of handling the problem ineffectively or turning clients away, some professionals convince clients that they did not really want the service in the first place. For clients the result is the same whether they are rejected as ineligible or "cooled out" of the system.

Goals of a Service Delivery System

Now that we have discussed the barriers to coordinated service delivery systems, it may be useful to clarify what goals should guide a humane delivery system.

FIGURE 10–2
A bureaucracy is typically hierarchical and centralized.

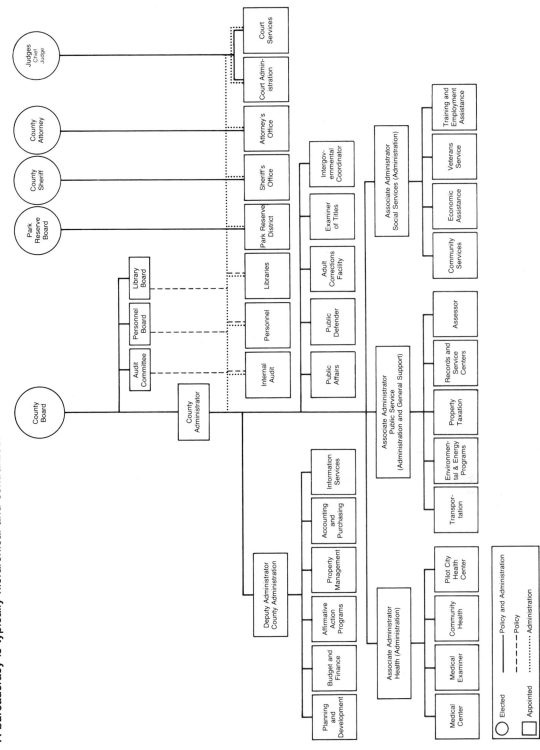

The goals of a service delivery system include accessibility, coordination, compatibility, cooperation, efficiency, effectiveness, accountability, and comprehensiveness.

Accessibility. No matter how potentially effective the service, clients cannot benefit unless they gain access to the service. Different states and even different counties within states vary tremendously in how accessible they make client services. Satellite offices in poor and rural areas where transportation is a problem help address this problem. Making agencies or meal sites accessible to the handicapped by removing physical barriers also helps. Sometimes it may be necessary to have bilingual staff to communicate with groups who do not speak English. Accessible services are services that are obtainable.

Coordination. Coordinated services treat the client as a whole person. Fragmentation of care is avoided. Case management is one technique that has been used effectively to assure coordination of services — notably in community care programs for the elderly and the "fixed point of referral" for the developmentally disabled. For a chronically impaired older person to remain at home, it is frequently necessary to use the resources of many agencies — nutrition programs, visiting nurses, county social service agencies, day care centers. In community care programs the case manager works with the client to determine what programs he needs and then arranges contracts with appropriate agencies to provide those services. The case manager makes certain that all of the services the person receives are compatible with each other and with the client's needs. Without a case manager the individual might be scheduled for many social activities on one day and none for the rest of the week, or may be scheduled for social activities yet have his health needs overlooked.

Compatibility. Services to clients need to complement each other. Clients need to experience services as making their lives more harmonious, not more complicated. The welfare recipient who is told by her protective service worker that she must be home more because her teenage children need supervision will be confused and frustrated when she is told by the income maintenance worker that she must accept employment or lose eligibility for the AFDC program, since her children are over six years of age. If services are to be appropriately linked and sequenced, they cannot be standardized and routinized; they must remain flexible. Linkage must be achieved by cooperation and coordination. Inappropriate standardization of programs creates no-win situations for the complex problems clients must face.

Cooperation. While coordination refers to a quality of the system, cooperation speaks to the quality of relationship of actors within the system. Cooperation takes place when professionals share goals and values, accept a mutual understanding of the problem, and have the ability to work together on a common task. The more conflict clients experience between helping professionals, the less confident they will be that the service plan is sound. Professional ideological differences should not be indulged at the client's expense. Cooperation and coordination should also lead to increased efficiency by obviating duplication of services.

Efficiency. An efficient service delivery system is organized in such a manner that no other way of organizing the system would produce greater output (benefits) for the amount of input (resources) expended in the process. Efficiency is a term borrowed from the business literature, and it continues to be much easier to measure when dealing with profit-oriented organizations. The more efficient a business is the more profitable it is. In the human service area efficiency is equally important but much more difficult to measure. Efficiency is usually achieved by routinization. Any part of the process that can be standardized provides at least the possibility of increased efficiency. One recent attempt at efficiency in hospitals involved having patients fill out their own medical history by responding to computerized questions. Early results seem to indicate this approach is cost efficient; whether this approach is conducive to improving the patient's overall health is still under study. If the computer system fails to get all the pertinent data or causes undue anxiety in the client, the efficiency of the system is decreased.

In addition to viewing efficiency as the relationship of inputs to outputs in the human service, it has also been defined as the ratio of service extended to results produced. Whichever way one defines efficiency, it is basically related to such things as personnel, time, money, materials, and equipment. Rino Patti lists some ways efficiency has been viewed in the human service arena.

1. The costs associated with units of program output (e.g., placing a child in a foster home, or delivering a treatment interview).
2. The costs entailed in achieving program objectives, with specific information regarding the component costs attributable to personnel, material, or equipment.
3. The relative costs of different services or approaches used in achieving the same outcomes (e.g., the comparative costs of chore and homemaker services in preventing institutionalization of the elderly).
4. The expenditure entailed in delivering a program compared to the monetary nature of the benefits realized (e.g., the costs of a training program for welfare clients in relation to the savings achieved as a result of reduced welfare benefits).[10]

Effectiveness. Effectiveness is traditionally defined as the degree to which the program meets its objectives, but this definition assumes consensus on program objectives. In reality funders may have one set of objectives, professionals another, and clients still another. For instance, a jobs program could be set up to get people off the welfare rolls. Policy makers would review the program's effectiveness according to how many fewer people received welfare. The professional would address a more complex measure of effectiveness and would look at both costs and benefits to clients and society. The client would view the program as effective if it improved his standard of living or quality of life. As administrators or providers of service, social workers cannot afford to overlook any of these assessments of program effectiveness. The indicators of effectiveness identified by Patti have a different emphasis from the indicators of efficiency.

1. The extent to which the program objectives have been achieved, including, for example, whether changes in client behavior, skill, attitude, or status that were expected to occur as a result of program interventions have, in fact, occurred. Client satisfaction with services received is also sometimes used as indicator of program effectiveness.

2. The extent to which treatment or service objectives established for individual clients have been attained. These are outcomes particularized to each case and are generally more specific than program-wide objectives. For example, the latter may focus on the reduction of recidivism among all delinquents served in a program, while individual treatment objectives might be targeted at the acquisition of certain social skills or a reduction in parent-child conflict for specific cases.

3. The variable effects of different kinds or levels of service on subgroups of clients. Such comparisons might involve the relative success of two methods of treatment—e.g., behavioral vs. milieu—or the same method applied for varying periods of time to two comparable groups in an institution for delinquents.

4. The differential impact of services on clients with different characteristics. A uniformly administered service, such as job counseling, may prove to be more effective with some clients (e.g., those with prior employment history) than others.

5. The comparison of outcomes for clients exposed to a program, with those for similar persons in the target population who have received no services.[11]

Accountability.   Both efficiency and effectiveness are related to the goal of accountability. In discussing the different views of program effectiveness we have already alluded to some of the different groups to which we are accountable. Traditionally social workers were accountable to their agency and their profession. The client movements of the 1960s made workers more aware of the importance of client satisfaction. The late 1970s ushered in a new era of accountability that all but ignored client satisfaction and professional concerns and instead stressed cost efficiency. Agencies hired individuals with academic training and experience in business rather than services. Many simplistically hoped that these managers would make the welfare system as efficient as the private sector. What has become increasingly clear is that the private sector is not nearly as efficient as we would like to believe and that efficiency is only one of the many goals human service agencies strive for.

For social workers being accountable means responding to the goals of the client, the profession, the agency, and larger society while providing services as humanely and efficiently as possible. While social workers cannot ignore any of these constituencies, they must recognize that there will be conflict between constituencies. A system's accountability will include policy makers, various professional groups, agencies within the system, clients and potential clients, and taxpayers. Whether accountability is viewed from the level of the individual social worker or of the service delivery system, the lack of agreement on what objectives to be accountable for remains. In spite of this disagreement, however, program administrators and social workers must continually strive to make services and programs more accountable.

Comprehensiveness.   Comprehensiveness addresses the goal of developing a system that meets all the client's needs. A job paying $25,000 a year will not help the mother of two-year-old twins unless she can obtain adequate child care for her children. Becoming an ace welder is not going to take a person's family off welfare unless a welding job is available. Generous scholarships will not help an underprivileged minority student if he has not received the basic education required for successful college work.

Comprehensiveness has sometimes been equated with cradle-to-grave security. A humane and comprehensive system certainly would remove the fear of economic insecurity and want, but it could never remove all of the worries associated with medical problems, learning disabilities, handicaps, and the like. Presently our society would not even consider offering such a comprehensive array of services. In reality the goal of comprehensiveness is limited to providing enough services so that what we do provide has maximum effect. The judicial system, for example, is (at least in theory) comprehensive. It provides punishments that range from fines with complete physical freedom, to probation with supervision, to many graduated levels of security all the way to maximum isolation. Prisons also have a range of programs from hard labor to college courses. Of course, our prison system is not necessarily an example of a coordinated, comprehensive delivery system, but it does suggest how complex a comprehensive system would be if client, institution, and societal needs were addressed.

Interorganizational Coordination: A Summary

This discussion of the service delivery system was designed to illustrate briefly the existing gaps in the service delivery system, to demonstrate the barriers that face service providers, and to identify the goals service providers strive to achieve. The practice principles summarize the important points of this discussion.

SUMMARY

If your practice goal is administration, you will become a specialist in service delivery; if your goal is direct practice you can contribute to making the service delivery system run more efficiently and effectively.

Knowledge of the structure and functions of the social welfare institution comprises another area of expertise for social work practice. Some social

Service Coordination

1. Services must be accessible.
2. Services must be coordinated.
3. Services must be compatible.
4. Service providers must cooperate.
5. Resources must be used as efficiently as possible.
6. Services must be accountable.
7. Services must be effective.

PRACTICE PRINCIPLES

work programs devote a whole course to this area; others teach this material as part of a policy class. Understanding the context of practice is essential to effective social work practice.

The Importance of Structures: An Application

Our final presentation is a very sad instance where bureaucratic structures protected social workers, but did not protect the client. Certainly no one would suggest that the social workers involved meant any harm. However, you may question whether they pursued their assigned tasks with appropriate diligence. Although this is a true case, the names of the individuals involved have been changed. Information has been provided by the Johnsons' attorney.

CASE STUDY
Josh: A Bureaucratic Tragedy

Mr. and Mrs. Johnson and their son Josh resided in a middle class neighborhood in a small midwestern city of about 50,000 people. The Johnsons were both in their early 20s and Josh was eight months old. Mr. Johnson was on Social Security Disability because he had Hodgkin's disease and was unable to work. Mrs. Johnson worked and required child care for Josh because Mr. Johnson was unable to care for him. Both work and child care were going well until Mrs. Johnson's regular babysitter became ill. Mrs. Johnson looked in the newspaper to find temporary care for Josh; she found an ad that Mrs. Olson had run soliciting babysitting jobs.

Mrs. Johnson, although nervous, was reassured when Mrs. Olson told her that she worked closely with the Department of Social Services and even did public speaking on child care. Since this was only to be temporary and Mrs. Olson seemed well qualified, Mrs. Johnson felt it would be okay. On the fifth and last day that Josh was to stay with Mrs. Olson, he was murdered by Mrs. Olson.

There were many things Mrs. Johnson did not know. Most significant, she did not know that two children had died previously at the Olson home. There were notations in the police file that an investigation should be completed particularly after the second child died. The Department of Social Services not only had failed to investigate the home, but even had Mrs. Olson speaking to parents of Sudden Infant Death Syndrome (SIDS) children.

Mrs. Johnson was also unaware that two women had made more than 45 telephone calls to the state Office of Day Care and Licensing, asking that Mrs. Olson be investigated for tending more children than licensing allowed. More important, these women had arrived at Mrs. Olson's unexpectedly and found their children in boarded-up playpens in a dark basement. These mothers removed their children from the home and started a campaign to investigate Mrs. Olson. The state never investigated their complaints, nor did they refer them to the local agency.

Mrs. Johnson also did not know that Mrs. Olson had been investigated for abusing her own son. Nine years earlier Mrs. Olson had received services from the county for personal problems of a "rather severe nature." This case had been kept open for four years. One year after the first child had died in the Olson home (a year prior to the death of Josh), city police records indicate that officers were called to the Olson home on potential abuse of the Olsons' natural child. The Olsons stated that they had agreed in disciplining Johnny Olson, "he will not be struck more than ten times." The file also disclosed that as of 1984 (the year Josh died), the school had made several inquiries about signs of physical abuse of Johnny. The county social worker inquired "numerous times" about Johnny's safety in the home. The case record indicates that the social worker was aware that Mrs. Olson was doing babysitting, but no investigation was made. The social worker was also aware of the two previous SIDS deaths.

Mrs. Olson was criminally charged with the deaths of the three children and subsequently convicted on charges relating to two of the deaths. Mr. and Mrs. Johnson brought a lawsuit against the agency hoping that this would prevent another child from meeting Josh's cruel fate.

The agency was found not negligent. The rationale was that the child care licenser had no obligation to investigate Mrs. Olson because she had never received the 45 complaints that were called in. The calls came in to the receptionist and it is not clear where she referred those calls. The agency supervisor testified that the receptionist herself can make the decision not to have a case investigated. However, state law requires that such reports be investigated.

There are many questions raised by this case, and social workers should consider them carefully.

1. Do you think the agency or the social worker should have been held legally responsible? Ethically responsible?

2. Do you think this case should be reported to NASW? (In Chapter 5 we discussed the procedures for such reporting.)

3. What part of the NASW Code of Ethics applies to this case?

4. Does it seem believable that more than 45 calls about a person with a record of suspected abuse went unheeded?

5. What changes need to be made in this agency? What do you know about service delivery systems that might help you plan protective services more effectively?

NOTES

1. Koya Azumi and Jerald Hage, *Organizational Systems* (Lexington, Mass.: Heath, 1972).
2. Robert Pruger, "The Good Bureaucrat," *Social Work* 18 (July 1973): 26–32.
3. Ibid.
4. Max Weber, *The Theory of Social and Economic Organization,* ed. and trans. A. Henderson and Talcott Parsons (New York: Macmillan, 1975), 328; "The Essentials of Bureaucracy," in *Reader in Bureaucracy,* ed. Robert Merton (New York: Free Press, 1967), 21–22.

5. Robert Scott, "The Factory as a Social Service Organization: Goal Displacement in Workshops for the Blind," *Social Problems* 15, 2 (Fall 1967): 160–175.

6. Viktor E. Frankl, *Man's Search for Meaning* (New York: Washington Square Press, 1963).

7. J. Kenneth Benson, "The Interorganizational Network as a Political Economy," *Administrative Science Quarterly* 20 (1975): 229–249.

8. Michael Aiken, Robert Dewar, Nancy Ditomaso, Jerald Hage, and Gerald Leitz, *Coordinating Human Services* (San Francisco: Jossey-Bass, 1975), 1–12.

9. Paul Adams and Nancy McDonald, "Clinical Cooling Out of Poor People," in *Things That Matter*, ed. H. Rubenstein and M. H. Bloch (New York: Macmillan, 1983), 139–145.

10. Rino Patti, *Social Welfare Administration* (Englewood Cliffs, N.J.: Prentice-Hall, 1983), 180.

11. Ibid.

Chapter

11

Biopsychosocial Functioning

Is being filthy, alone, totally without structure and without human contact better than being in humane, unlocked institutional housing of some kind?[1]

U nderstanding of human behavior is an essential component of any human service profession. Since behavior takes place in a diverse range of contexts, we need a general understanding of the demands and life tasks confronting individuals, families, and groups at all phases of their development. Without this understanding of stressful life events, professional intervention will be significantly hampered. In fact, many times well-meaning citizens and policymakers make life more difficult for the very people they are trying to help.

Common sense and good intentions are necessary but not sufficient to help distressed people with inadequate social functioning. Effective practice also requires understanding the biopsychosocial influences on the behavior of our clients, an understanding of the history of our client's problems, and knowing how to intervene to change the problems experienced by our clients. These different levels of knowledge are categorized as general theory, practice theory, and theories of practice. In this chapter we concentrate on general theories of biopsychosocial functioning and relate this general theory to social work practice and the forms of knowledge needed by all social workers.

All human service professionals need a basic grasp of their clients' problems or needs, yet each profession tends to carve out its own territory or domain of expertise. In social work, the focus of knowledge has traditionally been on social functioning concerns. Social functioning is a technical term in social work that refers to any biological, psychological, or sociocultural response pattern that results from the interactions between individuals and their environments. Social workers are trained to assess and intervene in these social functioning problems. In particular, social workers seek to help people change in order to enhance their social functioning or to resolve problems in social functioning.

Accreditation standards require that social work students be exposed to knowledge relevant to people as individuals and as members of groups. Groups include families, communities, and organizations. In studying individuals, we are required to examine their characteristics at multiple levels: social, biological, and psychological.

SOCIAL SYSTEMS

The social level of functioning refers to all the social systems within which an individual lives, relates, and is influenced. It consists of all interpersonal, familial, social support, institutional and sociocultural systems that regulate behavior. At the social level of functioning, social workers must acquire knowledge of how individuals relate to family, friends, enemies, authorities, school, job, the social service system, majority culture, and other systems. They must also assess whether these social relationships are acting as a resource or an obstacle to an individual's achievement of their life tasks.[2] In order to make these assessments, they must have knowledge of individuals in various sized groups: families, formal organizations, communities, and societies.

Life tasks were identified in Chapter 9.

In Chapter 9 we discussed the importance of society and how methods of socialization, social control, and social integration affect the individual. In Chapter 10 we looked at formal organizations and their effect on the individual and professional practice. Another level of social functioning critical to practice is understanding groups and group behavior. Each of us participates in many kinds of groups. Some of us live with our parents, sisters and brothers, who constitute a special kind of group—the family.[3] We also participate in other personal groups such as a group of close friends, work associates, or a neighborhood gang. These personal or primary groups and their membership present individuals with different demands from those encountered by individuals participating in secondary groups such as the National Association of Social Workers, the military, or a social work agency. In particular, social workers must understand how these different types of groups influence behavior and must understand the fundamental characteristics of commonly encountered groups in their practice.

In-groups are important variables in social integration.

Primary and secondary groups are not the only types of membership groups that are relevant to practice in social work. Individuals are also members of what sociologists have termed in-groups and out-groups. An in-group refers to "any association—either primary or secondary—in which there is a sense of solidarity, loyalty, friendliness, and cooperation."[4] It is generally the kind of group in which a person feels a sense of being at home or of experiencing what one might term a "we" feeling. In social work, many individuals come to agencies with problems that are a result of being denied membership in a desired group or groups. These individuals are typically treated as outsiders—as members of what sociologists have termed an out-group. It is important for the social worker to understand that this stranger or out-group status can be created by a variety of circumstances, such as lack of proximity to a particular place (living in a foreign country), or lack of proximity to a culture (having different values and norms, or membership in a minority group).[5]

Minority groups may be based on race or religion, such as the Amish.

Individuals are typically treated as outsiders because they do not share characteristics that determine whether or not they should be included within a particular group. Some of these characteristics are ascribed to individuals and others are based on their actual behavior. For instance, individuals might not be treated as members of a neighborhood because of their skin color. In this circumstance, they are denied membership in the neighborhood because they are members of a group with negatively valued characteristics. The neighborhood in this case is a source of alienation rather than support. This exclusion from group membership occurs in spite of the fact that membership in a neighborhood is traditionally determined by where a person lives.

Skin color is an ascribed status.

Group membership can also be based on achievement or performance. Children may be denied entrance into an extracurricular group at their school because they did not achieve the scholastic requirements. In this situation denial of membership is not based on characteristics that are ascribed to an individual, but instead on factors associated with an individual's performance. Social workers must have an appreciation of the processes and factors associated with the inclusion and exclusion of individuals in various types of groups and how this affects individual functioning.

In addition to knowing why people are included or excluded from groups, social workers must have an appreciation of the dynamics or forces that influence an individual's behavior in various groups. This allows the workers to identify which forces need to be modified to assist clients in meeting their life tasks.

To identify as a group member, an individual must be attracted to the group and must see himself as attractive to the group.

Further, the factors and processes commonly associated with group identity are critical components of social work knowledge. Group identity is typically associated with life tasks that confront most individuals during the stage of adolescence. It involves the search for membership in groups or the questioning of groups in which one is naturally a part.[6] During adolescence, for example, teenagers confront the task of evaluating their membership in various peer groups both in their neighborhood and at school. Adolescents also confront the issue of whether to identify with the religious organization that their family belongs to and whether to take on the behaviors and values associated with their family's ethnic group.

Knowledge of group development also helps clarify individual functioning. Group development refers to the changes over time in how a group is structured, how it interacts, and its culture.[7] Family development is a specific form of group development that has received substantial attention in social work programs of study. One approach to the study of family development is

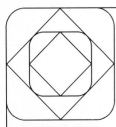

**DIAGNOSTIC
QUESTIONS**

Family Systems

1. What is the family composition? Are the children natural, adopted, fostered, from a previous marriage? Who else lives at home? Do grandparents or other extended family play a significant part in family life?

2. At what developmental stage is the family functioning? Is it newlyweds just beginning a family? Is it an elderly couple who are relinquishing the caretaker role and finding themselves in need of care?

3. What functions are being met by this family in terms of education, nurturance, economics, and other needs?

4. What roles are being played by each family member? Which roles are conducive to family functioning? Which are dysfunctional?

5. Where does decision-making power lie within the family? Is this appropriate? What are the rules and who makes them?

6. What are the values and beliefs that guide family functioning?

7. What are the family goals and aspirations?

8. How do family members communicate with each other? Directly or through intermediaries? Positively or negatively?

9. How cohesive is the family? Is it under stress? On a daily basis?

10. What are the family's coping mechanisms?

11. Is the family a closed or open system? Does it interact with outsiders or do the members keep to themselves?[9]

to view it in terms of certain stages that occur throughout the life of a family unit.[8] Another approach is to study how families are structured, and what functions are associated with family systems. Nurcombe and Gallagher suggest that to understand family systems social workers must be able to answer certain diagnostic questions as shown in the box.

These questions are important to social workers in recognizing the relative contribution of the external characteristics of a family to its functioning. In other words, what is the effect of class standing, religious persuasion, and ethnicity on the functioning of any type of family, whether it be single parent, nuclear, or extended?

Identifying the developmental stage of a family informs the worker of the issues confronting the family unit. For example, if a family is in the launching stage, children will be departing one by one. This situation requires parents and children to make major changes in fundamental relationships. Each stage represents different demands, different issues, and different tasks. Social workers must understand what knowledge, skills, and resources the family must secure to meet these changing demands.

BIOLOGICAL SYSTEMS

The biological level includes multiple systems that support the biological integrity and functioning of the human organism. It consists of biochemical, cellular, organic, physiological and nervous systems (peripheral and central nervous systems). Students are expected to take courses in human biology to understand the impact that disturbances in these systems have on the coping behaviors of clients. Once you become involved in practice, you will have a much clearer picture of how significant biological systems are to social functioning.

Although the social work curriculum does not stress biological knowledge to the same degree as psychosocial, it is very important. All social workers need a general knowledge of basic biological functions, regardless of their agency or field of practice. In addition, advanced knowledge of biological norms is important in special populations we might deal with.

Biology for the Child Welfare Worker

Child protective service workers in particular must have knowledge of the developmental norms regarding physical and maturational norms for children. Without this information, you cannot realistically assess when to intervene to protect a child. For instance, current data on infant biological norms prescribe age-appropriate expectations for when children should be able to hold their heads erect and steady, without bobbing.

If an infant deviates significantly from that norm, some type of intervention is warranted. This intervention may be limited to obtaining a thorough physical examination from a qualified pediatrician, or it could result in hospitalization for thorough neurological study. If there is no organic basis for this deviation, lack of nurturing, lack of physical stimulation, poor nutrition, or neglect must all be considered.

There are many simple assessment tools you can use to identify whether further testing is necessary. For instance, the early childhood assessment literature suggests the social skills normal for children beginning at 24 months.[10] This knowledge would lead you to ask the questions about a two-year-old that are presented in the accompanying box.

Whatever the stage of development, there are simple assessment tools you can use on a preliminary basis to determine whether you need further evaluation by experts. The questions identified address behavioral and developmental skills. Other assessment instruments could be used to assess communication and motor skills. Again, you could do the preliminary assessment. You are not expected to become an expert in each of these areas, only to recognize when development is far enough from the norm to be an area of concern.

Motor skills are related to the development and use of muscles and limbs.

Assessment can be made watching children at play.

Biological Impact on Adolescence

Psychological and sociological functioning change with changes in physical functioning.

The biological changes of puberty frequently impact on adolescent behavior. As puberty begins youngsters tend to exhibit disorganized behavior and a decreased willingness to accommodate the expectations of their parents or other adults. Puberty is marked by wide mood swings and periodic bouts of feeling picked on. Along with the physical changes goes a change of allegiance from parents to friends. As these allegiances become stronger we frequently see adolescent rebellion against the parents. Adolescents may become more irritable and have rapidly changing feelings and strong conformity to peer standards. Sexual exploration follows soon after bodily changes take place.

The combination of physical changes, peer conformity, and developing sexuality all make adolescents extremely self-conscious about their physical appearance and any deviations from normality. There are numerous assessment scales that can be used with adolescents to evaluate their biological development. Adolescents who develop at rates different from those of their peers may experience feelings of loneliness and depression. Sometimes development is even within the normal range, but when a youth feels different, it is still a problem.

Disorders of biological functions for adolescents tend to center in the areas of eating, sleeping, elimination, and sexual functioning. There is likely to be great fluctuation of these areas in adolescence, but if the problems per-

DIAGNOSTIC QUESTIONS

Early Childhood Development

1. Can the child independently choose a toy and play with it?
2. Does the child know how to pretend to do common activities such as calling Grandma on the phone?
3. Does the child like to play *near* but not *with* other children?
4. Does the child know the difference between boys and girls?
5. Does the child recognize self in the mirror?
6. Is the child strongly possessive of loved ones?
7. Does the child display dependent behavior, clinging and whining?
8. Is the child shy with strangers and in new situations?

sist, interfere with functioning, or cause family friction, intervention is necessary. Resolution of issues concerning sexual interests, friendships, values, relationship with parents and family, and educational and vocational choices leads young people to develop a sense of their own identity.

Biological Aging

> **Senescence is biological aging.**

Just as understanding adolescence and the related biological developments is important to the juvenile worker, understanding of senescence is important for the gerontological social worker. The study of senescence is the study of a group of processes which lead to a decrease in viability and an increase in vulnerability. In other words, as one ages there is an increased probability of death as a result of natural processes. The reduction in viability occurs at all levels within the organism; the increase in vulnerability to disease results mainly from declines in the functioning of the immune system.[11]

> **A functional approach to aging assesses how people function rather than their chronological age.**

Like adolescence, senescence produces obvious changes in the appearance and functioning of the person. There is even greater variability in the elderly as to when these changes actually take place. Most individuals are capable of maintaining an independent lifestyle until age 75; some can do so until well past 90. This variability makes it important for social workers to take a functional rather than a chronological approach to age. Instruments such as the Geriatric Functional Rating Scale can identify the functional age. It is also important to understand chronic medical problems. The elderly are frequently faced with maximizing their functioning in spite of deteriorating physical health, rather than hoping to regain the physical condition of an earlier stage of development.

We have discussed how normal biological development guides us in dealing with three different stages of the life cycle — infancy, adolescence, and

Culture and economics affect biological aging.

senescence. In many ways normal biological development is more clearly defined than psychosocial functioning. This is very useful for us as social workers, since we have access to simple instruments to help us assess biological functioning. We caution students, however, that these instruments are to be used only for preliminary assessments. Dealing with biological problems is outside the scope of social work expertise.

Biology and Human Behavior

Another important area of knowledge is understanding how biology affects mental functioning, which cuts across the different age groups. The interaction of biology, psychosocial variables, and environment is very complex. The environment can affect both biological and psychosocial functioning. For instance, poor nutrition (environment) can lead to birth complications (biology) that have at least a tentative relationship with schizophrenia (behavior). A clearer example of environment affecting biological factors might be the individual with Parkinson's disease who clearly has a brain disease and as a result, can move only at a snail's pace. Yet this same person caught in a burning building will race to the exit. He still has the brain disease, but the environment was more powerful than the disease in determining how the brain would function.[12]

Environmental factors that cause psychosocial stress to families include divorce, day care problems, lack of parental leave policy, teenage pregnancy, unemployment, underemployment, frequent moves for job advancement or job dislocation, and unsafe neighborhoods. These same environmental factors might cause biological problems such as birth defects, postpartum depression, or organically based mental illness.

The current thinking on mental disorders is that most cases of schizophrenia, manic depression, and, to a lesser extent, major depression have genetic (biological) factors as prerequisites. Heredity also contributes to panic and obsessive-compulsive disorders.[13]

Oxygen deprivation at birth has been shown to be related to the characteristics of attention-deficit hyperactivity—hypermotility, impulsivity, marked mood swings, short attention span, impaired memory, and math difficulty.[14]

Hypermotility is the inability to remain still.

The influence of genetic factors on behavioral disturbances has been supported by studies of adopted children. Adopted hyperactive children had a high prevalence of hysteria, sociopathy, and alcoholism among their natural parents. These characteristics were not found among the adoptive parents. Histories of full siblings and half siblings show a significantly higher correlation of hyperactivity between full siblings.[15]

Biology and Psychopathology

High levels of testosterone are related to aggression, low frustration tolerance, irritability, and impatience in boys aged 15 to 17.[16] A recent text on psychopathology summarizes the current literature on psychopaths, noting that "empirical evidence suggests that heredity does play a role in the development of psychopathy, though it cannot be considered the only factor.[17]

PSYCHOLOGICAL FACTORS IN ILLNESS

Just as biology is related to psychosocial functioning, psychosocial functioning impacts biological functioning. Physicians used to feel that certain medical illnesses could only arise if particular psychological events occurred. When these events contributed to pathologically altered tissues or organs the resultant diseases were called *psychosomatic*. Today that thinking has been revised; instead of only some illnesses being considered psychosomatic, they *all* are. The question now is how and to what degree psychosocial factors influence disease.[18]

The *DSM* III is the American Psychiatric Association's system of diagnosis.

This new outlook is reflected in the *Diagnostic and Statistical Manual* (*DSM* III-R), which uses the term *psychological factors affecting physical condition* (PFAPC) rather than psychosomatic illnesses. PFAPC may apply to any illness; the purpose of diagnosing PFAPC is to focus attention on the environmental factors influencing the patient's medical condition. Even though we know that psychological factors affect illness, we do not know how this happens. Explanations have ranged from unconscious conflicts[19] as a cause for psychosomatic illnesses such as hypertension, asthma, neurodermatitis, and peptic ulcers, to the idea that certain personality profiles produce specific diseases.[20]

Stress of any type is thought to activate a person's susceptibility to disease. Some suggest that instead of psychological factors producing physical conditions, it may be just the reverse: physiologic events may give rise to ingrained personality traits.[21] For instance, a colicky baby may require more feedings and more attention, and therefore develop more conflicts over dependence. Another possibility is that both physical ailments and personality traits are determined by gene structure.[22] Although we can expose you to the array of theories on how the biopsychosocial systems interact, the reality is that we know the interaction is significant but we do not comprehend how it operates.

SOCIOCULTURAL FACTORS IN ILLNESS

People's ethnic heritage and social class shape how they experience, understand, and deal with illness. Some ethnic groups exaggerate pain and some are overly stoic; some want relief from pain and some want to understand the meaning of the pain. Not every member of the same ethnic group responds in the same way; however, culture does influence how people perceive and cope with illness.

EVALUATING PSYCHOSOCIAL FACTORS

There are so many psychosocial factors that might affect illness that we have to limit our inquiry to those that are most pertinent. Maxmen has identified the psychosocial factors that are most important to physicians.[23] The factors he identifies suggest that the social worker gather information to assist the physician in the medical treatment. Depending upon what social functioning problems the social worker will address, there will be many additional variables important to the social work assessment. Refer to the diagnostic questions for a framework to guide social workers in making a medical assessment.

Again, we want to stress that the diagnostic questions address the psychosocial factors most closely related to treatment of the disease. There may be more significant social problems that need not concern the physician. This brief summary of ways in which the environment, biology, and psychosocial variables interrelate is not comprehensive. Our goal has been to make you aware of

**DIAGNOSTIC
QUESTIONS**

Psychosocial Medical Assessment

1. Does the patient understand the presenting illness?
   a. Can the patient describe to you what the illness is and what medications are to be taken?
   b. Does the patient understand the prognosis of the illness?
2. Does the patient trust that the doctor has told the whole truth?
3. What has been and will be the effect of the illness on family, lifestyle, and job?
   a. Has the illness caused financial strain?
   b. Will the illness necessitate a change in living style? If so, what is the patient's attitude? What is the family's attitude?
   c. Does the family believe that the patient is trying to recover?
   d. How will the illness affect employment?
4. Has the patient experienced any major emotional changes during the course of or just prior to the onset of the illness (e.g., divorce, remarriage, childbirth, new job, geographical move)?
5. What has been the patient's prior experience with illness?
   a. overreaction
   b. denial
   c. withdrawal
   Is coping adaptive?
6. What has been the prior experience with hospitals, medical personnel, and medical care?
   a. Suspicious? Dependent?
   b. Was there avoidance?
   c. Has the patient been maltreated?
   d. What kind of behaviors reassure or threaten the patient?
7. What kind of experiences have people in the patient's social network had with illness and the medical profession that might influence the patient's attitude toward care?
8. What type of social network does the patient have to aid in the recovery? Who might be dysfunctional?

the importance of biological knowledge to social work practice. By training and by inclination, we tend to understand the importance of psychological and sociological variables, but too often see the biological factors as outside our field of expertise. Few social workers master a thorough knowledge of human biology, but we wanted to illustrate and stress the fact that there are assessment tools available to assist you. A common rule of thumb is to assess the impact of organic causes of behavior before beginning our interventions. In spite of its contribution to illness, removal of a psychosocial problem will not cure the disease.

PSYCHOLOGICAL SYSTEMS

The psychological level of individual functioning involves "all mental functions that are conscious or have the potential for being brought to awareness."[24] These mental functions help individuals mobilize their internal and external resources to satisfy personal needs and to avoid internal and external threats. These functions are

1. Information processing
2. Motor control
3. Communication
4. Attitudes and emotions
5. Internal controls and aspirations
6. Social competence
7. Coping techniques[25]

These functions have been further defined by Nurcombe and Gallagher. *Information processing* involves orientation, attention, concentration, perception, memory, abstraction, problem-solving, judgment and insight. *Motor control* regulates motility, whereby the individual orients toward, seeks, finds, and manipulates the objects required to satisfy needs. *Communication* includes gestures, language, and the use of language as a tool of thought. *Attitudes and emotions* represent the subject's affectively laden impressions and ideas of the self and of significant people from the past or in the present.

Internal controls, rules and *aspirations* (superego and ego ideal) involve the controls, rules, guidelines, and goals that regulate behavior and give coherence and purpose to life. *Social competence* involves the capacity to discern the emotions and purposes of other people, to predict the social consequences of one's actions, and to resolve social dilemmas. *Coping techniques* are the repertoire of coordinated thoughts and activities used by the individual when subjected to stress.[26]

All of these functions are manifested in behavior. Social workers must learn to identify the behavioral manifestations for each of these psychological functions. Further, they need to understand how these psychological functions are influenced by biological and social factors.

Since the psychological system is the component of human functioning that directs the system to achieve its goals, it has historically received the most attention in social work training. A recent study indicated that almost 90 percent of schools of social work offered courses on theories of personality.[27] In these courses the focus of attention is primarily on identifying biological, psychological, and social tasks relevant to the life span development of individuals. It is assumed in these courses that social workers need to know the common tasks confronting individuals at each stage of the life cycle, as well as variations in development because of either culture or gender.

As an introduction to this area of social work knowledge, we present a brief discussion of three theories of personality that have had a profound effect on social work practice. Each of these theories continues to guide a significant portion of social work practice. We follow this presentation with a case study chosen to illustrate how these theories apply in practice.

The personality theories we have chosen to present are Freudian or psychoanalytic theory, Rogerian or humanistic theory, and learning or behavioral theory.

FREUDIAN OR PSYCHOANALYTIC THEORY

Freud recognized the importance of biology and environment in individual functioning.

Psychoanalysis suggests that human beings are naturally unhappy because of inadequate or traumatic experiences in early childhood. Unhappiness arises from inherent conflict between basic instinctual drives and the requirements of the social structure. Freud suggested that individual well-being or mental health is dependent upon a harmonious relationship among the various parts of the mind and between the person and the real world.

Successful psychoanalysis provides self-knowledge and understanding. "Cured" patients can use this knowledge in various ways: they may replace the unhealthy repression of instincts by rational, conscious control of them (suppression rather than repression), divert them into acceptable alternative channels (sublimation), or decide to satisfy those instincts. Freud did not believe that there was any danger that psychoanalysis would unleash uncontrollable primitive instincts. Self-knowledge would increase individuals' ability to control their unconscious.[28]

The diagnostic or Freudian school of thought was most prominent during the 1930s and 1940s, but still retains many adherents.

Freud's influence is most apparent in the techniques of psychiatric caseworkers, but his most profound effect has been the acceptance by social workers that insight into emotions and psychic life is a key element in all social work.[29] Freudian explanations of the unconscious were welcome additions to the rational model of social diagnosis outlined by Mary Richmond. Psychoanalysis helped to explain the irrationality that these workers observed in their practice.

ROGERIAN OR HUMANISTIC THEORY

Therapy in the Rogerian model is frequently referred to as client-centered therapy.

Carl Rogers's impact on social work has been significant enough to warrant mention in almost every social work text. Recent analysis of Rogers's work suggests that it may be especially relevant for radical social workers committed to human liberation. Though client-centered therapy has traditionally been considered conservative and apolitical, recent analysts have suggested that its basic tenet, client empowerment, is fundamental to radicalism. Rogers himself concluded in 1974 that he had been practicing and teaching politics all of his life but did not realize it.[30]

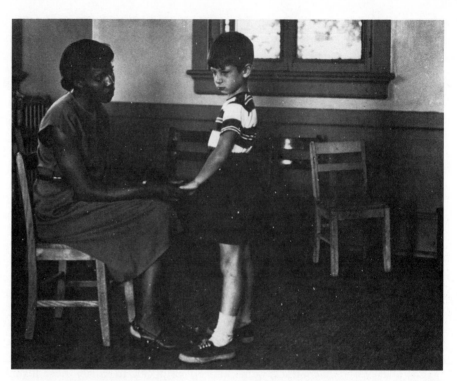

Understanding human behavior is a key element that affects the nature of the work done with clients, whether adults or children.

While Freudian theory is based on a genetic framework, client-centered therapy centers on immediate relationships. From birth, the world of the infant is the world she experiences. Within her world the infant has one basic drive — the tendency toward self-actualization. Self-actualization is the "inherent tendency of the organism to develop all of its capacities in ways which serve to maintain or enhance the organism."[31] The infant has the inherent ability to value experiences that enhance him. This "organismic" valuing process directs the infant's behavior toward self-actualization.

> **Self-actualization is the driving force of client-centered therapy.**

As the infant grows, he acquires a sense of self (the "self concept") derived from his own being and function within the environment. The development of self-concept is strongly dependent on the individual's perception of her experiences and environment, and her perception is influenced by her need for positive regard, a pervasive and persistent human need. The individual's need for positive regard can only be satisfied by others, and the effect of significant others is particularly potent. The total of these experiences produces a sense of self-regard, a learned sense of self based on the individual's perception of how others regard him. The sense of self-regard becomes a pervasive influence on his behavior.

> **Freud was more concerned with biological determinants of behavior. Rogers was more concerned with the person's social environment.**

Rogerian theory stresses empathy, positive regard, and genuineness, not technical skills or knowledge. *Empathy* is understanding the client's world as the client sees it. Empathy entails reaching for feelings, developing understanding of the client's feelings, and putting the client's feelings into words.[32] Reaching for feelings is the skill of asking the client to share the affective portion of the spoken message; empathy involves summoning an affective response that comes as close as possible to the experience of the other.

Empathy, positive regard, and genuineness are the sine qua non of socal work practice.

Positive regard is an unconditional affirmation of the individual's life and needs. The therapist genuinely cares for the client and remains nonjudgmental in words and actions. The therapist does not express approval or disapproval but instead trusts the client's ability to discover what is best for herself. The therapeutic effect of unconditional positive regard is that the client allows into awareness those portions of inner experience inconsistent with the self-concept. The patient receives confirmation of genuine understanding from another person and positive acceptance of the changing, new self.[33]

Genuineness requires the therapist to rely on moment-to-moment experiencing of feelings in the therapist–client relationship. The understanding arising from the therapeutic relationship is not only intellectual, but also organismic. Genuineness and empathy combine as the therapist experiences what the patient is feeling.[34]

Genuineness is a biopsychosocial phenomenon.

LEARNING OR BEHAVIOR THEORY

Behavior theory sees human behavior as determined by the environment. Behavior is learned from situational factors, not from within the organism. Since behavior is learned, it can be unlearned. Difficulties occur when learned maladaptive behavior results in anxiety; the anxiety is learned as a contingency (conditional response) of the learned maladaptive behavior. Behavior theory assumes that the individual has no inner control of behavior, no self-determinism. Values, feelings, and thoughts are ignored, and only concrete, observable behaviors are considered.[35]

Behaviorists are most concerned with environmental determinants of behavior and least concerned with biological determinants.

The following assumptions are basic to behavior therapy.

1. Behavior therapy concentrates on the maladaptive behavior itself rather than on underlying causes. This is in stark contrast to Freudian and Rogerian theory.
2. Maladaptive behaviors are acquired through learning. Both adaptive and maladaptive responses follow the general principles of learning.
3. Learning principles can be effective in modifying problem behaviors. Some behaviorists believe so strongly in this principle that they assert that autistic, schizophrenic and even epileptic children can be taught new behaviors with these principles.

4. Behavior therapy involves setting specific, clearly defined goals. This principle has affected social work practice by moving it toward an outcome-oriented approach in which evaluation is based on specific, observable, measurable criteria.

5. The therapist adapts the method of treatment to the client's problem. This principle puts the burden of effectiveness squarely on the therapist. Behaviorists suggest that blaming patients for lack of motivation is mere rationalization for their own ineffectiveness.

6. Behavior therapy concentrates on the here and now. Case histories are only of interest to the extent that they explain how the problem behaviors have been developed and reinforced.

7. Any techniques labelled as behavior therapy must be empirically tested and found to be relatively effective.[36]

Behaviorists have incorporated research as an essential practice component.

Behavior therapy, more than any other, has been concerned with scientific validation of its techniques. Since behavior therapy stresses observable and measurable outcomes, behaviorists are in a better position to document their findings than therapists dealing with "conscious states." But behavior therapies are still limited primarily to case studies and short-term outcomes. Laudable efforts have been made to test effectiveness, but behavior therapy cannot yet make definite statements of cause and effect.

SUMMARY

This chapter has addressed the biopsychosocial approach to understanding human behavior. We began by looking at the social determinants of behavior. We discussed the importance of genetics and physical development for children and the elderly. We also addressed some recent findings on how biology is related to mental illness and psychopathology. The reciprocal effects of disease and psychosocial functioning were noted. Finally, we looked at individual personality theories and showed how these theories assume differential impacts of biology and the environment.

In keeping with our goal of helping you conceptualize how the knowledge base applies to practice we have chosen an excerpt from *A Solitary Dance*, a novel by Robert Lane. This excerpt was chosen because it shows how theory relates to practice, how important it is to continually assess the effectiveness of our interventions, and to be aware of what kinds of therapies are effective with different kinds of clients. This excerpt deals with a psychosocial intervention with an autistic, psychotic, and hyperactive child. Autism is a psychotic disorder that is usually noticed in early infancy. Although there are different manifestations of autism, the common denominator is an inability to relate to people and situations from the beginning of life. While this condition has a clear genetic base, psychosocial interventions are necessary

to teach these children social skills. In addition to the psychosocial intervention, these children customarily receive antipsychotic medication.

In the novel, although Michael has been in the state hospital for three
years, none of the staff has been able to establish a relationship with him.
Patrick McGarry, a student intern, has been assigned to work with Michael
and is becoming frustrated with his inability to establish a relationship with
Michael. The excerpt is an exchange between Patrick and Scott, Patrick's
supervisor; Scott speaks first.

CASE STUDY
A Solitary Dance
Robert Lane

"Beginning therapists like you are always in such a
hurry, always expecting immediate success. You're
so ingrained with the American ethic of quick results
for little effort—of instant change when it suits
you—that you can't stand the thought of little or no-
progress, no overnight success stories like in the
movies!

"It takes time to build a relationship, Patrick,
to gain an understanding of the patient's psychody-
namics, to earn his trust. It's taken little Mike eight
years to get to where he is now. How can you expect him to change it all in a few months? Especially
when you're clambering over the mountainside for
only four or five hours out of each week? If it were
truly that simple, don't you think someone around
here would've stumbled on that solution and helped
Mike long ago?"

Still, in spite of Scott's lecture, I was rapidly
approaching my wit's end. Three months in the
trenches were getting to me. All that time I had been
chasing that kid, and he still wouldn't come a jot
closer, talk to me, or for that matter, even recognize
that I was any different from one of the rocks he
liked to rest on. Except that he'd get closer to
them . . .

"Well at least you're getting in shape," Scott
commented.

"I'm afraid the little guy has really got my
number, but good."

"Want to give up? Try one of the other kids?
Lots of other possibilities around here—"

"Of course not! I'm just getting started. I can
be just as stubborn . . . no, more stubborn, than
Mike. But what I haven't been able to figure out yet
is how to break the pattern—how to get him to relate to me."

"Maybe it's time you went back to square
one."

"What do you mean?"

"Perhaps you should begin to put some of
your knowledge of psychology to use: instead of allowing Mike to call all the shots, you start calling
some of them."

"I still don't follow, Scott. I've been trying to
do that all along, and I can't think of any other way
than I've already tried."

"What exactly have you been doing up to this
point?"

"Well, I've been trying to do what Rogers
advocates—provide unconditional positive regard,
acceptance, empathy. The emotional symptoms
and distress are supposed to subside as the innate
forces within the person strive for psychological balance. That's the theory, anyway. And it seems to
work for Rogers . . . "

Scott smiled. "Have you seen any evidence
that it's working with Mike?"

"No, not really. Maybe a look from him here
and there, but I can't even be sure of that, especially
at a distance of twenty-five feet."

"Okay, now. Are you ready to consider the
notion that perhaps one theoretical approach is just

not enough to cover all therapeutic situations? That there is no one method of therapy that is going to be applicable to every single patient we encounter?''

''I suppose.'' It was a grudging admission for me. Scott had broached the subject before, without much success.

''Boy, you're not kidding when you say you're stubborn! Patrick, do yourself a favor and ease up a bit. You've admitted that several months of work with Mike have gone nowhere, so you've got nothing to lose by considering other possibilities, have you?''

''I'm not sure. What do you have in mind?''

''You know how I feel about Rogers' approach. It's an excellent attitude to have toward the people you work with, but there are some patients who need much more than an interested, supportive listener. I suspect Mike is one of them.'' Scott gave me a wry smile. ''As a fellow humanist I can wholeheartedly agree with the sentiments behind Rogers' ideas, the fact that his concepts are based upon a deep respect for the person and his or her life situation, and that the therapeutic relationship is then constructed upon that premise. But remember, self theory falls far short of being a universal explanation of human behavior.''

''What's the alternative, then?'' I said, sensing what was coming. ''You don't think behaviorism is the answer, do you?''

''Not entirely. But the principles of learning and conditioning have been demonstrated very nicely in studies, especially those by B. F. Skinner.

''Behaviorism does have its uses and some very good techniques. In spite of what you might think. Of course, it has its limits of usefulness, too, like any other theory. But we know that in certain situations positive and negative reinforcement work extremely well in changing specific types of behavior patterns. So you don't want to disregard learning theory simply because it may be anathema to your humanistic notions.

''Psychoanalysis, too. Many of Freud's concepts—such as the unconscious, the defenses—have certainly withstood the test of time. The empirical data may not have supported some of the major hypotheses of his theory, but the fact remains that many of the psychodynamic constructs, as well as the therapeutic techniques, have proven extremely useful.''

''Scott, it's our same old argument!'' I broke in. ''I'm a dyed-in-the-wool humanist because I can't buy either the behavioristic view of people as mechanized creatures of reflex or the analysts' notions of unconscious motivation, that behavior is ruled by base instincts. I really believe in the integrity of the individual, and that each person has a choice. Anyway, I'm familiar with the principles of the various theories you've mentioned—that's the easy part. The problem is that I can't apply the techniques of any of these theories to a little buzz bomb named Michael Harris who runs up and down hills like a mountain goat and won't let me near him!''

''All right,'' retorted Scott. ''The problem is that you have yourself prematurely committed. There are no absolute applications of any of the theories yet—that's why they're still theories. Psychology as a science is, to put it mildly, in diapers. We have a lot of promising leads, some well-conceived studies, some good data, and the start of a body of knowledge. But we are a long way from fully understanding human behavior, much less predicting it with one-hundred-percent accuracy.''

''That's for sure. I'm beginning to wonder why I spent so much time in graduate school.''

''Well, it's not as hopeless as it may sound. But when you make the jump from the rudiments of science to applied work you have to stay loose, flexible, and accept the fact that you're not always going to be perfectly on target. What the theoretical framework does is increase your chances; it allows you to be objective, to plan, even to predict what should happen during the course of psychotherapy. What I'm advocating you do with Mike—with anyone you work with professionally—is concentrate on understanding him and assessing the situation. And be open to using any of the theories that might seem appropriate. So when you first start working with a person, begin by picking out the theory that seems to fit the individual's dilemma best, whether that theory is called self, behaviorism, psychoanalysis, whatever. Use those explanations, but be ready to look elsewhere when they don't seem to account for what's going on. Or when there doesn't seem to be any progress. Stay loose, flexible, open to anything.

''That's what sets true professionals apart: they draw upon their knowledge of science, using their skills to objectively evaluate what is needed, and then they choose a course of action. It's rarely very clear precisely what that should be; sometimes several treatment alternatives would be appropriate. One simply has to make a choice and, if things don't work out, be prepared to switch to another approach.

"And remember, Pat, all the while the patient may very well sense what is best: the Wisdom of the Mind, if you will. Some people, for example, need to dig back into the trauma of their formative years and work through unresolved issues and long-buried troublesome feelings—as the psychoanalysts advocate—while others simply blot out the past and deal with learning a more adaptive style of living that is future-oriented. More along the lines of a behavioral approach. But most, the majority I would say, want a combination. You have to learn to mold yourself, to shape yourself to whatever will best help your patient—an accommodation between what you sense they need, and what you think they sense they need, and what therapeutic approach will be most suitable for that purpose."

I was shaking my head by this time, but Scott pressed on.

"What I'm suggesting therefore, Pat, is that you be more eclectic. Be aware of the value of trying different things instead of being locked into one theory and approach. Mix a little Rogers with some Skinner and maybe add a dash of Freud. Okay?"

"At best I think I see what you're getting at, Scott. But I still don't see how using a goulash of theories and techniques is going to help me know what to do with my particular little id kid."

"You like challenges—that's another one for you. Think about what I've said, then try to put it to use."

From *A Solitary Dance* by Robert Lane (New York: Signet, 1983), 53–60. Used by permission.

NOTES

1. M. Wasow, "The Need for Asylum for the Chronically Mentally Ill," *Schizophrenia Bulletin* 12 (1986): 164.
2. R. Berger and R. Federico, *Human Behavior: A Social Work Perspective* (New York: Longman, 1982).
3. J. Lloyd, R. Mack, and J. Please, *Sociology and Social Life* (New York: D. Van Nostrand Co., 1979), 199.
4. Ibid.
5. L. Harman, *The Modern Stranger: On Language and Membership* (New York: Mouton de Gruyter, 1988), 12.
6. Barbara Newman and Philip Newman, *Development Through Life: A Psychosocial Approach* (Homewood, Ill.: Dorsey, 1984), 294.
7. R. Sarri and M. Galinsky, "A Conceptual Framework for Group Development," in P. Glasser, R. Sarri, and R. Vintner, *Individual Change Through Small Groups* (New York: The Free Press, 1974), 71.
8. B. Sheafor, C. Horejsi, and G. Horejsi, *Techniques and Guidelines for Social Work Practice* (Boston: Allyn and Bacon, 1988), 242.
9. B. Nurcombe and R. Gallagher, *The Clinical Process in Psychiatry: Diagnosis and Management Planning* (London: Cambridge University Press, 1986), 502.
10. For example, see D. Bailey and M. Wolery, *Assessing Infants and Preschoolers with Handicaps* (Columbus, Ohio: Merrill, 1989).
11. R. Atchley, *Social Forces in Later Life*, 3rd ed. (Belmont, Calif.: Wadsworth, 1980).
12. J. Maxmen, *Essential Psychopathology* (New York: Norton, 1986), 63.
13. Ibid.
14. H. Johnson, "Disruptive Children: Biological Factors in Attention Deficit and Antisocial Disorders," *Social Work* (March 1989): 137–144.
15. Ibid., 138.

16. D. Olweus, "Aggression and Hormones: Relationship with Testosterone," in *Development of Antisocial and Prosocial Behavior: Research, Theories and Issues*, ed. D. Olweus, J. Block, and M. Radke-Yarrow (Orlando, Fla.: Academic Press, 1986).

17. D. Doren, *Understanding and Treating the Psychopath* (New York: Wiley, 1987), 105.

18. Maxmen, *Essential Psychopathology*, 295.

19. F. Alexander, *Psychomatic Medicine: Its Principles and Applications* (New York: Norton, 1950).

20. H. Dunbar, *Emotions and Bodily Change: A Survey of Literature on Psychosomatic Relationships*, 3rd ed. (New York: Columbia University Press, 1946).

21. Maxmen, *Essential Psychopathology*.

22. Ibid.

23. Ibid.

24. Nurcombe and Gallagher, *Clinical Process*, 308.

25. Ibid.

26. Ibid.

27. W. Brooks, "Human Behavior/Social Environment: Past and Present, Future or Folly?" *Journal of Social Work Education* 22 (1986): 20.

28. R. Lubove, *The Professional Altruist* (New York: Atheneum, 1971), 89.

29. Ibid.

30. C. Rogers, *On Personal Power: Inner Strength and Its Revolutionary Impact* (New York: Delta, 1974).

31. C. Rogers, "Client-Centered Therapy," in *American Handbook of Psychiatry* Vol. 3, ed. Silvano Arieti (New York: Basic Books, 1959), 196.

32. L. Shulman, *The Skills of Helping* (Itaska, Ill.: Peacock, 1979), 40.

33. B. Meador and C. Rogers, "Client-Centered Therapy," in *Current Psychotherapies*, ed. R. Corsini (Itaska, Ill.: Peacock, 1973).

34. Ibid., 127.

35. B. Okun, *Effective Helping* (Belmont, Calif.: Wadsworth, 1982), 123.

36. D. Rimm and J. Masters, *Behavior Therapy* (New York: Academic Press, 1974), 6–17.

Chapter

12 Research in Social Work Practice

No profession can, or should, expect to survive without building into its training and practice the capacity for ongoing evaluation.[1]

Research skill is essential to effective practice.

The major concern of this textbook is to introduce you to the field of social work as a knowledge-based, applied professional field guided by a unique value base. Research is critical to building our knowledge base through evaluation of techniques reported in the literature. It is also the means by which we evaluate our own practice. We owe it to our clients and ourselves to constantly question what interventions are working and to stop using ineffective methods.

In an introductory text, you might expect that we would provide you with some of the basics of the research method. We will leave that to the research class. Instead, our goal is to convince you of the importance of the research method to practice. We hope to motivate you to see research as an integral part of your professional practice. We do this by presenting two types of social work interventions that show how important research skills are to effective social work practice.

The examples we use are an intensive in-home supervision program for serious juvenile offenders and an intensive case study of an emotionally disturbed adolescent. The first example incorporates casework with the individual juvenile and his family; group work is used in the remedial model as a therapeutic device; community organization skills are essential to eliciting cooperation from the schools, the police, and the courts. The use of these different methods is usually assumed in social work interventions. We chose this example to show that research (evaluation of the intervention) is also an essential part of the social work process.

The second example, an individual case study, was chosen to show how the assessment process is equivalent to doing research. An intensive case study is an exercise in problem-solving. It is an application of the rules of systematic thinking.

TREATMENT AS A PRESCRIPTION BUILDING CYCLE

The first step in any intervention is to clearly identify what the treatment variables are going to be. The treatment variables are determined by what has been found to be effective in dealing with the population or problem at hand. In this case it is serious juvenile offenders. To develop a treatment plan we draw upon the literature and practice knowledge.

The next step is to identify how we will know if the program is working. As agency employees we will be accountable on a program level, which means showing that the overall program is working. On an individual practice level we need to know to what degree each program variable is working for each individual client. Not all interventions work with every client, and not all social workers are effective with all interventions. When we build the means to measure effectiveness right into the program, we greatly enhance our effectiveness.

When we consciously measure the effects of our work, we are building our own professional skills and knowledge by identifying what types of clients will respond to what types of treatment and what our unique abilities are with each type of intervention. Just as each client is unique, each social worker is unique. The more you learn about what you are good at, the more rewarding practice will become.

Given the complexity of the problems we deal with, be aware at the outset that with each client you will need to recombine treatment variables to develop more effective treatment. As new prescriptive combinations are offered, evaluated, and revised, increasingly effective interventions are generated.

Figure 12–1 outlines the steps in the prescription building cycle.

RESEARCH BASED PRACTICE: AN EXAMPLE

Serious juvenile offenders are a major societal problem. They cause a great deal of property damage and make people concerned for their own safety. This group has not responded well to many of the programs that have been developed. Careful analysis of the studies that have been done with this group provides a sound theoretical and empirical base on which to develop a program.

Causal Theory

There are many theories about the causes of juvenile delinquency and little agreement among theorists. There are also many different types of delinquents. The program Juveniles in Jeopardy was developed to deal with a very specific population—serious juvenile offenders. Almost all of these children fall under the category of antisocial children. We believe that failure to understand antisocial children has led the profession to be ineffective in dealing

FIGURE 12–1
Program Development Cycle

1. Identify treatment variables.
    a. What has been shown to be effective in the literature?
    b. What have you found to be effective in your practice?
    c. What interventions have worked for your colleagues?

2. Identify outcome variables.
    a. What outcomes are predicted on a program level?
    b. How will you know each intervention is effective?

3. Based on your evaluation, how do you need to change the program or recombine variables to increase effectiveness?
    a. What works with which individuals?
    b. What are you most effective at?
    c. Do you need to use other professionals with other skills to improve the program?

4. Identify the needed changes and restart the cycle.
    a. Identify new variables.
    b. Identify evaluation measures.
    c. Redefine the program.

with these children; worse yet, we have contributed to their destruction of their family life by placing unwarranted blame on their parents. Many of these parents are kind, generous, hardworking people who are very committed to their children.

Who are the serious juvenile offenders? Boys outnumber girls in this category six to one. Over 90 percent of them have been in trouble by the age of 8, when many of these children first come into conflict with law enforcement. Yet the antisocial tendencies are there even earlier. In fact, antisocial children are different from birth. They tend to resist physical affection and show more crying and tantrums. Research has shown that antisocial children show a differential response to others' pain at a very young age.[2] A normal child will cease activities that they see as causing pain to another. With antisocial children, the stronger the victim's reaction to pain, the more the child will increase the behavior causing the pain.

This theory of antisocial children incorporates a biopsychosocial approach.

Normal children are relatively aggressive until the age of two—they take whatever they want. At this age, however, we see a decrease in aggressive behavior and the development of an array of more socially acceptable means of having their needs met.

Antisocial children do not achieve life tasks at the pace of normal children.

Antisocial children have a different development pattern. Rather than decreasing their aggressive behaviors, they train others to behave in ways that maintain their aggressive behavior. At the age of 9 they display the same number of aggressive behaviors as a normal 2- to 4-year-old. Antisocial children are noncompliant. They will risk rejection for short-term goals and in

A social worker talks with juveniles at school.

fact have an inability to sacrifice for long-term goals. They also suffer from an inability to "read" people.

These children are not pleasant to be around. As their control over the family increases, anarchy ensues. A common response to their behavior is avoidance. This can take the form of workaholism for fathers and alcoholism for mothers. A working father can usually remove himself from the situation, but it is much more difficult for the mother because babysitters are extremely difficult to find for these children. Once the child starts attending school, there is added pressure on the parents as teachers and social workers tend to blame the parents for the child's behavior.

The result of this process is a delinquent lacking in personal, interpersonal, and social cognitive skills. Antisocial children are deficient in anger control, have adopted erroneous systems of thinking, and are impulsive and over-reliant on aggression as a means of problem-solving. A program that allows (pressures) the delinquent to change his behavior has the greatest likelihood of decreasing delinquency. Intervention needs to be restrictive but at the same time it can be healthful for, and helpful to, the delinquent and his family.

Interventive Theory

Goldstein and Glick, Ferraro, and Agee, have all used aggressive replacement training in secure juvenile institutions.[3] Kohlberg developed and tested the cognitive-developmental approach to dealing with serious juvenile

TABLE 12–1

Program Variables	Intervening Variables	Outcome Variables
Cognitive	Decreased aggression	Decreased criminal activity
Behavioral	Improved school performance	Decreased cost of supervision
Affective	Improved family functioning	Decreased institutionalization
Control	Improved self-concept	Decreased threat to community

offenders.[4] Goetter developed a model for intervening with suicidal delinquents.[5] Each of these programs has documented considerable success in changing delinquent thinking and behavior. Juveniles in Jeopardy was built on the premise that a combination of the components (treatment variables) in each of these programs, plus a sex education and family mediation component, would be successful in treating and supervising high risk juveniles.

Treatment Variables: The Research Hypothesis

Juveniles in Jeopardy is a program that combines behavioral, affective, and cognitive skill training with control by sanctions. It was predicted that this program would result in decreased aggressive behavior and improved interpersonal relationships. Decreasing aggressive behavior and improving interpersonal relationships would lead to improved personal functioning, which includes decreased criminal activity, better school performance, and less institutionalization. Table 12–1 illustrates the relationship of these variables.

Evaluating the Intervention

The first step in the program was to determine who the appropriate target population would be. In other words, serious juvenile offenders must be conceptually and operationally defined so that others would know what was meant. Then they would have a basis on which to judge what types of juveniles they might treat using these program components. The target population was seriously delinquent youths between the ages of twelve and sixteen and a half, living in their own homes. There had to be a court order to participate and the juvenile had to have a minimum score of 16 on the Arizona Juvenile Risk Assessment Scale.[6] This instrument is a formalized device for estimating continued delinquency based on actuarial principles of prediction, past research, and delinquency theory. It allowed the social workers to compare the candidates against success and failure rates of youth with similar characteristics. Use of this scale ensured that the program was serving the targeted population—children with a high probability of committing further serious crime.

Decreased criminal activity and decreased use of institutionalization were the primary outcome variables for this program. Decreased criminal activity was measured by police reports (serious and minor) and court actions; this was compared with the child's behavior two years prior to the program. Decreased institutionalization was measured by the number of children placed in treatment and/or correctional institutions by the county agency; the comparison was made with the three years prior to the implementation of the program.

The intervening variables were also measured. Aggression was measured using the Spielberger Aggression Scale.[7] School performance was measured by reports from teachers. Special forms were developed for the teachers to evaluate the youth on assignments completed, attitude, effort, and attendance. These are very simplified forms developed to get the necessary information with as little inconvenience to the teacher as possible. Family functioning and self-concept were measured on Hudson Scales.[8] These are easily administered, nonthreatening instruments that can be answered in a very short period of time.

Feedback from these measures is frequently useful to the clients to see what kind of progress they are making. The program administrators found that using these measures as part of the treatment process was well worth the extra effort required.

As we stated, overall program effectiveness measures are important to the agency and to funding sources. If the overall program is to be successful, we need to maximize the effectiveness of each program component.

The Program

The first program module is aggression control. Anger is a controlling emotion for most adolescents in trouble. Anger arises out of frustration and leads to aggression. Breaking the cycle of aggression is a primary step in decreasing delinquent behavior. Using a program developed by the Texas Youth Commission,[9] the administrators gave the youth an overview of the skills they would be taught in this treatment program. These modules were designed to prepare and motivate the youth and their families to become active participants in the program. We introduced the program concepts and began role playing on an individual basis.

The goals of this module are: (1) to introduce the concept of aggression, (2) to help the child inventory his aggressive behaviors, (3) to begin to empower the youth to control impulsivity, and (4) to get the youth to recognize the detrimental effect of aggression on her life. Before and after measures were used to determine the degree to which these goals were accomplished.

The second treatment module is structured learning. Since lack of basic social skills interferes with social functioning of aggressive youth, teaching social skills increases their options for problem-solving and social interaction. Structured learning consists of modeling, role playing, performance feedback and transfer training. The specific model used in this program was developed by Goldstein and his associates.[10] This model has been found to be particularly effective with dysfunctional families, especially working class and lower class children.

This component is didactically presented. It includes role-taking training, providing immediate feedback, and early, continuous, and frequent reinforcement for correct enactment of behaviors being taught. As these basic social skills are mastered, the youngster moves into more self-regulated, inner-controlled behaviors.

The treatment goals for this model are: (1) to identify skill deficits in the youth, and (2) to teach social skills. The program modified Goldstein's social skills assessment scales to determine what skills needed to be taught and to measure the degree to which the youth learned the skills.

The third program module is teaching contingency management to the parents. The goal of this treatment is to teach parents to understand and control the aggressive behavior of their children through appropriate rewards and punishments. This is a social learning approach to behavior. Parents inventory their own behaviors prior to learning the skills and record their rewarding and punishing behaviors. Family functioning is measured prior to the contingency management classes and upon completion of the treatment.

The self-control unit (module four) combines teaching relaxation techniques, assertiveness training, and cognitive restructuring. Relaxation techniques are taught because it is impossible to feel intense anger during deep relaxation. This allows the youth to learn self-management of intense anger or anxiety.

Assertiveness training is designed to increase the youth's self-worth and help him develop more satisfying relationships. Nonassertion leads to lowered self-esteem and increased anger and tension, which in turn leads to increased aggression. It is a vicious circle, but it can be broken. Through assertiveness training the youth learns: (1) how to develop satisfying interpersonal relationships rather than domination, (2) the difference between aggression and assertion, and (3) to reduce anxiety and anger with assertiveness.

Cognitive restructuring is a method to help youths challenge the self-defeating nature of their beliefs. Cognitive restructuring is based on rational emotive theory.[11] Irrational thoughts lead to inappropriate emotions, which lead to anger, depression, and anxiety. Individual feelings and behaviors can be changed by influencing patterns of thinking.

An adapted version of the Kendall-Wilcox Self-Control Scale[12] was used as an evaluative device. Both the child and the parent provided pre- and post-test data. For the assertiveness training the Gambrill Richey Assertion Inventory was used.[13]

Adolescence presents conflicts for many teenagers.

Module five, the advanced anger control unit, combines all the skills learned to use anger constructively. Anger can energize behavior by increasing intensity, help express negative feelings, inhibit anxiety, and initiate coping behaviors. Anger can also disrupt behavior, facilitate impulsivity, and instigate aggression.

Self-assessment of progress was made by the youths, who filled out behavior incident reports to measure behavioral change and to chart their own aggressive behavior.

Moral reasoning (module six) is designed to develop cognitive conflict regarding genuine moral dilemmas. The purpose of this module is to promote self-discovery through exposure to higher levels of reasoning. Success in this module will lead to valuing fairness, equality, justice and respect for others, which would lead to a decrease in antisocial behavior. Kohlberg has developed pre- and post-tests to evaluate the youths' level of moral reasoning.[14]

The final module is based on the "errors in thinking" concept, an advanced model of cognitive restructuring.[15] It motivates the youth (1) to become aware of their faulty thinking patterns, (2) to become aware of how their errors in thinking relate to their delinquent behavior, and (3) to make a commitment to change their patterns of behavior and thinking. This is the final stage to prepare the child and parent to function without outside supervision. This process takes place in a group setting.

First, the child identifies herself and other family members and gives a detailed account of her chemical usage and criminal behavior. She then receives honest feedback from other parents and peers. The process is designed to let the child know who she is without trying to make her feel good about past behavior. The therapist must be matter-of-fact, honest, and direct, rather than confrontive.

The second part is essay writing. Each child must write at least five essays for the group. The essays reflect on how the youngster's thinking errors and crimes have affected his life, family, and friends. The social worker needs to be aware of learning problems that may affect this assignment. Even if the children cannot write fluently, they can verbally reflect on these issues.

The group responds to the presenter in regard to effort, honesty, and accuracy of the assessment. The child is forced to take a long look at the direction his life is going. Both the child and the family must confront the consequences of what happens if the child chooses not to change. Some families recognize that the child is not willing to change and begin to detach themselves emotionally from the child. They make the decision that if the child is not willing to change, they are unwilling to let that child ruin the family.

As with any social work intervention, the termination phase is critical. In this program termination entails a series of meetings in the home with the parents and the child. Each home visit involves a written contract for tasks to be accomplished and issues to be discussed and resolved. Parents write the child's rules, and the social worker develops a contract that provides the necessary care and supervision of the child in the home, building on all the skills the child and parents have learned. The goals are: (1) to restructure the family unit with the parents in control, (2) to have the child cease delinquent activity, and (3) to have harmonious family functioning.

Following completion of the seventh module, post-test measures are taken. These include:

1. Spielberger Aggression Scale
2. Hudson Scales measuring:
   parental relationships
   marital relationships
   sibling relationships
   self-concept
   life contentment
3. Criminal activity—policy referrals
   serious
   minor
4. Court actions
5. School records
6. School behavior

7. Number of runaways

8. Types of placements
   home
   foster home
   secure institution

9. Cost of services — savings

Program Results

One program using the Juveniles in Jeopardy model of treatment produced the following outcome.[16] A total of 24 children (87 percent male and 13 percent female) were served over a two-year period. Thirty-eight percent of the children successfully completed the program and are no longer receiving any type of social work services. Seventy-nine percent of the children, who were highly vulnerable to an out-of-community placement, continue to live in the community, and 21 percent were placed in institutional care. Eighty-four percent of the children who remained in the community are currently enrolled in school.

As a group, the most significant changes occurred in the areas of parental relationships, self-image, self-contentment, sibling relationships, extra-curricular activities, school attendance, and attitude toward school. The findings on delinquent behavior were skewed by the fact that two individuals committed major crimes within the first month of program implementation. This is not unusual when a new program is introduced; there is, predictably, testing by some participants. Following the sentencing of those two juveniles to correctional institutions, there was a distinct decrease in delinquency among other program participants.

By using research knowledge and skills it was possible to identify what treatment variables were likely to be successful and to measure exactly which interventions were effective. In the case study LeCroy and Ismail show how research skills aid social workers in making a complete and accurate assessment, which is a prerequisite to effective intervention.

CASE STUDY
An Intensive Case Analysis[18]
Craig LeCroy and Bian Ismail

One of the frequent pitfalls of the case study method is that the social worker tends to pay attention to the information that supports a preconceived idea or theory about why a person is functioning in a certain way. In contrast, using research methods makes the intensive case study more of an exercise in problem-solving. It applies rules of systematic thinking in order to understand the total situation and respond in an effective manner.

Bromely summarized the scientific aspects of a case study in the following way:

> The basic aim of a quasi-judicial case-study is
> to formulate a cogent argument, i.e., a rational
> and empirical argument, which explains the

behavior of the person under investigation. Such an argument is, in effect, a *theory* or *explanation* about that person's adjustment, and is therefore open to question and subject to continual revision in the light of the fresh evidence and new ideas. Ideally, the case-study eventually reaches a stage at which it makes good sense; it is internally coherent; it corresponds with the empirical evidence; it successfully predicts how the individual will behave; and it is accepted by competent investigators working independently of one another.[13]

An effective case study must follow certain steps, outlined in Figure 12–2.

ABBREVIATED CASE DESCRIPTION

JB is a 15-year-old adolescent from a troubled family who now lives in a residential treatment center. He was abused as a child, has had numerous foster home placements, and is diagnosed as having attention deficit disorder with hyperactivity. He has a history of abusive and aggressive behavior toward others. There are indications that he is self-destructive, having attempted suicide when quite young, taken dangerous risks, and abused drugs. He has not made much progress since being placed in the residential treatment center.

JB's mother, Mrs. Z, was using both LSD and amphetamines while she was pregnant with him. Although JB's parents were cohabitating at the time, they were not married. Shortly after JB's birth, his mother broke off the relationship because the father was involved with another woman. There has been no contact with the father since.

Soon thereafter, JB's mother married Mr. E, who adopted JB. Mr. E was physically and emotionally abusive to JB. At the age of two, JB was diagnosed as hyperactive and placed on Ritalin. Records indicate that at the age of four, JB attempted to hang both himself and his sister. Other self-abusive behaviors included throwing himself against walls. At the age of four he was placed in foster care. The next year his adopted father died of cancer. JB was returned to his family the day of Mr. E's funeral.

During the next three years JB was hospitalized twice in a children's psychiatric program. JB's behavior continued to be abusive toward his siblings and mother. Finally, JB's mother brought him to the child

FIGURE 12–2
Steps in a Case Study

1. Narrative or case description
2. Listing of the problems
3. Grouping of the problems
4. Reasons for the groupings
5. Diagrams of events and relationships
6. Final narrative understanding
7. Conclusions

protective agency, saying that if he were returned home she would end up killing him. JB's behavior remained uncontrollable through three foster home placements and he was placed in a residential treatment center. At the center JB is reported to be impulsive and in need of constant attention. He demonstrates little social maturity or sense of responsibility. He has had difficulty relating to peers and authority figures. There have been numerous incidents of abusive behavior and sexual misconduct.

LISTING OF THE PROBLEMS

At this stage the emphasis is on laying out all the problems. Later, the list can be reexamined to eliminate problems that do not have supporting evidence. This step helps to identify and clarify the problem. It lets the social worker determine what needs to be analyzed further and see what connections begin to emerge between the problems and what problems are most important. Listing the problems also begins the process of rearranging the information to encourage new and alternative viewpoints about the problem. Figure 12–3 presents a list of the problems for JB.

GROUPING OF THE PROBLEMS

The next step is to study the list of problems and begin to organize the data. In order to obtain a better understanding of the client, the procedures of structuring and restructuring can be used. This facilitates a better description and interpretation of the data and is similar to exploratory data analysis. Figure 12–4 presents one way of structuring data using

FIGURE 12–3
List of Problems

Asthma	Limited impulse control
Hyperactivity	Poor peer relationships
Oppositional to authority figures	Attention deficit disorder
Grand and petit mal seizures	Provokes others
Poor self-concept	Sees world as against him
Aggressive behavior	Compulsive liar
Manipulates others	Substance abuse
Low trust level	Inappropriate sexual behavior
Poorly developed conscience	Difficulty completing tasks

FIGURE 12–4
Organizing the Data

Prenatal complications
Disrupted family (father left)
Reconstituted family   Background issues
Physical abuse
Self-destructive behavior (attempted suicide)
Abusive and aggressive behavior
Poorly developed self-concept   Foreground issues
Lack of social skills
Poor peer relationships
Opposition to authority
Residential treatment

the case example. The table shows some initial ideas about how to understand the functioning of JB within a life history perspective. It also presents data on the sequencing of events that led up to JB's current status as a client in long-term residential treatment. At this point we have little empirical understanding of JB's functioning. Vague and general terms are being used and their empirical basis still needs to be established.

An alternative way to organize the data is to sort the problems into categories that fit together conceptually. This process should be a result of both inductive and deductive approaches to the problem. Using the inductive method classifies the information without much concern for meaning. The deductive approach attempts to look for patterns of meaning from the data. This step requires the social worker to have knowledge of normal and pathological development. Table 12–2 uses the case description and knowledge of human behavior to begin the process of sorting problems into categories.

Table 12–2 presents the mechanism by which the data begin to acquire meaning. Patterns of meaning or theories begin to come into play as one attempts to group problems into conceptual categories. To make interpretations of the data, it is helpful to make explicit the reasons for the conceptual groupings. This analysis also forces the social worker to examine implicit beliefs, judgments and inferences. By making statements explicit we are more compelled to justify our actions.

TABLE 12–2
Problems Sorted into Categories

A. *Physical Problems*	D. *Poor Self-Control*
Hyperactivity	Little impulse control
Asthma	Oppositional to authority
Seizures	figures
	Aggressive behavior
B. *Poorly Developed Conscience*	Difficulty completing tasks
Compulsive liar	
Provokes others without cause	E. *Relationship Problems*
Sees nothing wrong with anti-	Manipulates others
social behaviors	Low trust level
Negative concept of women	Provokes others
	Oppositional behavior
C. *Poor Self-Concept*	Poor peer relationships
Lack of identity	
Sees world as against him	
Substance abuse	
Takes risks	
Aggressive behavior	

REASONS FOR GROUPING

Group A: Physical problems

Hyperactivity, grand mal seizures, and asthma can all be treated with medication. It is important to know what kinds of medications JB is taking and what the intended and unintended effects of the medication are.

Group B: Poorly developed conscience

JB exhibits several behaviors that infer a poorly developed conscience. JB lies for no apparent reason and will not admit to lying when confronted. JB antagonizes younger children and enjoys seeing the resulting pain. JB has a hard time distinguishing right from wrong. JB has a negative concept of women. He buys pornographic material whenever possible, makes derogatory remarks to women, shows no respect and will not accept authority from women.

Group C: Poor self-concept

Evidence of JB's poor self-image include lack of self-care and his inability to accept positive feedback. JB takes life-threatening risks. He engages in behaviors that will inevitably lead to injury. JB will also substance abuse whenever he gets a chance. JB is developing aggressive tendencies and is physically assaultive. He suffers from paranoia, feeling that the world is out to get him.

Group D: Lack of self-control

JB shows little impulse control. When agitated he will strike out without thinking. He often blurts out things that are inappropriate, hurtful or unrelated to anything. JB is unable to follow directions or complete tasks.

Group E: Relationship problems

JB has a long history of abusive behavior toward others. There is little affection between JB and his mother; she does not want him back in the home. JB has had numerous incidents of aggressive behavior and inappropriate sexual conduct at the residential treatment center. Staff describe JB as someone who manipulates and provokes others for no apparent reason.

    Five problem areas have been grouped together in this case analysis. The assumption is that these five areas fit together in some functional sense, that is, there are some causal factors suggesting the grouping.

CAUSAL FACTORS: DIAGRAMS OF EVENTS AND RELATIONSHIPS

The reasons for the groupings need to be made clear. The supporting evidence for each grouping must be rigorously evaluated and reviewed; therefore, the next step is to examine closely the possible reasons for each of the groupings.

This process is facilitated by the use of diagrams. Each grouping is diagramed in order to examine the nature of the relatedness of the problems. This diagraming process is similar to that used in path analysis. (Path analysis is a special form of statistical analysis that attempts to show not only what variables are associated with each other but in what sequence and how strongly they are associated.) The purpose of this step is to explore the causality—the exact manner in which problems may be related to one another. Figure 12–5 presents a series of diagrams that show causality for each of the different problem groupings.

The information in this case study consists of narrative, statements, test results, and diagrams organized in certain ways. It is important to point out that this information is composed of various facts, assertions, suppositions, inferences and judgments. This data has been taken from numerous sources and organized in different ways.

The *intensive* case analysis examines the data carefully. What is based on fact and what is based on opinion? What interpretations are being made from the data? What judgments are lacking empirical support? Validity is of concern in the case analysis. For example, we have independent correspondence substantiating JB's aggressive tendencies. There are self-reports in which JB talks about being "mean," staff reports of aggressive behavior, family reports of aggressive behavior, and psychological evaluations suggesting an overly aggressive disposition. The reliability of the data is also of interest; do observers report behavior in an internally consistent manner? The scientific method in an *intensive* case analysis is critical; "a case-study is to be judged by its internal coherence, by the extent to which its empirical

content can be independently and objectively verified, and by the validity of its conceptual framework."[18]

In order to make the knowledge, assumptions and arguments understood it is important to write out the reasons for the problem groups. This step brings us closer to putting together the pattern. At this point the major issues are refined and a justification of the person's functioning is beginning to develop substance. The following section demonstrates this process with JB.

Group B Category—Poorly Developed Conscience

Possible Reasons:

Mrs. Z was a poor role model. Frequently she substance abused; she moved from relationship to relationship, and she has lied to JB on several occasions.

There is a lack of positive relationships in JB's life. JB has a poor relationship with his family. He does not get along with siblings or parents. There has not been much nurturing, caring or love in his family.

JB's inability to see right from wrong may stem from his experience of child abuse. JB was often hit for no apparent reason; as a result, consistency of punishment vs. reward is not related in his mind. Inappropriate parenting may have led to a low level of moral development.

The problem of JB provoking others without cause could result because JB wants rejection to maintain a negative outlook on himself.

Group C Category—Poor Self-Concept

Possible reasons:

JB feels unwanted by his mother, partly because she did not protect him from his stepfather's abusive behavior. JB was removed from the home and has experienced much rejection from home. Also, failed placements in several foster homes may lead to a feeling of constant rejection.

Constant abuse for no reason is likely to lead to a poor self-concept. The abuse also causes JB to see the world as being against him. JB was taken out of the home because of his acting out; however, his stepfather who was abusing him remained in the home. Constant relocation may have made JB think the whole world is out to get him.

FIGURE 12–5
Examination of causality of relatedness (pp. 277–278)

Group A: Physical Problems

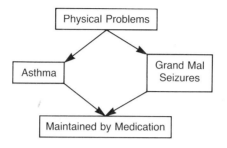

Commonality = maintained by medication

Group B: Lack of Conscience

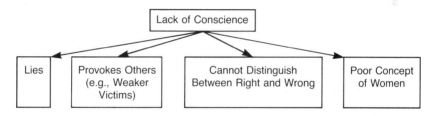

Commonality = sees little value in others

Group C: Poor Self Concept

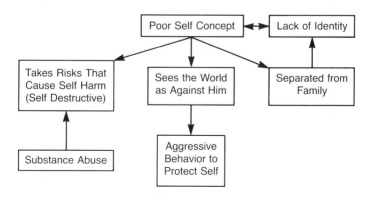

Commonality = does not see himself as valuable

FIGURE 12–5 (continued)
Examination of causality of relatedness

Group D: Poor Self Control

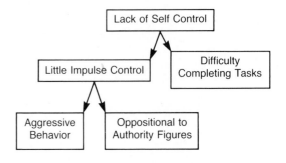

Commonality = cannot control impulsive tendencies

Group E: Relationship Problems

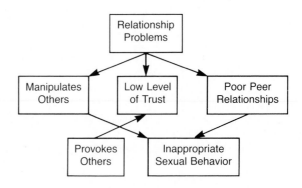

Commonality = has not established meaningful and
satisfactory relationships with others

Substance abuse may have been a way to take risks, deal with anger, or rebel. The child abuse and lack of nurturing may have caused this.

JB's risk-taking behavior can be seen as a result of a poor self-concept resulting from early experiences. His self-abusive behaviors early on in life have translated to risk-taking in early adolescence. This self-destructive behavior could be a way of punishing himself because his stepfather died as soon as JB was placed in foster care. JB may feel responsible for his stepfather's death; self-abuse may occur as a means to punish himself.

Group D—Poor Self-Control

Possible reasons:

This may have been caused by an unstructured, abusive home environment and lack of positive and consistent discipline. JB was hit whenever his stepfather fancied.

Parents showed little impulse control, thereby

FIGURE 12–6
Overall Understanding of Events and Relationships

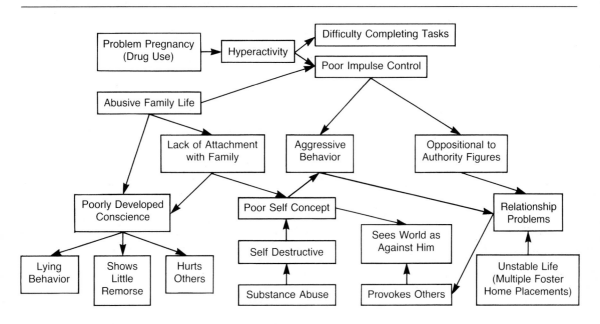

providing a role model for a lack of self-control. JB may be defiant as a result of his parents' abusive nature. His opposition to authority figures may also result from this. His inability to complete tasks may be related to his oppositional state. Clinicians see this as lack of impulse control.

Group E — Relationship Problems

Possible reasons:

JB developed a basic lack of trust early in his life. Because of an abusive home environment he did not receive appropriate nurturing or attachment. He began life unwanted and without a father. Since few people in his life have given him love he may believe he can only get attention through provoking others. The many disruptions in his life have not allowed him to become attached to any adult figures, which explains some of his lack of self-control. JB's early tendencies toward aggressive behaviors have also contributed to generally poor peer relationships. Inappropriate sexual behavior results from

the lifelong lack of attachment and the tendency to manipulate others.

FUNCTIONAL ANALYSIS OF CLIENT'S PROBLEMS

The final step in an *intensive* case study is to put together a final understanding of the person. This is best done in a diagram or graph that shows the theoretical or supposed relationships between causes and effects. The graph should represent a functional analysis of the events and relationships.[19] The strength and direction of the factors and their relationships should be shown. The procedure of making a diagram of the relationships forces one to grapple with important assumptions about the case. It can act to forestall premature problem-solving and can provide a broader perspective. This final diagram should represent the visible end product of a long process of thinking about the case.[20] Figure 12–6 represents this process of analysis in JB's case.

By permission of the author. A version of this case study will appear in *Case Studies in Social Work Practice*, ed. Craig LeCroy (Wadsworth, in press).

SUMMARY

Since a major goal of social work intervention is to help clients achieve more satisfying personal and social functioning, it is imperative that we develop techniques that can be replicated from one setting to another. Knowledge of research provides the method for structuring our interventions, evaluating the outcomes, and sharing the findings with our colleagues. Research is critical to developing a sound knowledge base. Research allows us to observe the relationship between antecedent and resultant elements in a particular problem situation and provides evidence of what types of interventions have been able to change problem situations and bring about the desired effects. Research knowledge and skills introduce certainty, dependability, and control in making those changes. Even more important, it ensures that those changes are consistent with the integrity and values of the client and the profession.

NOTES

1. J. Fischer, *Effective Casework Practice* (New York: McGraw-Hill, 1978), 3.
2. G. Patterson, *Coercive Family Process* (Eugene, Ore.: Castalia Publishing Co., 1982; K. Magid and C. McKelvey, *High Risk* (New York: Bantam, 1988).
3. A. Goldstein and B. Glick, *Aggression Replacement Training* (Champaign, Ill.: Research Press, 1987); M. Ferraro, workshop presented at American Correctional Association, January 1988; V. Agee, workshop presented at American Correctional Association, January 1988.
4. L. Kohlberg, "Moral Stages and Moralization: The Cognitive-Developmental Approach," in *Moral Development and Behavior,* ed. T. Lickona (New York: Holt, Rinehart & Winston, 1976).
5. R. Goetter, *S.O.S.: A Suicide Prevention Guide* (in press).
6. J. Ashford and C. LeCroy, "Placing Juvenile Offenders in Residential Treatment: A Decision-Making Model," *Residential Treatment for Children & Youth* 5, 4 (Summer 1988).
7. C. Spielberger, G. Jacobs, S. Russel, and R. Crane, "Assessment of Anger: The State-Trait Anger Scale," in *Advances in Personality Assessment,* Vol. 2, ed. J. Butcher and C. Spielberger (Hillsdale, N.J.: Lawrence Erlbaum Assoc., Inc., 1983).
8. W. Hudson, "Elementary Techniques for Assessing Single-client/Single-worker Interventions," *Social Service Review* 51 (1977): 311–326.
9. Ferraro workshop.
10. Goldstein and Glick, *Aggression.*
11. A. Ellis, *Reason and Emotion in Psychotherapy* (New York: Lyle Stuart, 1962).
12. P. Kendall and I. Wilcox, "Self Control in Children: Development of a Rating Scale," *Journal of Consulting and Clinical Psychology* 47 (1979): 1020–1030.
13. E. Gambrill, *Behavior Modification: Handbook of Assessment, Intervention, and Evaluation* (San Francisco: Jossey-Bass, 1977).
14. Kohlberg, "Moral Stages."

15. C. Shea of Hennepin County Home School Program in Minnetonka, Minn. presented this adaptation at American Correctional Association, 1988.

16. R. Goetter is a primary author of the Juveniles in Jeopardy program. These data are from his practice experience.

17. Dennis Basil Bromely, *The Case Study Method in Psychology and Related Disciplines* (New York: Wiley, 1986), 37.

18. Ibid., 95.

19. Ibid.

20. Ibid.

Chapter

13

Social Welfare Policy

As individuals, Americans tend to be a generous and helping lot. We respond to loneliness, impoverishment, and hardship through our communities, churches, and secular charities.

As a nation, the story is somewhat different. Given the persistence of poverty and serious social problems in the face of affluence, it is difficult to argue that we have a deep and long-standing national commitment to social justice and equality, even though we claim to believe in both.[1]

S ocial welfare policy is an essential component of the social work knowledge base. To study social welfare policy is to study the history, politics and economics of social welfare, social services, and other societal decisions that directly affect people. Policy is both a process by which a society sets a course of action to accomplish certain goals and the product of that process. Social policy can promote change or it can protect the current conditions; it can support existing power structures or redistribute power. It can take from one group and give to another; it can make opportunities for certain groups and create obstacles for other groups. It is not only the poor who benefit from social welfare policy. The Food Stamp program, for instance, injects some $12 billion annually into the retail and wholesale food industry, as well as into agricultural production.[2]

Policy is both a process and an outcome.

THE ROLE OF THE SOCIAL WORKER

Historically, social workers have played an important role in developing social welfare policy. We were instrumental in the development of the first White House Conference on Children in 1909, the Social Security Act and other relief programs of the 1930s, and the War on Poverty in the 1960s. Today social workers serve on city and county governing bodies, in state legislatures and the U.S. Senate, lead election campaigns, and direct state human service agencies. Never before have so many social workers held high government positions—both elected and appointed.[3]

Social workers need to understand and at times disagree with social policy that affects their practice. In 1968, for example, social workers protested against U.S. involvement in the Vietnam War.

No professional group is more directly affected by social welfare policy than social workers. Salaries, working environment, availability of jobs, and resources for clients are all provided through and limited by what legislation is passed and what degree of funding is provided to support the legislation. Understanding the economic significance of human services programs often is essential to knowing how and why government policies are made.

In addition to your self-interest as a social worker, you will also have a professional obligation to be informed and to contribute to the formation of humane policy. As a professional social worker you will be expected to have an expertise in social welfare policy. Both the general public and lawmakers frequently look to the profession for leadership in this policy area.

Progressive social change is enhanced by empowerment of social workers and clients in the policymaking process. Understanding the nature of politics and the process of policymaking is a source of power. It is truly amazing how many educated people do not understand how political decisions are made. Understanding the process increases your ability to affect the process and anticipate the effects of new policies.

Social welfare policy is the means by which social workers and other humanitarians strive to redistribute resources to improve the quality of life for the poor, the disabled, the elderly, and the handicapped. Whether manifested in health care, housing, or hunger, the overriding problem tends to be poverty. The causes of poverty are systemic. They derive from a combination of individual talents, motivations, upbringing, conditions of the labor market, heritage, and inequalities of opportunity.

In order to facilitate our discussion of poverty and social welfare policy, we begin by briefly describing the major programs that have been developed to deal with poverty and hunger in America. The two major health policies, Medicare and Medicaid, are discussed in the health care policy section.

POVERTY PROGRAMS

Aid to Families with Dependent Children (AFDC)

AFDC is the present version of Aid to Dependent Children, which was part of the 1935 Social Security Act. Eligibility requires the presence of one or more children who are deprived of the financial support of one of their parents because of death, disability, or absence from the home. Some states also have AFDC-U, which allows the family to receive income assistance even if there are two parents in the home. Eligibility is based on meeting a predetermined needs standard; the amount of payment depends upon how many people are in the household. There is also a limit on how many assets the family can own. Each state has different eligibility and payment standards. Most AFDC families receive food stamps and medical assistance. AFDC payments in real dollars decreased by 35 percent between 1973 and 1983; while the cost of living increased, AFDC payments decreased.[4] In addition, AFDC has increasingly been tied to the labor force. In 1967 mothers with children over six years of age were required to register for employment; this has since been lowered to three years of age.

Nutrition Programs

Child Nutrition. These include the School Breakfast Program, the Child Care Food Program, the National School Lunch Program, Special Milk Program, and the Nutrition Education and Training Program. All of these programs receive funding from the federal government to provide nutrition to day care or school age children. They also reduce the amount of commodities the government must store.

WIC. The Special Supplemental Program for Women, Infants, and Children was tested in 1972 and adopted in 1974. This program provides vouchers for the purchase of prescribed foods for pregnant and nursing women and children under five years of age. WIC is administered by the U.S. Department of

Agriculture nationally and by state governments and Native American tribes locally. Women and children must be recertified at a health center every six months. This program was drastically cut under the Reagan administration.

Elderly Nutrition Program. The Older Americans Act, a 1965 amendment to the Social Security Act, was amended in 1972 to provide congregate meals for people over 60 years of age. In 1978 it was again amended to include a system of home-delivered meals for functionally impaired elderly (Meals on Wheels). This program is funded primarily by the federal government, but has some state and local matching as well as participant contributions.

Food Stamps. The Family Nutrition Program is administered by the USDA. Originally, recipients had to purchase food stamps, which could then be redeemed for significantly more than people paid for them. In 1977, the Food Stamp Act mandated that free food stamps be made available to low-income households lacking the cash to buy stamps. Coupons are now issued directly to eligible households, eliminating the purchase step. This program is federally funded; the USDA pays the full value of food stamps and provides states with half of the costs of administering the program.

Supplemental Security Income (SSI)

This is a means-tested cash benefit program for the indigent aged, blind, and disabled. It is funded and administered by the federal government through the Social Security Administration.

Each of these poverty programs has its origin in the Social Security Act and its amendments. In this chapter we discuss the passage of the Social Security Act and some of the important amendments. We then look at the problem of poverty and how it affects housing, hunger, and health care.

These policy areas have been chosen for two reasons: to introduce you to basic policies that all social workers must be familiar with, and to illustrate the kinds of choices that are made in the policy process.

POLICY ANALYSIS

It would be difficult to overstate the importance of political activity to large numbers of people, including the profession and those it serves. Policy has tremendous potential for benefiting or harming people. The policy process is the backdrop before which the major decisions about social welfare are made and implemented.

If we see policy analysis as a problem-solving process we can identify steps very similar to the process identified in Chapter 3.

To examine an existing social welfare policy there are certain steps to follow. These steps reflect what is known as the rational approach to policy analysis. We briefly identify a framework that will help you analyze policy, and then we look at the passage of the Social Security Act and subsequent policy developments affecting the poor. Our discussion is structured by these questions.

**DIAGNOSTIC
QUESTIONS**

Rational Policy Analysis

1. What is the problem? Develop a clear statement of the problem. Every policy is developed to respond to what a significant portion of the general public views as a problem. The problem statement should identify both the severity and the incidence of the problem. (*Severity* is a measure of how much people are suffering; *incidence* measures how many people are suffering because of the problem.)

2. What is causing the problem? Identify the true cause of the problem. For example, is the cause of unemployment lack of jobs or lack of skills? If there are no jobs available, training welfare recipients will be a waste of time. If there are jobs available, but the poor do not have skills, training programs will be beneficial to the individual and the economy. Some people believe that permanent unemployment for a large portion of the working class is the wave of the future. This would require a very untraditional approach to clients. In the past we have always tried to motivate clients to work. Should technological advances make permanent unemployment the norm, we would need to teach clients to live fulfilling lives, to engage in satisfying activities, and not to feel stigmatized even if they are unemployed.[5]

3. What are the intended effects of the programs? Identify policy goals. For instance, Medicare was intended to provide health care for the elderly. However, an unintended side effect made health care so costly that the goal has not been achieved.

4. Identify the target population. Who is the policy intended to serve? If we develop nutrition programs for the poor, *poor* must be clearly defined. The Department of Labor uses a different indicator of poverty than does the Older Americans Act. Some people who are eligible for services under the Older Americans Act are not eligible for Supplemental Security Income (SSI). There

Social policy analysis, like any other educational application, requires that you become familiar with a new set of terms. Understanding these terms will make our presentation of the material clearer and will prepare you to analyze other policies.

Dimensions of Choice

Who benefits? This is one of the most basic decisions about any reallocative policy. Some programs are set up on a selective basis, whereby only certain people receive the benefits. This is true of medical assistance and food stamps. These programs are usually means-tested; other benefits might be set up on a universal basis. Public schools, public libraries, and parks are just a few of the social benefits available to everyone regardless of income.

Another way to view the difference between universal and selective programs is to compare social insurance programs to public assistance programs. Social insurance programs are available to everyone who belongs to

Selective programs are usually means-tested, which means they are available only to people with income below a predetermined amount.

fore, an elderly couple who have too much income to receive SSI might be eligible to receive Meals on Wheels or free meals at the senior center.

5. Identify the predicted effects of the policy. Is the policy going to hurt one group and help another? For example, is sentencing reform going to provide increased protection for the victim or the criminal? Will it change the quality of life for any particular group?

6. Study the history of the policy. How and when was the policy instituted? What prompted lawmakers to adopt this policy? How have administrative actions and judicial decisions changed the policy or its original intent? Abortion policy is a good example of how court decisions, state legislatures, and federal funding have all had major impact in a policy area. Many state legislatures have shied away from setting clear policy on such a volatile issue. As a result, the Supreme Court has had to decide cases such as Roe v. Wade. Roe v. Wade granted women the right to a safe, legal abortion. Anti-choice groups have tried to get state legislatures to outlaw abortion. In some states they have been successful in keeping poor women from having abortions by passing laws to limit public funding and prohibiting abortions in government-supported hospitals.

7. Compare the proposal to alternatives. For each policy that is developed, there are many options that could have been chosen. Some questions to compare proposals include: (a) Who benefits? (b) What will the benefits be? (c) Will the policy goals maximize on equality, equity, or adequacy? (d) Who pays and who decides? (e) What portion of the money goes to administrative costs? (f) Which plan is greater on target efficiency? (g) Which is greater on allocative efficiency? (h) Are the services stigmatized? (i) What choice or sovereignty is built into the program? (j) How flexible is the program?

Public assistance programs are income-tested, short-term and stigmatized.

a certain group, regardless of income. They are nonstigmatized and seen as a natural function of government. Public assistance programs require that the recipient be poor; the services are stigmatized and the benefits are assumed to be short-term, until the person can be self-supporting. Public assistance is seen as a stopgap measure, rather than an ongoing function of government.

What will the benefit be? Redistribution programs can be structured to give the recipients cash to buy a certain service or commodity, or they can be given the service/commodity itself (in-kind). In-kind benefits can include such things as housing, food, clothing, jobs, or opportunities. A client in need of housing can be given money to find housing or can be provided an apartment in a low-income housing project. An example of an opportunity is when hiring agencies expand their eligible hiring lists to include veterans, handicapped, women, or minorities who have not qualified through the normal testing procedures. Scholarships and veterans' educational programs are also opportunities.

Will the benefits be equal, equitable, or adequate? Although each of these goals is important to social welfare programs, they are often in conflict with each other.

Equality suggests that everyone be treated equally in the program. But there are two types of equality. One type, which we call numerical equality, suggests the same treatment for everyone. *Proportional equality* suggests the same treatment for similar persons. If numerical equality were the goal, programs would be developed that strive to equalize resources and benefits available in society. In reality, we design programs that more closely adhere to the proportional equality goal. We identify groups that should be given assistance and then attempt to treat those groups relatively equally. As an example we can look at the AFDC and food stamp programs. Each state sets a benefit level for each different size family. The federal government attempts to equalize benefits between low-paying states and high-paying states by making more food stamps available to families in low-paying states.

Equity is the idea that individuals should receive benefits based upon their contributions to society. Related to that is the concept of less eligibility. Most social welfare programs reflect the equity concept by making assistance available to those who cannot work, but making it less than the income the family or individual would receive if they were active in the labor force.

Social security and unemployment compensation reflect the equity concept by paying more to recipients who have paid more into the fund.

Adequacy implies that it is desirable to provide a decent standard of living for all people, whether or not it is earned. Decent standard of living means different things to different people; in recent years the standard below which no one should fall has itself been steadily dropping. When Ronald Reagan became president a family of four with an income of $14,000 could still receive food stamps. Reagan and his policymakers decided that this standard was too high and lowered the income limit for a family of four to $11,000. By 1983, real per family benefits from AFDC had dropped to only two-thirds of their former level.[6]

Each of these different goals influences some policies more than others. As a general rule, income assistance programs tend to respond to the equity issue. As a society we are very concerned that no one receive money without working, if at all possible. Equality is pursued more aggressively in health care and educational policy. When adequacy is the primary goal, policies tend to develop in-kind rather than cash forms of assistance. This is to make certain that beneficiaries get the designated benefit rather than using welfare money for other purposes.

Who pays? Who decides? Who pays refers to what level of government finances the program. When Democrats are in power the tendency is to move social welfare programs to the federal level. President Nixon's revenue sharing program sent large portions of money that had gone for social welfare programs back to the local level. President Reagan aggressively pursued a

---

Proportional equality is a goal of social welfare policy.

Less eligibility suggests that no welfare recipient should receive more than the lowest-paid laborer.

policy of sending both the cost and the decision-making power back to state and even local decision-making bodies. This trend is clearly continuing under President Bush.

The two questions are closely related. There is clear evidence that clients receive fewer benefits and more stigmatized services, the closer the decision-making is to the local level. Members of Congress are less threatened by irate opponents of welfare programs than are mayors. Further, there is a real benefit to states in bringing federal money into the state. One way to do this is through welfare programs. So, if states have to develop welfare programs to get federal money they are likely to do so. If they can get federal money without developing the programs, the money will frequently be channeled into other areas such as highways, police, or reduced taxes.

Once these choices are made, the additional criteria on which social policy must be judged include administrative costs, target efficiency, allocative efficiency, stigmatization, sovereignty, and flexibility.

Administrative costs include all the expenses incurred in operating a program that do not directly benefit clients. You may argue that administrative costs are not lost because they provide an important source of employment, but it is still not channeling money to the intended recipients. Administrative costs have become a major issue for private charities. *Sixty Minutes,* the television show, has done a number of reports on charitable fundraising that suggest less than 10 percent of the money collected by some charities is used for the purpose collected. The rest goes to administrative costs — especially the hiring of professional fundraisers.

Target efficiency concerns how well the benefits are distributed to the intended groups and is measured in horizontal and vertical efficiency. *Vertical efficiency* is the degree to which benefits reach only the target group. *Horizontal efficiency* is the degree to which all of the target group is served. As a rule, we are much more concerned about vertical than horizontal efficiency. There is more concern over ineligible people receiving benefits than over how many people do not receive them who should.

Perhaps the elderly are one exception to that rule. The federal government actually runs advertisements encouraging the elderly to apply for SSI. The ads stress that SSI is not a welfare program; no such ads have ever been aired for poor families.

Allocative efficiency assesses how the policy affects such issues as the work ethic, birth rates, and integration. For example, will a policy encourage people to accept employment? Will the level of AFDC benefits encourage women to have more children? Will educational policies encourage integration?

Stigmatization is the degree to which society sees the service as demeaning. Social workers believe that poverty itself is demeaning and work for programs that improve rather than destroy individuals' self-concept. Conservatives tend to believe that the more demeaning the program, the greater the

Public housing programs have been more successful for the elderly than for families.

vertical efficiency. They reason that if programs are stigmatized, only the neediest will apply. In actual practice, it appears that the more difficult benefits are to obtain the less likely the elderly, the sickly, and mothers of small children will take advantage of the programs designed to help them.

Sovereignty refers to the degree of choice. Taxpayer sovereignty refers to the degree to which clients' choices are limited. In other words, medical assistance programs are high on taxpayer sovereignty because the only thing the recipients can use the eligibility for is to get health care. On the other hand, SSI for the disabled is high on consumer sovereignty because the clients or consumers get a check, which they can then spend on their own priorities.

Health care is an interesting area to look at in terms of sovereignty. Why have we historically provided in kind for the health of the poor, rather than simply giving them the money these services require and letting them spend it as they see fit? This would be much more in the spirit of the free enterprise system. Our discussion of policy provides some insights in this area.

Flexibility is the degree to which programs can respond to changing conditions. The policymaking process takes time; often, by the time a policy is finally passed, changing social and economic conditions have already outdated the policy.

Consider the difference in programs for the elderly versus those for families. Social Security benefits, because they were indexed to the rate of inflation, nearly tripled in real spending power from 1967 to 1985. In other words, as inflation went up, benefits went up proportionally. By way of comparison, spending in the AFDC program was at about the same real level in 1985 and in 1967, despite the fact that the number of poor children needing assistance had risen.[7]

As social welfare policy has developed many decisions have been made. On what basis will benefits be distributed? What will the benefits be? How will programs be administered? How will they be financed? Once these decisions were made they affected what percentage of the money would go for administrative costs, how important horizontal and vertical efficiency would be, how much choice clients would have, and how accessible and flexible the programs would be. As these programs were developed, equality, equity, and adequacy were given differential emphasis. These questions and concerns were paramount in the development and passage of the Social Security Act.

THE SOCIAL SECURITY ACT

In a message to Congress on June 8, 1934, President Franklin D. Roosevelt stated the problem when he declared that the American people "want some safeguard against misfortunes which cannot be wholly eliminated in this man-made world of ours. . . . I am looking for a sound means which I can recommend to provide at once security against several of the great disturbing factors in life—especially those which relate to unemployment and old age."[8]

The 73rd Congress passed a large number of emergency relief and recovery measures. These were a heavy drain on the treasury, and recovery came very, very slowly. Roosevelt realized that longer-term solutions were needed. He instituted a study of social insurance to formulate proposals for the 74th Congress. Social insurance was well developed in Europe by this time. European governments had begun as early as the 19th century to develop social insurance methods to protect industrial workers against the economic hazards of unemployment, accident, illness, premature death, and old age. They built upon trade union and other voluntary action, and upon their systems of poor relief. By 1934 nearly all European governments had developed a variety of state-operated and subsidized social insurance institutions.[9]

In the U.S. at this time, there were only small beginnings of social insurance programs in some of the states. In 1907 Massachusetts created the Commission on Old Age Pension, Annuities and Insurance. Between 1911 and 1916 nearly two-thirds of the states enacted worker's compensation laws. There was great resistance to social insurance, for a variety of conflicting reasons. On the one hand, some thought social insurance reform was inadequate — they were looking for more revolutionary changes. On the other hand were those who were afraid of social insurance because of its socialistic implications. These people were convinced that social insurance would lead to the decay of American society.

Among those who feared social insurance but still believed that individual security was a social problem, the answer seemed to be voluntarism rather than compulsory insurance. The labor unions tended to push company welfare plans rather than compulsory government insurance.

Even among the social insurance advocates there was considerable acrimony. Social workers such as Jane Addams of Chicago's Hull House and Paul Kellogg, editor of *Survey,* championed social insurance. The National Conference of Charities and Corrections provided forums for discussion of social insurance and impetus for social insurance programs. The social workers tended to favor gratuitous programs rather than contributory insurance programs. They were committed to including the poor regardless of whether they could contribute to the funding of these programs.

A second group of advocates wanted to spread the risk among individuals, employers, and government. They believed that wages were not high enough for workers to meet the risk through savings. One such individual suggested that "the class which needs social insurance cannot afford it, and the class which can afford it does not need it."[10] Social insurance, they argued, should be seen as an effort to readjust the distribution of the national product, perhaps not absolutely equitably, but justly enough for "national vitality."[11]

A third group had tremendous faith in the capitalist system. They sought to eliminate or at least mitigate the harshness of capitalist institutions by inducing owners and managers to reduce the economic hazards to industrial workers.[12]

In spite of the great interest in social insurance programs, the systems developed in the United States were a relief or public assistance system for the poor and an insurance system for the elderly and unemployed. In fact,

The National Conference of Charities and Corrections became the National Conference of Social Work in 1917.

Gratuitous programs require no contribution by the recipient.

Categorical aids are means-tested income programs for the blind, disabled, elderly, and families with dependent children.

The political and social environment determined the policy goals.

The Social Security Act was the first real federal intervention into the social welfare arena.

the framers of the Social Security Act believed that the categorical aids or public assistance programs would only be necessary for a short time. Once the economy started to function more effectively, these programs would not be necessary.

The political and social realities of the day made the Social Security Act a modest beginning of social assurances against economic risks. The preamble to Public Law No. 271 reflects the political climate of the times. The Act is to provide for the "general welfare by establishing a system of Federal old-age benefits, and by enabling the several States to make more adequate provision for aged persons, blind persons, dependent and crippled children, maternal and child welfare, public health, and the administration of their unemployment compensation laws."[13]

The Social Security Act established a dual system of federally supported income maintenance programs. The unemployed and the elderly with previous connections to the work force were to receive federally administered social insurance programs. These social insurance programs were unemployment insurance and Old Age, Survivors Disability and Health Insurance. The "worthy" poor were to receive federally assisted, state administered relief programs. The concern with allocative efficiency is reflected in the fact that social insurance was to cover only those with previous connections to the labor force. These programs were to encourage work. The strong emphasis on "workfare" today reflects this same concern.

Federally aided categories of assistance (categorical aids) were designed to help those classes of the poor whose poverty could not be readily attributed to personal shortcomings. Therefore, state programs for the aged, the blind, and the widowed were generally not seen as stigmatized. There was also a belief that the need for these programs would wither away as social insurance took hold. The unworthy poor—the able-bodied—were left at the mercy of local government.

The Social Security Act of 1935 was the first major piece of federal social welfare legislation. The act has been amended many times, but still contains both social welfare and public assistance programs. The social insurance programs today are for the same groups as the original insurance programs—the Old Age, Survivors, Disability and Health Insurance, unemployment compensation, and Medicare. The public assistance or categorical aids are Aid to Families with Dependent Children, Supplemental Security Income (SSI), and Medicaid. SSI replaced Blind Aid, Disabled Aid, and Old Age Assistance. These programs are now administered by the federal government through the Social Security Administration. This reflects the concern that these "worthy" poor receive benefits that are not stigmatized by the welfare label. However, since the public views the primary recipients of AFDC as divorced women, this program remains locally administered and highly stigmatized.

Putting Blind Aid, Disabled Aid, and Old Age Assistance under the auspices of the Social Security Administration was designed to cut administrative costs and stigmatization.

The values and decisions that shaped the Social Security Act continue to shape social policy today. The value dimensions and choices available structure our discussion of poverty, and we then discuss how our views of poverty and societal values have shaped a specific area of policy—health care.

POVERTY

"This time I am angry, saddened, deeply troubled by what I saw. The lives of individuals reflect the reemergence of armored racism and governmental meanness disguised as bureaucracy. Bureaucratic red tape of the food stamp program makes it almost impossible for them to get what they need."[14]

Poverty was first officially defined by the Johnson administration in 1964. The poverty line was created by using a 1955 survey that found the average family of three or more spent about one-third of its income on food. The poverty line was set at three times the cost of the cheapest nutritionally sound diet the Department of Agriculture could devise.

Beginning in 1968 flexibility was built into the figure as it was adjusted upward annually to reflect inflation. However, today the poverty line figure is only 33 percent of the median family income, whereas in 1964 it was 44 percent of the average family income.[15] Some people believe the poverty line should reflect the median family income, rather than three times a minimally healthy diet. The U.S. Department of Labor's Bureau of Labor Statistics has developed budgets for three hypothetical standards of living in the United States: lower, intermediate, and higher.

Instead of using three times the minimal healthy diet, the procedures used assumed that maintenance of health and social well-being, the nurture of children, and participation in community activities are both desirable and necessary social goals for all families. The budgets used to construct these standards included projected food, housing, transportation, clothing, personal care, medical care, other family consumption costs, occupational expenses, and taxes. This more realistic standard has never been used for public assistance programs.

In 1986 the poverty lines based on the Department of Agriculture formula were:

- $5,701, one person under age 65
- 7,370, two persons, head of household under 65
- 8,738, three persons
- 11,203, four persons[16]

Using this standard, the poverty rate in the United States has never gone below 11 percent. The poverty rate was 22.2 percent in 1960 and was cut in half by 1973. From 1973 through 1979 it remained right around 11 percent. In 1983 it reached 15.2 percent, but declined to 13.6 percent in 1986. Decade by decade,

- 1960s—poverty rate dropped 10.3 percent
- 1970s—poverty rate dropped 0.4 percent
- 1980s—poverty rate rose 1.9 percent (1980–86)

In 1986 there were 32.4 million people in poverty; two-thirds were white. Nearly 40 percent of the poor had incomes 50 percent less than the poverty line. Poverty rates by age show that children are the most vulnerable.

Age	Percent of poor
Under 15	21%
15–24	16%
25–44	16%
45–54	8%
55–59	10%
60–64	10%
over 65	12%

Minority Poverty

The poverty rate for blacks has consistently been about three times higher than the rate for whites. According to a report from the Children's Defense Fund, in 1979 the poverty rate for white children was 11.4 percent; by 1987 it was 15 percent. The poverty rates for black and Hispanic children far outpaced those for white youngsters. In 1979 the poverty rate for black children was 40.8 percent; it rose to 45.1 percent by 1987. In the same period, the rate for Hispanic children rose from 27.7 percent to 39.3 percent. The Children's Defense Fund has called on President George Bush to fulfill his campaign pledge to invest in the nation's children.[17]

Many people move in and out of poverty each year. Poverty is both a more persistent and a more pervasive problem for black people. About 25 percent of the total population lives in poverty or receives welfare benefits at some time. About half of these individuals get out of poverty within a year or two. Half of all AFDC recipients are off in less than one year; only 16 to 18 percent last five years or more. Blacks represent only 12 percent of the population, yet make up 62 percent of the long term poor and 58 percent of the latent poor—those who would be poor except for welfare.[18]

In 1983, 58 percent of black infants were born to unwed mothers. Over 50 percent of children being raised by a mother alone live in poverty. By 1985, half of all black families were headed by single women; 60 percent of these children live in poverty. Of black children today, one in two lives in poverty and one in two grows up without a father.[19]

If instead of using the absolute poverty line we use the concept of "needy," which is defined as 125 percent of the poverty line, half of all black and Hispanic children were needy in 1985, while 6 in 10 black and Hispanic single mothers were needy. More than 7 in 10 children in fatherless black families were needy; if the family was Hispanic, then almost 8 in 10 children were in need.[20]

Housing

Between 1980 and 1987 the Department of Housing and Urban Development (HUD) budget was cut from $35.7 billion to $14.2 billion. Federal subsidies for low-income housing were reduced by 60 percent between 1985 and 1990, and virtually no new public housing was built. Currently the federal government subsidizes 4.2 million low-income households, in one way or another. But over the next decade, according to some estimates, up to 900,000 of those privately owned, federally subsidized rental housing units could vanish. As these units reach their 20th anniversary, the owners may, without government approval, dispose of the property in any way they choose — converting units into high-rent condos or razing them to make room for shopping malls. Additionally, it is estimated that nearly 100,000 nonsubsidized low-income units will be lost every year through abandonment, foreclosure, arson-for-profit, and condominium conversion.[21]

> The nature of our homeless population is largely misunderstood. The lives of most of them are like the lives of the people we all know in our families, in our own communities. They are homeless because they are unemployed . . . because of chronic poverty . . . or simply because of the nationwide shortage of affordable housing.[22]

Robert Rigby, executive director of Jersey City Public Housing Authority (PHA), says that he gets a dozen phone calls a day from people who are desperate for housing. Jenann Olsen, of Milwaukee Public Housing Authority, reports that the number of poor people locally has risen 160 percent since 1980. Olsen speculates that this is because of the shift in Milwaukee's job market, which has lost many high-paying industrial jobs to lower-paying positions in the service sector. Kansas City has long waiting lists, with people begging to get into any kind of public housing. The worst cases are Baltimore, with 13,000 families waiting for openings in 17,000 housing units; Chicago, where 44,000 have been waiting for openings in 49,000 units; and Sacramento, where there are 2,700 waiting for 2,800 units.[23]

Serious and often dangerous conditions are not being repaired, forcing residents either to live with broken heaters and plumbing or sue to get them fixed. Units are often in dilapidated condition. A woman in New Orleans sued the Public Housing Authority because her six children were going to be removed due to the conditions of the home.[24]

Many buildings are being torn down because repairs are too expensive. The Philadelphia Housing Authority closed two 15-year-old towers last year because the estimated $18 million repair costs were prohibitive. A 286-unit building was closed recently in Washington, D.C. because structural damage would have cost $8.5 million to repair. HUD estimates that about 70,000 units are rendered unusable every year because of repair costs.[25]

Reagan's goal at HUD was to do away with government-built and managed housing and privately built but government-subsidized housing in favor of programs to direct subsidies to low-income tenants. Under this program,

A food commodities program was a forerunner of the food stamp program and was seen by some as inefficient and demeaning.

tenants would be given a voucher and then would find their own housing. Reagan liked this because it was much simpler than building government-owned housing or subsidizing private construction of low-income units. He insisted that vouchers were less expensive than new construction subsidies and gave tenants more choice about where they live.

Vouchers are paid for by federal dollars but administered through local public housing authorities. In this program the government pays recipients the difference between 30 percent of their income and the *fair market rate,* a standard amount established by HUD as the maximum a low-income household should pay for rent.

While there is some appeal to the voucher system, the major problem is that it does not respond to the problem. In many areas of the country, housing is just not available. It is estimated that about 25 percent of vouchers today go unused because housing is not available. Another problem with the voucher system is that the clients themselves have to negotiate the rents. In many areas it takes a great deal of sophistication and skill to negotiate effectively.

Political perceptions are also important to the housing problem. The federal deficit is usually cited as the major reason for reining in public hous-

The middle and upper income groups have been receiving more housing assistance, while housing assistance for the poor has been decreasing.

ing spending. Yet what some people call "housing assistance for the rich" — tax subsidies — increased during the Reagan administration. Subsidies for low-income housing are more visible than tax breaks, but they actually constitute only about one-quarter of all housing subsidies. The largest of these — middle and upper-income subsidies — are interest deductions for property taxes and mortgage interest payments. These deductions caused the government to lose about $37 billion in potential revenues in 1987, compared to $20 billion in 1980.[26]

The most recent development, which is likely to have a long-term effect on housing, was the scandal which has been referred to as the "Robin HUD" scandal. At the outset it looked as if one or a few people were illegally channeling funds to low-income people. In reality, it seems that a tremendous amount of graft was taking place, and huge amounts of money were being channeled to politically influential developers and consultants, such as former Secretary of the Interior James Watt. Jack Kemp, secretary of HUD for the Bush administration, vowed to get to the bottom of the scandal. Since Mr. Kemp favored the voucher system from the outset, this scandal may prove to be the impetus he needed to get his pet policies implemented.

Hunger

In 1977 members of the Physicians Task Force on Hunger had reason to believe that the hunger problem in America had virtually been eliminated. Just six years later, in 1983, it was clear that hunger had returned. When research staff from Harvard University interviewed emergency food providers and the hungry themselves, they found that many of the hungry were recently unemployed, or were people who had been terminated from food assistance programs such as food stamps and school lunch. Hunger appeared to be associated with federal policy and economic changes.[27]

The Physicians Task Force on Hunger in America was established in 1984. It was composed of prominent physicians and health experts from around the nation, academic and religious leaders, and human service professionals. The task force was asked to go into different regions of the nation to carry out the following tasks: (1) Document how widespread hunger is and what groups of Americans are hungry; (2) Analyze regional variations in hunger; (3) Assess the effects of hunger on the health of children, pregnant women, and the elderly; (4) Determine why hunger is a problem and make recommendations to remedy the problem and prevent it from recurring.[28]

The task force spent nearly ten months studying hunger in the Deep South, the Mid-Atlantic region, the Southwest, and the Midwest. The major findings of this study are sobering.

Hunger in America is a problem of epidemic proportions across the nation. No one knows the exact number of people who may be hungry at some period each month, but it may be as many as 20,000,000.

Hunger in America is getting worse, not better. In spite of reports that the economy is improving, there seems to be little impact on the problem of hunger. Emergency food programs across the nation report significant increases in the number of hungry people.

Malnutrition and ill health are associated with hunger. Today there is compelling evidence that vulnerable groups, particularly children and the elderly, are at considerable health risk due to hunger. Malnutrition is a problem that impacts somewhere in the vicinity of a half-million American children. Growth failure and low birth weight are associated with inadequate nutrition and are serious problems among low-income pediatric populations. Chronic health problems are associated with undernutrition and are serious among the elderly poor.

Hunger is the result of federal government policies. Hunger occurs because policies either produce it or fail to prevent it. Today our leaders have permitted poverty to reach record levels by cutting back on programs that help our citizens. Not since the Great Depression have we seen so many bread lines.

Present policies are not alleviating hunger in America. Poverty in this country is at the highest rate in twenty years. Purchasing power for the poorest 40 percent of the population is lower than it was in 1980.

Changing Ideology

In 1977 teams of doctors retraced the routes they had covered the previous decade, when they had found serious hunger and malnutrition. These medical professionals suggested that there were far fewer "grossly malnourished people in this country today [1977] than there were ten years ago."[28] This did not seem to be due to an overall improvement in living standards, because living standards overall were not better. Only the area of food was different. The food stamp program, the nutritional component of Head Start, school lunch and breakfast programs, and to a lesser extent the Women, Infants and Children (WIC) program had made the difference."[29] These gains have vanished.

"The inauguration of Ronald Reagan as President of the United States in January 1981 ushered in a new era in terms of the conditions of the country's poor and the prospect for their integration into the American social system."[30] Waxman's observation describes the overall effect of Reagan-era policies. The Reagan administration made unprecedented cuts in the nation's domestic programs, which served the most vulnerable people in our society. Aid to Families with Dependent Children, public housing, food stamps, WIC, and Medicaid were all drastically reduced.

Another major initiative of the Reagan administration was the attempt to have both the funding and administration of welfare taken over from the federal government by the individual states. This assumes that states are capable of administering welfare, and that states are more or less comparable in their needs and resources.[31]

HEALTH CARE POLICY

At least one-tenth of the population does not have necessary health coverage.

Just as hunger and housing became more serious problems for the poor, adequate health care has become inaccessible to many. Despite tremendous expenditures for health care, we have failed to provide public or private health coverage for between one-tenth and one-sixth of the population. Of those below the poverty line, roughly one-quarter are uninsured, and access of the uninsured to medical care seems to be diminishing.[31]

The allocative efficiency of present programs is in question.

Forty percent of government funds for the poor are earmarked for medical services. Government medical programs have displayed a strong institutional bias; hospitals and nursing homes receive far more money than do ambulatory or community health services.[32] When such a large portion of welfare expenditures is going into medical care, there are difficult questions that need to be asked. Clearly, there are some who think the poor would be better served by allocating the money differently. Originally, policymakers asked whether health services to the poor had improved their health care. There appeared to be a consensus that improvement was taking place. The expansion of health care costs has become so great that policymakers are now looking for ways to cut back with the least clinical and political cost. Instead of asking whether more would help, they are now asking, "Would less hurt?"[33] Some people are redefining the problem, claiming that lack of health care is not the problem, but rather the proportion of the budget that goes into health care.

Institutional services include hospitals and nursing homes.

Certain developments within the medical arena are likely to have important implications for health care for the poor. Expansion of medical schools and overbuilding of hospitals over the last three decades has led to a glut in the marketplace of both institutional and physician services. As a result, health services are increasingly being conducted as for-profit enterprises. Employers and government, as major purchasers of health care, are increasingly cost-conscious.

Why are health care services provided in-kind rather than in cash?

Perhaps we should begin a discussion of health care with the basic question of why we have historically provided for the health care of the poor rather than giving them cash so they can purchase insurance or health care. One probable answer is that spending on health care for the poor is good public policy for the collective interest. The collective interest is served by keeping disease down and the work force healthy. This was certainly the motivation for setting up public health agencies.

The common view of health care as a need carries significant moral overtones. Need asserts an obligation on others. Health care need is limited to care perceived as effective in preventing or restoring deteriorations in someone's health status. Unnecessary health care, such as cosmetic surgery, is not a need.

Perhaps the most important reason we earmark funding for health care is that there are certain areas such as education and health care where we are unwilling to tolerate huge inequalities between social groups.

The U.S. Public Health Service has been blocked from performing direct medical services or assuming a role in its financing or coordination.[34]

If we consider alternative proposals, health care for the poor could take three different forms. Health care could be provided by government through a National Health Service.[34] It could take the form of social insurance, such as the elderly have with Medicare. Finally, it could remain as a public assistance program.

Federal financing of health care for the poor did not exist prior to the Depression. Before 1930, health care was entirely a local responsibility. The Social Security Act provided some matching support to the states for maternal and infant care, handicapped children and dependent children. In 1950 Congress extended support to local governments to purchase medical care for those on cash assistance. In 1960 the Kerr-Mills Act increased the level of federal support for the needy aged who did not qualify for welfare.

Medicare is sometimes referred to as Title XVIII of the Social Security Act.

In 1965, the passage of Medicare shifted elderly health care into the social insurance framework. Medicare is the federal health insurance program serving principally the elderly, but also younger persons who are either disabled or have end-stage renal (kidney) disease. Medicare consists of two parts, financed by separate trust funds with different sources of revenue. Revenues for part A, the hospital insurance portion that helps participants pay for inpatient hospital care and post-hospital skilled nursing facility care, are obtained primarily from the Social Security payroll tax. In contrast, revenues for part B, the supplemental medical insurance component that assists beneficiaries to pay chiefly for physician services and outpatient hospital services, come from premiums paid by (or on behalf of) participants and from general revenues.

Medicaid is referred to as Title XIX.

Medicaid, the program of medical assistance to poor families, stayed within the framework of public assistance. It provides comprehensive health care coverage—regardless of age—for those who qualify for public assistance or who might become indigent as a result of medical expenses. Financing for Medicaid is shared by the federal government through general revenues, the state, and in some cases even the local government.

Institutional racism affects Medicaid.

Medicare enjoys the political protection created by a span of eligibility that includes the middle class and pays much more generously than Medicaid. Medicaid suffers from reimbursement rates so low that many physicians refuse to provide services to the poor. Political perceptions and values play a large part in the adverse connotations of Medicaid. Most Medicaid benefits are seen as going to black AFDC families. In reality two-thirds of Medicaid expenditures go to the aged and disabled (much of it for nursing homes). We can contrast that with the perception of the Veterans Administration, which is perceived as treating veterans' war injuries. In fact, three-fourths of admissions to VA hospitals are for nonservice-connected conditions. Hospital benefits of Medicare are additionally protected by the fact that its financing comes from an earmarked payroll tax that cannot be tapped for other purposes, whereas Medicaid must compete for general revenues at both the federal and state level.

Entitlements are benefits people have a right to that cannot be limited by availability of funds.

When employers receive a tax subsidy, they do not have to pay the tax. Of course, the tax must be paid by someone else, or else government must spend less.

Regressive programs provide the most benefits to the least needy.

Federal funding provides an incentive for states to participate.

The general public is very concerned about the costs of Medicaid. It is seen as an uncontrollable benefit because the legislation granted certain entitlements. Actually, the tax subsidy that employers receive for providing health care to their employees is greater than the cost of Medicaid.

When people are concerned about allocative efficiency, we have serious problems in health care. The tax subsidy is highly regressive. The more likely one is to receive health insurance through employment, the more generous the benefits are likely to be, and the greater the value of any tax exemption. Employees prefer health care benefits rather than cash because the benefits are not taxed.

Another problem in allocative efficiency was the Hill-Burton Act. The Hill-Burton Act was a major impetus in the growth of hospitals and medical schools. Hill-Burton subsidized hospital construction and set up the National Institutes of Health to support medical research and expand schools and teaching hospitals. This act stipulated that hospitals receiving these funds must provide a reasonable amount of free care to the poor; however, the requirement was neither defined nor enforced for two decades.

One attempt to target the poor was the creation of the National Health Service Corps, which provided scholarships to medical students in return for commitments of service in underserved areas after graduation. In return for financing of their medical education, recipients owed the government service in poverty stricken areas. Many rural areas, particularly American Indian communities, were served through this program.

Even though there have been problems of inadequacy in Medicaid since its inception, it does represent an advance over earlier federal grants-in-aid to the states for health care for the poor. It provided for a generous federal match of state spending (from a minimum of 50 percent of total expenditures to a maximum of 77 percent, the proportion of federal support varying inversely with state per capita income.) Medicaid created a zone of adequacy and a degree of flexibility for the states. States had to include recipients of AFDC and the blind, disabled, and aged on SSI. Flexibility was built into the extent to which the working poor who have incomes no more than one-third above the cutoff for cash assistance or who have "spent down" their assets in the face of overwhelming medical bills can be included. If the states choose to cover these latter groups, they get federal matching funds. They can cover additional groups, but without federal matching money.

Medicaid required the states to cover inpatient hospital care, physicians' services, laboratory tests, and other items; it did not specify the amount of such services that had to be covered. There were 32 optional services. Anyone who met the eligibility requirements was to have a free choice among providers (consumer sovereignty).

The growth in Medicaid was rapid. From $2.5 billion in 1967, it rose to $9 billion in 1973 and about $30 billion in 1982. Early increases in expenditures were from increased numbers of people being covered. After 1973 the increases came from growing costs of services, especially a rise in intermediate care facilities.[35] It should be noted that coverage of intermediate care facilities came about as an attempt to keep down the cost of expensive skilled nursing care costs. There is some question about whether expanding the coverage to elderly who only needed intermediate care reduced the level of care to what was needed, or whether it created a whole new group being served that had not been reimbursed before. Today it can be said that the expenditure drift toward hospitals and nursing homes has effectively taken money away from primary and preventive health care.

Almost all states have had to respond in some way to fiscal pressures caused by increased costs. Some states have reduced or eliminated eligibility for optional groups such as unemployed parents or the medical needy; some have reduced the numbers eligible by not raising income cutoffs during a period of inflation.[36] Other states have set arbitrary limits on the length of hospital stays or number of physician visits.

The decrease in the number of families covered illustrates how our definition of adequacy changes with the political climate.

An unintended side effect of Medicaid was that it built in the means to limit physician payments, while hospitals and institutions were on cost-based reimbursement. This led many physicians to choose not to participate in Medicaid. Many poor people had no choice but to use hospital emergency rooms and outpatient departments, which would be paid considerably more for providing the same service.

The Reagan administration tried to cap federal support for Medicaid and to give the states greater flexibility in running their programs. Congress rejected the cap, but there was a series of reductions in federal support. A key provision was the decision to cut public assistance for the working poor, which disqualified about a million people from Medicaid. In the early years of the Reagan administration, Medicaid expenditures decreased although the number of people under the poverty line in the United States increased.[37]

In terms of allocative efficiency, Medicare created some problems by the reimbursement methods used. Since hospital reimbursement was on a per cost basis, inefficient hospitals were paid more. Since physicians were paid on a "usual, customary, and reasonable" basis, the program paid more for doctors who charged high fees. The result was that these programs inadvertently caused costs to rise. The program also redistributed money from poorer to wealthier areas of the country.[38]

In 1983 an amendment to the Social Security Act threw out cost-based reimbursement and introduced a new prospective payment system (PPS) to hospitals by diagnosis-related groups (DRGs) — a fee-per-case system, as opposed to the fee-for-service. This was aimed at providing hospitals an incentive to reduce costs per admission. This new method of payment is already having a significant impact on hospitals' treatment of Medicare recipients, as well as on internal management and relationship to physicians.

The initial evidence is that the prospective payment system is positive. The average length of hospital stay on Medicare has fallen. Hospital admission rates have also dropped slightly, in spite of the fact that the new payment system actually offers an incentive for overadmitting.

Over the long term there are dangers to watch for. Hospitals could develop strategies to maximize revenue by putting patients into high-yield categories. Rather than treating patients for what they need, doctors might treat them for the disease that is most profitable. There can also be problems for the poor. The poor tend to have longer hospital stays, because their health status is worse and they suffer from more overlapping conditions. DRGs do not fully reflect differences in severity and the existence of multiple problems. Therefore, the system may encourage hospitals to shun the elderly poor, just as they generally have an incentive to shun more complicated and expensive cases.

A doctor will generally make about ten times as much profit for running $500 worth of tests that give 98 percent certainty of diagnosis as for $50 worth that give 97 percent certainty. The doctor who chooses only the $50 test could also be bankrupted by a malpractice suit in the one out of a hundred cases where opting for the $500 tests would accidentally have proven right.[39]

In terms of reimbursement, 37 state Medicaid programs have dropped Medicare's cost-based approach in favor of different types of incentives.[40] Congress also modified the "free choice of provider" requirement for Medicaid programs. States can now "lock in" (limit the choice of physicians) overutilizing recipients and "lock out" overprescribing or inferior-quality service providers. The most common use of "lock in" is to obtain waivers to use HMOs or case-management systems in which services are restricted to what the plan or doctor advises. Some states use a flat payment plan per recipient, and the provider is then at risk for the cost of service. In a flat payment plan the physician group is paid a certain amount for each client and they are then responsible for providing medical care. If they get a healthy group, they make money; catastrophic illnesses could cost the physicians money.

The Future of Health Care for the Poor

For a number of reasons access to health care for the poor and the uninsured may get worse. The number of low-income groups covered by insurance is dropping. A smaller percentage of the poor is now eligible for Medicaid. Over the last decade a larger portion of the population has fallen below the poverty line, but programs have been cut back. There has also been a drop in private insurance coverage, which reflects the long-term trend of job losses in the primary labor force. New jobs being created are primarily in the service sector and do not carry health insurance.

The National Health Service Corps is running out of physicians who owe service to underserved areas. The Hill-Burton free-care obligations of hospitals are also running out—some hospitals that have provided free care to the poor will no longer have a legal obligation to do so. The case against

The primary labor force involves high-paying jobs in manufacturing and industry that carry fringe benefits such as health insurance.

decreased health care for the poor suggests that the glut of physicians and hospitals will drive them to serve the less affluent.

Clearly, the policy for the future should not be to train more physicians or build more hospitals, but rather to distribute the health care resources we have available more efficiently. Some of the options available are: (1) to cover everyone with adequate health insurance but require them to get care in "managed care" programs that keep down hospital and specialist costs; (2) to require premium payments from recipients (This has always been the practice in Medicare, but is a problem in Medicaid, because only the very poor are eligible for Medicaid); (3) to raise taxes on alcohol, tobacco, and gasoline, all of which take a toll on health; (4) to require the beneficiary to do cost-sharing (This too creates problems for the very poor. Even if the amount they have to pay is very low, they cannot receive health care if they do not have it.); (5) to tax employer-paid health benefits, "one of the major remaining tax shelters."[41]

Each option available has both negative and positive characteristics. Each suggests different values and priorities, and different outcomes would be produced by each. "Almost every advanced country's system of medical finance is bringing results that are the opposite of those predicted by its politicians, professed by its doctors, believed by its voters, and hoped for by its saints."[42]

The seriousness of the problem in the U.S. has been graphically portrayed by Harold P. Freeman, the president of the American Cancer Society, who called for a "guerilla war" to extend cancer therapies to the poor and minorities, who have the highest death rates in the country from the disease. For every other group, survival rates for many cancers have increased dramatically, but the poor and minorities do not get early and adequate cancer treatment.

In the general population, half of cancer patients are expected to survive their disease. Americans living below the poverty line have a cancer survival rate 10 to 15 percent below that for other Americans. The American Cancer Society estimates that 178,000 people with cancer who might be saved through early diagnosis and treatment will die each year. Because these people lack access to quality health care, their cancers are more likely to be diagnosed in advanced stages, when treatment options are more limited and survival rates are lowest.

The poor are also less aware of the warning signs of cancer, and the medical system discourages preventive health care. For the 37 million people who have no health insurance and do not qualify for Medicaid, the emergency room is their entry to the health care system. This leads to a serious problem in continuity of care. The American Cancer Society found that fewer than 45 percent of those living below the federal poverty level are eligible for Medicaid. Some patients are driven into poverty to get treatment, but for many poor and near-poor people, the stigma against public assistance prevents them from applying.[43]

SOCIAL WORK VALUES, KNOWLEDGE, AND SKILLS: A SUMMARY

Throughout this book we have stressed the importance of values in social work practice. Individual dignity and worth of every individual are two values critical in the area of poverty and social welfare policy. Social workers must incorporate a belief in the legitimacy of universal services.[44] Poor people are very much like economically secure people. Life circumstances, often beyond their control, have caused them to be unable to meet their basic needs. Thus, programs that define them as "unworthy" or "deviant" will be stigmatizing, demeaning, and underutilized.

Social workers should understand that most individuals recover from poverty within a relatively short period of time. For this group, services should be developed that shorten the length of time even more. The persistent or long-term poor are a small percentage of the total poverty population. For this group, we need to learn more about the causes of persistent poverty and tailor programs to people's needs. Social workers must become involved actively in the field of income maintenance, including policy formulation. No other service field is more important to the poor. If social workers would play a stronger, more enlightened role in policy formulation and implementation, the poor could receive benefits more appropriate to their economic and social needs.[45]

Throughout its history social work has been the primary profession sanctioned to alleviate the suffering caused by poverty. Social work education must expose students more fully to the income maintenance programs and the importance of these benefits to the lives of the poor. Students need experience in income maintenance and employment settings. They need to study poverty and social stratification and how these lead to discrimination and unacceptable levels of inequality.[46] Students need to be taught the skills of policy analysis, development, and implementation that will enable them to uphold the profession's tradition.

NOTES

1. R. Haveman, *Starting Even* (New York: Simon and Schuster, 1988), 17.
2. E. M. Wells, "Food Stamp Program," in *Encyclopedia of Social Work*, 18th ed. (Silver Spring, Md.: NASW, Inc., 1987), 628–634.
3. L. Ginsberg, "Social Workers and Politics: Lessons from Practice," *Social Work* 33, 3 (May–June 1988): 161.
4. Haveman, *Starting Even*, 220.
5. D. Macarov, "Re-evaluation of Unemployment," *Social Work* (January–February 1988): 23–27.
6. Haveman, *Starting Even*, 75.
7. G. Falk, "1987 Budget Perspectives: Federal Spending for the Human Resource Programs" (Washington, D.C.: Congressional Research Service, February 1986).
8. F. D. Roosevelt, *Review of Legislative Accomplishments of the Administration and Congress* (Washington, D.C.: United States House of Representatives Document #397 (73rd Congress, 2nd session), 2.

9. T. Schlabach, *Edwin E. Witte: Cautious Reformer* (Madison, Wis.: State Historical Society, 1969), 74–75.
10. A. Epstein, *Insecurity, A Challenge to America: A Study of Social Insurance in the United States and Abroad* (New York, 1913), 38–39.
11. Ibid.
12. T. Schlabach, Witte, 81.
13. U.S. 74th Congress, Public Law No. 271.
14. Dr. William Beardslee, quoted in Physicians Task Force on Hunger in America, *Hunger in America* (Middleton, Conn.: Wesleyan University Press, 1985).
15. Haveman, *Starting Even*.
16. Ibid.
17. "Poverty Rising Among Young," *New York Times* Service, 1989.
18. N. Wyers, "Economic Insecurity: Notes for Social Workers," *Social Work* (January–February 1988): 18–22.
19. Haveman, *Starting Even*, 78.
20. "While Most Gain, Millions Suffer," *Washington Post* (20 January, 1986), A1, A11.
21. T. Riordan, *Common Cause Magazine* (March–April 1987): 26–31.
22. Ibid.
23. Ibid.
24. Ibid.
25. Ibid.
26. Ibid.
27. Physicians Task Force on Hunger.
28. Ibid.
29. N. Kotz, *Hunger in America: The Federal Response* (New York: The Field Foundation, 1979).
30. C. Waxman, *The Stigma of Poverty* (New York: Pergamon, 1983), 129.
31. Ibid.
32. P. Starr, "Health Care and the Poor: The Last Twenty Years," Paper presented at the Institute for Research on Poverty Conference, Williamsburg, Virginia, December 7, 1984.
33. Ibid.
34. Ibid.
35. P. Starr, *The Social Transformation of American Medicine* (New York: Basic Books, 1982), 235–289.
36. T. Moloney, "What's Being Done About Medicaid," (New York: Commonwealth Fund, 1982).
37. J. Holahan, "The 1981 Omnibus Budget Reconciliation Act and Medicaid Spending," Urban Institute, May 1984.
38. K. Davis and C. Schoen, *Health and the War on Poverty: A Ten Year Appraisal* (Washington, D.C.: Brookings, 1978).
39. Ibid.
40. N. Macrae, "Health Care International," *The Economist* (April 28, 1984): 17.
41. Starr, "Twenty years."
42. V. Cohn, "Bitter Pill for Health Insurers," *Milwaukee Journal,* Washington Post Service, (26 February, 1989).
43. Macrae, "International."
44. Oshkosh *Northwestern* (17 July, 1989), 11.
45. Wyers, "Insecurity."
46. Ibid.

Chapter

14

Special Populations — Special Issues

In America, one of the most dangerous ways to be different, is to be black.[1]

The profession of social work strives to combat oppression in many different forms. In spite of our rhetoric to the contrary, our society is relatively intolerant of diversity. People are uncomfortable with others who are different from themselves. This is a natural tendency for many. However, some people strive to bridge the gap between themselves and others by increasing their understanding and appreciation of differences. Others try to control diversity by limiting the options of those who are different.

Clearly, if you are to be involved in the profession of social work you must make the commitment to fight oppression and expand opportunities for all other people regardless of their ethnic heritage, their sexual preference, or handicapping conditions they must overcome.

Social work programs are required to teach cultural diversity in the curriculum. There are a number of methods by which this can be done. One of the most common methods is to teach ethnicity or diversity as a categorical phenomenon.[2] In this approach cultural differences are explained according to the degree to which individuals manifest specific distinctive traits. While this approach may teach you to value diversity, it does not develop your sensitivity to how individuals experience their ethnicity. What you are left with is typically a new kind of stereotyping.

An alternative way to study ethnicity is to use a transactional approach.[3] In a transactional definition of ethnicity, we identify the ways in which people who are communicating or interacting maintain their sense of cultural distinctiveness. Transactional definitions treat ethnicity as an element of behavioral and cognitive participation in the decisions and symbolic constructs that supply meaning to communication. Ethnicity, then, is not a group of traits we need to memorize and a set of responses appropriate to those traits; rather, ethnicity must be seen as a situational phenomenon. It is this situational approach to the issue of cultural distinctiveness that can make a difference in social work practice.

In this chapter we are fortunate to have contributions from six individuals who have experienced the categorical approach to treatment as a member of a minority group. Each of them knows the frustration of being stereotyped, sometimes benignly and sometimes maliciously. Each has a desire and a commitment to have you understand his or her treatment on a personal, not a categorical level. The authors deal with oppression in three different areas: ethnicity, sexual preference and lack of recognition of the effects of Post-Traumatic Stress Syndrome. The common element in each of these situations is the personal feeling of oppression for being different and the writer's desire for social workers to understand this on an experiential level. Each of these writers has completed at least an undergraduate social work degree. They are sharing their experiences with you as an attempt to decrease the oppression others might suffer.

ETHNIC DIVERSITY

There is no question that there has been a significant upsurge in racial hatred toward minorities. This is especially evident against middle class blacks. Some of the most serious and publicized incidents include the Howard Beach incident in Queens, New York, the Ku Klux Klan demonstration in Cummings, Georgia, and a recent slaying in Brooklyn. Howard Beach is a middle class neighborhood where three black men were assaulted by whites. In fleeing the situation, one of the men, Michael Griffith, ran into the path of an automobile and was killed. In Georgia the residents of Forsyth County boasted on national television of their willingness to engage in violence to maintain their racial homogeneity. Yusef Hawkins, 16, was shot to death in the Bensonhurst area of Brooklyn when he and three friends ventured into the area to look at a used car for sale.

Some people believe that this racism is being bolstered by right-wing rhetoric. Benjamin Hooks of the NAACP suggested that there was "a steady drumbeat from the Reagan administration that somehow white males are being mistreated."[4]

Social issues and needs raised by minority or oppressed groups are as diverse as the groups represented. One common thread is that to eradicate oppression will require a redistribution of resources and power. In addition to understanding the discrimination individuals have suffered as members of a minority group, we need to be cognizant that group membership itself adds to the difficulty of coping in American society. Racial minorities suffer double jeopardy because each social problem they face is exacerbated by racism.

Some minorities suggest that one cannot adequately understand discrimination without having experienced it. As educators we believe that

It is important that professional social work education include experience and information in preparing workers for ethnic sensitive practice.

one way to help you experience racism is through the lives of our guest writers.

Janet Davenport graduated with honors from an accredited BSW program. After spending three years as a paraprofessional in the Midwest, she was finally able to obtain a social work position in an eastern city. Janet left social work to become a city news reporter. Her special areas of interest are minorities and women. Janet's essay was written in 1984 but her message is still timely.

Edwin Gonzalez-Santin is a social work educator at Arizona State University. Ed's experience with racism was complicated by being uprooted from his own culture, difficulty with a new language, and skin color. In contrast to Janet's middle class but painful upbringing as a black American, Ed's life was filled with fear for his very survival. Ed suggests that social work educators must take the lead in fighting racism.

Our third author, Toby Ferrell, gives us both his personal response to his own social work education and guidelines for what he believes must change. Toby is another honors graduate from a BSW program who was unable to find employment in the field. Toby is involved in operating a small business in a metropolitan area.

CASE STUDY
American Racism

Janet Davenport

The best way for me to describe or talk about my feelings on discrimination, race prejudice, and racism is to talk about my own personal experiences growing up black in America. I can vividly recall how I felt about being treated unfairly as far back as four years old. This is one of the reasons I strongly reject the notion, too often expressed by white adults, that children are color blind. Although my consciousness was not as fully developed as it is now, I was very aware of color differences in people and gradually learned how these differences could so affect a person's destiny. My trusting and innocent view of the world was shattered quite early.

What does it feel like to be the target of discrimination in a racist society? It is like calling out in the middle of the night with your voice left unheard. It is like being chained to a curse which had its foundation well laid before your birth. It is like living with a disease which you know the cure for, but treatment lies outside yourself and in the hands of other people. It is over four centuries of coping with a problem when mental health "experts" say if you have been coping with the same problem for a year, that is too long. It is turning around and finding yourself in the same predicaments as past generations — a spot you never really thought you would be in, because you convinced yourself you would be so much more in control of life forces. It is having your stomach muscles tighten while you grope for the words to explain irrational white hatred to your preschooler, who you desperately want to grow up positive and healthy in a hostile society. It is being hungry knowing if you were white there would be less chance of it being so. It is sitting and listening to white liberals tell you all about your culture and your history as if whites are smarter about you than you are about yourself — the ultimate insult by white intellectuals. It is being angry and in a cage. Paul Laurence Dunbar and Maya Angelou, the noted black writers, say a lot about black people's frustrations in *We Wear the Masks* and *I Know Why the Caged Bird Sings*. Blacks have been slaves in this country for a long time. And, while a lot has changed — a lot more has not or has merely taken a different form.

Naturally we are all unique individuals, shaped by the experiences we have lived. It should go without saying, blacks are no different. It is interesting, however, that blacks have been pushed into the position of having to qualify themselves first as human beings before they can move on to any other social level. It does something to a person having to qualify first as a member of the human race, before moving to square two. It fills me with indignation when I am placed in that position. When it is a one-on-one interaction then at least I can confront my offender. When it is hidden behind a tangle of policies, rules, and laws, it takes a longer time to confront. It is so much more difficult to figure out exactly who is attacking or restricting your freedom to be a human being when the culprit lies hidden behind traditions.

Before I entered kindergarten, I was curious about everything. I could not wait to read so I could understand all the words bouncing off the walls around me. A white woman screamed the word nigger at me one day for peering at her red-faced, squealing infant in a stroller. I truly did not understand the full weight of the name she selected to assault me with, but I knew it had something to do with her being white and me being black. I was so hurt and then angry for the obvious reason — I had done nothing to deserve the attack. My eleven-year-old brother was also in the playground. He saw this woman screeching obscenities at me at the top of her lungs. He quickly grabbed my hand, cursed her back loudly, and took me home.

The black parent's job is not an enviable one. It is not easy explaining prejudice or countering racism. I remember my sense of disbelief upon learning I could expect similar scenes (like the playground scene) and worse as well as things too complicated for me to fully understand. It all seemed so stupid. It did not make sense. It was a bad joke, unfair, and painful. Could skin color be that important? I was confused. It did not seem possible that color was a valid reason for hating an entire race of people and relegating them to an inferior rank.

I thought that by learning more about black people, my people, I could learn the deep, dark secret or terrible thing we had done to bring about what appeared to be a social curse. I went to the dictionary for a definition very early in my elementary school education. The dictionary described a Negro as one of the black race with negatively described physical characteristics such as flat noses, kinky hair, big lips, rather than broad noses or curly hair or full lips. Negatives surrounded me.

During this period of my childhood, a teacher selected me to read the paragraph about blacks in our social studies reader. For several weeks we had studied about the different states, the fascinating people who made this country strong and brave and beautiful. Then we came to the era of the Civil War. I wanted to die as I read about Negroes and that all they did was pick cotton as slaves and make themselves a burden and source of trouble by setting off a Civil War. I did not know whether to believe this shocking bit of information, but I was furious with the teacher for having me read it in front of all my white classmates. I have no doubt that she did it to humiliate me. I hated her and hated white people for making my people slaves and then I was angry at my people for being slaves. I grew more ambivalent.

It was a mixed bag of sitting in back of classrooms, false accusations, being ignored or given the wrong kinds of attention. One teacher patted my head and then had the nerve to tell me she was dying to see what my hair felt like. She was surprised it was soft. I wondered what she expected—barbed wire? I resented this form of recognition. I know too well what it is like to sit in a class and starve for positive attention.

Name calling and rejection by teachers became a pattern. I developed a sixth sense for who cared and who didn't. Too often they did not care. The few who did care helped sustain me. I grew

less passive and more rebellious, rejecting adults in general, whites in particular. I developed defenses to shield me from all the negative information I was receiving about myself (always thankful for caring parents and friends). I saw the ugly light whites persisted in casting on me reflected on them. I was not the animal—they were. I was not ugly—they were. I was not dumb—they were. And so the defenses grew.

By the time I was in junior high school, I was angrier, but I began to learn just how unhappy and miserable life could be if you do not have choices or options. Because of a zoning law, I was left with no alternative but to walk well over a mile to a ghetto school where the majority of students were both black and poor. It took little time to understand why our books were outdated, torn and defaced; why the school was infested with roaches and the teachers were terrible. One teacher kept a vodka bottle in his briefcase and sipped out of it all day long. Another teacher hung a child by his feet outside a window. There were some so apathetic and burned out it did not make any difference whether they came to the class. It was a nightmare. I felt helpless—totally victimized. What could I do? I was only twelve years old. My parents did not seem sure whether to believe my accounts of a typical day at school. I was enraged, but frightened by what I saw. When my parents finally realized what was happening (we were new to the city), and saw my fears were based in reality, I felt it was almost too late. A whole school year had gone by and I was cheated out of a seventh grade education, which was very important to me. Not that I was such a scholar or loved school so much, but I believed then education was the only way I would achieve social and economic equality. This was being denied to me. My family, the black community, my black role models had stressed getting the "white man's education."

I was also confused by the messages I got in school, such as "you deserve straight *A*'s for being mannerable and well dressed." It did not seem to matter what the quality of my work was. Nobody cared whether I learned anything. By the time my parents were ready to accept the financial burden of sending me to a private school (at great personal sacrifice), a new zoning law was passed and I was bused to a suburban school which was in a much safer and better maintained environment.

It took over half of the next school year for me to be placed in a classroom that provided any learning. As my dear racist guidance counselor explained twice, since I was from an inferior school and of minority background I belonged in the lower half of the eighth grade class. I resented her assumption, but was glad to finally be at a "real" school. Before the end of the year I was finally placed in the advanced class. Imagine the shifting around and adjustments for an eighth grader merely because of skin color.

This school also assumed that all black children needed to talk to a special counselor. Are your parents living together? Is your home noisy? Do you have a place to study? Much later, in college, I was required to read the results of these findings in social science courses. I was a subject for the cultural deprivation theorists of the sixties. A white girl who sat behind me in homeroom said, "I've never seen a black person before." Fourteen years old—I had been looking at them, learning their ways all my life, and she was going to tell me she had never seen a real live one like me before. I told her that was her problem and it must be sad to be so stupid. My tolerance had come to an end. Evidently the other black children's patience had also worn thin, because they were openly hostile to not only the white students, but the teachers as well. There were fistfights every other day. The school administration did not know what to do with us. They did not know how to talk to us. They did not know how to teach us. We rebelled. A black face was always in the principal's office, including mine.

I brought some poems to social studies class. The teacher had suggested we share poems of social relevance. They were poems by Don L. Lee. One began, "A rat done bit my sister Nell and Whitey's on the moon." These poems were confiscated from my locker and I was called to the principal's office. The social studies teacher, whom I will never forget, came out of the principal's office blushing. In a phony voice he said, "How in the hell did they find out?" I knew how they found out. This teacher had come across so supportive, so liberal, and so encouraging. He taught me to mistrust in a way

more profound than words can express. A "militant" tutor, a black college student who wore miniskirts and a large Afro, said, "I told you so; you can't trust white folks ever. Now let that nice liberal be a lesson to you." She had warned me and he was a lesson to me. And, it all became sort of a game of risks and survival.

High school proved to be more of the same but on a different level. It was 1969, and I was not only questioning the education system, but white America as a whole. I was fully aware of the double standard—one for blacks and another for whites. I hated the hypocrisy around me. I did not like the unrealistic expectations. I needed space to grow and make mistakes. It was as if a black person making a mistake, being less than perfect, was evidence of inferiority. It was like being measured against a foreign set of ideals that the foreigners themselves could never measure up to. It was enough to make people sick in the head, but survival was primary.

Why did we not have black teachers? Why were we not taught black history? Where were the black counselors? Why were we punished for doing the same things as white kids, while they went free? Why were we unheard? Ignored? We were fed up. We boycotted classes. Tensions rose. Violence increased. Black students were arrested. Police were in the schools checking for weapons. There were skirmishes in the city. Racial tension was the name the papers gave it. Curfews were set. Anger took center stage.

After a couple of deaths, and numerous injuries, the city began negotiations with black community leaders. We wrote up a list of demands—not requests as our parents had urged—and presented them to the superintendent of schools and the mayor. I will never forget that confrontation as long as I live. Our voices were finally being heard. What do you people want? This was the question of the hour. It seemed so hollow. What did they think we wanted? We wanted to be treated as human beings.

Well, we got a black history course, two black teachers, one black counselor and an Afro-American studies club. My energy focused on seizing the time, placing my creativity in directions other than hatred. I directed a play about religion, drugs, and the black community. I danced African dances, wore African clothes, and had a wonderful time being my black kinky-headed self. But, the redundancies in being black and being female began to hit me. I'm not a chick, a broad, a ho'e, or a hammer, I screamed. The more things changed the more they remained the same. If we do not learn from our history we are destined to repeat it.

All I wanted was to get out of high school, my hometown, and my parents' home. By the time I stepped on a college campus as a full-fledged student, it was being said my generation caught the tail end of the action that had gone on at campuses across the nation. Boston University did have a solid Afro-American studies program, the Martin Luther King Center, black fraternities and sororities, Afro-American orientation week, and a black student government organization. I became involved in both white student government and black student government. I began to see how I had to play a game in order to get through the system. Do what I had to do to retain my dignity and identity, but conform to white folks' ways of doing things to get what I wanted. I began to see how blacks and whites really have different values and ways. Basically nonconformist, I struggled with conformity. There was so much to learn about how to figure the mess out, live my life, and be happy.

I searched for answers to the problems of race—being black in America. The more I searched the more I ended up right back where I started. I am a black woman who made it through white America's education system, but I did not make it through in one piece. I have had to compromise too many of my true values and ideologies, and that has taken a little something away from me. But one thing white America will never take away and that is my dignity and human spirit—they did not give it to me. You cannot take back what was never yours. While I may have some semblance of sanity, the inequities around me put me in a headset of preparedness to kill or be killed. I still get called nigger. Sometimes by little children, but mostly by men in fast-moving cars. I am immune. They reinforce what I have known for a long, long time. Bigots have no guts,

just blind hatred. I am a product of American socialization. I manage my emotions very well, but it is inevitable I will have hypertension like my father. I carry stress in my back. There is a price to pay for being so-called educated by white schools. I am so tired, but will never give up the cause. The cause for freedom for every black woman, man, and child in these United States of America.

P.S. If you should feel that this struggle is part of the past, let me relate a recent incident to you. I was asked by the local university department of social work to be a respondent to a panel presentation on Racism in Field Placements. Although I am very tired of being the resident minority in this community, I felt obligated to do what I could to make education more accessible to minority students. I was told that four field supervisors would do short presentations and I would be asked to respond. From the outset it appeared that the agenda was very different from what I had been told to expect. Much to my surprise, the panel deferred to my "minority" status and allowed me to give the first presentation. Swallowing my feelings of betrayal by the organizers, I extemporaneously addressed race issues in field placements. As I feared, the panel of "experts" then went on to say they could not relate to race discrimination but they wanted to address discrimination against the elderly, the mentally handicapped, and the learning disabled. My anger was further exacerbated as I had to sit and listen to the local professionals relate their difficulty in hiring minorities in this area. Here I was an honors graduate of this social work program, qualified to speak as an expert on racism in field placement but unable to secure a professional position in the community in spite of endless interviews and applications. Strangely, I could muster no sympathy for their efforts to recruit black professionals. It seems the only function I served was that the social work department could now document that it sponsored a full-day conference to deal with issues of racism. I am sure the Council [CSWE] will be impressed with these efforts. After all, isn't that what Affirmative Action is about— effort, not results. Racism marches on!

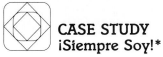

CASE STUDY
¡Siempre Soy!*

Edwin Gonzalez-Santín

My family were campesinos in Mayaguez, Puerto Rico. My father, like his father, was a sugar cane cutter. My father dreamed of taking his family to the United States of America. In Mayaguez we lived in low-income housing near the cane fields. Our community was a rich mixture of the descendants of Spanish colonists, Dienos and Carib Indians, and African slaves. This mixture of Spanish, Indian, and African blood continues to characterize Puerto Rican society today. This mix of race and culture fosters equality and tolerance.

I had to leave my country to learn about racism. Shortly after reaching New York at the age of six, an awful, hurtful feeling attacked my very being. It seemed that white people did not like me. I was spat upon and called "nigger." In Puerto Rico "negrito" was a term used with warmth and affection. The popping veins and red, twisted faces that accompanied this new, strange-sounding word "nigger" haunts my memory to this day.

My new country became more confusing and scary to me as my cousins showed me where the baseball bats (my protection) were "stashed" around the neighborhood. This did not make me feel safe. I was terrified and confused: "Why did Mom and Papi work so hard to get us here? Papi does not want us to cut sugar, but is this better? Is Papi right? Are there more opportunities here?"

I felt we had been cheated. No one told us they hated Puerto Ricans here! Papi and Mom had made great sacrifices so we could come to the United States, and we were met with hatred and resentment because of our skin color. This was the beginning of what would become a lifelong education on racism.

Things got worse when we moved to Petersburg, Virginia. We had to ride in the back of the bus and go in the rear door of the restaurants. I kept

wondering what had happened when we boarded the plane to come to the U.S. We didn't change, but we were no longer treated like people. We were *things,* objects of other people's hate.

Painful memories still burn—like going swimming with some friends at a public pool in Doedoe Park in Lawton, Oklahoma. I paid my quarter and jumped in the water. The sound of that whistle still sends chills up my spine. Everyone hustled out of the water and the man came over to me and said I had to leave because I was offending other swimmers. Shame swept over me as I left the pool. I felt so alone. I never told my parents what had happened. The anger still gnaws at my being.

Other strange things happened after we came to the mainland. My mother told us not to go out in the sun so our skin wouldn't get any darker. This didn't make sense—sun felt so good. School days were a mixture of confusion and humiliation. In the first grade, I had to go to the bathroom but did not know how to ask permission. Other children had told the teacher they needed to go to the office and then left the room. I tried that. Fear, confusion, and embarrassment struck when the teacher yanked me out of the bathroom, screaming derogatory racial comments. What had I done wrong? I did not know the language.

In high school I was ordered to the principal's office for explaining to the teacher that Don Juan was not pronounced "Don June." The principal added to my humiliation by telling the class that the teacher knew more about my language than I did. My own brother's name was Juan.

Adolescence brought new forms of racism. Dating was a source of agony. I had a crush on a white girl but knew her parents would not allow her to date me. An Anglo friend arranged a secret date and I had to hide in the bushes down the street while my friend picked up my date. I could not even be in the car with him. A week later her parents found out the truth and punished her for seeing me.

---

[1] "I am always," that is, "I will always be who I am."

Ed Gonzalez-Santin meets with future social workers.

The most torturous racist image I carry with me is the day my oldest sister was knifed on the playground by a white boy who did not like "niggers." As of that day I was convinced we were going to be killed by these "crazy Americans." My father warned us, "You've got to stick together to survive!"

As a family, the event brought us closer together, but it also instilled a siege mentality. I felt I had to fight my way out of this thing. In this new place, if you were white, you were valued as a human being. If you were of color, forget it! I was surrounded by feelings of isolation, self-doubt, confusion, and fear of being physically or verbally attacked. I became further withdrawn and angry. I decided if these people were afraid of me, they would leave me alone. I would learn to fight. I would meet their meanness with my own. I would overcome my fear by causing fear in others. I would no longer tolerate being called "nigger," "chili pepper," or "pepper belly." I was further incensed at the inappropriateness of their insults. Didn't they know

Puerto Ricans do not use chilies in their cooking? No one would listen when I tried to tell them I was Puerto Rican. I felt proud of my heritage but I just kept being lumped with all the "bad" dark-skinned people who "sounded Spanish."

Learning to fight back only created more problems, especially with the school system. Inadvertently, I was reinforcing their already negative stereotypes of me. As I grew older I realized I was not the problem — they didn't hate me, they didn't even know me — my color was the problem. Today, I try to explain these things to my children. My children continue to suffer pain and confusion over the same things I suffered 27 years ago. Joan Baez sings it for us: "It's hard to be a princess in America, if you are brown."

I hope my pain has not been in vain. It drives me to try to explain and protect my own children from racism. Sadly, I tell them racism does not exist just in America — it is worldwide. People of all colors hold racist views. Prejudice, racial stereotypes, lack of acceptance, and misinformation are passed from one generation to the next. Fighting racism seems like a never-ending battle.

My daughter asks if she will quit being hurt by racism when she grows up. I tell her I am still hurt by it and am still fighting it. One of the ways I fight racism is within my chosen profession. I am a social work educator who works actively to recruit and retain minority students and faculty. I experience considerable resistance to the infusion of minority content in the curriculum. With great sadness I read articles in university newspapers such as "Minorities Bite the Hand that Feeds Them." Minority professors are few in number, seldom tenured, and not in key leadership positions. Universities spend a great deal of time setting up recruitment plans and little time or effort in actual recruitment. The social work profession has not done any better than other professions. How can we advocate for the poor and oppressed if we cannot resolve this basic issue within social work education?

I believe that social work must play an active role in addressing racism. We must be vigilant to the dangers that racism poses to the very fabric of society. Fighting racism starts with an examination of ourselves, as individuals and as a profession. We must teach students to think critically about the racist structures of society. We must find ways to provide experiential learning for students so that they may be immersed in the visceral experience of being the victim of racism. Hearing the tale may not be as effective as feeling the sting. We must be courageous enough to speak out boldly against racism while being sensitive to those who are victimized by it. Social work is an applied field. We must be actively involved in the struggle. Social work educators are in a position to lead this charge.

 ## CASE STUDY
Modifying Social Work

Toby Ferrell

Social work as a profession has not responded to the needs of the black population. This must not be allowed to continue. There must be fundamental change in the social work curriculum, practice, and thought if we are to be effective in moving blacks into the mainstream and advantages of our society.

One of the reasons conventional social work methods have been ineffective in the black community is the setting in which it developed. Settlement houses, youth agencies and other early forms of social services were appropriate for white immigrants and poor whites who were only in need of financial assistance. They were of little use to blacks who were seeking to gain acceptance as human beings.[5] There is no service capable of remedying this problem.

Another reason social work has been ineffective in responding to black need is its inherent function in the present political and economic system. Social work has been given the mandate to make our society more humane. In order to do this social workers most frequently function as social control agents, keeping things rolling along with minimal change. For blacks to become equal, major change must be not only allowed but facilitated. Capitalism as an economic system is dependent upon low wages. Low wages occur only if there is competition for jobs. Therefore, there must be fewer jobs than people, requiring a segment of the population to be unemployed. Over the past 200 years, this segment has been the black population. Therefore, any agency or profession in the business of maintaining such a system will come into direct conflict with black equality.

REDEFINING THE BLACK IMAGE

The black's role in the labor force presents conflict for blacks from a very early age. The urban black child is lectured by social workers and teachers to attend school, study, work hard, etc. The values upheld by white society are drilled into their heads but the avenues upon which to achieve them are not open to these children.[6] The inner city school which the child must attend is frequently substandard; as he gets older, jobs that are available will most likely be at substandard pay and the cycle will be repeated with the next generation. Social work must share in the responsibility for stopping the perpetuation of this cycle.

To uphold its share, social work must first revolutionize its thought patterns toward black clients and practitioners. One of the prerequisites for being a social worker has been the ability to view people from a "color blind" perspective. This is an error. Black clients must be viewed as black clients with problems and causes distinctly different from those of other racial groups. For instance, black children have a totally different lifestyle from white children. White kids enjoy a carefree childhood while black children are preparing themselves to enter the adult phase of life — the maturing process is much quicker in the ghetto than in suburbia. This should not be viewed as a fault or weakness in the black family. Social workers need to understand and appreciate the strengths of the black family. Early maturity is a means of survival in the ghetto.[7]

Finally, if radical change in the analysis of black problems is to occur, there must be a reanalysis of black history. This is a history of frustration and betrayal by white institutions in which blacks have placed trust. Now the white social worker comes into the black community offering ideas and methods that sound faintly similar to those of the white missionaries who came to Africa years ago; they brought the Bible but took the land.

Social work must also re-analyze its relation to black history. What assumptions have programs and services to blacks been based upon? Most services were given with the basic belief that blacks were lazy, subhuman and in need of patronage by the superior white race. This negative concept must be changed to a positive concept of blacks. Black poverty is not genetically inherited, but environmentally and socially thrust upon blacks. As Malcolm X once said, "We didn't land on Plymouth Rock, it landed on us!"

The history of blacks must be appreciated as a history of struggle and survival.[8] The strength exhibited by blacks' ability to survive, and in fact "progress," should be viewed as a positive char-

acteristic. Social workers should recognize and value the undeniable strength of the black race.

SOCIAL WORK CURRICULUM

To allow this reversal of attitude toward the black race, the social work curriculum must be "blackened," i.e., the black experience "must be incorporated in social work curriculum and practice."[9] The black experience is translating all occurrences and events and how they impact on the black community. It is an increased emphasis on black culture, black heritage, and the basic realization of what it means to be black.[10] This is a condition which is remarkably absent from social work but it is a situation which can be rectified.

There are three basic components of the social work curriculum: human behavior and the social environment, social welfare policy and services, and the practice sequence. Each of these can be injected with the black experience. The human behavior sequence should examine the idea that it is socioeconomic factors such as institutional racism that cause stress in the black community and decrease the chance of blacks' receiving either a good education or job. Human behavior should stress the black experience as unique to overcome the long-held view that sees blacks as inferior. It is also necessary to look at the social controls that manage to keep blacks "in line," such as law enforcement agencies, educational systems, and the pacifying profession of social work.[11]

Social policy should emphasize the impact profit, power, and privilege have on policies, and that since blacks are scarce in these categories the cycle has consequently been able to sustain institutional racism.[12]

Social work practice courses should train students to be able to work in the black community. This must start with studying the history of black culture, black religion, family development, marriage patterns and customs, etc. Students should be taught how to study and learn to understand the individual black communities. The political, economic, and social institutions and their impact on black development must also be included in this analysis.[13]

It is essential that social work thought and curriculum be blackened to the extent that the problems of blacks are accepted as unique and different from those of any other group. Only then can social work methods be revised to effectively attack these problems and their causes. Current methods are too passive. Social work needs to be more action-oriented. Services must be taken to the people. It is not important how attractive the office is but how much it can help people.[14]

The advocacy role should be more widely adopted. This can take the form of participating in boycotts, pickets, and if necessary fear-inducing and violent tactics. Social workers can also be responsi-

ble for monitoring the programs in their agencies that are funded for a specific purpose to insure that the funds are appropriately used.[15]

BLACK VS. WHITE ROLES

There is one thing to remember when examining all these changes that should take place. *The bulk of the work for black liberation must be done by blacks, not whites!* Whites are to be responsible to themselves because the problem is not a black problem but a problem of white racism. Social work is but one of the many societal institutions that can contribute to the remedy.

POST-TRAUMATIC STRESS DISORDER (PTSD)

PTSD is a disorder that begins with an external stressor that is great enough to produce traumatic symptoms in most people.[16] Whether the victim is a battered woman, an abused child, a rape survivor, or a combat veteran, PTSD characterizes normal people reacting to an extreme situation.

PTSD causes the victim to experience self-blame and feelings of powerlessness and immobilization. The most profoundly damaged are brainwashed and tortured to the point where reality and fantasy are blurred.

Sadly enough, experience has shown us that battered women suffering from PTSD are likely to receive neglectful or punitive responses from the helping professions. Professionals frequently blame the victim by attributing her plight to personality deficits such as masochism.[17] To the contrary, most battered women make efforts to escape the violent victimization, often to find their options minimal or nonexistent.

Vietnam Veterans

The group first and most often associated with PTSD is Vietnam veterans. Their plight is in some respects similar to that of battered women. Neither our government nor the American people have wanted to deal with the aftermath of the war in Vietnam—a painful experience everyone wants to forget. However, over 500,000 veterans cannot forget. This is a conservative estimate of the number of veterans suffering from post-traumatic stress disorder.[18]

The formal definition of PTSD offered by the Veterans Administration is "a survivor reaction to catastrophic stressors experienced in war, having a prolonged effect on personality development, patterns of adjustment, coping styles, and interpersonal functioning."[19] This disorder can be acute, chronic, and/or delayed.

The actual psychiatric casualties during the Vietnam War were low compared to previous wars. Psychiatrists felt that the method of deploying and replacing men as individuals and not as units would prevent psychiatric casualties.[20] In retrospect, it seems as if this assumption was not only premature but grossly in error. The implications presented by PTSD have had devastating consequences for some veterans traumatized by the battlefield or combat experiences. The acute subtype of the disorder is synonymous with disorders labeled shell shock or combat fatigue in previous wars. Combat fatigue manifests itself earlier and generally responds to treatment. It seems that the chronic and delayed subtypes are more prevalent in the Vietnam veterans.

In spite of the many people suffering from PTSD little research has been done on the problem. This section draws on both the personal experience and research of Ron Cross and Beverly Gudex to illustrate the problems and potential strategies in dealing with victims and their families. Ron is a Vietnam veteran presently pursuing a social work degree. Bev is a hospital social worker. Bev and Ron have been married for ten years. Since PTSD has had such a powerful effect on their marriage, they want to share this experience with future social workers to increase knowledge and understanding of the problems. First, Ron presents his story and the findings from his research; this research itself has been an important component of Ron's therapy. Then, Bev presents her view of this relationship. Though their accounts are personal, both Ron and Bev believe important practice principles can be drawn from their experiences.

CASE STUDY
A Personal Account of PTSD
Ron Cross

Perhaps the best way to illustrate some of the symptoms of PTSD is to describe two victims. I will describe my own experience and then my wife will describe hers. While my wife did not serve time in Vietnam, she too is a victim of PTSD, as it has had a devastating effect on her life.

My story begins as a Marine in Vietnam. I spent thirty-two months in combat. After returning from my third duty in 'Nam, I felt the horror was behind me. Then, twelve years ago I experienced acute depression.

My marriage was falling apart. I spent most of my time at home alone upstairs, my wife and children downstairs. My wife tried to tell me that she cared for me, but I got real uncomfortable talking

about things like that so I would get up and leave. I would hit my wife for no reason. I didn't have any friends. My children tried to get close to me. I just wanted to get away. They didn't understand. There were times when I drove real crazy, screaming and yelling.

There were times I was so depressed that I couldn't even go downstairs. As I became more depressed, I drank more. Frequently I thought about committing suicide.

Sometimes, my head still replays some of my experiences in 'Nam. Regardless of what I want to think about, it comes creeping in. It's so hard to push it out. It's old friends, their faces, the ambush, the screams, their faces (tears) . . . children dying, blood, helicopters, and death. You know, every time I hear a chopper (helicopter) or see a clear, unobstructed green treeline, a chill goes down my spine—instant memory. When I go hiking now, I avoid green areas. I stay above the timberline. When I walk down the street, I get uncomfortable with people behind me. I feel most comfortable in the corner of the room, with walls on both sides of me. Loud noises irritate me and sudden movement or noise makes me jump.

Night is hardest for me. I go to sleep long after my wife has gone to bed. I think of so many of my 'Nam experiences at night. A number of times, my wife has awakened me with a look of fear in her eyes. I'm all sweaty and tense. Sometimes I've grabbed her neck and started choking her before I realized where I was. Sometimes I remember the dream, I guess most of the time I do. It's always the war or the enemy is chasing me and I can't run anymore.

My experiences are not unusual—I know that now. One of my friends recently shared a similar experience. He had fallen asleep on the couch watching TV. He woke up sopping wet from a cold sweat. When he awoke he was in elephant grass and saw eyes, faces—they were coming and he was shooting and shooting, but they just kept coming. He didn't have enough bullets so he ran and ran and ran. When he came to, he was exhausted.

The literature on PTSD documents thousands of similar cases. I hope that sharing my personal experience will increase your sensitivity to the agony of the Vietnam veterans who are suffering from this disorder. Personal experience provides a meaningful backdrop, but it is also important to look at this problem in a broader spectrum. Mine is not an exceptional case. For this reason I will present a summary of what is known to date about PTSD.

There is some evidence that not all Vietnam veterans with intensive combat experience are disturbed by delayed stress. The veterans who have combat-related disorders appear to have been younger men with high intelligence, high levels of education, considerable verbal ability, middle-class urban backgrounds, who may have either volunteered or been drafted but who had achieved no high rank and who had been discharged from the military.[21]

The nature of post-traumatic stress was different from the stressors of the previous wars, as it did not emerge until after the war was over and personnel had returned to civilian life. The symptoms also differ from previous war-induced traumas. PTSD is a group of symptoms, large and small, specific and vague, and with affective, attitudinal and adjustment components. Guilt is a major component: guilt for atrocities performed, guilt over transgression of traditional morality (specifically in reference to sex, drugs, and violence), guilt for having failed buddies, and survivor guilt. In addition there are feelings of rage, feelings of betrayal by the country, which sent soldiers to war, self- and societal alienation, apathy, depression, anxiety, obsessive tormenting memories, nightmares, insomnia, sensory hypercuity, extensive use of the ego defense mechanisms of denial and suppression. Other symptoms include confusion, nihilism, ideological disillusionment, uncontrollable hostility, wanton violence, flashback experiences, drug and alcohol addiction, unemployment, lack of goal orientation motivation, reentry shock, inability to adapt to the banality of civilian life after the excitement of war, and suicidal tendencies.[22]

The incidence of psychiatric syndromes among veterans is difficult to determine from the literature. Some veterans with emotional problems have received discharges which preclude treatment services from the Veterans Administration. There have been no resocialization programs for veterans where such problems might surface. The psychic numbing or numbed guilt syndrome is more than likely to escape notice as long as it leads to no overt disruptive behaviors, and as mentioned previously, the full-blown syndrome tends not to occur until after return to a civilian environment and is in some cases ten or more years later. For these reasons, the incidence of psychiatric syndromes remains difficult to estimate.

Rage is one of the more common syndromes. There are many reasons for the rage I personally feel. For me Williams sums it up best in the following words.

> Military training equated the rage with the masculine identity in the performance of our military duty. Whether in combat or not, the military experience stirred up more resentment and rage than most had ever felt. Finally, when combat was experienced, the combatants were often left with wild, violent impulses and no one upon whom to level them. The nature of guerilla warfare—with its use of such tactics as booby traps, land mines,

and surprise ambushes with enemies' quick re-
treat — left the combatants feeling like walking time
bombs; the veterans wanted to fight, but their
enemy had disappeared. Often they unleashed
their rage at indiscriminate targets.[23]

Such experiences are much more common
than most people believe. Other symptoms such as
flashbacks, sleep disturbances, anxiety reactions, and
survival guilt are also common. Re-experiencing feelings and experiences is especially troublesome for
those of us who are still numb and attempting to
avoid these feelings. For others, it is just a constant
reminder of their time in Vietnam, something they
will never forget.

Thus far I have presented some of the most
common effects of these problems in everyday life
and in interpersonal relationships. Now I would like
to discuss some of the techniques that have been
developed to treat PTSD.

The extent to which PTSD affects the individual varies. The variables which account for the level
of disruption in the veteran's life are unknown. The
best predictor of the intensity of symptoms tends to
be the extent to which the veteran was exposed to
actual combat.

Before the publication of Wilson's *Forgotten
Warrior Project* the vast majority of the affected veterans were ultimately diagnosed as having personality disorders such as schizoid, paranoid, or antisocial tendencies. The major focus was apparently
on etiological factors other than the intrinsic traumatic qualities of combat.

In treating a PTSD victim, it is particularly important to be empathetic to the horrors of the combat situation. Many veterans have struggled end-
lessly to suppress these feelings, in part because of
the refusal of society to even acknowledge their existence. Anyone involved with veterans is aware
that the veteran's ability to talk about his wartime
experience is diminished by fear of losing control. If
professionals ignore this important issue then the
veteran is harmed again. The wound caused by the
professional is called the "second wound."[24]

The "second wound" connotes the delayed
emotional damage that is inflicted by the hostile and
insensitive responses of hospital personnel, social
workers, criminal justice personnel, and even by
friends and family. It is the failure to acknowledge
the trauma the veteran is suffering. For this we ex-

cuse ourselves and alleviate our fear by blaming the
victim, i.e., deciding the problem is caused by mental imbalance, not social injustice.

Exploration of the veteran's combat experience
and evaluation of how the veteran views his present
affective experience is important to problem assessment. Some veterans will continue to express numb-
ness to their combat experience and current affective
issues. Yet, on close examination of present-day activities, they do suffer feelings of remorse and sadness. As already described, a great many veterans
with this disorder have periods of intensely violent,
impulsive behavior, very often directed at close family members and friends. These veterans question
their own sanity. In contrast, those veterans with personality disorders almost invariably blame something external to themselves in order to provide some
justification for their behavior. They suffer no remorse or horror for their actions. This is very different
from veterans suffering from PTSD.

Most veterans had minimal problems before
their combat experience and were totally unprepared for the Vietnam experience. In fact, the key
components in an accurate diagnosis are: a good
premorbid history, an exploration of the veteran's
combat experiences, and an examination of his
coping skills immediately after the war and to the
present time. Many veterans with PTSD also have
significant problems due to multiple substance
abuse. It appears that some have habitually medi-
cated themselves and compounded their problems.
Not only does the stress problem prevail, but also a
dependency on substance abuse. These problems
must be dealt with before any lasting treatment for
PTSD can begin.[25] Successful treatment of PTSD requires a recognition that this disorder is not an underlying psychosis or a simple or complex hysterical
reaction but rather a dynamic survivor's syndrome.

There is growing consensus among professionals as to the etiology of the disorder among
combat veterans of the Vietnam War. There is strong
feeling that a primary cause of PTSD was the young
age of the combat soldier. The average age was only
nineteen — normally the time when a young man
seeks personal identity and forms ideological commitments. The average young adult experiments
with education, jobs, travel, lifestyle and other activities during this period. Vietnam asked too much
of young men in the period of psychosocial mora-

torium. The soldier in Vietnam, especially the combatant, was faced with a series of moral, social, and political conflicts which resulted in a strong personal need to justify his experience and to find existential meaning in actions. Furthermore, this task of cognitive reorganization and search for meaning in the role of warrior required ideological change in order to cope with the situation psychologically while fighting to survive physically.[26]

The length of tour in Vietnam also contributed to the soldier's problems. The Army, Navy, and Air Force tours lasted twelve months. Marines stayed thirteen months. During World War II the average time in combat was six weeks. This and the nature of guerilla-type warfare created a constant stress of unknown magnitude. The time element in getting to and from the war contributed further to the problem. A soldier was transported from the United States to Vietnam and vice versa within seventy-two hours. This left no time for preparation or debriefing.

There were no funerals or ceremonies for the dead, so friends that were present one day were gone the next. There was no time to grieve—no rites of passage. Originally the average soldier did not question his patriotic duty; in fact, the majority of the soldiers volunteered. Patriotism waned as the war dragged on. A hill was taken one day, left the next, and retaken a month later. Nothing was gained and many friends lost. One goal remained constant—getting home. Personal problems were magnified by the hostile reception of the American public—veterans were now called baby killers. Veterans internalized these conflicts.

In addition to the causes of PTSD identified by professionals, I feel there are additional causes. One

problem for the soldier was a lack of professional leadership. During the 32 months that I participated in combat, there was an officer in charge of our platoon for only six months. The leadership was then placed upon young soldiers untrained in leadership.

Another problem in combat was intelligence reporting. This information was often incorrect and demoralizing. A unit would be told that there were only small units of enemy forces. Upon entering the area, large units were the norm, and loss of buddies was a common experience.

Finally, the lack of compassion of higher ranking officers, members of Congress, and the public in general, during and after the war, numbed and disillusioned the soldier. Only recently have people and the media begun to consider the effect of the war on the veterans.

My plea to you as future social workers is to understand this disorder. Statistics show that over 59,000 veterans have committed suicide since the war. The prison population is over 25 percent Vietnam veterans; their unemployment rate is 31 percent higher than the national average; 38 percent have divorced within six months of returning home; 38 percent are experiencing drug dependency.

PTSD is a reality. Unfortunately, not all veterans recognize this. Some are still stuck back where I was twelve years ago. I have been lucky. I have participated in one of the few treatment programs available. I have not received any magic cure. I know dealing with PTSD is a process—I take one day at a time. I hope that sharing my personal experience will make you better able to help other veterans cope with this disorder.

CASE STUDY
Coping With The Effects of PTSD
Beverly Gudex

It always helps to know that you are not alone. I am sharing my story with the hope that some of you will understand and then try to help the Vietnam veterans and their families.

OUR STORY

We met in January 1979; I was a naive twenty-four-year-old social worker in a nursing home. He was a thirty-nine-year-old traveling salesman from an out-of-state company. When he first told me he had been in Vietnam it did not seem important.

Life was happy. I was oblivious to Ron's attempt to share his suffering. I remember one evening he asked me to read a book entitled *A Rumor of War* by Philip Caputo. Ron was a character in that book. I was simultaneously horrified and engrossed by what I read. And angry — angry at the thought that anyone had to endure such a horrifying experience. He was intensely interested in my response. He seemed to feel he was on trial as a human being.

Our first few months were happy and fun-filled. Ron was desperately struggling but I assumed this was related to his recent divorce. I thought divorce was the explanation for the deep hurt in his eyes and the detached way he spoke of three children. Whatever the cause of the pain, I thought our love could conquer it. And, just as his pain would heal, so would his employment record. He would not quit jobs and disappear.

As our relationship grew more serious I introduced Ron to my parents, who immediately disliked him. As I watched my father quiz Ron, I knew the battle had begun. He saw fifteen years' age difference, a divorced man with three children, a job-hopper. Ron was desperately seeking acceptance. He tried to tell my father of his capabilities. The harder he tried, the worse it got. To all those adjectives was added "exaggerator."

After that fateful meeting, Ron was hurt and I was angry. Hard feelings and harsh words ensued; the more my parents attacked Ron, the more committed I became to marrying him. My parents finally relented.

Back home Ron and I began to socialize more with my friends. I noticed that he had no friends. I was his best and only friend. He did not understand my need to be with other people. He would not look people in the eyes. These problems seemed small and we proceeded with our wedding plans.

Ron continued to work for the same corporation doing heating and air conditioning. He traveled each week but was home weekends. The pay and benefits were good and we had frequent warm phone conversations during the week and great weekends. There was even talk of a promotion for him. About a month after we were married, he took a week's "vacation" to work on our house. After several days he announced his intentions of staying home. There was no reasoning with him. He even refused to call his boss to make a formal termination. His rationale was, "I want to be home with you."

Within a couple of weeks he began a lower-paying job locally. He was excited, productive, and got along well with his co-workers for six months. Then it went downhill. I knew what was coming — by spring he was laid off.

By now Ron had developed a fairly good rapport with my parents. He wanted to try dairy farming with my dad. I saw problems, but Ron was as insistent upon trying farming as he had been upon leaving the other two places. Needless to say, the cycle repeated, complicated by emotions involving family. I saw the relationship gradually deteriorate. Ron was angry and hostile both at himself and my father. I heard the target of Ron's accusations change from my father to me — I was choosing my parents, or I would not let them treat him as they did. We moved back to our own home.

Ron began to search for a job. The search was longer this time. He was tense, hostile, volatile, and depressed. This was the first time in his life he was unable to walk from one job to another. His work record, age, and the economy were against him. I began to notice an increase in his alcohol consumption. He was also beginning to admit to frequent nightmares about Vietnam.

Ron did find a job by late spring, but the job was taken out of desperation. His new employers were engaged in very shady practices. Both men drank on the job and Ron followed suit. Work was not steady. When I began to find him drunk, sometimes he would try to offer an explanation; other times he would just cry and promise to quit. I was repulsed. My responses ranged from crying and self-pity to anger. The promises were always broken and the behavior repeated. It was no longer just the drinking. He began to contemplate suicide. I remember coming home one night and finding a folded white note on the stove. I feared this was "the note." Fortunately it was not.

The intensity of the situation continued to grow. One Saturday morning I found a knife sticking in the floor on his side of the bed. I removed it and said nothing. He demanded it back. When I asked why he needed it the reply was, "I'm not going to let those 'gooks' kill me in my sleep."

He refused to discuss his problems, other than a sentence or two about hatred of God and religion, fear of losing me, self-hatred or fantasies of retaliation against his present employer. It was now June, warm and raining. He would get tense and pace like a caged animal. "Smells like 'Nam, God I hate this," was all he would say. He seemed to be in Vietnam more than he was in reality.

At this time we heard about a couple of other Vietnam veterans in Fond du Lac who were beginning to organize. I made a few phone calls and found out about rap groups for Vietnam vets. Together we hesitantly walked through the door the first evening of the meeting. It was obvious that the meeting was for veterans only. I left. That night he came home almost happy. He had a pamphlet about delayed stress. He kept saying, "It's not just me. I'm not crazy. Look at this, it's me." The pamphlet listed the symptoms: depression, anger, anxiety, sleep disturbances, and many more. He fit all of them! At the rap group he also heard of an inpatient treatment program just for Vietnam veterans. It was one of three programs available in the country at that time. He had to go—everything was crumbling around him.

Ron entered treatment in August 1981. When I called his dad and let him know of Ron's admission, his father's voice broke. He said, "His mom tried to tell me Ronnie was not the same when he came back from Vietnam, but I did not want to believe it." At least I could talk to them about it. I had so few friends who understood.

We knew little of what to expect from the treatment program. The day of the admission I left filled with fear because the staff had treated Ron rudely and then admitted him to a locked ward with some pretty strange characters. I remember seeing real fear in his eyes as I left.

Time went fast. Ron changed. He seemed to be calming down, and he began to talk about his future. He talked of the Veterans Administration sending him to college to study social work. He began to compare himself with the twelve vets in his treatment program. He saw himself as being a lot more together than they were and this strengthened his self-image.

Ron came home a new man. He was happily making plans to start college. He started on schedule and seemed to enjoy his classes.

But we did not live happily ever after. Initially Ron had been sent home on tranquilizers. He was a zombie. In the follow-up outpatient appointments, his medications were switched often. He reacted poorly to most of them. I nagged, he quit taking them, and for a while he functioned better. I was not prepared for the consequence of taking that crutch away.

His alcohol intake after treatment was minimal. Then he went on a couple of binges in late spring. I called the program director frantically to ask what I should do. He told me that Ron was well aware of the fact that he should not drink—not even one. He explained that inside Ron was a trained killer, and under the influence of alcohol anything could happen. I pleaded with Ron not to drink, and told him what the director had said, but he denied it.

By now Ron had established a network with other Vietnam veterans in Fond du Lac. Few of these men acknowledged that they had any problems and chemical use was common. They saw the Vietnam experience as the problem and chemical use as relief. One particular vet was always available when Ron wanted to drink. They reinforced each others' dependencies.

The worst came in early June. It was "Walleye Weekend," and Ron was going to help man the Vietnam veterans' booth. He went early Sunday morning; I went on an outing with my family. When I got home at 4:00 p.m. and he was not home, I was worried.

He came home with his "enabler" friend. He was highly agitated and violent. He had seen one of his most recent employers at the park and decided to "get even." From Ron's disjointed talk I gathered that he had broken into his former place of employment but decided that was not enough. He was bent on getting a Coke bottle and gasoline, making a molotov cocktail, and going back to the shop to destroy the building. He tried to get into the garage to get the things he needed. I tried begging, reasoning, and physical restraint. His buddy Bruce wrestled him to the ground. Ron did manage to get to the garage door and punched out one of the wooden panels with his fist. The sight of blood was no deterrent. Between the ranting and ravings about the destruction of the shop were sobs and repeated, "I'm crazy." It was unreal. His behavior had regressed to before treatment times. In desperation I called the program director at home. Before putting Ron on the phone, I briefed the program director on the situation. He told me that Ron should not be allowed any more alcohol and encouraged to sleep. Because his behavior was so bizarre, the program director suggested emergency admission with treatment in the alcohol rehabilitation unit. The problem was a two-and-a-half-hour trip, and he was too crazy to take anyplace safely. I could not call the cops on my own husband.

Ron talked to the program director. He calmed down enough to consent to going for a walk. My hope was that he would get tired enough to go home and sleep. Bruce walked with us. Once we started walking it became clear that the only reason he had consented was to get another bottle of alcohol. When I objected he became violent again. As we neared the house on the corner of our block, he grabbed one of the wooden slats on the porch trim and ripped it off. Bruce restrained him from doing any more damage. We walked a couple more feet. He again pleaded for booze. I said no. Bruce disagreed with my approach and suggested I allow Ron to drink himself into oblivion. Ron then proceeded to change his mind and headed home. When he got to the house he found two sleeping tablets, took them, and fell asleep.

Filled with anger and sobbing hysterically, I watched him sleep. How could this man who said he loved me put me through this kind of terror? How could he show so much growth over the past ten months and regress so rapidly? Why was this happening? Was he ever going to be cured? How much more did he expect me to endure? How much could I endure?

I had two friends I confided in. They asked questions that included, "Is he an alcoholic?" I said no and repeated to them what Ron told me, namely, that the delayed stress was the primary problem and while he used alcohol it was only in response to the primary problem. One close friend who had been through some bad times with her husband, now a recovering alcoholic, said, "Bev, the bottom line is what are you willing to put up with, the cause of his drinking be damned."

It was now summer of '82. I kept repeating the question my friend had asked: What are you willing to put up with? I began to ask myself my limitations. I was aware that my power or influence base with my husband had eroded over the past three years. I tried to evaluate Ron's situation. I saw progress in his ability to relate to people (he had even begun a few friendships of his own); he was able to complete one semester of college, was now in summer school and doing well scholastically. He no longer seemed suicidal and was less dependent upon me. He had begun to talk and write about his Vietnam experience. On the negative side I saw his irrational, sudden explosions of anger. While these were not easy to deal with, they were nothing in comparison to the combination of violence and despair that I saw during periods of intoxication. He continued to be negative and nasty towards my family. He continued to complain of memory impairment, especially in regard to school activities. There were also times when he drew away from any intimacy for extended periods of time.

It was like living with a time bomb. I never knew what to expect. When things were good they were exceptionally good. However, the reverse was equally true. I knew that I could not live like this forever. I again tried to find additional help for Ron because I knew that he still had not resolved a lot of things about his Vietnam experience.

Ron joined a Vietnam vets' rap group and I began to see further progress by the end of 1982. He was beginning to blossom at school and was elected to the student government. He began to develop new interests and more friends. The drinking decreased, as did the frequency of his fits of rage.

Things were going so well that my confidence in our relationship grew. By spring of 1983, I knew we had it together now. Except for periodic, normal arguments that go with living together, things were fine.

Then he had two drinking binges in August. The violence and irrationality were at the danger limit. Then, one weekend in September Ron accompanied me on a weekend up north. I was attending a conference and planned to mix business with pleasure. When I left for my meeting Saturday morning, Ron was already on the lake doing what he did best—fishing.

I came back at 4:30 p.m., to find a full bottle of Blackberry Brandy on the table and him drunk on the floor. He was barely conscious. There was no pity left in me, only anger. I told him I was leaving.

He was alert enough to say, "You mean you would leave me here like this?" In a flash I knew that if I left him he would end up on the bottom of the lake. I threw all of Ron's gear into the car, gave away the fish he had caught, and went back into the cabin to collect my drunk husband. He begged me to stay there. I could not. I hated the cabin, the bar, Ron, and everything that went with this fiasco of a weekend.

It was 6:00 p.m. when I got him settled into the car and began the three-hour trip home. What a trip! We were on the road for about two minutes and the terror began. I realized he was in Vietnam, not on the way home. The sun was beginning to set and he was busy scanning the horizon, looking for "gooks." He kept saying, "It's too green, they're here, I can feel them." Then he began grabbing at the wheel or behind the seat, looking for his gun. When unable to grab at anything else, he would fiddle with the radio knobs until he had it between stations and had no reception. Then he began to frantically scream, "We're out here. Can't you hear us? Come in, please come in," getting even more frantic when he received no reply on the radio. For the first time I was unable to get him to realize that he was in Wisconsin, not Vietnam, and for the first time I was actually afraid of him. I stopped in the next town and got him two cups of coffee. He was better momentarily but as soon as we were on the road again he was back in 'Nam. Now he would not drink the second cup of coffee because he was saving it for Indian, a fellow Marine pointman in Vietnam. This scenario continued for two hours until he began to doze off. We made it home by 10:00 p.m., and then I fell apart.

That episode solidified a decision in my mind. I would take one last stab at getting help for Ron. If he refused help and insisted upon drinking, he could do so but I would not be around to pick up the pieces. I called his social worker again and told him of the problem. He was surprised because Ron never let on in group that he was having any problems. There Ron cast himself in the role of the helper and professional.

The social worker agreed to meet with Ron and me. For three Thursdays, Ron recounted in great detail his Vietnam experience. I was not shocked by what he was saying. By now I had either heard it or read it in his papers before. Once

this was established, we moved on to the subject of his alcohol abuse. The social worker helped me clarify my feelings and then spell out my position to Ron. Ron saw his alcohol use like this: Bad Vietnam dreams/nightmares/thoughts + alcohol = relief. I tried to point out that the real equation was Vietnam + alcohol = temporary relief followed by long-term pain and destruction. He agreed and said he would quit using booze if that made *me* happy. The social worker interceded and said the decision must be based on his needs, not mine. Ron agreed to quit using alcohol. Again I thought the decision was made and life would be wonderful.

One Saturday afternoon in February I came home to find Ron and a Vietnam veteran friend smoking dope in the basement. It took me only one minute to notice that Ron had also been drinking. After a heated emotional discussion the bottle came out from behind the washer. I did not pour it out or do any of the other things I had done in the past. This time I was ready to leave. Circumstances prevented it, but never before had I spelled out my feelings as I did then. I let him know that I loved him, had given him what I was capable of, and from then on he was on his own. If he chose to drink or to smoke pot, he had every right to do so, but if he did I would leave.

What does all this mean? What conclusions have I reached about living with a Vietnam veteran with post-traumatic stress? What advice would I give other women married to Vietnam veterans? I think it is extremely important for all women who have Vietnam vets as husbands to read all they can about Vietnam. Vets usually refuse to talk about 'Nam. This only buries the problem deeper, and it does not help to work out the difficulties. Be ready to listen, but do not force the issue. If one can convey warmth, caring, and understanding despite the horror stories, the vet will talk, if only in small segments. I learned the hard way that the spouse should also be extremely attuned to signs of chemical dependency. Vietnam veterans tend to deny any problem with addiction. My experience with PTSD victims is that healthy coping mechanisms develop only when the veteran stops using all chemicals. The key ingredients needed to make a relationship work are patience and strength. You must learn and accept the fact that one learns to cope with PSTD, but one is not cured. The poor coping mechanisms may have been learned from childhood, traumatized during Vietnam, and reinforced thereafter. I had been expecting my husband to change behaviors that he had learned over the past fifteen years. The other thing a wife must do to survive is to establish a strong support system of her own. This support system is vital for when things get rough (as they inevitably do).

The ultimate decision for the wife is what she is willing to take and capable of giving. She can increase her capacities by developing support systems; she cannot change what her husband has suffered, and she should not waste time feeling guilty about it. She must allow herself to place expectations on her spouse. While he cannot stop the terror PTSD causes him, he can stop the use of alcohol and other drugs which exacerbate the pain and spread it to those around him.

I have found pity to be destructive to our relationship. As difficult as it sometimes is, I know I can only help Ron by demanding that he remain strong and help him in every way to maintain that strength. Because I love Ron I am frequently overcome with feelings of sympathy and understanding for his destructive behavior. But I have learned that this understanding must be channeled to constructive expectations, not destructive sympathy. While I am feeling confident about our future, I remain aware of the continuing threat PTSD holds over our life. We approach life one day at a time, balancing our expectations—neither allowing ourselves to despair nor anticipating the impossible dream. Life is what we make it on a day-to-day basis. Life is enhanced by our concern for each other, loving friends, and qualified professionals who can provide the support and guidance we need in difficult times.

HOMOSEXUALITY

The term "gays and lesbians" is used in place of "homosexuals" because it focuses less on sexual behavior and more on lifestyle.

Analyzing societal response to homosexuality or gays and lesbians brings the potential of oppressive labeling to bear on a current phenomenon. Within the last thirty years, homosexuality has been defined as a crime, as an illness, and as an individual's choice. As recently as the 1950s gay men were being imprisoned for their sexual preference. Along with this punishment they were likely to receive "treatment" for their "problem." Treatment often consisted of aversive and frequently painful stimuli being presented simultaneously with homoerotic stimuli.

In 1963 Karl Menninger, one of the most progressive psychiatrists of the time, suggested that homosexuality was a condition that called for treatment to transform the homosexual into a heterosexual.[27] Within twenty years of Menninger's statement the American Psychiatric Association, the American Psychological Association, and the National Association of Social Workers had all taken a public position in support of homosexuality as a choice and removed it from their classification of disorders.

An estimated 5 percent to 15 percent of the U.S. population is homosexual.

Though social workers as a group were the last to speak out for the rights of gays and lesbians, they also voiced the most active commitment to overcoming their oppression. An excerpt from the policy statement adopted by the delegate assembly of the National Association of Social Workers on May 22, 1977, reflects the tone of the commitment.

> The profession of social work is uniquely suited to assist American society in understanding the relationship between environmental conditions and human functioning. The burden of the eradication of homophobia—the fear of homosexuality—cannot be placed on the homosexual minority. . . . The ultimate

responsibility for the eradication of discriminatory practices which impinge on the lives of the homosexual minority falls on the social work profession, together with other groups in the society.[28]

Since 1977 legislation has been passed to protect the rights of gays and lesbians from discrimination in jobs and housing, but there have also been attacks on homosexual rights by groups such as the Moral Majority. Conservative politicians led by Senator Paul Laxalt (R-Nevada) have introduced legislation, The Family Protection Act, that would define homosexuality as deviance and would condone oppression of gays and lesbians as individuals and as a group.

Changing views of homosexuality illustrate how society defines and redefines behavior as deviant or normal. These phenomena are also reflected in changed legal and societal responses to abortion, marijuana, and mental illness. For the prospective social worker, it is important to be aware of the needless oppression society may be inflicting on certain groups of people. This understanding can decrease the potential of unknowingly becoming a part of that oppression. History provides a powerful lesson. The case study selection illustrates how liberating practice can help overcome oppression and what kinds of knowledge and skills are needed to work with gays and lesbians. This case study illustrates a positive social work response to a lesbian client; the author chose to remain anonymous.

CASE STUDY
Gay and Lesbian Counseling Services

Kay Sullivan, 32, realized that her inability to sleep, loss of appetite, and periods of crying were symptoms of depression she had experienced on previous occasions. Now the depression seemed overwhelming and it took all her energy to make it to her job as a third grade teacher in an elementary school where she had taught for the last seven years. Kay was fairly certain about the source of her depression, yet she was uncertain about whom she could go to for help. Rather than talk to her friends or colleagues, she looked in the yellow pages of the phone book and found an agency called the Gay and Lesbian Counseling Center. She called the phone number, and after a brief interview she made an appointment for two days later.

Kay arrived early at the appointment and drove around the building several times before entering. Once she was in the waiting room, she nervously looked around her at two men and one older woman who were also waiting to be seen. Soon a small, dark-haired woman about Kay's age entered the room and introduced herself as Susan Williams — Kay's social worker. Susan spoke briefly about the purpose of the agency and the different services that were available — coming out groups, individual counseling, support groups, couples' groups, family counseling, and community education. Susan also explained that there were both male and female counselors as well as both gay and straight counselors, and if Kay would feel more comfortable with someone else, that could be arranged after the initial intake interview.

With gentle encouragement from Susan, Kay began to tell her story. When Kay was in graduate school working on her degree in education, she met a woman named Elizabeth. She and Elizabeth became good friends, studied together and eventually moved in together in order to share expenses. As the two women became closer they began to engage in sexual fondling and sleeping together. Elizabeth told Kay she had been involved with two other women when she was younger and considered herself to be a lesbian. Kay was not even sure that she understood what the word lesbian meant or that she had ever known anyone who was lesbian.

Kay went on to explain that she fell in love with Elizabeth and convinced her not to tell anyone about their relationship. She and Elizabeth found jobs teaching together in the same school and bought a small house together near the school. In the past two years, Elizabeth had grown increasingly restless with her job and her relationship with Kay. She moved out of the house and began seeing other women. Kay panicked that as Elizabeth became more "out," their colleagues at school as well as Kay's family who lived in the community might find out about her. At the same time there was a part of Kay that envied Elizabeth's openness and wished to experience new relationships too.

Susan, the social worker, allowed Kay to cry and ventilate her feelings of loss over an important relationship. Susan explained that Kay was going through a grieving process and at the same time being forced to consider her own "coming out" process. Both of these problems were contributing to Kay's depression and to periods of great anxiety. Kay felt some relief after telling the worker her problems and agreed to come back for another session.

Over the next six months, Kay was seen eight times in individual sessions, and twelve times in group sessions. Elizabeth attended one session and some old issues of anger and guilt were resolved, so it seemed possible that the two could continue to remain friends. The social worker suggested that Kay join a lesbian coming out group when she felt ready to do so. Kay found the group to be very helpful and as a result came out to her parents and to a friend at work. Although her parents had some resistance to Kay's behavior, they agreed to attend a family support group. Kay has been dating other women and has made new friends in the group she attended. Although she continues to worry about some of her work colleagues finding out about her sexual preference, she is considerably less depressed and feels more comfortable with herself.

Based on the work of Moses and Hawkins,[29] we have developed practice principles for social workers working with gay and lesbian clients.

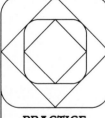

PRACTICE PRINCIPLES

Practice with Gay and Lesbian Clients

1. Accept the reality that being gay is a normal, nonpathological form of human sexual and affectional expression.

2. Recognize that many gay and lesbian problems arise from societal oppression, not individual weakness.

3. Move beyond helping gays and lesbians cope and adjust. Develop innovative and satisfying ways to grow as a gay or lesbian person.

4. Support gay and lesbian clients in moving beyond stereotypical gender role definitions, if they so choose.

5. Recognize that gay primary love relationships may not be lifelong or monogamous. Many prefer a more independent relationship.

6. Be willing to facilitate the "coming out" process.

SUMMARY

This chapter focused on problems of being different in a society that praises diversity but rewards conformity. We have looked at special groups from a knowledge standpoint—why these people suffer oppression and discrimination—and we have used this knowledge to develop practice principles.

Janet Davenport, Edwin Gonzalez-Santin, and Toby Ferrell provided insight into the American black and Hispanic experience and made suggestions for the social work profession. Ron Cross and Bev Gudex provided rich insight into post-traumatic stress disorder as it affects Vietnam veterans—how it feels, what social workers need to know, and how social workers can intervene. Finally, we looked at gay and lesbian counseling services. We drew upon an individual experience and the literature to develop practice guidelines for working with gay and lesbian clients.

Each of these groups has unique characteristics, yet each suffers from the pain of being different. It is important to you as a future practitioner to be sensitive both to individual discrimination suffered by your clients and to institutionalized oppression which they endure as members of minority groups.

We close this chapter with the words of the great Dr. Martin Luther King, Jr., from the Centennial Address delivered at Carnegie Hall in New York City, February 23, 1968. No one has more eloquently summarized what we feel should be the social worker's creed.

> Today we are still challenged to be dissatisfied. Let us be dissatisfied until every man can have food and material necessities for his body, culture and education for his mind, freedom and human dignity for his spirit. Let us be dissatisfied until the empty stomachs of Mississippi are filled and the idle industries of Appalachia are revitalized. . . . Let us be dissatisfied until our brothers of the Third World—Asia, Africa and Latin America—will no longer be the victims of imperialist exploitation, but will be lifted from the long night of poverty, illiteracy and disease. Let us be dissatisfied until this pending cosmic elegy will be transformed into a creative psalm of peace and "justice will roll down like waters from a mighty stream."

NOTES

1. W. Ryan, *Equality* (New York: Pantheon, 1981).
2. J. Green, *Cultural Awareness in the Human Services* (Englewood Cliffs, N.J.: Prentice-Hall, 1982), 9.
3. Ibid.
4. D. D'Souza, "Racism in the 1980s," *Social Problems 88/89* (Guilford, Conn.: Dushkin Pub. Group, 1988).
5. Eugene Perkins, *Home Is a Dirty Street: The Social Oppression of Black Children* (Chicago: Third World Press, 1975), 114.
6. Ibid.

7. Charles L. Sanders, *Black Agenda for Social Work in the Seventies* (Atlanta, Ga.: Atlanta University School of Social Work, 1971), 21–22.

8. Ibid., 36.

9. Ibid., 1.

10. Ibid., 4.

11. E. Aracelis Francis, *Black Task Report: Suggested Guides for the Integration of Black Content into the Social Work Curriculum* (New York: Council on Social Work Education, 1973), 6.

12. Ibid.

13. Ibid.

14. Sanders, *Black Agenda,* 22.

15. Ibid., 32.

16. D. Saunders, "PTSD: A Label That Does Not Blame," *Wisconsin Coalition Against Domestic Violence Newsletter* 9, 1 (March 1990): 5.

17. E. Stark and A. Flitcraft, "Personal Power and Institutional Victimization: Treating the Dual Trauma of Woman Battering," (New Haven, Conn.: Domestic Violence Training Project).

18. John P. Wilson, *Identity, Ideology and Crisis: The Vietnam Veteran in Transition* (Cleveland, Ohio: 1978).

19. *Diagnostic and Statistical Manual,* III (Washington, D.C.: American Psychiatric Association, 1980).

20. Tom Williams, *Post-Traumatic Stress Disorders of the Vietnam Veteran* (Cincinnati, Ohio: Disabled American Veterans, 1980).

21. Charles Figley, *Stress Disorders among Vietnam Veterans* (New York: Brenner/Maxell, 1978).

22. Williams, *Post-Traumatic Stress,* 32.

23. Ibid., 78.

24. Ibid., 87.

25. Figley, *Stress Disorders,* 202.

26. Wilson, *Identity.*

27. Karl Menninger, *The Vital Balance: The Life Process in Mental Health and Illness* (New York: Viking, 1963).

28. Quoted in Bernice Goodman, "Some Mothers Are Lesbians," in *Women's Issues and Social Work Practice,* ed. Elaine Norman and Arlene Mancuso (Itasca, Ill.: Peacock, 1980).

29. A. Moses and R. Hawkins, Jr., *Counseling Lesbian Women and Gay Men* (Columbus, Ohio: Merrill, 1986).

PART

V

FIELDS OF PRACTICE

Social work may be said to be traveling towards maturity as a profession when it is capable of assimilating knowledge and skill from many sources without loss of integrity; . . . it has achieved consistency between its goals and its methods and is willing to subject itself to self imposed standards of conduct; it recognizes its sphere of social responsibility [fields of practice]; it evolves methods for merging its empirical and theoretical knowledge; and it is able to recruit its candidates from the higher levels of intelligence.*

W here do social workers work? Social work offers services in nearly every area of human life where social stress and dysfunctioning are found. With such a wide range of areas of social concern, the profession has continually had to address how to describe and how to amalgamate its diversity. Social work service patterns have traditionally been differentiated by the specific locations or settings (e.g., hospitals, mental health clinics, public welfare departments), the general areas of concern or fields of practice (e.g., child welfare or health care), and the characteristic methodologies used in day-to-day practice (e.g., casework, group work, and community organization).

Shortly after the turn of the century, when social workers were nearly exclusively associated with programs of public and private welfare, a movement was begun to separate practice into specific fields of practice. General welfare was joined by efforts in child welfare, family services, general medicine, psychiatry, and recreation. In the 1920s and 1930s social work concerned itself with elaborating the differences between those who worked in the various settings. After World War II, social work became preoccupied with developing specializations based not only on the specific work place and methodology but also on the theoretical orientation of the work being done. Developing these specializations was part of a general strategy to increase the

---

* Eduard Lindeman, "Social Casework Matures in a Confused World," paper given at the annual meeting of the New York State Conference on Social Work, 1946 (Albany, N.Y.: 1947), 51.

profession's prestige. By narrowing its focus social work could build respect as a profession in its own right, rather than depending on medicine and law. While people helping people is as old as the human race, professional social work, as a disciplined and skillful method of helping people, is less than a century old.

In 1957 the Council on Social Work Education delineated nine areas of practice for social work. Designated as "fields of practice," this list included public assistance, family social work, child welfare, corrections, psychiatric social work, medical social work (including public health), school social work, group service agencies, and community planning. By using the concept of "field of practice" it was hoped that the tendency to measure specific practice activities by attributes found outside the actual practice could be avoided, thus leaving the door open for evaluation of the social work tasks. This assumes that significant variations should be found in the social work process itself and not in the environment in which it takes place.

Throughout this text we have striven to show the uniqueness of social work practice. We started by discussing a variety of human service professions and how each of them contributes to the betterment of the individual and society. We compared each related profession to social work. We then discussed social work methods, the profession of social work, its historical development, and the knowledge that lies at the core of social work practice. Included in this discussion was the role of values and politics in social work practice.

Basic Questions

In this section we build upon everything you have learned about social work. We demonstrate how the knowledge, skills, methods, values, and politics translate into the specific fields of practice. This section will be especially helpful to those who have only a general sense of wanting to work with people but do not know the types of opportunities that are available and what kind of preparation you may need. These chapters will answer many questions you may have. What settings might I work in? What kinds of skills will I need for a particular field of practice? What roles will I be expected to fill? Is there a licensing or certification process that makes a certain kind of training or education necessary for this field? What other kinds of professionals will I collaborate with?

Where Social Workers Practice

This section answers some of these basic questions as they relate to the most popular fields of social work practice. Child and family welfare, gerontology, health, mental health, criminal justice, and public social service departments employ approximately 98 percent of the social workers in the field. We examine these fields in terms of what social workers do, what types of knowledge they need, the roles and functions appropriate to the field, the historical development of the field, and the impact of legislation and policy on this field of practice now and in the future.

General and Specific Knowledge: The Application

Even though we separate the chapters into fields of practice, the social work skills and methods are consistent across the fields. In Part IV we looked at knowledge in terms of general and specialized knowledge. Part V can be seen as an application of this material. No matter the field of practice, the general knowledge of individuals, families, groups, organizations, systems, and communities is necessary. The generic skills contained in the social work process are also necessary. However, depending upon the specific role you play or the field in which you practice, you may need specific knowledge and skills required by that setting and the problems unique to it.

Social Work Frame of Reference

Throughout this book we have referred to social work's unique frame of reference. By this we mean the guiding principles of viewing problems from the dual perspective of private troubles and public issues, using a systems approach to problem assessment, and viewing people in interaction with their environmental resource system. You will experience this frame of reference in the fields of practice by observing how social workers help colleagues think beyond the individual to the broader problem, bring order into the delivery of social services, and seek to avoid inappropriate decisions born of crisis and frustration. Such analysis of policy and planning issues on the part of social workers has often led to better policymaking and planning on the part of management.

Direct vs. Indirect Service

By discussing the role of the individual social worker in improving policy and service delivery we want to avoid confusing the roles of direct and indirect practitioners. Clearly, a different level of expectation and expertise is inherent in the role of administrator. Administration (indirect practice) requires specific knowledge, skills, and attitudes that are qualitatively different from those of direct practice. However, the social work frame of reference leads all social workers to have an impact on policies and procedures of their own agency, and many times even in the political area.

Chapter

15

Family and Child Welfare

Why is it that despite timesaving devices, an unprecedented degree of affluence, and universal education, the family's ability to nurture children seems to be diminishing? How can it be that more time, money, and knowledge lead to decreased capacity for childrearing?[1]

Considerable alarm has been expressed about the deteriorating status of millions of children and their families. Social service agencies, courts, welfare departments, hospitals, mental health centers, special education professionals and district attorneys say they are overwhelmed by the crush of cases of desperate children they are encountering. Perhaps the most conspicuous problem is physical and sexual abuse of children, with over 2 million cases being reported annually — including more than a thousand deaths.[2]

Drugs have become a significant factor disrupting family life. Almost one-third of the Kenosha, Wisconsin, schoolchildren in grades 6 to 12 say they are worried about their parents' use of alcohol, and 15 percent to 20 percent are concerned about parental abuse of another drug.[3]

Child death in the U.S. is three times higher in poor families than in non-poor families, and the U.S. child death rate is the highest overall among 23 developed nations.[4]

Teenage pregnancy has become so prevalent that one out of ten teenaged girls in the United States becomes pregnant every year, and almost half of these pregnancies result in births — 30,000 of them to girls under the age of 15.[5] In addition to being at high risk psychologically, the babies of teenagers are at higher risk medically. Infant mortality is 200 percent higher among babies born to teenagers than to those born to women in their twenties.[6] Low birth weight babies are at increased risk for serious mental, physical, and developmental problems, and teens are 23 percent more likely to have premature babies.[7]

Suicide is the second-leading cause of death for people between the ages of 15 and 19. One study of teen suicide found that 60 percent of all high school seniors have seriously considered suicide by the time they graduate.[8]

The National Advisory Committee for Juvenile Justice and Delinquency Prevention identified the serious violent chronic delinquent as the major problem confronting our nation in the juvenile justice arena. Today more than half of all juvenile arrests are attributable to only six to eight percent of the youth population.[9]

Abused children, dysfunctional families, drug abuse, teenage mothers, and juvenile offenders are some of the most important problems child welfare social workers must confront. Social work is uniquely designed to address these problems. As a profession we have always been at the forefront in developing family interventions and policies.

Child welfare is a specialized field of social work concerned with providing social services to children and parents to help them fulfill childrearing responsibilities, and to obtain from the community the resources and protections necessary for healthy family functioning. Child welfare services reinforce, supplement, and substitute some of the parental functions that are not met by parents. Children and families frequently need social services to support and strengthen family life, to supplement parental care, or to substitute for inadequate care by the child's own parents. They are also designed to make existing social institutions and programs more responsive to family needs, or to develop new services when necessary programs do not exist.

HISTORY

"The social work profession traditionally has been a leader in seeking to eliminate the obstacles that often prevent children from receiving the help that could make the difference between wholesome development and a life of hopelessness and despair."[10]

The problems of child abuse and neglect did not suddenly appear in the 20th century. Throughout history, children have been abused and mistreated. English common law stipulated that fathers had the right to inflict arbitrary or severe discipline.

Early poor law in the colonies saw no inherent value in the family structure other than as an economic unit. Hence, those families who were unable to provide for their children were seen as a moral and economic threat. These children were to be "bound out" or placed with families who were self-supporting so they would not be tainted by parental failure. Dependent children could be placed with anyone willing to take them; the adults, in turn, were to recoup their expenses from the child's labor.

The first American institution for children was founded by the Ursuline Sisters in 1729. Children's institutions did not proliferate until the 1800s. With the Industrial Revolution, mass immigration took place and religious groups became involved in developing children's institutions. These institutions were relatively militaristic in design, but did provide bare necessities while preserving the children's religious heritage.

In the 1850s Charles Loring Brace of the Children's Aid Society of New York started the practice of placing vagrant children from the streets of New

Children develop most effectively in a safe, nurturing environment.

York on rural farms. Brace believed that it was futile to work with delinquent children without placing them in a new environment. To him the ideal family setting was the farm family.

Government intervention in family life began during the first half of the nineteenth century. The thrust was twofold: (1) to prevent neglected children from becoming criminals and (2) to intervene as guardian when minors were deprived of parental care.

The first child protective society began in New York in 1874. Originally, these societies removed abused children from their homes. Child welfare agencies initiated legislation designed to prevent maltreatment of children and punishment for the perpetrators.

The early development of protective service agencies was on a two-track system. Most agencies stressed the enforcement tradition and were closely related to the courts. However, others joined a movement to create an administratively separate child welfare system of services. They stressed prevention of delinquency, abuse, and neglect through skill and professional expertise. However, they were in actuality largely a child placement agency.[11]

The juvenile court movement was led largely by social workers who believed that children needed to be treated differently by the court system. This movement led to the development of juvenile probation services designed to provide casework services to juvenile probationers.

In 1909 President Theodore Roosevelt called the first White House Conference on Child Dependency. The theme of the conference was the virtues of home life. As a result of this conference, the Children's Bureau was established in 1912 to report on dangerous occupations, accidents, and diseases of children. The bureau's investigations identified the need for child protection, and efforts to obtain federal regulation of child welfare followed. By 1930 all the states had taken legal measures to safeguard the working conditions of children.[12]

Child welfare services moved even more decisively from the voluntary service sector into the public sector with the passage of the Social Security Act. Today, even though many child welfare services are provided in the voluntary sector, the bulk of the costs are borne by the public treasury.

The experience of black children in the child welfare system has been separate from the white system. Black children were served primarily by separate self-help mutual aid systems. When they were served by the white system and placed in almshouses, evidence suggests that their treatment was harsher than that of white children.[13]

Following the Civil War, black child welfare services were provided through the Freedmen's Bureau, the first federal welfare agency. (See Chapter 7 for a description of this agency.) Its offerings included educational programs, protective services, child placement, and reuniting children with former-slave parents.[14] Black children were largely excluded from the charity organization societies and settlement houses, although some white agencies did establish branches in black neighborhoods.[15]

In spite of the many reforms of the Progressive Era (1896-1914), these gains did not affect the lives of black children. It was only after World War II that black children started to be included in the white child welfare system.[16] In the tremendous growth of civil rights and child welfare programs of the 1960s the child welfare system continued to be highly exclusionary and discriminatory. Interest increased in black control of services through participation on agency boards and a push to hire minority staff.[17]

In 1982 Billingsley and Giovannoni noted that "overt discrimination of the early system had been replaced by covert discrimination via maldistribution of services."[18] They contend that although the *policies* of exclusion have ended, adequate services are still not available to black children, and therefore little meaningful change has occurred since the 1940s.

American Indian children have also been denied the benefits of the white child welfare system. In 1879 a boarding school system was developed for Indian children between the ages of 5 and 20. These schools prohibited the use of native languages and the observation of cultural customs. Placement rates for Indian children have been exceptionally high because of inadequate protection of both parent and child rights and use of culturally biased standards. Some indicators of the vulnerability of American Indian children include a high infant mortality rate, increased number of orphans because of high adult mortality, and high placement rates.[19]

Child welfare services have been especially destructive to Indian families. Children have been placed disproportionally out of their own homes, and transracial placements have been overused in both foster care and adoptions. Few Indian families can qualify as foster or adoptive parents under white cultural standards. The Indian Child Welfare Act (P.L. 95-608) was funded inadequately and has been controversial for primarily political reasons.

Social work practice in child welfare is strongly influenced by the political and economic environment. When the economy is healthy and families are able to meet their financial needs, there is a decrease in crime, drug usage, and child abuse. As the environment creates increasing pressure on families, social workers intervene on a protective as well as a problem-solving basis. Today, the whole family structure is at great peril as a result of tremendous changes taking place both in society and within the family.

VALUES

The National Association of Social Workers has clearly delineated the values that guide child welfare practice, regardless of the historical time or setting in which it takes place. The NASW standards for social work practice in child protection were prepared by the NASW Task Force and approved by the Board of Directors of the National Association at its meeting in 1981. We draw from this report to examine how values affect both protective services and juvenile court services.

The NASW Code of Ethics establishes the ethical responsibilities for social workers with respect to themselves, to their clients, colleagues, employees, and agencies, to the profession, and to society. Acceptance of these responsibilities guides competent social work practice in all child protective tasks and activities. The task force report also delineates the values most critical to child welfare social workers.

The acceptance of one's own humanness with a commitment to continued pursuit of personal and professional growth. As we discuss social work in terms of values, knowledge, and skills, we can lose sight of the fact that we as human beings are an integral part of the social work process. Social workers trained in Freudian models of practice are made aware of this through concepts such as transference. These therapists are taught to be very aware of how they personally affect the treatment process and when clients are attributing characteristics of significant others to the therapist. In some cases the therapist becomes a parent figure, a resented sibling, or even a rejecting lover. Even though many social workers today reject Freudian concepts, this example illustrates how important the individual doing the treatment is to the process.

Acknowledgment of one's own values, attitudes, and biases about children, families, childrearing practices, and ethnic and cultural differences, along with awareness of the potential impact of these personal feelings upon professional decision making.

Some recent findings suggest that institutional and individual racism is still an important factor in child welfare services. "The system responds more

An example of transference is when the client sees the therapist as the reincarnation of or substitute for a parent or sibling.

slowly to crises in minority families; such families have less access to support services such as day care and homemaker services."[20] On an individual basis minority children receive less comprehensive service plans, and minority parents are viewed as less able to profit from support services. A recent study concluded that, although the child welfare system is more tolerant of certain problems in minority families, assessment and intervention are harsher once a situation is defined as problematic.[21]

Belief in the capacity of people to change and the desire of most parents to be good parents. While this seems like a straightforward and easily held belief, it can at times be very difficult to maintain for the social worker who has to deal with child molesters or highly dysfunctional families on a daily basis. It takes a great deal of professionalism and knowledge to continually recognize strengths and potential in abusive and neglectful parents. And, since the environmental conditions impacting on these parents seem so difficult to change. it sometimes becomes easier to blame the parent for what may be environmental problems.

Recognition of the dignity of the child as an individual with both a right to adequate care and a stake in a continuing family relationship. One area in which the dignity of the child can be improved is foster placement of adolescents. Seldom is the adolescent's opinion sought, and it is frequently discounted when offered. As Taber and Proch observe, "Involving suspicious, alienated adolescents in case planning is difficult and time-consuming. However, adolescents who have not been consulted easily can subvert case plans."[22]

Even more important than the child subverting case plans is the fact that we miss important opportunities to help the adolescent learn decision-making skills. "What better way to prepare adolescents for adult autonomy than to allow them to make decisions and accept the consequences?"[23]

Commitment to the child's family as the preferred unit of childrearing and nurturing. When a social worker is faced with an antisocial child, it is too easy to see the family as the problem and place the child in an institution or foster home. This can be very destructive. We must recognize that parents hold the key for these children. Parents must learn to control these children, and it must begin at an early age. Never again will anyone have the awesome power a parent has over a young child. In addition, parents are the only people who love a child enough to go through the hundreds of learning trials necessary to socialize the child.[24] It is up to the family to teach the child how to relate to others, how to accomplish tasks, and how to survive in the school setting. Schools, peer groups, and society at large must assist in this function, but unless the parents prepare and then support the child in polishing these skills, the child will not profit from later socialization agents. Parents need knowledge, support, and resources to handle these children. Social workers can be an important linkage in helping parents obtain these resources.

Commitment to assist in meeting the physical, emotional, social, educational, moral, and vocational needs of children. Healthy children must have nurturance, care, protection, guidance, and control; they must develop a sense of trust, belonging, and security. Security needs must be met by adults who protect them from harm and teach them to control themselves.

Commitment to fostering the rights of children and parents. This includes the right to confidentiality and privacy. Children have the right to be protected against abuse, neglect, cruelty, and exploitation; parents have the right to determine for themselves, within the limits set by society, how they will rear their children. One area in which these rights have been vigorously debated is with gay and lesbian parents. Historically, homosexuality would have been grounds for removal of children; case law and many state statutes now protect the custody rights of gay and lesbian parents.

Belief that child neglect, abuse, and exploitation are more likely to be symptoms of social and economic deprivations and personal problems rather than of willful, premeditated malice. You will recall that this approach to social problems was identified as one of the unique characteristics of the social work frame of reference. Rather than assuming that child abuse is a psychological problem of the abusing parents, the social worker assesses the social environment to determine which social stressors are contributing to the abuse and what resources need to be developed to prevent further abuse.

Recognition of society's responsibility to children and the need for social workers to be accountable to the community. Social workers do not operate in a vacuum in determining what is in the best interests of children. Child welfare is a socially constructed concept, and any intervention in the family system must be socially acceptable. Americans' commitment to family privacy and responsibility at times makes prevention of abuse and neglect more difficult. The whole concept of community sanction can become very difficult when neighbors want children removed from what they view as an unacceptable environment. Yet state statutes protect parents' custody rights unless significant abuse or neglect can be established in the legal sense. Child welfare is a constant effort to balance protection, privacy, and justice.

FUNCTIONS

A function is an activity that contributes to the operation of a system. Chapter 3 discusses social work functions.

In discussing the values that underlie child welfare practice we frequently alluded to the essential functions that child welfare services meet within the society. Child welfare workers deal with problems caused by dysfunctions in the family system. When juveniles commit serious crimes, there is either a breakdown in the families' ability to socialize or control the children, or the children themselves are experiencing a breakdown in social functioning skills. When parents abuse their children, social, psychological, and possibly biological functions have broken down. Social workers strive to "fix" the problem by helping individuals lead a happy and socially acceptable life; that is, they attempt to maximize the well-being of individuals and to protect society. These are very general functions that are translated into practice in various ways, depending upon the setting in which the intervention takes place.

The functions of child welfare workers can be summarized under the categories of prevention, protection, support, control, individual treatment, and situational intervention.

The prevention function refers to programs and policies that are developed to prevent problems in family functioning. This may include development of parenting classes for young, inexperienced parents. Or it might be the development of respite care homes for severely disturbed or diseased children. Respite homes allow the natural or foster family to take time away from the demands of children who require round-the-clock care. The assumption is that by maintaining the mental health of the caretakers, you are not only providing the children with better care but also preventing abuse or neglect that may occur if the caretakers are overwhelmed by the demands of caring for special needs children.

The prevention function tends to be a favorite among social workers, since it is a proactive approach—one in which social workers experience a lot of positive feedback. Most families are happy to receive such services, and the professional-client relationship tends to be consensus-oriented, in contrast to the protective function, which is frequently highly stressful and conflictual.

The protection function relates to the federal statute that requires all reports of child abuse and neglect to be investigated. Even though we have a federal statute that requires investigation, we have no clear guidelines of what constitutes abuse or neglect. "To protect children at risk and to identify non-maltreating families in need of other services, policies are needed that more specifically set forth the definitions of child abuse and neglect."[25] This brief quote points out another aspect of the protection function. Child welfare workers frequently find themselves in the position of protecting a family that is *not* abusive or neglectful from unwarranted interference. Unwarranted complaints may come from divorced spouses, extended family members, or neighbors who simply do not approve of the parents' lifestyle, even though it may not be harmful to the children. Even if these families do not need protective services, they may benefit from support services.

The support function refers to any action to help parents solve or mitigate personal or social problems. For social workers attached to family court, this may consist of explaining to the newly divorced parent how to obtain financial assistance. Juvenile court workers may provide important support to parents who are faced with court proceedings against their child.

The control function refers to activities directed toward regulation of clients' behavior. This can include any statement or activity designed to induce clients to conform to socially acceptable standards of behavior. This function is most apparent in dealing with juvenile offenders. Juvenile court workers function very much like adult probation officers in setting rules that delinquent children must observe. Another instance of the control function is with parents who have sexually abused their children. The court may decide that the family is better off if the offender receives treatment rather than punishment. While social workers provide treatment, they usually maintain some responsibility for seeing that the client's behavior is controlled. They may require that the offender abstain from alcohol, or an abusing parent can be limited in terms of contact with the child. In fact, most child welfare workers have an extensive list of conditions the offender must follow in order to remain in the family. It is the social worker's responsibility to monitor and enforce these rules and to invoke the appropriate consequence when they are violated.

Individual treatment activities focus primarily on the individual, as in the example just cited, when the child welfare worker "treats" the abusing father in an attempt to help him control his aggressive behavior. The treatment may be a combination of behavior modification, relaxation therapy, and assertiveness training. Individual treatment tends to be a contractual agreement between the client and the social worker to change some aspect of the client's behavior and perhaps even his value system.

Situational treatment refers to activities that are focused primarily on the social environment of the client. Recently, a baby was born in a hospital in a middle-Atlantic state who tested positive for the human immunodeficiency (HIV) virus that can develop into AIDS. The mother was imprisoned shortly after the baby's birth and his father disappeared. Responsibility for the baby reverted to the child protection service (CPS) in that city. After six months the CPS had failed to make any provisions for the baby, who was still in the newborn nursery. The hospital social worker had repeatedly asked that CPS find more suitable placement for the child. When these appeals did not bring the desired results, the hospital social worker threatened to file charges of neglect against the city CPS. That threat produced action; within one week a foster home was found for the baby.[26]

The primary function of direct practice in child welfare is helping dysfunctional families alter their behavior, obtain necessary support from their environment, and maximize their social functioning. Our unique expertise in working with families is to assess the social problems contributing to their dysfunctional behavior, the environmental stressors, and how interpersonal and community relationships are affecting their behavior. Our interventions are based upon knowledge of childhood development, family functioning, the public welfare system, the court system, motivation, and emotional and environmental factors.

Social workers are likely to remain primary service providers in this field. Our systemic orientation to family functioning is unique; neither courts nor psychiatrists nor psychologists practice from this perspective. Our understanding of the environmental contributors to family functioning is essential.

In fact, one of the problems identified in child welfare practice is that social workers repeatedly defer to the judgment of psychiatrists in case planning, even when "based on their knowledge of the child's social situation they disagreed with psychiatrists."[27] While this may remove the onus from the social worker if the case plan fails, it also increases the probability of failure because it does not benefit from the insights of the person most familiar with the family functioning.

Social work contributions can be in the area of direct service—helping families improve parenting competence, promoting the development of children, and enhancing self-support and self-sufficiency. However, the profession must continue to play an important role in indirect service—the development of "public policy and child welfare services that strengthen the ability of vulnerable families to raise healthy children."[28]

KNOWLEDGE

Child welfare, like each field of practice, requires social workers to have knowledge of *general* theory of human behavior and the social environment; *practice theory,* which includes knowledge of policy, services, programs, institutions and how social work practice relates to each of them; and a *theory of practice,* which is the specific social work methods or interventions they will use. The practice method used will depend upon the systematic interpretation of those principles that help social workers understand phenomena and a clear delineation of principles for producing change. In simpler terms, interventions are based on knowledge of what is happening, why it is happening, and how we can change what is happening.

Specialized knowledge needed for this field includes expertise in intervening with families, frequently on an involuntary basis. Such intervention requires knowledge and acceptance of the unique legal responsibilities and constraints and knowledge necessary to work simultaneously with the child, the parents, other child welfare services, and the courts.

Standard 3 of the NASW Standards for Social Work Practice in Child Protection states: "Social workers in CPS shall display knowledge basic to the social work profession and an understanding of the social institutions, organizations and resources serving children and families." This standard refers to general knowledge. Included in this component are the history and development of social work in general and child welfare specifically.

Human growth and behavior is another area of general knowledge. Child welfare workers need to know what normal development is; if a child is not progressing through the appropriate stages, the social worker needs to know when intervention is indicated. Understanding human behavior implies understanding the human needs and motivations, feelings, behaviors, and activities of children. This includes problems of childhood or the effect of school difficulties upon children and their families.

Theories of practice such as the principles and methods of casework, group work, community organization, and research are important to all child welfare workers. Indirect practitioners will need to have knowledge of administration, supervision, and planning as well.

Understanding the cultural, political, and legal structures, processes, and practices is essential to child welfare practice. Today, child welfare agencies are experiencing drastic budget cuts at the same time we are seeing an increase in reports of child abuse and neglect. On top of this we have widespread abuse of alcohol and drugs, increased poverty among children, high numbers of high school dropouts, and high rates of adolescent pregnancy.[29] Given the lack of economic commitment to the field of child welfare, social workers must frequently fall back on invoking legal processes to obtain the resources needed for clients. An example of this is special education classes for a handicapped or incarcerated child. (We discuss this further under Relevant Social Policy.)

Family functioning is inherently related to the economic factors impinging on individuals and the community in which they live. The cost of living, the standard of living, employment opportunities (or lack thereof), and the accessibility of benefits and services will all affect the degree to which parents can meet the needs of their children. Social workers cannot ignore these critical variables.

To address these problems the social worker has to know the purpose and structure of public and child welfare service agencies, the functions of each agency, how they relate to each other, and on what contingencies their funding is based.

Effective resource linkage requires knowledge of the agency and a professional working relationship between the social worker and professionals in the fields of education, health, mental health, special education, child guidance, and vocational services. Since services never fully meet the needs of the targeted population, it requires knowledge and skill to acquire needed services and resources for your clients.

Finally, we cannot overlook the importance of understanding how the individual relates to the family, the community, primary and secondary groups, the neighborhood, and wider social systems.

We are increasingly learning about how personality develops. We now know that it involves a combination of congenital endowments, experiences in family living, environmental opportunities, and cultural influences. In spite of our ever-expanding knowledge, we still do not know to what degree nurture or nature is prevalent in personality development. For the social worker the primary area of expertise will be the contributions of nurture, or environmental influences. However, the presence of organically based disturbances can also have a strong impact on social functioning and the social worker needs to be able to recognize these conditions, understand what medications are taken for the conditions, and what the side effects are likely to be. In fact, a critical step in dealing with an emotionally disturbed child is to have a thorough physical examination by a qualified pediatrician.

Methods of childrearing can vary widely across the families we serve. We need to be aware of cultural differences in raising children. For instance, in some American Indian cultures, children are raised by the maternal grandmother. This is the norm, rather than a problem. Problems can be created when social workers object to this norm and view the absence of the parents as neglect. Whatever the variation in cultural norms, there are certain basics that need to be met in the childrearing process. Basic health care and social experiences appropriate to different stages of development must be provided. Children need guidance and discipline in order to form values and ideals.

A realistic understanding of family culture, the emotional aspects of parent-child relationships, and what factors affect parental capacity to meet children's needs is essential for the child welfare professional. Knowledge of the parent's responsibilities, obligations, duties, and rights provides the framework in which protective services operate.

NASW Standard 4 states, "Social workers in CPS shall possess specialized knowledge and understanding about children and families and about the dynamics of child abuse and neglect." There is a host of research and theory that guides the social worker in understanding the interrelationships between physical, sexual, and emotional abuse and neglect. This knowledge base also provides assessment tools to determine when neglect and abuse are present and whether interventions need to be directly with the family or whether lack of resources is causing the neglect.

Some of the factors that contribute to child neglect are: high divorce rates and the resultant impoverishment of women and children, lack of adequate day care, teenage pregnancies, and medical problems. Many child welfare problems result from parental incapacity to function adequately as a parent; an individual may be motivated, but still unable to function effectively. If parents have personality disturbances themselves, are heavily involved in marital conflict, or are seriously in debt, their capacity to parent will be severely constrained.

High mobility is another problem area for many children. It can be caused by frequent job changes by the parent, broken homes, foster placements, or even evictions. Most children need to experience a secure living environment to develop trust and security. While some families may be able to move often and yet instill that security, it is an almost impossible task for parents who face a multitude of social stressors.

Recognizing feelings and attitudes associated with being a "client" will also lead to a more constructive relationship. For the parent who asks for assistance, there is likely to be a tremendous sense of helplessness and failure. The community and culture the parent lives in will also have an effect on how he or she feels. For the involuntary client who feels the social worker is an intruder, there is likely to be anger and hostility. Working with involuntary clients is an important skill social workers are taught.

One of the most disturbing facts about the child welfare field is that in spite of the tremendous body of knowledge necessary for effective practice, only 25 percent of public agency child welfare social workers have any formal training in social work.[30]

ROLES

Child welfare can present role conflicts for the social worker. Protective service social workers experience ongoing conflict between parents' rights to privacy and children's rights to protection. Much of child welfare is uncharted territory, and decisions about life-threatening situations have to be made with limited information. Another role conflict comes into play when the social worker is "treating" an abusive parent. The social worker is required by law to report any further abuse. Some social workers feel that this interferes with the professional-client relationship.

Some social workers in corrections have dealt with this dilemma by insisting that treatment would be provided only if no reporting would be done that would ultimately hurt or even help the client. This approach is designed to facilitate open communication and eliminate the element of manipulation. However, when the protection of a child is involved, this option is not feasible.

Other social workers have taken the opposite view and used their power in the supervision process as a source of motivation. Knowledge and experience have taught some social workers to recognize and use authority as an important variable in treatment. Child welfare workers are involved in normal social work roles.

Social workers serve as brokers when they make linkages between the client and a community agency such as a community mental health center. Child welfare workers are likely to work closely with pediatricians or public health nurses to determine the impact of the child's physical development on behavior. If a child has an organically based personality disorder, a psychiatrist will be needed to prescribe and monitor medication. A psychologist might be called in to perform intelligence or personality testing. Each of these professionals has specific and important roles in the child welfare arena. Social workers need to understand the differences in these roles and to manage the services in such a way that the client gets the correct services at the most appropriate time.

Social workers' advocate role is a familiar one to child welfare workers because the complexity of the programs, the fear of rejection, the lack of communication between agencies, and the high degree of stratification and depersonalization in social agencies can create special problems for even the most knowledgeable and capable individuals. Since programs are never adequately funded to meet the need identified, only the most adept at advocating will get the desired services. Most dysfunctional families need assistance in this area.

The enabler role is evident when the social worker helps the patient and the family find strengths and resources within themselves to solve their problems. In this role the social worker enables the family to change or to achieve the desired goal by concentrating on their own strengths and abilities and helping them apply these strengths to the problems at hand.

The teaching role introduces information to the family that was not previously available. A social worker may teach human sexuality to a group of schoolchildren, parenting and communication skills to parents, or survival skills to a group of teenagers. Family planning and dependency prevention are two other areas where social workers frequently develop teaching programs.

As a mediator the social worker acts to reconcile differences and to intervene between conflicting parties in order to promote reconciliation or compromise. Family court workers are frequently involved in mediation with families when there is dispute concerning custody or visitation. In this situation the worker must be primarily concerned with the welfare of the child, but mediate the conflict between the parents in a way that decreases the negative impact on the child.

In most child welfare settings social workers have primary responsibility for direct practice and program administration. In many ways social workers have more status in the child welfare area, because we have long been recognized as experts in this area. It is primarily social workers who uphold the authority to protect children vested in state law.

RELEVANT SOCIAL POLICY/LEGISLATION

Child abuse reporting laws are in effect in all 50 states. These laws vary in terms of both who must report and what must be reported. Most state laws are in compliance with the federal statute that requires that all reports of child abuse and neglect be investigated (Child Abuse Prevention and Treatment Act, 1974).[31] One motive for compliance is to be eligible for federal funds derived from the act. Two key criteria in the act are the requirement that the states define abuse and neglect and that they conduct prompt investigations upon receipt of a report.

Public Law 94-142, the Education for the Handicapped Act, and Public Law 99-457, the 1986 amendments to PL 94-142, have had a far-reaching impact on child welfare, both for handicapped preschoolers and juvenile offenders. The intent of the laws is to: (1) ensure that a free and appropriate education is available to all handicapped students; (2) help local and state education agencies provide this education; (3) assess the effects of these efforts; and (4) provide due process assurances to handicapped students and their parents.[32]

Children are at increasing risk as family and community structures break down.

The passage of this act has led states to develop and implement public awareness programs focusing on early identification of handicapped infants and toddlers. Most states have also developed some type of "child find" system for referring and screening children who need further evaluation.[33]

Another group that should be affected is incarcerated juveniles. The federal mandate specifically extends to correctional education programs. The response for this group has not been as effective for a number of reasons. First, the law is more difficult to implement in a correctional setting because it was written for the public school system. For example, it is almost impossible to allow parents to be involved in treatment planning because of travel logistics. Second, the unavailability of qualified personnel is a serious problem. Only 28 percent of juvenile correctional education teachers are certified in special education.[34] Third, there is the feeling that delinquents just do not deserve the same benefits as law-abiding citizens.

Since scarce financial and human resources must be allocated according to fluctuating national priorities, the prevalence of handicapped persons in any human service program tends to be skewed by sociopolitical variables. Special education needs estimates range from "nearly all delinquents have learning disabilities," as seen from a special educator's view, to "nearly all delinquents are normal," a sociologist's view.[35]

The importance of special education programs for juvenile offenders becomes especially critical when one views certain statistics. The probability of adjudication is 220 percent greater if the young offender is learning handicapped;[36] periods of incarceration last two to three years longer for retarded inmates because they do not understand prison rules or know how to advocate for their rights;[37] retarded inmates are more frequent targets of physical, sexual, and economic abuse by other inmates.

The third area of policy essential to child welfare workers is juvenile corrections. Every major jurisdiction in the United States has two discrete legal systems for responding to criminal acts: a juvenile court, which is given responsibility for most offenders who fall under a specified age, and a criminal court, which is responsible for all the rest. Juvenile courts were first established in 1899 and were designed to be treatment-oriented rather than punishment-oriented. The goal was to provide protection and rehabilitation for juveniles. The underlying assumptions were that children were not totally responsible for their behavior and that the state had some duty to help socialize its children.[38] Juvenile dispositions (sentences) tend to be indeterminate. That is, juveniles remain under supervision until authorities think they are rehabilitated or until they reach legal adulthood. Juvenile courts are guided by the least restrictive principle: whenever possible, children should serve their sentences in their own homes. If this is not feasible, options range from foster care to residential treatment to juvenile correction agencies. Because of the commitment to rehabilitation that permeates the statutes in the juvenile arena, social workers tend to hold a primary place in providing supervision and in program development.

Some recent concerns have suggested that the juvenile system itself might become a "two-track" system. Research studies have found that there is a small group of offenders who, while legally juveniles, have demonstrated a sustained commitment to serious criminal activity and for whom the probability of continued involvement is extremely high regardless of rehabilitation efforts. There is also a slightly older group of high-risk offenders who are only one or two years past the transition from juvenile to criminal courts; since their juvenile records are closed, the present system obscures their true level of criminal activity. As a result, these serious offenders receive more lenient sentences than their records warrant.[39]

Waiver is when juveniles are charged as adults in the adult system.

This concern is likely to be translated into reforms in the juvenile system. Some of the reforms being considered are: changing the bases for waiver of juveniles into adult court, increasing the minimum amount of time that serious juvenile offenders must remain in secure custody, forming special juvenile career criminal prosecution units, and making juvenile proceedings and records more accessible to public scrutiny and criminal courts.[40] At the present time the ability to waive juveniles is severely restricted by most state statutes; children must be released when they reach the age of majority, and juvenile records are "closed," that is, not available to the courts or prosecutors.

In this section we have identified just three areas of policy that are important for the child welfare worker: abuse and neglect, handicapping conditions, and juvenile justice. We recognize that almost every social policy and program adopted or proposed will impact on family functioning. For instance, national health policy and income support programs are both vital to effective family functioning. Our goal was not to be all-inclusive, but rather to illustrate how integral the social and political climate is to the development of policies that benefit or constrain child welfare practice.

THE FUTURE OF FAMILY AND CHILD WELFARE PRACTICE

Social workers have been involved in child protection, child care, foster care, adoptions, institutionalization, teenage pregnancy, and juvenile delinquency for over 100 years. Most of these service areas are highly valued by society in general, even though funding is far from adequate. By and large we have a large base of theoretical and practice knowledge to draw on in providing these services.

We believe there are three pressing problems that society and social work must face for which we do not have adequate answers. These three problems are: (1) the spread of AIDS to infants and children, (2) the increasing numbers of antisocial children who are wreaking havoc on families and communities, and (3) the unprecedented number of children raising children.

Children born with AIDS have emotional and physical needs that require resources far beyond the capacity of their parents to provide. Most of these children will die within 3 years of birth.[41] Will our answer be to set up orphanages filled with dying infants? Will these children be kept in newborn nurseries? Can we find foster homes that can provide loving care throughout the child's short life and dying process? As a profession, do we have a responsibility to support legislation to limit the rights of people who are likely to transmit AIDS to children?[42]

What are we to do with high risk children such as the 5-year-old who pushed his playmate off an apartment house balcony to his death? The child recounted this deed with a smile. The prognosis for this child is very bleak. The parents are unable or unwilling to put adequate effort into socializing the child, and the state is a poor substitute. He was placed in a long-term residential center, which is to determine when he can be released. If he is typical of such children he will grow up in a series of foster homes with little or no treatment, and will ultimately end up in prison after causing serious harm to more than one individual.[43]

Many areas need to be studied to probe the reasons for these dangerous children. Among the list of suspected causes are marital discord; physical, sexual, and psychological abuse or neglect; overly harsh, inconsistent discipline; genetic influences; poverty and social disadvantage; family position of the child; temperament; and childrearing practices.[44] While the justice system seems to be prepared to handle this problem through punishment of parents or children, social workers will continue to try to understand and change the behavior.

The problems of teenage pregnancies and births are compounded by adverse health, social, and economic outcomes. Teen mothers drop out of school at alarming rates. They can expect to earn half as much as women who first give birth in their 20s. Studies have shown that many children of teenage parents suffer from educational and cognitive deficits, and they tend to have lower IQ and achievement scores.[45]

Caring for a young child is normally a struggle. For a single parent the task is truly formidable. If that parent is a mother still in her teens—an unusually stormy period of development—the demands of childrearing are often beyond her capability. Teenage mothers have excessively high rates of child abuse and neglect; the incidence of Sudden Infant Death Syndrome is 68 percent higher among children of teenage mothers than in the general population.[46]

Given that successful teenage parenting is almost an impossibility without considerable outside support, we need to develop programs and policies that ensure teenage mothers are receiving the needed support. Given their youth, they may need more than support. There is some evidence to suggest that these children raising children should be given supervision and education. Rather than assuming that because they can conceive and deliver a child, they can rear that child, we may want to build in some kind of assurance of that capability. Clearly, the best response to the teenage pregnancy problem would be effective birth prevention education. This response seems unlikely; in the meantime we are allowing millions of children to raise their children under conditions that almost ensure delinquency, mental illness, and poverty.

SUMMARY

"A diminishing level of family care during the early years of childhood has left the young more vulnerable to physical harm than at any period in recent decades."[47] To counter this trend, social workers have been pushing for more governmental support to assist families in caring for their children. Intervening in the functioning of families is tricky business for government. Social policy objectives are muddled by incompatible goals of protecting children and protecting parental freedoms.

"The old value of the sanctity of family and the right of parents, within limits, to rear their children without outside intervention is still valid."[48] However, we cannot use these values to justify ignoring the lack of social services and the need for protection of children. Rather, we must recognize the problems that come to bear upon parents and fight just as strongly for their right to obtain essential social supports to combat family dysfunction.

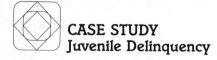

CASE STUDY
Juvenile Delinquency

The treatment of serious juvenile offenders provides an example of how knowledge, functions, values, and roles translate into practice with one client. A diagnosis of antisocial personality disorder usually suggests extremely serious psychological and social functioning problems for both the victims and their families. Antisocial personality disorder* is the diagnosis given to those people who tend to operate without a conscience. "There does seem to exist an identifiable personality type, the joining of genetic and environmental factors, that is highly prone to criminal behavior. The type that . . . is known most commonly as antisocial personality."[49]

The protection function is primary. Parents and other children in the family need to be protected and so does the community. "The central feature is a personality disorder in which there is a history of continuous and chronic antisocial behavior in which the rights of others are violated, persistence into adult life of a pattern of antisocial behavior that began before the age of 15. . . . Lying, stealing, fighting, truancy, and resisting authority are typical early childhood signs."[50]

Since juveniles are dealt with separately from the adult correctional system, society expects social workers to set up treatment programs that protect society and prevent further acts of delinquency. Knowledge of how the juvenile court functions is important—social workers must know their responsibilities and constraints.

The prevention function in this instance covers the goal of minimizing further delinquency, but for the social worker involved with this child's family, it should also include prevention of family dysfunctioning. When families produce antisocial children, the parents frequently find they are blamed for the child. Social workers can prevent family deterioration through education, support, and situational intervention.

The support function may entail listening to the parents' needs and fears. The sharing of intense

fears helps to dilute feelings of isolation and anger. The social worker will understand the difficulty of coping with an antisocial child and understand that empathy combined with education is often the most effective tactic. There needs to exist an honest, direct relationship between the parents and the social worker. The parents must feel that the social worker truly understands the pain the child is creating in their lives.

The support offered must be reliable, consistent, and continuous. The social worker must make a commitment to the parents to be available. Families are likely to become overwhelmed in caring for this type of child. The support function cannot be fulfilled on a 9-to-5, Monday-through-Friday schedule. Arrangements for backup staff should be understood by the parent.

In discussing the support function we addressed the needs of the family of the antisocial child. In discussing the control function, we are primarily concerned with the control of the child's behavior. Clearly, the parents will be our most important resource in achieving this goal. This function is very difficult with antisocial children, because they do not respond to the same types of socialization mechanisms that motivate normal children.

Teaching the parents skills such as contingency management, assertiveness training, and relaxation therapy provides some possible means of helping them control the child. These children cannot tolerate other people's limits on them. They are constantly testing and baiting—constantly pushing the limits. Such children create major disturbances when asked to comply with reasonable requests.

At a very early age they develop obnoxious means of controlling situations. For instance, one such child who was unhappy about the attention her brother was receiving from the parents' guests announced that a neighbor boy had pulled down her pants and played with her. The child grinned smugly as she observed the adults' embarrassment.[51]

The more severe the character disorder of the child, the more control problems the parents will

_____
* Social workers must understand the condition known as antisocial personality disorder.

have. Extreme cases have included a 15-year-old* who unremorsefully bludgeoned an 80-year-old woman to death, and Ted Bundy, who was executed in 1989 as a result of his murderous rampages. In controlling these children, the social worker needs to have very specific knowledge about this character disorder. The intervention must be based on proven techniques that have been tested on the appropriate target population. Sending the parents to the typical parent training program will only lead to more frustration and guilt on their part.

Individual treatment will take the form of treating the antisocial disorder with therapies specifically designed for this problem. Some of the treatments that have been found to be effective with these children are the social learning approach, rage

---

* This 15-year-old was the first child under age 16 to be convicted of first degree murder in his state.

therapy, Wilderness Therapy, aggression control, and Juveniles in Jeopardy.[52] Traditional psychotherapies have not been very successful. Pharmacotherapy has not yet been developed that impacts on antisocial behavior. This may be an important trend in the future, however, since abnormalities in the brain waves of antisocial individuals have been found. Diet is also being investigated as a contributor to antisocial personality. Once again we see the importance of biology to social functioning.

The situational treatment function can be seen as the social worker deals with the stress in the child and the family environment. Parents can feel as much stress from family, friends, and schools as they do from the child. Social workers should obtain the parents' permission to consult with significant individuals and organizations to make them aware of the parents' need for support. Everyone involved needs to be educated about what is fact and what is myth in dealing with antisocial children.

NOTES

1. N. Gilbert, "The Unfinished Business of Welfare Reform," *Society* (March/April 1987).
2. M. Petit, "Advancing a Family-Centered Agenda in Public Policy," Special Conference Empowering Families '88 Prevention Report, National Resource Center on Family Based Services, University of Iowa, Winter/Spring, 1989.
3. Milwaukee *Journal*, 28 May 1989, 1B.
4. M. Petit, "Advancing a Family-Centered Agenda."
5. E. Stark, "Young, Innocent, and Pregnant," *Psychology Today* (October 1986): 28.
6. J. Sanko, "Children Having Children," *Rocky Mountain News*, Denver, Colo. (16 July, 1986), 21.
7. C. Wallis, "Children Having Children," *Time* (9 December, 1985): 79–90.
8. *Suicide Prevention: A Resource Planning Guide*, distributed by the Wisconsin Department of Public Instruction.
9. *Serious Juvenile Offenders* (Washington, D.C.: Office of Juvenile Justice and Delinquency Prevention, U.S. Department of Justice, March 1984), 3.
10. D. Harris, "Renewing Our Commitment to Child Welfare," *Social Work* (November–December 1988): 483–484.
11. S. Kamerman and A. Kahn, *Social Services in the United States* (Philadelphia: Temple University Press, 1976).
12. J. Axinn and H. Levin, *Social Welfare: A History of the American Response to Need* (New York: Harper & Row, 1982).
13. A. Billingsley and J. Giovannoni, *Children of the Storm: Black Children and American Child Welfare* (New York: Harcourt Brace Jovanovich, 1972).

14. P. Hogan and S. Siu, "Minority Children and the Child Welfare System: An Historical Perspective," *Social Work* 33, 6 (November–December 1988): 493–498.
15. P. Jackson, "Black Charity in Progressive Era," *Social Service Review* 53, (1978): 400–417.
16. Billingsley and Giovannoni, *Children of the Storm*.
17. Ibid.
18. Ibid.
19. Hogan and Siu, "Minority Children," 494.
20. Ibid., 493.
21. M. Close, "Child Welfare and People of Color," *Social Work Research and Abstracts* 16 (1) (1980): 26–33.
22. M. Taber and K. Proch, "Parenting: An Essential Child Welfare Service," *Social Work* (January/February 1988): 63–64.
23. Ibid.
24. G. Patterson, *Coercive Family Process* (Eugene, Ore.: Castalia, 1982).
25. S. Wells, T. Stein, J. Fluke, and J. Downing, "Screening in Child Protective Services," *Social Work* (January 1989): 45–48.
26. J. Miller and T. Carlton, "Children and AIDS: A Need to Rethink Child Welfare Practice," *Social Work* (November/December 1988): 553–555.
27. M. Taber & K. Proch, "Parenting," 63.
28. D. Harris, "Renewing."
29. Ibid.
30. P. Hogan & S. Sui, "Minority Children."
31. S. Wells et. al., "Screening."
32. A. Blackhurst, "Issues in Special Education," in *An Introduction to Special Education,* 2nd ed. (Boston: Little, Brown, 1985), 45–85.
33. D. Bailey and M. Wolery, *Assessing Infants and Preschoolers with Handicaps* (Columbus, Ohio: Merrill, 1989).
34. C. Nelson, "Handicapped Offenders in the Criminal Justice System," in *Special Education in the Criminal Justice System,* ed. C. Michael Nelson, R. Rutherford, and B. Wolford (Columbus, Ohio: Merrill, 1987).
35. C. Murray, *The Link Between Learning Disabilities and Juvenile Delinquency: Current Theory and Knowledge* (Washington, D.C.: National Criminal Justice Reference Service, 1978).
36. M. Santamour and B. West, *Retardation and Criminal Justice* (Washington, D.C.: President's Committee on Mental Retardation, 1979).
37. R. Snarr, "The Criminal Justice System," in *Special Education in the Criminal Justice System,* 24–52.
38. P. Greenwood, "Differences in Criminal Behavior and Court Responses among Juvenile and Young Adult Defendants," in *Crime and Justice: An Annual Review,* ed. M. Tonry and N. Morris (Chicago: University of Chicago Press, Vol. 7, 1986).
39. Ibid.
40. Ibid.
41. S. Wells et. al., "Screening."
42. Ibid.
43. K. Magid and C. McKelvey, *High Risk: Children Without a Conscience.* (New York: Bantam, 1987), 33.
44. Ibid.
45. Ibid.

46. Gilbert, "Unfinished Business," 115.
47. Ibid.
48. L. Costin, "Is the Family Neglectful or Neglected?" *Society* 24, 3 (March/April 1987): 27.
49. C. Cloninger, "The Anti-social Personality," *Hospital Practice* (August 1978), 97–103.
50. *Diagnostic and Statistical Manual* III. (American Psychiatric Association, 1980).
51. F. Cline, *Understanding and Treating the Severely Disturbed Child* (Evergreen, Co.: Evergreen Consultant in Human Behavior, 1979).
52. For full descriptions of these treatments, see Patterson, *Coercive Family Process* (social learning); Magid and McKelvey, *High Risk* (rage therapy). The variety of Wilderness Therapy programs in existence are basically programs that provide an opportunity for children to test themselves against the elements. Juveniles in Jeopardy is a program of Special Offender Services, Oshkosh, Wis. developed in 1989; see also A. Goldstein and B. Glick, *Aggression Replacement Training: A Comprehensive Intervention for Aggressive Youth* (Champaign, Ill.: Research Press, 1987). The Texas Youth Authority has also developed a program of aggression training.

Chapter

16

Health Care

O ver 50,000 social workers practice in the health field today. The types of clients they deal with range across the age, ethnic, and social class spectrum.

Some of the current challenges to health care social workers are: the development of programs and policies to meet the needs of people with AIDS and their families, discharge planning, treatment of eating disorders, and development of hospice programs.

Health care social work started in the hospital setting, which is the most common setting for health care social workers today. However, community health centers, family planning clinics, health maintenance organizations (HMOs), industry, and labor unions are increasingly employing social workers in direct practice roles. The U.S. Public Health Service, the Veterans Administration, and state health agencies hire social workers for indirect practice—planning, policy development, and administration.

HISTORY

The original sanction for social workers to engage in direct practice in a health setting was provided by Dr. Richard C. Cabot in 1906, when he established a social services department at Massachusetts General Hospital. Ida Cannon was the first hospital director of social services. Dr. Cabot perceived that the physical illnesses presented by the poor immigrants he was treating were strongly related to the poor nutrition, inadequate housing, and overall economic plight of his patients. Dr. Cabot assigned a small group of social workers to work with immigrant mothers on these problems.[1] Hospital social workers formed the first specialized professional association in 1918.

In both England and the United States, the nineteenth century settlement movement was involved in health issues. They developed numerous programs and worked for health policy to combat the pollution and dirt in the environment. Impure water, lack of garbage disposal, poor ventilation, and inadequate quarantine procedures were just a few of the problems settlement workers tried to resolve. In addition they set up neighborhood health clinics, well baby clinics, and sanitariums.

VALUES

In Chapter 4 we discussed social work values as identified by the National Association of Social Workers. Clearly, the general social work values apply in health settings. To summarize the generic social work values, we can say that (1) society has an obligation to ensure that people have access to resources they need to meet various life tasks; and (2) in providing these resources, the dignity and individuality of the person should be respected. In addition, there is also a distinct set of values held by social workers with regard to health care.

1. Total health care is a right.
2. Access to health care should not be limited by lack of financial resources.
3. Quality of life should be considered in prolongation of life decisions.
4. Caring and coping are as important as technological advances.
5. Health care should be based on models of wellness, rather than strictly a disease focus model.

Values are a part of every professional's action system. One of the unique characteristics of practice in health care is that other professions in the system have values that differ from those of social work. Fundamental values establish the outer boundaries of each profession.

The social worker in health care experiences value conflicts. The client's values always need to be at the center of attention. Yet there will legitimately be times when what clients want is not consistent with their own best interest or that of their family and/or community. Self-awareness assists the social worker in meeting the responsibility for explicating a value framework. Values can help control the anxiety inherent in the social work role.

Values and knowledge are related systems of thought and action. It is important for the social worker to understand when an interventive action is based on values or knowledge or a combination of the two. When planning for the care of an Alzheimer patient, there are certain things we know about the disease and about the effect of the disease on family functioning. Yet the recommendation of the social worker and the ultimate decision of the family will largely be determined by values. The social worker acknowledges to the patient when a suggested plan of action is based on values rather than on objective reality.

In the social work role we need to maintain a balance of flexibility, integrity, self-awareness, and technical expertise.

FUNCTIONS

Health care social workers: (1) deal with social problems involved in disease management and health care; (2) work to return temporarily or permanently disabled patients to the community and normalize functioning to the extent possible; (3) become involved in policy and program decisions to humanize service delivery; (4) educate the community in wellness and understanding of disease; and (5) conduct research.

The primary function of direct practice in health care is helping patients negotiate the health care system and maximize their personal health. Although this function has not changed dramatically over time, our knowledge and skills have become more refined. Just as new medications are discovered, the social work profession discovers what the effects of these medications are on the social functioning of the patient and how the family can help manage the disease.

Our unique expertise is to work with the patient to quickly and accurately assess the social problems contributing to health problems, the environmental stressors, and how interpersonal and familial relationships are impinging upon physical illness. Our interventions are based upon knowledge of physical, emotional, and environmental factors. We have a continually increasing base of knowledge to draw from, and methodological advances in dealing with individuals, families, and groups allow us to enunciate with some accuracy a rationale for appropriate intervention and to predict the case outcome. The case study of Mrs. R illustrates the importance of social work knowledge to patient care.

CASE STUDY
The Case of Mrs. R.: Reframing a Problem

Gary Rosenberg

Mrs. R., 48 years old, white, Jewish, married, mother of one child, and bearing a history of chronic paranoid schizophrenia with multiple psychiatric hospitalization had been admitted to a general surgical service for repair of bleeding hemorrhoids. Diagnostic tests had been completed for this "routine" procedure when Mrs. R. unexpectedly refused a final pre-op blood test and became loudly and verbally abusive to nurses and house staff. Mrs. R.'s resident physician reacted angrily and discharged her on the basis of noncompliance and the nonemergency nature of her illness just as the social worker arrived on the floor. Yet, three weeks later, Mrs. R. was readmitted by mutual choice to the same service to undergo surgery successfully.

This change did not happen magically! Rather, Mrs. R. offers a nice example of the delicate balance between meeting patient and staff system needs. Borrowing the technique of positive reframing from the field of family therapy enabled the social worker to accomplish this task. Positive reframing attempts to place a symptom or behavior in a different light, connoting it positively. Thus, it changes the cognitive and perceptual view of the symptom.

To Mrs. R., whose habitual tendency had been to view the world as hostile, the prospect of surgery with its aggressive, painful, and visible effects seemed unacceptable at first. For a person with little sense of control, losing more control risked going out of control. It can easily be forgotten just how much patient status alone implies heightened dependencies. For surgical patients undergoing general anesthesia, it implies total dependency. The first effort, therefore, was to learn from Mrs. R. what her primary concerns were. It was assumed that she wished for treatment whether or not she could presently tolerate the stress of receiving it (an attitude that immediately and helpfully separated the social worker from other staff and permitted the engagement of Mrs. R.). Though at first she regarded the worker with skepticism, the social part of the service won out! She agreed to talk and identified her physical pain, her mistrust of physicians and other strangers in the hospital network, the long delays in completing a diagnostic work-up, her loneliness for husband, son, home, and her clearly articulated fantasies (even conviction) of death or mutilation as surgery proceeded under general anesthesia. Most of all was her repetitive worry that she had failed to be a "good" patient as evidenced by her discharge. It was from her own perception that the worker molded her main intervention. Her "failure" to comply could be reframed; perhaps she and staff could both benefit. By the end of the first discussion (interrupted by her husband who thereafter participated in her treatment), it was agreed to try for a series of meetings over the next few weeks. These appointments would include, at times, a liaison psychiatrist attached to the service, her attending surgeon, resident surgeon, anesthesiologist, and various persons in the preadmission and admission offices who proved most cooperative re: room and floor assignment as well as date and length of readmission. These meetings allowed Mrs. R. to receive psychotropic medication under psychiatric guidance in order to diminish her anxiety, and to review again the surgical procedure planned and the type of anesthesia to be used. These issues were now discussed in a clinical setting, and there-

fore, were much less threatening. It was arranged for her to be readmitted to the floor best known to her and for a deliberate less-than-usual time, that is, 48 hours.

In working with staff, the social worker helped nurses and doctors to depersonalize Mrs. R.'s earlier attacks and to understand her behavior as defensive and a regression (particularly her low frustration tolerance and mistrust of strangers). Seen in this way, Mrs. R.'s first admission and "failure" to comply was newly and usefully reframed to staff and Mrs. R. as a "rehearsal." Second admissions, routinely endorsed on a pediatric service, are less acceptable (although occasionally as necessary) for those persons who are chronologically older.

The interventions outlined were chosen primarily for the following reasons: as a more neutral staff member, the social worker's agenda for Mrs. R. differed from both the nurse's and physician's. Mrs. R.'s submission to authority was not required, only her alliance in gaining good care. The thrust was, therefore, chiefly towards heightening her self-esteem, self-control, and autonomy. Knowledge of the mechanisms of defense permitted explaining Mrs. R.'s initially belligerent and aggressive behavior as a mask for much deeper fears to staff less familiar with such a perspective.

Finally, Mrs. R. illustrates the point that there is no such thing as a "routine" surgical procedure since each patient anticipates in a unique manner based on his personality and character structure, prior experience, and a host of other internal and external variables. There are also real limitations to the expenditure of time and energy involved in helping a Mrs. R. through a surgical experience. For each success story we ought not forget the very real number of patients who are either lost to care or whose silence (unlike Mrs. R.'s roar) is mistaken for trust, but they may be hurting just the same.

From Gary Rosenberg, "Practice Roles and Functions of the Health Social Worker," in *Social Work Issues in Health Care,* Miller and Rehr, eds., © 1983, pp. 167–168. Reprinted by permission of Prentice-Hall, Inc., Englewood Cliffs, New Jersey.

As we have repeatedly stressed, the methods and principles of social work practice are common to all social work settings. Our sanction to remain a vital part of the health care field is dependent upon our maintaining a social orientation to patient care. No other health care provider circumscribes practice from this perspective; it is our unique domain.

The practice of social work in the health field requires that other health professionals recognize our contributions to the tasks and responsibilities of defining and meeting the health needs of individuals and certain designated groups. The goals of the health care system include: (1) promoting wellness; (2) preventing disease; (3) treatment of illness; (4) optimum rehabilitation from disease or disability; (5) humane care for the terminally ill. In each of these areas social workers' knowledge of the psychosocial and environmental contributors to these goals is essential. Social work contribution can be in the area of direct service—empowering people to maximize the health system and their own abilities—or indirect service—teaching, planning, and policymaking.

KNOWLEDGE

Effective health care social workers must have an eclectic knowledge base. They need knowledge of issues in health care and knowledge of problem-solving. It requires one type of knowledge to understand the issues; it takes practice knowledge to be effective in resolving the problems related to these issues. The best test for knowledge in practice is whether it is useful. Useful knowledge helps us recognize and organize observations in the environment, suggests what things can be changed, and provides direction on how to go about producing the change.

For example, we know that prevention activities require the following: (1) a target condition that can be observed and measured; (2) a population at risk; (3) a clearly outlined plan of intervention; and (4) measurement of incidents following the intervention.

The problem of teenage pregnancy is one that social workers might be asked to address. The target condition is observable and the population at risk is defined in general terms. For the intervention to be effective, the social worker must limit the measurement to a more circumscribed population. If the intervention is a prevention program within one high school, then the social worker needs a baseline measure of incidence in that high school. If it is a statewide education program the measurement and the intervention must take place on a state level. Based upon the clearly stated goal of the program, the social worker must determine what intervention will be the most effective, under what condition, and why. The development of this intervention will draw upon her knowledge of human behavior, adolescence, the immediate and larger social environment of the target group, community mores, sensitivity to cultural variables, and her knowledge of human sexuality and family planning methods and devices.

This is not an exhaustive list of the types of knowledge the social worker needs, but it does convey the importance and complexity of knowledge in each social work intervention. In hospital settings, social workers must understand the organizational and administrative structure of the agency because they are likely to take on the functions of intake, liaison, and referral. They work with the administrative arm of the hospital, which is concerned with fiscal accountability, plant management, labor policy, and public relations. In addition, they deal with the clinical arm, which is concerned with service delivery.

Hospital social workers must understand that social, cultural, and economic variables have a significant impact on illness and recovery. Knowledge of families and how illness and hospitalization disrupt family functioning is essential. Many times medical treatment alone is insufficient to reverse health problems, even if they are physical in origin. Hospital social workers must thoroughly understand their own role and function and that of each of the other professions. Knowledge of individual and group behavior is critical to effective participation on the health care delivery team. In this setting social workers are never the primary caregivers.

Community medicine is concerned with incidence, prevalence, and risk factors in health care. "Community medicine practice involves the use of epidemiology, behavioral and management science, knowledge of the organization and coordination of health services, and of primary, secondary, and tertiary levels of care."[2] Practice in community medicine is likely to be in the area of research and policy development. Social workers involved in this arena need very specific knowledge such as epidemiology and biostatistics. These are tools to identify social and psychological characteristics of high-risk populations. Although this field may seem far removed from the typical approach to social work practice, social workers also need this type of knowledge to provide the social evidence related to disease.

If only medically oriented professionals are involved in the assessment and resolution of health problems in population groups, the proposed solutions are likely to be limited to medical solutions. If illness is a function of the interaction between a person's adaptive capacity and infectious agents in the environment, we must be committed to studying how the person and the social components of that environment can exacerbate or avert disease. Social workers must remember that no amount of individual change will offset the effect of long-range social problems that have contributed to the poor health of many groups in our society. Germ theory has long seen disease as lying solely within microbes. Susceptibility to disease is increasingly being seen as part of the larger ecology affecting the person. This ecological concept of disease is consistent with the social work frame of reference and holds great potential for the proper formulation of the problem of disease, its treatment, and its control.[3]

Once again in community practice we see the importance of knowledge of human behavior and the social environment. We must be concerned with the growth, development and potential of the human being and with the understanding of the properties of the social environment that assist or interfere with human potential.

Particularly in the area of community health, it is easy to see the importance of understanding the sociological components of disease. While direct practice social workers must be familiar with the sociological components, they deal on a much more consistent basis with the psychological components of disease.

Most social workers have a basic knowledge of psychoanalytic, behavioral, and cognitive theories of behavior. None of these theories offers a total understanding of human behavior. The social worker will not find easily identified prescriptive measures in how to deal with patients, but must carefully seek to understand the individuals' functioning guided by knowledge generated in these theories.

Stress theory is important to health care practice. For stress to be handled, the patient's coping capacities must be activated. For social workers to be effective, they need to understand the individual's motivation, how much he knows about his illness, what are his problem-solving abilities, and what is his level of self-esteem. The social worker must recognize defenses against anxiety and depression. Strengthening the patient's coping skills can lead to stress reduction. Perlin and Schooler identify three ways in which coping behavior can be improved: (1) by eliminating or modifying conditions giving rise to problems; (2) by perceptually controlling the meaning of experience in a manner that neutralizes its problematic character; and (3) by keeping the emotional consequences of problems within manageable bounds.[4]

One area in which social workers have specific skills and knowledge is helping families of terminally ill children cope. The social worker must ensure that the child gets quality medical care and access to as normal and full a life as possible. There is a tendency for medical professionals to give dying children less attention than children who may survive.[5] Families are hesitant to confront this situation for fear of jeopardizing even the minimal care the child is receiving. The social worker's goal is to ensure that proper care and attention are given to the child and family by medical staff and to share in the dying process with the family. Frequently the social worker must obtain additional information to enhance the family's decision making, and must help protect the patient's autonomy and individuality. Most important, the dying child should be allowed to externalize her fears and frustrations, receive adequate pain control, enjoy unrestricted visitation, and receive affirmation of her self-importance.[6]

Social workers maximize the patient's ability to cope by recognizing how the person's problems are related to environmental fit, by humanizing the service delivery system, by teaching and assisting in problem solving, and by supporting positive adaptive behaviors of both the patient and the family. Frequently social workers also have the ability to make available resources to aid in coping that patients or their families were unaware of or had found inaccessible.

Family theory is critical to health care. The patient who appears at the hospital or clinic is rarely an individual seeking help, but rather a member of a family facing a problem they do not have the internal resources to solve. Strain and Beallor have identified five prerequisites if the family is to be of assistance.

1. The ability of the family to accept the fact that the patient may regress physically and mentally as a consequence of the illness;
2. Their ability to help him ward off the stresses evoked by the illness;
3. Their ability to tolerate the patient's expression of his fears and feelings, for example, that he is going to die, that he will never be the man he once was, that he will recover, and so forth.
4. Their ability to enlist the patient's basic trust, that is, his confidence that they will not abandon him and at the same time to support his efforts to function as autonomously as possible;
5. Their ability to mobilize outside support on behalf of the patient when necessary.[7]

The importance of each of these prerequisites can be seen in caring for terminally ill children.

ROLES

Throughout our discussion of health care social workers we have alluded to a number of roles that social workers are called upon to fill. As in other settings social workers are brokers when they serve as a linkage between the client and the hospital or other community resources. The hospital discharge planner, particularly, will be involved in brokering services. The patient may need help in finding a suitable nursing home, home nursing, or housekeeping services.

The advocate role is familiar to the hospital social worker because the complexity of the system and the high degree of stratification and depersonalization in a hospital can create special problems for even the most knowledgeable and capable individuals. Within the nursing home setting the advocacy function has been formalized by setting up the Nursing Home Ombudsman program, which is supported by federal funds under the jurisdiction of the Department of Health and Human Services. The Ombudsman program sets up a review service for those individuals with grievances against any part of the health care system.

The enabler role is evident when the social worker assists the patient and the family to find strengths and resources within themselves to aid in recovery, rehabilitation, or acceptance of terminal illness. In this role the social worker enables the client to change or achieve the desired goal by concentrating on the patient's and the family's own strengths and abilities and helping them apply these strengths to the health problem at hand.

One of the most important roles of the medical social worker is teacher and provider of important information.

The teaching role introduces information to the patient or family that was not previously available. A health care social worker may teach human sexuality to a group of adolescents. We see social workers in some hospitals involved in teaching parenting skills to teenage parents. Wellness programs are another setting in which social workers are teachers.

As a mediator the social worker acts to reconcile differences and to intervene between conflicting parties in order to promote reconciliation or compromise. Hospital social workers are frequently involved in mediation with families when there is dispute concerning who will care for a family member with a long-term illness. For example, a sixty-one-year-old man has suffered severe brain damage and will need a high level of custodial care for the rest of his life. This man had nursed his first wife, the mother of his children, for fifteen years before her death from multiple sclerosis. His grown children feel that he now deserves to be cared for in his home by his present wife. His present wife feels that his needs can best be served in group foster care. She is not prepared to provide twenty-four-hour care to her husband. Since he does not even remember her, she feels that group home staff will provide a better quality of life than she can provide. This family has spent many hours in mediation with a social worker. At the present time, the patient is living in his home, attending a day care center, and spends every other weekend with one of his five children. The mediation continues as long-term plans are developed.

RELEVANT SOCIAL POLICY/LEGISLATION

Since financing health care is a major problem for most families, health care social workers need to be familiar with Medicare, Medicaid, and other third party reimbursement plans such as private insurance, health maintenance organizations (HMOs), or prepaid group practice. Many states have special medical assistance programs for indigents who do not qualify for Medicare or Medicaid. How these payment plans are structured has far-reaching effects on the type of health care service delivery social workers will be reimbursed for providing.

The 1972 Social Security Amendments established Professional Standard Review Organizations to review the health care provided under the Medicare, Medicaid, and Maternal and Child Health programs and to make judgments on the medical necessity and quality of the care. Overall this legislation was designed to achieve cost containment and has had extensive impact upon health care service delivery.

Since nutrition is such an important part of health, social workers need **Means-tested programs** to be aware of means-tested programs that provide either money or food to **are available only to** the poor. The Women, Infants, and Children (WIC) program was developed **people who fall below** specifically to provide nutritious food to pregnant women and children. One **a certain level of in-** social worker used the WIC program to procure orange juice for African- **come.** American children who were victims of sickle-cell anemia. Although there is no cure for sickle-cell anemia, large quantities of orange juice diminish the pain associated with this condition.

THE FUTURE OF HEALTH CARE PRACTICE

In addition to the roles and functions already identified, hospital social workers will increasingly develop new services in health care. Individuals suffering from substance abuse, child abuse, spouse abuse, parent abuse, AIDS, and eating disorders cannot be adequately responded to if one limits the view of the health care system to the biological training of the physician. The increasing incidence of these social problems has led to an increase in health care workers. Even medium-sized hospitals tend to have social workers involved in the emergency room and in discharge planning.

As health care financing swallows an increasingly larger portion of the gross national product, social workers will be among the professionals called upon to develop preventive measures and cost effective alternatives, and to debate the ethical and moral issues involved in the new technology.

SUMMARY

Throughout this chapter we have tried to illustrate the complexity and importance of social work values and knowledge in health care settings. At this point we present you with an actual case study in which to apply what you have learned. The whole concept of faith healing creates dissonance for most social workers.

This brief case study should make you think about the role of values, knowledge, and skill in a complex problem formulation that requires not only an inventory of knowledge and skills available for intervention, but some basic questioning of the extent to which we really value client self determination. To what degree are we willing to force the medical model of disease control on resistant clients? We strongly recommend that the discussion questions be analyzed very seriously.

CASE STUDY
Exploring Social Work with a Faith Healing Family
Ann Stirling Frisch

Phillip and Rose Johnson discovered that their first child, a boy, had an abdominal tumor. They treated it by praying, laying on of hands, and by massaging his legs. When this child was sixteen months old, a sister was born. Although she was reported healthy at birth, she developed problems breathing and nursing at about nine days of age. The family gathered to pray. They administered mouth-to-mouth resuscitation, enabling her to breathe again, but she died at eleven days. Autopsy revealed the cause to be pneumonia.

When authorities were told about the death, they seized the boy and the court gave permission for surgery to relieve the pressure on his spine. He died.

The prosecutor charged the parents with involuntary manslaughter in the death of the infant, but did not charge them with the death of the boy.

When Phillip came to trial, authorities learned that Rose was again pregnant. Alleging that there was the possibility of blood (Rh) incompatibility, the court assumed custody of the fetus to ensure a medically supervised birth, claiming that the child would have a ninety-five percent chance of being retarded or worse if not treated medically. The child, however, had already been born at home. He was seized, rushed to the hospital, and found to be healthy. He was placed in a foster home temporarily, then placed in the home of the maternal grandparents (non-faith healers). The mother was ordered to have a complete postpartum physical exam; the child was provided medical postnatal care. The maternal grandparents reported that the child had a runny nose; when no problem was found, the grandparents arranged for the child to have allergy testing (normally done after children are three years of age). No problem was found. The parents thought the runny nose was caused by a woodburning stove.

During the first year of the child's life, Rose lived with her parents in order not to be separated from her child. Phillip was in the county jail, having been convicted on the involuntary manslaughter charge. Rose was not brought to trial.

At the age of two, the child was placed in the custody of his parents, though he remains a ward of the court.

DISCUSSION QUESTIONS

1. What value dilemmas can you identify? Are there areas where these dilemmas overlap with knowledge?

2. Identify each of the roles the social worker might use in this setting.

3. What general types of knowledge must the social worker bring to this case? What specific knowledge might a health care social worker have that a family and court social worker might not have?

4. What conflicts might arise between the social worker and other professionals involved in the case?

5. What social welfare policy or legislation guides the social worker in this case?

6. Who would be the client in this case—the court, the hospital, the child, the parents?

7. Identify environmental resources available to this family.

8. What would be the goal of the social worker's intervention? Is this compatible with the goal of the parents? Is it in the best interests of the child?

9. How would you measure the effectiveness of the social worker's intervention?

NOTES

1. Rosalind Miller and Helen Rehr, *Social Work Issues in Health Care* (Englewood Cliffs, N.J.: Prentice-Hall, 1983).

2. Gary Rosenberg, "Practice Roles and Functions of the Health Social Worker," in Miller and Rehr, 129.

3. Carel B. Germain and Alex Gitterman, *The Life Model of Social Work Practice* (New York: Columbia University Press, 1980).

4. Leonard Perlin and Carmi Schooler, "The Structure of Coping," *Journal of Health and Social Behavior* 29 (March 1978): 2–21.

5. Kathy Price, "Quality of Life for Terminally Ill Children," *Social Work* (January 1989): 53–54.

6. Ibid.

7. James Strain and Gerald Beallor, quoted in *Psychological Interventions in Medical Practice,* ed. James J. Strain, (New York: Appleton-Century-Crofts, 1978), 166.

Chapter

17

Mental Health

Two out of every ten persons in the United States suffer from one or more mental disorders.[1] A mental disorder is technically defined as any clinically significant behavior, condition, or personality trait that results in subjective distress or in impairment of one or more important areas of an individual's functioning.[2] The results of a recent survey indicate that 29.4 million Americans suffer from mental disorders such as anxiety disorders (13.1 million), substance abuse (10.0 million), affective disorders (9.4 million), and schizophrenia (1.5 million).[3] Earlier studies specify rates "that range from a low of 10 percent to a high of 23 percent."[4] Regardless of the accuracy of these estimates, a relatively disturbing finding from this recent survey is that fewer than one-fifth of those diagnosed as having mental disorders have ever sought services from a qualified mental health professional.

Social workers, psychiatrists, psychologists, and mental health nurses are recognized as "the four core disciplines in the field of mental health."[5] Other than nurses, social workers provide more mental health services to children, adolescents, and adults than either psychiatrists or psychologists. If we were to include in our definition of mental health any services that involve mental health-related problems addressed in child welfare, health care and other social work fields of practice, then social workers would probably surpass even nurses as the primary mental health providers. However, in this chapter we only explore social work concerns relevant to practice in the specialty mental health system. This system includes services provided at child guidance clinics, community mental health centers, state or county hospitals, veterans' hospitals, private psychiatric hospitals, care and board homes, crisis clinics, and psychiatric wards in general hospitals. In this specialized system of human service delivery, social workers provide a variety of clinical services, consultation and education, research, planning, administration, and community organization.

The term mental health *defies a uniform definition.*

The target of concern in this specialty system is mental health problems.

HISTORY

In order to appreciate the role of social workers in the current mental health system, it is helpful to have an understanding of the evolution of practice and of treatment in this rapidly changing field of practice. Although mental disturbances have troubled humanity throughout its history, the scientific treatment of mental disorders is a relatively recent development in the history of societal responses to mental problems. During feudal times, "the Church and the feudal lord took total responsibility for the needy."[6] This included individuals who had what we would today call mental disorders. At the end of the feudal period in Europe, different systems of care began to develop for the poor and the rich. The rich were generally treated at home, whereas the poor were treated in hospitals run by religious orders. The oldest mental hospital from this period that is still in operation was started in Valencia, Spain, in 1408.[7] A distinct characteristic of this hospital was its philosophy of care. Staff sought to treat and to protect patients without isolating them from members of their community. This philosophy of care, practiced in the 15th century, has much in common with community care models in our present system of mental health.[8]

Historians assume that the emphasis given to humane modes of treatment in Spain was in part a result of the cultural contacts that the Spanish had with Moslem beliefs and practices. That is, historians speculate that the "first asylums for the insane in the world were built by the Moslems."[9] In Moslem communities it was assumed that mental disturbances were a result of natural rather than supernatural forces. Unlike Christian Europe, the Moslems maintained many of the classical philosophical beliefs of the Greeks and Romans regarding the natural causes of illnesses. In addition, their religion stressed that God loved the mentally ill. As a consequence, the mentally disordered were treated as sick persons and subjected to many of the treatments prescribed in the classical period of Greek and Roman history by Hippocrates, Galen, and Soranus. These early physicians prescribed treatments for illnesses believed to be caused by natural forces. The majority of the treatments prescribed by these early medical men involved either purging techniques or herbal remedies that were designed to place the person's humors back into an appropriate state of balance. Today some of these treatments are still employed on individuals who seek help from traditional folk healers. For example, *curanderos* or folk healers in traditional Mexican villages and communities still employ herbal treatments to restore a person's system to a proper balance.

Although there were religious hospitals that provided care to indigent individuals with mental disturbances in non-Moslem Europe, the care that was provided in these hospitals was far from humane. Treatment consisted primarily of either ceremonial rites or of severe regimens of punishment. These ceremonies and punishments were designed to exorcise individuals of their demons or evil spirits. During the Middle Ages, it was widely believed

Feudalism was the form of social organization that characterized European society between the 9th and 14th centuries.

Community mental health dates back to the early 15th century.

Religion has been an important cultural variable in determining how we care for the mentally ill.

Humors were bodily fluids such as black bile.

Some religious beliefs support humane treatment; others justify punishment for the mentally ill.

that mental disturbances were caused by demons. In fact, a major source used to guide priests in the treatment of mental disorders was the *Malleus Maleficarium*, or *Witches' Hammer*. This book, which prescribed practices for the identification and treatment of witches, resulted in the torture and burning of thousands during the Inquisition.

When the feudal system began to erode in the late 1400s, many of the care functions provided in religious monasteries were shifted to the local communities. Since the communities were not prepared for this responsibility, many indigent individuals were subjected to severe forms of punishment and custody. In particular, the role of the Roman Catholic Church in the care of disturbed individuals was dealt a severe blow in England. Henry VIII dissolved the monasteries and other forms of church property in 1539.[10] Because of his position toward the Church, the community and the family in England had to play a more significant role in the care of disturbed individuals than was true of most countries in southern Europe. There, the Church retained more of its influence as well as its system of care.

The dismantling of the Church's role in England resulted in a number of social problems. The response of English society to these problems was to pass secular laws designed to regulate the poor. These were the Elizabethan Poor Laws of 1601, which were discussed in greater detail in Chapter 6. In these laws, responsibility for the care of the mentally ill and the poor was delegated to local authorities, who appointed overseers in each parish to collect taxes to assist them in their care functions.

In the American colonies, the Elizabethan Poor Laws also played a significant role in how the mentally disordered were treated.[11] As in England, the mentally disordered in the colonies were generally treated as if they were criminals. They were placed in jails and punished, and in some circumstances received capital punishment. The ideology of the Protestant Reformation also played a significant role in how the mentally disabled were treated in the colonies and in England. This reform movement in Western Christianity assumed that discipline was needed to achieve a godly society on earth. As a consequence, strict discipline was often prescribed to rid disturbed individuals of their sins and to return them to a favorable relationship with God.

Changing ideologies lead to changes in treatment.

The eighteenth century brought enlightenment to the care of the mentally disordered. In this period there was a rebirth of the role of philosophy and of science. As in the time of ancient Greece and Rome, mental disturbances began to be conceived of as illnesses resulting from natural causes rather than as possession caused by supernatural forces. William Tuke in England and Phillipe Pinel in France were instrumental in regenerating humane approaches to the care of the insane. In fact, it was their view that medical personnel had the moral duty to treat disturbed individuals in as humane a fashion as possible. Their efforts resulted in what was known in the history of mental health as moral treatment.

Moral treatment resulted in radical changes in societal views regarding appropriate treatments for the mentally ill. It was assumed that the environment was so unstable that programs were needed to buffer the effects of the stresses and strains of everyday life. That is, some individuals needed retreats or asylums from the pressures of day-to-day life. It was also assumed in this treatment approach that the insane needed more humane conditions than had been previously provided.

Pinel and Tuke were especially known for advocating the release of disturbed individuals from the customary practice of placing them in chains and from bloodletting practices. They also sought to provide disturbed persons with regimens of care that stressed sympathy and kindness. Their reforms had a significant influence on the field of mental health. In fact, the first asylums established in the United States were guided by their philosophies of care. However, their approach was significantly challenged when expenses began to rise to meet the needs of the marked increase in new immigrants to this country who needed the services of asylums.

Economics are another determinant of treatment.

These fiscal demands eventually resulted in decreased acceptance of humane techniques and in the creation of differential treatments for the rich and the poor. The rich were still exposed to humane treatments designed to cure their problems; the poor were subjected to custodial care without expectations that they would ever improve. In essence, hospitals for the poor shifted from humane practices and began to function once again as prisons.

The horrid conditions encountered by the insane in jails is what promoted the noteworthy reform efforts of Dorothea Dix in the mid-1800s. Dix is considered one of the key reformers in our country's history of mental health. Her efforts alerted legislators to the need for hospitals to care for the insane who were being abused in jails, workhouses, poorhouses and penitentiaries. After she informed the public of these gross abuses, a number of reforms were instituted that resulted in the establishment of thirty-two mental hospitals in the United States.[12] Unfortunately, history has repeated itself; in some jurisdictions in the United States such as Arizona, more of the mentally ill are being treated in jails than in mental hospitals.[13]

About the time that Dorothea Dix instituted her reforms, "the old notion that none, or at best very few of the mentally ill could be cured was suddenly discarded."[14] The ideology of progress began to take hold, as well as belief in the curability of mental disorders. This shift in ideology ushered in new interest and commitment to the scientific treatment of the mentally ill. Within this era of optimism, principles from the scientific method began to be applied to most problems in medicine. This ideological shift also influenced psychiatrists. They began applying scientific principles in their investigations and treatment of patient concerns. In doing so, they recognized that mental disturbances are "determined by a multiplicity of causes bound up in the physiology, psychology and social milieu of the individual."[15] This recognition encouraged them to seek associates such as social workers to assist them in obtaining a better understanding of patient problems.[16]

The importance of a biopsychosocial approach emerged in the early 20th century.

The formal involvement of social workers in the field of mental health did not begin until shortly after the medical social work program was estab-

Many of the present mental health institutions were built in the 1800s.

lished at Massachusetts General Hospital in 1905. This social service program was designed to provide services to medical patients who were treated at the hospital. The format of this program and its services interested Dr. James J. Putnam, who was the chief of neurological services at Massachusetts General. Dr. Putnam and Edith Burleigh, an experienced social worker, developed the first social service program that was explicitly targeted for individuals suffering with mental illnesses.[17] Social workers were used in their program to gather additional data to assist psychiatrists in making more accurate assessments and in improving the treatment of patients.

Following the development of the program at Massachusetts General, similar programs were instituted in New York at Bellevue Hospital and at Cornell Clinic.[18] After the establishment of these programs, other social service programs were established in Baltimore and Chicago in psychiatric settings.[19] In 1906, E. H. Horton, a graduate of the New York School of Philanthropy, was the first social worker to apply aftercare principles to the care of discharged patients from two hospitals in New York.[20]

World War I increased further the demand for overall psychiatric services, as well as for the involvement of social workers in these services. "Psychiatrists, aware of the potential value of social workers in the usual psychiatric services, saw an opportunity for developing valuable assistants in dealing with the large numbers of men who had developed conditions requiring psychiatric care under the strain of war service."[21] However, there were few professionally trained social workers available. This situation prompted special initiatives that resulted in the establishment of a special training program in psychiatric social work at the Smith College School of Social Work and at the New York School of Social Work.[22] Mary Jarret established Simmons's field program in psychiatric social work and was the first person to use the term. Prior to these accomplishments, Jarret was best known for having established the first social service program at the Boston Psychopathic Hospital.[23]

Besides the war, other events contributed to the involvement of social workers in the field of mental health. In 1908, Clifford Beers wrote an exposé entitled *The Mind That Found Itself.* It characterized the conditions that he witnessed in mental institutions while being treated for his own illness. Following the publication of his experience, he began organizational efforts that resulted in the formation in 1909 of the National Committee for Mental Hygiene. It is important to note that Adolf Meyer recommended the term *mental hygiene* for this new movement that was inspired primarily by the efforts of Clifford Beers. Adolf Meyer was the psychiatrist who included social workers in his holistic approach to mental illnesses at Johns Hopkins. In fact, some sources cite his efforts as the first inclusion of social workers in the field of mental health and the first use of the comprehensive case history.[24]

William James, a key figure in American psychology, was a staunch supporter of Beers.[25]

Beers's book was recognized by a number of distinguished persons in the history of mental health besides Adolf Meyer. His movement also influenced the education of many social workers; most of the early programs in psychiatric social work had courses explicitly on the topic of mental hygiene.[26] A key objective in Beers's movement was to reorganize the system of mental health and to foster new methods of treatment and prevention of mental disorders. Indeed, the mental hygiene movement was instrumental in promoting the relatively novel view, for this time, that mental problems could be caused by psychological and social phenomena.

The child guidance movement began in 1909 in Chicago under William Healy.

Another movement that emerged in this time period that is often regarded as part of the mental hygiene movement was the child guidance movement.[27] This movement suggested that many problems encountered by adults could be prevented by intervening in the early lives of children. By 1921, the Commonwealth Fund established a demonstration project for child guidance clinics throughout the United States. This organization, in collaboration with the National Mental Hygiene Committee, also funded field training experiences for students in psychiatric social work from the New York School of Social Work. In fact, there was a relatively rapid expansion of child guidance clinics in the country, which called for more and more trained social workers. The numerous social workers trained in these clinics eventually played a significant role in the field of community or social psychiatry.

As society recognizes
the importance of a
problem, financial re-
sources may become
available to respond to
the problem.

Following World War II, the demand for psychiatric services increased. In order to meet this need, the Veterans Administration, in collaboration with the Menninger Clinic, initiated a program to train mental health professionals. Today "the Veterans Administration as a single entity employs the largest number of trained social workers in the United States."[28] Shortly after these initiatives, Congress passed both the National Mental Health Act and, in 1949, the enabling legislation for the National Institute of Mental Health. This organization continues to play a significant role in the training of social work professionals in the field of mental health by providing stipends to train graduate students in social work.

Today many social
workers in the field
of mental health be-
long to the Federation
of Clinical Social
Workers.

The specialization of psychiatric social work continued to diversify up until the elimination in the 1950s of its professional association and in the 1960s of its special program of accreditation. However, many of the workers trained in the 1950s by NIMH and the Veterans Administration played an instrumental role in the community mental health movement of the 1960s. In fact, social workers constituted the largest group of mental health professionals who participated in the community mental health movement.

In the 1970s social workers also played a significant role in the movement to deinstitutionalize the mentally ill and in the establishment of community support programs. They have also contributed significantly to the development of new interventions for working with families with chronically ill members. Social work in the 1980s was still making significant contributions "in areas in which it pioneered, including aftercare, preadmission screening, family casework, and community organization, including the development of self-help and mutual aid groups."[29]

VALUES

There are a number of value dilemmas that are specific to the practice of social work in the field of mental health. These dilemmas reflect the nature and complexity of this growing area of practice. Although workers in this field of practice encounter distinct value conflicts, the general values that were identified by the National Association of Social Workers in Chapter 4 also apply to this area of practice.

Self-determination can
cause value conflicts in
the mental health field.

In social work we seek to affirm the worth and the dignity of our clients as well as to promote their self-determination. Yet friends, relatives, and neighbors of our clients may seek our assistance in initiating legal proceedings that conflict in many ways with these cardinal values. In most jurisdictions, mental health professionals are granted the authority to evaluate whether to hospitalize or civilly commit an individual for care and treatment. In these involuntary hospitalization procedures, social workers have to balance a number of competing interests or values. The interest in the safety of family members from a dangerous individual with a mental disorder must be weighed against the interest of the mentally disordered person to the right of self-determination. In this circumstance, mental health social workers are often presented with the problem of deciding who is their client. Since a third party initiated the request for the evaluation, the worker has to clarify her relationship with the identified patient. In particular, the social worker has an ethical duty to clarify for the person being evaluated the nature and purpose of his involvement. In order to resolve dilemmas of this nature, Frederick Reamer, a social work educator, has developed a list of guidelines to assist social workers in resolving all forms of dilemmas encountered in practice.[30]

In 1978 the President's Commission on Mental Health's Task Panel Report on Legal and Ethical Issues prescribed explicit guidelines for professionals in the field of mental health. These and other guidelines in the field of mental health clearly point out that the views of the client should always be respected unless the client lacks the mental capacity to consent or refuse to consent to treatment, or presents a clear danger either to self or to others that can be properly addressed by available treatment. In other words, a widely accepted value in the field of mental health is that it is not justifiable to forcibly detain persons for treatment simply because we disapprove of their way of life. Instead there must be a compelling reason, such as an emergency situation, before a social worker could ever invoke the power of the state to force a treatment action against the wishes of a mentally disordered person. It is important to note that this value applies to any form of clinical or treatment intervention and not just to matters surrounding involuntary hospitalization.

An emergency is generally perceived as a life-threatening situation.

Besides desiring to pursue actions that respect the wishes of any treatment client, social workers also place a high value on clients' right to treatment. That is, once people are detained in a hospital or have their liberty restricted to any extent, they are owed appropriate forms of treatment. In the past, some adolescents and adults have been placed in locked or secure units against their wishes for the purpose of treatment. However, the services they received on these units differed minimally from those found in a jail or detention facility. For this reason, mental health social workers are committed to the value position of restricting a person's liberty only if that person will receive some benefit from the forced treatment.

Most mental health social workers are also supportive of the recommendation by the President's Commission on Mental Health that special populations have a right to treatment, such as minority groups, children, adolescents, and the aged. In fact, the profession of social work has always voiced a stronger commitment to serving these groups than have the other core disciplines. In addition to the recognition of rights to treatment, social workers also assume that this treatment should be provided in the least restrictive environment possible. That is, social workers in mental health support the legal precedent that states that "though the government purpose be legitimate and substantial, that purpose cannot be pursued by means that broadly stifle fundamental personal liberties when the end can be more narrowly achieved."[31]

Confidentiality is also a key issue for social workers in mental health. Clients often reveal sensitive information that may be damaging if known by others. As a result, social workers in mental health settings devote substantial attention to protecting the sensitive information contained in all of their records. They also place a high value on keeping their level of inquiry in treatment and in evaluation processes within the boundaries of referral needs. They are thus committed to not soliciting information that would unnecessarily invade a person's privacy. Last, they value the use of procedures that will clarify for their clients the limits of confidentiality in the services that they provide. For example, if they are performing court-ordered evaluations, they should identify in advance how information shared with them during the evaluation may be revealed to others in the form of a report or court testimony. In essence, the social worker in mental health, as in other fields of practice, has to make a concerted effort to realize the profession's commitment to values that respect client confidentiality, self-determination, and individualization of needs.

FUNCTIONS

Mental health social workers address a variety of psychosocial adaptations and resource deficit issues that impede people's ability to meet their life tasks. They realize many of these functions by helping clients develop competencies or skills to meet the demands of their environment. For example, school-age children are often brought to a child guidance clinic because they fear going to school. After a clinical assessment, the mental health social worker may discern that the student is refusing to attend school primarily because he lacks the necessary social skills for relating with his peers. In order to respond to this problem, mental health social workers often teach the youth skills that will enable them to cope better with peer-oriented problems and with other demands presented by their school environment. They may also assist a youth with a school refusal problem by linking the child's family to resources that provide them with appropriate clothing and school equipment that minimize negative reactions by their peers.

Skill development for impaired individuals is a key function performed by social workers. Mental health social workers also assist individuals, families and groups with skill development issues in other mental health settings. For instance, they play a significant role in the provision of aftercare programing for the seriously mentally ill who suffer from persistent mental conditions. Individuals with serious mental disorders are often hospitalized for a significant period of time. When they are discharged from these periods of hospitalization, they generally need support in reestablishing relationships and in negotiating their environment. Because social workers are very knowledgeable about community resources, they are often expected in the mental health system of service delivery to help clients establish a supportive environment in the community. This may require that the worker develop new relationships for the client, such as establishing a linkage between the client and a receptive neighbor or friend.

In working with discharged patients, mental health social workers also work at enhancing client problem-solving abilities by functioning as a trainer or skill developer. In such a capacity, they are expected to teach the discharged person skills for avoiding being overwhelmed by day-to-day stresses. Lack of such skills is widely recognized in the mental health literature as a common characteristic of the mental disorder known as schizophrenia. The supportive and educational functions provided by mental health social workers play a significant role in preventing a relapse in a client's condition and in facilitating that client's readjustment to living in the community.

Schizophrenia is a major Axis I mental disorder (see DSM-III-R).

In addition to working on skill development issues with the seriously ill, the mental health social worker also is involved in numerous consultation and education programs in the community that are designed to help people manage the stresses and strains of everyday life. For instance, they may give workshops and training programs for mothers that are designed to improve their effectiveness as parents. Assertiveness training is another form of skill development that we find many mental health social workers providing to people who cannot assert their interests.

The multitude of skill development activities that mental health social workers are involved in serve other functions besides that of enhancing client coping and problem-solving abilities. They also play a significant social control function. For instance, when youth are referred to mental health clinics for conduct problems and aggressiveness, resolution of these problems not only enhances the adaptability of the client, but also ensures that the client is behaving in a socially appropriate fashion. In fact, a significant proportion of the tasks performed by mental health social workers is directed toward changing deviant forms of behavior.

Protection of the individual and the community is a social work function involving value conflicts.

We have already touched on some of the dilemmas encountered by mental health workers when they are asked to exercise their powers to hospitalize a person involuntarily. Without this control function, society would not have a resource to turn to for the protection of individuals who behave in a threatening or dangerous fashion. In this capacity the mental health social worker seeks to control the person's condition for the protection of either members of society or the client. Many individuals with severe mental disorders are also incapable of taking care of their food, shelter, and other essential needs. For these individuals, social workers in the mental health system devote considerable energy dispensing needed resources and in creating environments that are responsive to their needs.

The community support function often requires resource development.

Policy development is a function that is sometimes neglected by direct practitioners.

Mental health social workers are also involved in significant efforts directed toward policy reform and social change. For example, many social workers are currently lobbying for policy changes that are designed to provide services to homeless individuals who are suffering with mental disorders. They are also actively involved in reform efforts designed to ensure that adequate mental health services are available for mentally ill individuals incarcerated in our local jails. Furthermore, social workers have played a major role in reform efforts designed to reduce stressors in the environment that contribute to substance abuse and other mental health difficulties. They have also advocated for funds to support self-help and empowerment enterprises for substance abusers, women, and minority persons. These are just some of the societal maintenance, control, and change functions that are performed by social workers in the field of mental health.

KNOWLEDGE

The field of mental health demands that social workers have knowledge of generic social work principles and knowledge of issues specific to practice in the field of mental health. One area of significant import is classification. Social workers in the field of mental health need to have knowledge of existing systems for classifying and naming mental disorders. Without this knowledge, it would be impossible for them to communicate effectively with other mental health professionals.[32]

The dementias comprise a class of disorders that are characterized by a loss of various intellectual abilities such as memory or judgment.

In the field of mental health, the most widely used classification system is the *Diagnostic Statistical Manual*-III-Revised *(DSM-III-R)*. Social workers in mental health need to know something about this sanctioned system of classification not only for purposes of communicating with other practitioners, but also for assisting them in retrieving valuable information.[33] For instance, if a social worker is told that her next client has multi-infarct dementia, then she knows where to look in books and manuals to read about the client's probable symptoms and the likely course of the disorder. From this kind of inquiry, the worker would also learn that the client has a disorder that accounts for 10 percent to 25 percent of all dementias.[34] In addition, the information on this topic would inform her that multi-infarct dementia is caused by hypertension or small blood clots that block the supply of blood to the brain. She would also know that the client would probably show some loss of his intellectual abilities, and that these losses had a relatively sudden onset. Last, this information would enable her to predict the likely course of this disorder.

In order to apply the *DSM*-III-R effectively, social workers must also have a basic understanding of its underlying philosophy. Robert Spitzer and Janet B. W. Williams submitted a definition of *mental disorder* to the American Psychiatric Association task force that reflects the *DSM*-III's basic assumptions:

> In *DSM*-III each of the mental disorders is conceptualized as a clinically significant behavioral or psychological syndrome or pattern that occurs in an individual and that is typically associated with either a painful symptom (distress) or impairment in one or more important areas of functioning (disability). In addition, there is an inference that there is a behavioral, psychological or biological dysfunction, and that the disturbance is not

only in the relationship between the individual and society. (When the disturbance is limited to a conflict between an individual and society, this may represent social deviance, which may or may not be commendable, but is not itself a mental disorder.)[35]

This quotation illustrates the complexity involved in defining what is a mental disorder. Although there are benefits in using the *DSM*-III-R and its attendant definitions, social workers in mental health must also appreciate when it is inappropriate to use psychiatric labels or classifications. In particular, they must guard against the clinicalization or medicalization of deviations in thought, mood and behavior that are best characterized as social deviance.

Besides knowledge of the assumptions underlying the *DSM*-III, social workers in mental health must be able to differentiate between serious and minor disorders. They must also have a basic understanding of which disorders respond best to which interventions. This should include a basic understanding of the general characteristics of medications that are commonly used in the treatment of various disorders. For instance, many novice social workers have failed to develop good discharge plans for their clients because they did not understand the target or side effects of their clients' prescribed medication. These effects play a significant role in how clients comply with treatment.

The prior medication compliance issue touches on another significant area of knowledge that is useful to mental health practitioners. Social workers in this field of practice must also have knowledge of illness and help-seeking behavior. Illness behavior refers to the behavioral responses of people to the perception of having an illness or disorder. For instance, when people feel ill, they can potentially go through five different stages of behavior.

Sometimes illness and disorder are used interchangeably.

1. *Symptom experience:* In the initial stage, patients decide something is wrong because they feel ill. They may choose to medicate themselves or seek help from lay people or folk practitioners. The outcome of this state is recovery, uncertainty, denial or the acceptance of being sick.

Response to illness can be seen as a developmental process.

2. *Assumption of sick role:* At this point patients cease to function normally and seek from associates a validation of their assumption of the sick role.

3. *Medical care contact:* The patient seeks professional advice and negotiates treatment.

4. *Dependent patient role:* The patient accepts and undergoes treatment. Sometimes, however, patients will reject treatment, particularly if they disagree with the diagnosis or plan, or if they do not feel at ease with the physician.

5. *Recovery:* The patient relinquishes the sick role and resumes normal functioning. A less favorable outcome involves persistence in the sick role despite recovery from bodily disease.[36]

These five stages were developed to describe behavioral responses to illnesses or disorders commonly encountered by practitioners. However, the services of social workers in mental health are not limited to individuals with mental disorders or illnesses. Mental health social workers also help people

A Rogerian approach to counseling includes an emotionally meaningful relationship based on empathy, genuineness, and positive regard.

with problems in living, such as adapting to loss of a job or of a family member. As a consequence, they must also have a broad understanding of general responses to problems.

James Green, a social work educator, has identified stages for describing general behavioral responses to problem situations, which he has termed help-seeking behavior.[37] In his model of help-seeking behavior, he identifies four basic components:

> (1) the client's recognition of an experience as a problem, (2) the client's use of language to label and categorize a problem, (3) the availability of indigenous helping resources in client communities and the decision-making involved in the utilization of those resources, (4) client oriented criteria for determining that a satisfactory resolution has been achieved.[38]

Knowledge of these components is especially useful when a worker is practicing in a folk community or one with a different ethnic population. For example, some Native American people in the Southwest consider symptoms of not being able to sleep, sweaty palms, and constant fearfulness as evidence of a spiritual problem rather than of a possible anxiety disorder or emotional disturbance. In fact, they believe that many behavioral deviations considered disorders by social workers are instead spiritual problems that were created by a violation of sacred ways. In essence, it is critical for mental health workers employed in traditional communities to understand the kinds of symptoms that result in a person seeking the services of either a medicine person or a folk healer. Some Native American people would never think of seeking a counselor to assist them with manifestation of anxiety.

ROLES

In discussing the functions, knowledge, and values of social workers in mental health, we have already touched on their practice in hospitals, child guidance clinics, community mental health settings, and veterans' hospitals. However, several settings of practice were not touched on in this discussion. For instance, some masters-level social workers also work in the private sector providing needed social work services. They may work in private practice, where they see individual clients, families, and groups for a fee, or as consultants to public agencies or private industries. In these fee-for-service arrangements, social workers provide a variety of specialized services, such as counseling, therapy, case management, social histories, and evaluations. However, they are rarely involved in dispensing resources, which is a key role played by social work professionals in the public sector. Social workers' investigative, case management, and consultative expertise is invaluable to a wide range of clients and employers.

Although many social workers pursue independent or private practice, the majority of social workers in the field of mental health still work in public agencies or nonprofit corporations. Their skills are particularly needed in these service sectors to screen clients for admission to hospitals, residential treatment centers, and day treatment resources. Their brokerage abilities are also invaluable to just about any inpatient treatment facility that provides aftercare services or community support programing. Last, their networking and case management skills play a key role in virtually every public mental health setting, regardless of whether it is a hospital, child guidance clinic, or outpatient clinic.

RELEVANT SOCIAL POLICY/LEGISLATION

In the late 1960s California passed the Petris-Laterman-Short Act. This legislation reflected a major shift in ideology regarding the care and treatment of the mentally ill. Prior to this legislation, most jurisdictions in the United States supported legal standards that allowed for the involuntary hospitalization of the mentally ill for their own protection. In addition, there was minimal regulation of treatment, since treatment decisions were presumably best handled by doctors, rather than legislators or attorneys. Indeed, it was assumed that these benevolent procedures were inherently helpful, rather than abusive. However, evidence mounted during the 1960s of psychiatric abuses of authority that prompted recommendations by some civil libertarians to abolish commitment proceedings.

Parens patriae is Latin for father of the country.

Although civil commitment procedures were not abolished, substantial reforms were instituted in legislation such as the Petris-Laterman-Short Act. Many of these reforms were inspired by concerns surrounding the legitimacy of the civil commitment process. This process had traditionally been justified "under the state's parens patriae authority to act as the general 'guardian of all infants, idiots and lunatics'."[39] This paternalistic authority was rooted in the assumption that the state has a duty to protect those who are incapable of caring for themselves. It was this fundamental notion involving welfare ideology that was challenged by civil libertarians in the late 1960s and early 1970s. In particular, they were troubled by the abuses in this authority that resulted in the unjust confinement of individuals who were not suffering from mental disorders, such as the commitment of Earl Long, governor of Louisiana, for political rather than treatment reasons. They were also troubled by the conditions of the supposed treatment provided in these institutions. In many institutions, the treatment afforded clients had more in common with custody in a jail than treatment in a hospital.

After the assumption was successfully questioned that commitments to institutions were benevolent, reforms were instituted in the process and the criteria for involuntary hospitalizations. As in the Petris-Laterman-Short Act, many states began to enact legislation that severely restricted the state's parens patriae power for treating the mentally disordered. This was accomplished by restricting commitments to acts dangerous either to members of society or to the individual. Moreover, these new commitment standards in many jurisdictions tended to exclude nonsuicidal behaviors, as well as commitments for persons merely in need of treatment.[40] The upshot of these policy reforms in the early 1970s was the creation of an ideology of antipaternalism in the field of mental health.

The antipaternalistic policies instituted in the 1970s, plus the deinstitutionalization movement of the mid 1970s, have left an interesting legacy in the field of mental health. One noticeable result has been the presence in the community of mentally disordered individuals who live on the streets. Perhaps you have seen men or women wearing winter coats in the middle of summer, or carrying all of their possessions in a paper bag. You may also have seen a mentally ill person eating out of a garbage can or attempting to spend a night in a cardboard box when temperatures were expected to drop below zero. These circumstances present serious policy issues for society and mental health professionals. What role should society and the social work profession play in the care and treatment of these individuals? This is a key policy issue facing our society in the coming decades, especially in view of other policy reforms instituted by the Reagan Administration.

Block grants are grants that are noncategorical in nature, such as for specific mental health issues.

In 1981 President Reagan's Omnibus Budget and Reconciliation Act was passed. This legislation discontinued the government's practice of providing direct funding to community mental health centers. Instead, the government began to fund block grants, with the expectation that local authorities would divert some of this funding to community mental health concerns.

This marked an end to a longstanding direct involvement by the federal government in promoting community mental health that began with the passage of the Community Mental Health Centers Act of 1963. Moreover, it diminished federal responsibilities for the mentally ill and returned them to the states at a critical phase of the deinstitutionalization movement. As in colonial times, local authorities now have primary responsibility for the care and treatment of the mentally ill.

The shift in fiscal responsibility to the local community has significantly affected community mental health objectives for the chronically ill. Few communities are expending funds to support community programs for this population. They are also diverting federal dollars allocated to the states for this cause to other programs. These fiscal realities, coupled with the anti-welfare state ideology and antipaternalism in civil commitment policy, are consistent with the overall shift in American values away from notions of duty and community responsibility. It is within this ideological context that social workers in mental health will have to function in future years. Unlike the period of optimism in which the community mental health movement was fostered, present practice is within a highly conservative environment that is opposed to any paternalistic or welfare notions. The upshot of this situation has been a drastic reduction in care provided to individuals with serious mental disorders. In fact, jails and prisons are once again becoming the primary care facilities for the indigent mentally ill in our country.

THE FUTURE OF MENTAL HEALTH PRACTICE

The current revolutions in biological psychiatry and psychopharmacology are dominant trends that should continue to have a significant impact on social work practice in mental health. These trends should produce further innovations in the treatment of affective, schizophrenic, and other major mental disorders. As a consequence, social workers must maintain a basic familiarity with new medications on the market and biological discoveries. Since social workers will probably continue to play a significant role in future aftercare programing, they will need to have an even greater appreciation of common medications in order to engage in effective relapse prevention and basic case management.

Also related to advances in psychopharmacological and biological research are the new technological innovations in diagnostic procedures. Nuclear magnetic response (NMR) and positron-emission tomographic (PET) scanning are new techniques that will probably become common clinical and research tools.[41] NMR is a technique that produces high-resolution images of structures in the brain in extreme detail. This procedure will enable researchers to compare differences in brain structure without the risk of exposure to the levels of radiation associated with computerized axial tomographic (CAT) scanning. Positron-emission tomographic (PET) scanning is the technique that allows for an examination of blood flow in the various regions of the brain. The results of this technique, in combination with the results from NMR research, should lead to a number of new causal theories of mental disorders. These new theories will require new labeling by practitioners and clients of their presenting problems. These client labeling problems will produce new illness behavior reactions that social workers must be prepared to address.

SUMMARY

There is substantial evidence that the field of psychiatry will continue to emphasize and to address the medical aspects of client problems. This further medicalization of psychiatry will probably lead to less interest on the part of psychiatrists in specializing in problems in living.[42] Instead, they will engage in further specification of the medical aspects of psychiatry. This shift in focus in psychiatry will probably result in social workers taking on a greater role in doing psychotherapy and in providing psychosocial rehabilitation of chronically ill patients. To some extent, social workers and other mental health professionals will also take on more of these psychotherapeutic functions because of the "trend for less coverage of psychiatric services. For the third-party and out-of-pocket payers, lower-priced substitutes are more desirable."[43] That is, the cheaper social work services in psychosocial domains should be in greater demand in the future than they are today.

CASE STUDY
The Spinach Playwright

Mr. Abraham is a 50-year-old single white male who was referred to your psychiatric hospital by his family for involuntary treatment. Mr. Abraham was raised in upstate New York and lived there until his father died approximately ten years ago. He had apparently moved in with his father and lived in the basement following several hospitalizations for schizophrenia. He is now living with his brother's family in Phoenix, Arizona.

The family is alleging that Mr. Abraham is gravely disabled and that he is likely to come to serious physical harm because of his mental condition. The family is petitioning the court to have Mr. Abraham involuntarily hospitalized for several rea-

sons. He has been wearing two layers of coats for the last three weeks and refuses to take them off. The family is concerned about this because it is the middle of July. Mr. Abraham has also been refusing to bathe and has an "awful" body odor; the family also reports that his hair is severely matted. The family estimates that Mr. Abraham has not bathed in approximately one month.

Mr. Abraham has also positioned himself in a closet in their home for the stated purpose of writing a play. He has been in this closet for approximately one week. Since he has refused to leave the closet until he completes his play, family members began bringing him food. However, Mr. Abraham will only agree to eat green foods because his play is about spinach. The family also points out that he never stops writing. In fact, he writes over and over on the same lines, but will not let family members see what he is writing.

When Mr. Abraham was brought to the psychiatric hospital, he was very pleasant and cooperative with staff. His initial reaction was one of confusion. He did not understand why staff and his family were concerned about him. In fact, he could not understand why the police interrupted him from writing his play. When he was introduced to his court-appointed attorney, he told her that he knew that he wanted to make her a dancer in his play. Although it appeared that he had not bathed in months, Mr. Abraham never displayed any evidence of violence or anger toward staff.

DIAGNOSTIC QUESTIONS

1. What is the role of the social worker involved in evaluating Mr. Abraham?
2. What societal functions are played by the worker in this case?
3. Identify the value dilemmas presented in this case.
4. What do you think is the appropriate societal response in this case?
5. Under what circumstances is involuntary treatment appropriate?
6. What additional information would you need in order to make an appropriate judgment?
7. Do you think Mr. Abraham is an appropriate candidate for involuntary treatment?

NOTES

1. J. K. Myers, M. M. Weissman, G. L. Tischler, et al., "Six Month Prevalence of Psychiatric Disorders in Three Communities" *Archives of General Psychiatry* Vol. 41 (1984), 959–967.
2. R. L. Spitzer and J. B. W. Williams, "The Definition and Diagnosis of Mental Disorder," in *Deviance and Mental Illness*, ed. W. R. Gove (Beverly Hills, Calif.: Sage, 1982), 19–20.
3. Myers et al., "Six Month Prevalence."
4. E. G. Goldstein, "Mental Health and Illness," in *Encyclopedia of Social Work* (Silver Spring, Md.: National Association of Social Workers, 1987), 105.
5. J. W. Callicutt, "Contemporary Settings and the Rise of the Profession in Mental Health," in *Social Work and Mental Health*, ed. J. W. Callicutt and P. J. Lecca (New York: The Free Press, 1983), 30.
6. T. R. Vallance and R. M. Sabre, "Mental Health and Social Structure: An Introduction to the Current Scene," in *Mental Health Services in Transition: A Policy Sourcebook* (New York: Human Sciences Press, Inc., 1982), 18.
7. A. Deutsch, *The Mentally Ill in America* (New York: Columbia University Press, 1949).
8. B. L. Bloom, *Community Mental Health: A General Introduction* (Monterey, Calif.: Brooks/Cole Publishing Company, 1984), 35.
9. A. Deutsch, *The Mentally Ill in America: A History of Their Care and Treatment from Colonial Times* (New York: Columbia University Press, 1949), 15.
10. W. Trattner, "The Background," in *The Emergence of Social Welfare and Social Work*, ed. N. Gilbert and H. Specht (Itasca, Ill.: Peacock, 1981), 25–26.
11. Vallance and Sabre, "Mental Health," 18.
12. R. M. Suinn, *Fundamentals of Abnormal Psychology* (Chicago: Nelson-Hall, 1984), 44–45.

13. J. B. Ashford, "Offense Comparisons Between Mentally Disordered and Non-Mentally Disordered Inmates," *Canadian Journal of Criminology* 31 (1989): 35–48.
14. Deutsch, *The Mentally Ill* (1949), 132.
15. G. S. Stevenson, "Introduction," in *Psychiatric Social Work*, by L. M. French (New York: The Commonwealth Fund), x.
16. Ibid.
17. Callicutt, *"Contemporary Settings,"* 31.
18. Ibid.
19. S. H. Swift, *Training in Psychiatric Social Work* (New York: The Commonwealth Fund, 1934).
20. Callicutt, "Contemporary Settings," 31.
21. Swift, *Training*, 2.
22. Ibid.
23. Callicutt, "Contemporary Settings," 31.
24. R. K. Blashfield, *The Classification of Psychopathology: NeoKraepelinian and Quantitative Approaches* (New York: Plenum Press, 1984).
25. N. Ridenour, "The Mental Health Movement," in the *Encyclopedia of Mental Health* (New York: Franklin Watts, Inc., 1963).
26. L. M. French, *Psychiatric Social Work* (London: Oxford University Press, 1940).
27. Ridenour, "The Mental Health Movement," 1095.
28. Callicut, "Contemporary Settings," 35.
29. Ibid., 40.
30. F. G. Reamer, "Ethical Dilemmas in Social Work Practice," *Social Work* 28 (January–February 1983): 31–35.
31. *Shelton v. Tucker* 364 U.S. 479 (1960).
32. Blashfield, *Classification*, 4–6.
33. Ibid.
34. J. S. Maxmen, *Essential Psychopathology.*(New York: W.W. Norton & Company, 1986), 105–106.
35. Spitzer and Williams, "Definition and Diagnosis," 19.
36. B. Nurcombe and R. M. Gallagher, *The Clinical Process in Psychiatry: Diagnosis and Management Planning* (London: Cambridge University Press, 1986), 14–15.
37. J. W. Green, *Cultural Awareness in Human Services* (Englewood Cliffs, N.J.: Prentice-Hall, 1982).
38. Ibid., 31.
39. G. B. Melton, J. Petrila, N. G. Poytress, and C. Slobogin, *Psychological Evaluations for the Courts: A Handbook for Mental Health Professionals and Lawyers* (New York: Guilford Press, 1987).
40. Ibid., 218.
41. N. C. Andreasen, *The Broken Brain: The Biological Revolution in Psychiatry* (New York: Harper & Row, 1984).
42. L. J. Duhl, N. A. Cummings, and J. J. Hynes, "Introduction: The Emergence of the Mental Health Complex," in *The Future of Mental Health Services: Coping with Crisis*, ed. L. J. Duhl and N. A. Cummings (New York: Springer Publishing Company, 1987).
43. Ibid., 6.

Chapter

18

Criminal Justice

A ll societies develop methods of social control to limit human behavior. The family, school, church, and community provide many forms of informal control. Many social workers become a part of the formal mechanism of social control known as the criminal justice system. The system includes written laws and institutional structures that determine which behaviors are not to be tolerated and how violators will be identified, processed, and sanctioned.

There are three major components to the criminal justice field—police, courts, and corrections. The roles and functions vary across these different areas. In addition the justice system is divided into an adult system and a juvenile system.

The juvenile system is discussed in Chapter 15.

Criminal justice is big business. According to the Bureau of Justice Statistics, the total expenditure in 1985 for criminal justice in the United States was $55 billion. Forty percent ($22 billion) of the total expenditure went for police protection, twenty-four percent ($13 billion) for corrections activities, and thirty-six percent ($20.1 billion) for judicial and legal services. Between 1976 and 1985, the cost of police services increased by 100 percent; court costs increased by over 200 percent; and corrections by 197 percent.[1]

The most common setting for social workers in the criminal justice field is in corrections. Most states have social workers in correctional institutions and probation and parole agencies. Police departments are increasingly employing social workers to be involved in community liaison and family crisis intervention. Municipal courts sometimes hire social workers to help with diversion projects, particularly for mentally handicapped and substance-abusing offenders. Client service workers or client advocates in public defender offices usually have social work training. Many professionally trained social workers in corrections go into administration after having spent time in direct practice.

In spite of the long history of social work in the criminal justice system, there are still strident voices within the profession who do not see the role of social control agent as appropriate to social workers. Consistent with our analysis of the profession, we believe that social control is an important

391

function of social work and that social workers have important contributions to make in both working to rehabilitate offenders and humanizing the system. These goals need to be pursued by both direct and indirect service providers.

HISTORY

Surprisingly, "treatment" for criminals began with the practice of imprisonment. At the outset it was seen as a humanitarian alternative to the brutal corporal punishments of the day. Imprisonment was first practiced by religious groups in the Middle Ages. This practice was based on the belief that monastic life would provide the proper environment for redemption. These houses of corrections were not used for lawbreakers but rather for "fallen women." Corporal punishment continued to be meted out to men.

The first prison established to punish criminals was the Walnut Street Jail in Pennsylvania, established by the Quakers in 1790. John Howard (1726–90) was the first person to suggest that criminals should have educational training, congregate work, religious training, and follow-up care after release. Almost a century later reformers such as Enoch Wines and Zebulon Brockway were fighting for proper education and religious training for prisoners.[2]

Between 1870 and 1880, a dozen states passed laws permitting the construction of reformatories whose inmates would be subject to sentences based on how their "reform" progressed. For many reasons these reformatories did not live up to the great expectations of their designers.[3]

Throughout the 19th and 20th centuries we have seen the pendulum swing back and forth between ideas about the causes of crime. Classical criminologists argued that humans chose between the pleasure of crime and the penalties imposed, and that fixed schedules of penalties would deter criminals.[4] Social determinists argued that people had little control over the forces that induced criminal acts. Imprisonment could both remove the criminal from such forces and protect society. Both of these schools of thought assumed that imprisonment was an appropriate response to crime.

The pendulum also swings back and forth in terms of the effects of imprisonment. During the 1960s and 1970s some professionals suggested that long penal servitude was not an effective system either of deterrence or protection; imprisonment was seen as wasteful of human values and resources. From this evolved the idea that a more workable way to protect society would be to treat the individual, not punish the crime—to learn about the causes of his offense by skillful and experienced study and judgment, and to reeducate the offender when possible.

The 1980s saw another attitude reversal. Social workers, psychiatrists, and psychologists were severely criticized for their inability to predict or cure criminal behavior. The general public called for longer sentences and more severe prison conditions.

Social work practice is strongly influenced by the perceptions and policies of the day. When the emphasis is on treatment and alternatives to prison, social workers are likely to have a strong job market in community corrections or treatment departments within institutions. When the attitude changes, there are fewer treatment positions and more security and supervision-oriented positions.

VALUES

In no area of social work practice is there more debate about values than in the criminal justice field. There is both intraprofessional value conflict over the proper role of social workers and interprofessional conflict over what social work roles are appropriate and sometimes even over turf issues of who should provide what services.

Chapter 4 has a full discussion of social work values.

Clearly, the general social work values apply: (1) society has an obligation to ensure that people have access to resources they need to meet various life tasks; and (2) in providing these resources, the dignity and individuality of the person must be respected. Client self-determination becomes more complex in this setting. As social work practitioners we have a strong commitment to client self-determination; however, this is limited by the rights and protections of the rest of society. Offenders forfeit many of their freedoms and rights at the time of their conviction.

In addition to the generic social work values, there are some specific values held by consensus by criminal justice social workers.

1. Restrictive measures must guarantee public safety and encourage the personal growth of the client.
2. Access to rehabilitation and treatment programs should not be denied on ethnic or religious grounds.
3. Loss of freedom is the punishment for crime. Secondary punishment such as inhumane prison conditions is unacceptable.
4. Programs and policies need to respond to knowledge developed in the field, not popular sentiment.
5. Capital punishment is murder.
6. Supervision and rehabilitation can be complementary goals.

One area of value debate among social workers revolves around the dignity of the client. One faction argues that respecting the dignity of the client requires recognizing the free will of the client to commit crime and the necessity to hold the individual responsible for her behavior. Others argue that the social conditions in which some individuals must survive ensure they will commit crime; by holding the individual responsible, we are blaming the victim. Although there is little resistance to holding adults responsible for their criminal behavior and seeing crime as a choice, it is much less clear when we deal with juvenile offenders.

In criminal justice settings the dual responsibility to the individual and the agency or community is an ongoing source of value conflict. The criminal justice system has a special function of protecting and promoting the interests of the client and protecting the community. Social work is an important part of that system. Self-awareness assists the social worker in meeting the responsibility for explicating a value framework. Values can help control the role conflict inherent in criminal justice social work.

Interprofessional value conflict can be seen in the public defender setting. The attorney is committed to using the legal system to accomplish the goal identified by the defendant. Should an abusive parent want to be released to live with his family, it is the attorney's responsibility to present the case in a manner likely to produce that outcome. The social worker, on the other hand, must also consider the best interests of the children in the home. It would be unethical for the social worker to testify as a professional recommending home placement if the social worker believed this would place the children in jeopardy. In this situation the social worker can do a case assessment and develop alternatives to incarceration, but must not let the defendant's wishes dictate the professional recommendations.

Competency examinations determine whether the defendant is capable of participating in his own defense.

Another potential source of interprofessional value conflict is competency examinations. The request for competency evaluation is usually based on observations by police officers, jail officials, family, or attorneys that the defendant is disturbed and might lack competence to stand trial. This is an appropriate use of the evaluation. However, this process can be abused when individuals are sent to maximum security hospitals for a competency evaluation if the real motivation is to provide temporary incarceration and treatment.

Since involuntary civil commitment has become more difficult, some highly disruptive individuals are free to roam the streets and become a nuisance to the community. If the crimes they commit do not warrant imprisonment, one solution is to arrest them on a minor charge and then have them sent to a security hospital for evaluation of competency to stand trial. Since these evaluations sometimes last up to 60 days, the offender is at least temporarily removed from the community.[5]

Due process mandates that certain freedoms can be removed only by the courts.

This situation provides a value conflict for social workers, since they are being pressured by the community to do something about the problem. Yet, to cooperate in "pseudo-competency evaluations" is a clear infringement upon clients' due process rights. In other words, professionals are using "expertise" to deny clients freedoms that can legally be taken away only by the courts. Our system of laws says that judges—not psychiatrists, psychologists, or social workers—have the right to take away the liberty of a mentally ill person.

Values and knowledge are related systems of thought and action. Interventive action is based on values or knowledge or a combination of the two. In dealing with a mentally ill inmate who is being victimized in the prison setting, social work values indicate the individual should be moved to a hospital setting. Knowledge, however, would suggest that it is not uncommon for

Wisconsin Resource Center is a unique presence developed to meet the needs of mentally ill prisoners.

an inmate who is victimized in the prison setting to become the predator in the hospital setting, or that once the inmate is in the hospital, she will adopt a patient role to do easier time. This introduces a whole new configuration of values and knowledge, that is, short-term **values** of immediate individual safety vs. individual long-term prognosis and safety of other hospital patients.

FUNCTIONS

Criminal justice social workers deal with problems caused by dysfunctions of the social control mechanisms. When a crime is committed, there is a breakdown either in the social control system or in the behavior of the individual. Social workers strive to fix the problem by helping the individual lead a happy and socially acceptable life; that is, they attempt to maximize the well-being of the individual and to protect society. These are very general functions which are translated into practice in various ways depending upon the setting in which the intervention takes place.

Day[6] developed a useful categorization of the functions of the probation worker that can be used to describe the functions of most criminal justice social workers. The functions he identified were support, control, individual treatment, and situational treatment.

The support function refers to any statement or action to help offenders solve or mitigate their personal or social problems. For the social worker attached to the police department, this may consist of explaining to new arrestees how to obtain legal assistance. For the social worker in the public defender office, this may be assisting persons in finding employment, which will make them better probation risks at the time of sentencing.

The control function refers to activities directed toward regulation of the offender's behavior. This can include any statement of activity designed to induce the offender to conform to socially acceptable standards of behavior. Many times social workers require that the probationer abstain from alcohol and stay away from taverns. A probationer can also be limited in terms of friends he is allowed to visit. In fact, most probation social workers have an extensive list of conditions that offenders must follow if they want to remain in the community. The social worker's responsibility in probation and parole is to make certain these rules are followed and to invoke the appropriate consequence when they are violated.

Individual treatment activities focus primarily on the individual offender. A social worker might work with high-risk offenders to control their aggressive behavior. The treatment may be a combination of behavior modification, relaxation therapy, and assertiveness training. Individual treatment tends to be a contractual agreement between the client and the social worker to change some aspect of the clients' behavior and perhaps even their value system.

Situational treatment refers to activities that are focused primarily on the social environment of offenders, and that make active use of their relationships with other people. The Galveston County Mental Health Deputy Program was concerned that the needs of the mentally ill in the criminal justice system were not being met. Therefore, they established a special operations unit to deal with the mentally ill through crisis intervention, special screening, and information and referral to determine clients' needs for psychiatric evaluation and to meet their social service needs.[7] They used a variety of agencies to create an environment responsive to the needs of mentally ill offenders.

Theory into Practice

The treatment of people with AIDS in correctional institutions provides an excellent example of how each of these functions translates into practice with one client. A diagnosis of AIDS may cause extremely serious psychological problems for both victims and their families. The support function is primary. In fact, many times the treatment goal is just to be with the person, listen to her needs, and provide empathetic support. The sharing of intense fears helps to dilute feelings of isolation and grief. The social worker must understand the stages of coping with terminal illness and understand that empathy is often the most effective tactic. There needs to exist an honest, direct relationship between counselor and client.

The support offered must be reliable, consistent, and continuous. The social worker must make a commitment to himself and to the person with AIDS (PWA) to be available. Clients should be advised far in advance when the worker will be absent, and arrangements for backup staff should be understood by the client. Fear of abandonment occupies a central position in the mind of the client; fear of death is greater when faced alone.

Two frustrating but important points to remember are that it will take a considerable investment of time to establish the trust necessary to be effective; and as that trust develops the social worker may become a "dartboard" for all the anger the client feels. Social workers have to avoid personalizing these attacks. When they occur, the client should be encouraged to talk about his anger.

There are two types of control functions that must be met. The client has to understand the precautions necessary to avoid spread of the disease. Also, individuals with AIDS should be encouraged to take as much of an active role in treatment as possible. People with AIDS tend to become passive recipients of medical treatment; they need to be encouraged to do what they can for themselves. Exerting control (within the limitations imposed by the setting) can help ward off a sense of imminent decline.

Individual treatment takes the form of encouraging people with AIDS to be vocal and expressive. Family and friends frequently avoid talking about the very issue (their own mortality) that the PWA needs to discuss. Unlike many other treatment situations, the social worker should permit denial. Denial can be an effective defense mechanism as long as medical care is not compromised as a result. Denial reduces stress, assists in coping, and helps maintain a positive quality of life.

The situational treatment function can be seen as the social worker deals with the stress in the inmate's environment. People with AIDS can feel as much stress from family, friends, and other inmates as they do from the disease. Social workers should obtain the client's permission to consult with these individuals to make them aware of the infected person's need for support. These individuals also need to be educated about what is fact and what is myth in dealing with AIDS.

Another function the social worker can play is being a liaison with the primary physician. Since the patient is dealing with a great deal of anxiety, it often interferes with listening and comprehension. It is critically important that counselors obtain written permission from their clients to consult with the physicians and the hospital.[8]

The primary function of direct practice in criminal justice is helping offenders alter their behavior, obtain necessary support from their environment, and maximize their social functioning. Our unique expertise is to work with offenders to assess the social problems contributing to their criminal behavior, the environmental stressors, and how interpersonal and familial relationships are affecting their behavior. Our interventions are based upon knowledge of deviance, the legal system, motivation, and emotional and environmental factors.

Social workers are likely to remain as primary service providers in this field. Our systemic orientation to criminal behavior is unique: neither the police, the courts, the attorneys, the psychiatrists, the psychologists, nor security personnel practice from this perspective; it is our unique domain. Our understanding of the environmental contributors to criminal behavior and rehabilitation is essential. Social work contributions can be in the area of direct service — helping individuals alter their behavior — or indirect service — administering an institution or a program, teaching, planning, and policymaking.

KNOWLEDGE

The criminal justice area, like each field of practice, requires social workers to have knowledge of *general* theory of human behavior and the social environment; *practice theory*, which includes knowledge of policy, services, programs, and institutions, and how social work practice relates to each of them, and a *theory of practice*, which is the specific social work methods or interventions they will use. The practice method used will depend upon the systematic interpretation of those principles that help explain the phenomena and a clear delineation of principles for producing change.

Specialized knowledge needed for this field includes but is not limited to theories of punishment and theories of deviant/criminal behavior.

Theories of Punishment

Theory of punishment refers to the guiding rationale for dealing with adjudicated criminals.

Punishment means the infliction by the state of consequences normally considered unpleasant upon a person for committing a crime. Punishment theory considers the various points of view regarding the desirable objectives of punishment and the rationale that should sustain the sentencing and correctional system.

Punishment was instituted because it was thought by lawmakers that a system of laws impartially applied would have the long-term consequence of furthering the interests of society. Communities need to feel protected even while they maintain a sense of justice. The alternative to a justice system would be a vigilante system in which citizens took the law into their own hands.

Among opposing theories of punishment, there seems to be general agreement in at least two areas. We will continue to have punishment, and the purpose of punishment will be to protect society and deter crime. Theories of punishment are usually grouped under the headings of retributive, utilitarian (deterrent and rehabilitative models), and conflict.

Retributive theory stresses guilt and justice.

The two primary tenets of *retributive theory* are: (1) punishment must be imposed by the court as prescribed by law, and (2) punishment must be proportioned to the gravity of the offense committed. One looks only to the crime to justify punishment, and denies that the consequences of that punishment, whether good or bad, have any relevance to justification of punishment. Retribution must be paid because it is owed. Retribution is not the same as vengeance. Vengeance is self-serving; it is not defined by pre-existing rules and is not proportioned to the injury avenged. Policy based on retributive theory would include an emphasis on determinate sentencing. Determinate sentencing abolishes much of the discretion of the courts in sentencing, and severely limits adjustments to sentencing that were previously made by corrections professionals.

Vengeance is arbitrarily taken by anyone who feels injured and wishes to retaliate.

Determinate sentences, sometimes called flat sentences, are for a fixed length.

Utilitarian theory, by contrast, insists that punishment can be justified only if it has positive consequences that outweigh the intrinsic evil of inflicting suffering on human beings. This theory sees punishment as evil, to be allowed only insofar as it avoids some greater evil. This theory leads to the policy of least restrictive sanctions, which is contained in the Model Penal Code developed by the American Bar Association. This means that there should be no more loss of liberty than is necessary to achieve the protection of society. Any punitive suffering beyond societal need is defined as cruelty.

Utilitarian theory posits that punishment must be limited by marginal gain.

The *deterrent model* (one version of utilitarian punishment) suggests that punishment is necessary to the social order. In this model is an underlying belief that law-abiding citizens are honest because they are afraid of being caught. Deterrent theory stresses the wrongness of the crime and the means to deter potential offenders from committing crime. General deterrence is the ability of criminal law to make others refrain from crime through fear of punishment; individual deterrence is the effect of the punishment on the punished. This theory assumes that crime is rational. Criminals will engage in crime if crime pays. The most extreme form of deterrent punishment is capital punishment. Most deterrent theorists, however, suggest that punishment policy needs to emphasize certainty and swiftness rather than severity, as this would produce the greatest marginal deterrent effect.

Deterrent theories see the threat of punishment as necessary for social order.

The *rehabilitative model* is motivated by humanitarianism — a belief in the worth and dignity of every human being and a willingness to expend the effort to reclaim the criminal for his own sake, not merely to protect society. During the 1960s and 1970s many professionals saw rehabilitation as the primary goal of the correctional system. Emphasis on the rehabilitative model was especially strong after a very bloody uprising at Attica State Prison in New York in 1971. The rehabilitative model became closely aligned with the medical model of treatment. Psychiatrists such as Karl Menninger fostered the belief that we can diagnose offenders and pursue a course of treatment that will bring about a cure. The rehabilitative model is based on these assumptions:

Rehabilitative theory assumes that professionals can "cure" criminals.

1. Human behavior is the product of antecedent causes. We can identify these causes.

2. Knowledge of the causes of human behavior makes possible an approach to the scientific control of human behavior.

3. Measures used to treat offenders should serve a therapeutic rather than punitive function. Such measures should be designed to effect changes in the behavior of the convicted person, in the interest of the convict and society.

Indeterminate sentencing allows sentencing to be altered based on the progress of the offender and the professional's prediction of their recidivistic potential.

The rehabilitative model led to policies of indeterminate sentencing, which gave professionals a great deal of power in deciding the type of punishment and how long an individual would be incarcerated. The theory assumed that since crime was a "disease," the professional could recognize when the "cure" had been effected. It was both costly and unwise to retain the criminal once the cure had taken place. High costs and the inability to cure or even decrease crime have led to considerable disenchantment with the rehabilitative model. However, this still tends to be the guiding theory for most social workers practicing in the criminal justice area.

Conflict theory suggests that punishment is not related to the gravity of the crime, but to the interests of the wealthy. According to Ryan, imprisonment as punishment and the development of the penitentiary are contemporaneous with the beginnings of modern capitalism, and related to the need to control the idle poor.[9] Further, he suggests that the professional full-time police force developed in response to the necessity of managing restless factory workers who lashed out against working conditions by rioting. This analysis would lead to policies to change societal conditions rather than individuals.

Theories of punishment guide the field in setting policy to respond to crime. This body of knowledge is most useful to indirect practitioners who make policy. Theories of deviance are more pertinent to the daily practice of social work.

Theories of Deviance

Theories attempting to explain deviant behavior have ranged from attributing the cause to individuals' genetic makeup to socialization to larger environmental structures to the transmission of values from a subculture. These have generally been classified as biogenetic, psychological, psychosocial and sociological theories.

Biogenetic theory suggests that criminality is inherited.

Biogenetic Theories. The earliest biogenetic theories date back to the late 1700s, when phrenologists thought that bumps on criminals' heads were manifestations of irregularly shaped brains. In the early 1900s Lombroso's theory of atavism became popular. Lombroso claimed that some criminals were throwbacks to prehuman, apelike beings.[10] The 1950s saw a resurgence of attempts to relate body types to delinquency.[11] A more recent theory speculated that the presence of an extra Y chromosome adds to the aggressive tendency of some criminals.[12] While there is still much debate on this theory, there is evidence to suggest that some deviant behavior is at least partly due to a genetically inherited physiological predisposition. This has been shown to be true particularly for alcoholics.[13]

See Chapter 17 for a
related discussion of
causes of mental ill-
ness.

Psychological Theories.   The psychological theories tend to view crime as mental illness. Adaptation theory suggests that stress is an important variable. The most important stresses contributing to crime arise in disturbed interpersonal relationships. People must derive satisfaction in life through a constant process of interaction. When their needs are frustrated, this failure to find gratification of interpersonal needs engenders powerful and often maladaptive emotions.[14]

Freudian theory postulates that crime can be attributed to sublimation of humans' basic sexual, aggressive instincts.[15] Still others have suggested that crime is related to mental pathology,[16] maternal deprivation,[17] and hormonal imbalance.[18]

The currently popular psychological theory, developed by Yochelson and Samenow, concerns "the criminal personality."[19] They suggest that criminality is on a continuum. While all people exhibit criminal elements to some degree, these individual qualities and traits pervade the criminal's personality; the result of these qualities and thinking is crime. If one could place a video camera in the mind of a criminal, we would see a steady stream of illegal and destructive ideas. Most of this thinking is deterred by fear of apprehension. Yet, as the idea for a particular crime continues to emerge, the criminal embellishes her fantasy to the point that she is in a state of hyperalertness. This is a state that criminals find desirable, and it is this excitement that maintains criminal behavior.

In order for the criminal to maintain the cycle of violation, he must maintain an opinion of himself as superior. It is this sense of superiority which overcomes the fear of apprehension, because he feels he is so talented he cannot be caught. This thinking process is frequently aided by alcohol and drugs. This individualistic view of crime is consistent with the general societal attitude toward crime prevalent today.

Psychosocial Theories.   Whereas psychological theories look at variables that are a part of the individual's personality at birth, psychosocial theories emphasize factors that develop as a consequence of interacting with others. It can be said that psychosocial theory posits that a criminal is a normal person whose criminal behavior is learned in a process of symbolic interaction with other human beings. This type of theory typically looks at the family as a source of inadequate socialization of the child. If a child is not appropriately socialized, she will not accept and abide by the values of larger society. As such individuals become adults they refuse to accept their role as contributing members of society, and make their living through criminal activity.

Learning theory also suggests a psychosocial approach when it emphasizes imitation and role modeling. The example frequently cited is the ghetto child who sees that pimping and drug dealing lead to positions of power in the community. The concern with violence on television is based on the belief that children learn to imitate these behaviors.

Labeling theory is another example of psychosocial explanations for criminal behavior. Particularly in the literature on juvenile delinquency, there has been much concern over the phenomenon of labeling a child delinquent. The rationale is that once an individual is labeled, he tends to live up to that label, and further, that once he is labeled, opportunities are restricted. Once a child is labeled a drug user, for example, other users are likely to approach her at the same time that nonusers avoid her.

Sociological Theories.   Sociological approaches to deviance analyze how social structures tend to pressure people to engage in criminal activity. Sociological theorists study the manner in which criminal behavior arises, is maintained, and is controlled in a given community. This theory does not search for defects within the individual but assumes that crime arises out of either the functioning of society or social units within that society.

The two major sociological traditions of thought about the problem of crime can be consolidated under the anomie tradition and the differential association tradition.

Durkheim first used the concept of anomie.[20] He focused on the way in which various social conditions lead to unlimited goals or ambitions that produce a breakdown in the social control norms. Merton and Cloward have each expanded this theory by adding the concept of differentials in access to success by illegitimate means.[21] Cloward's opportunity-structure theory had a forceful impact on the development of social reform programs in the 1960s.

Early theorists were implying that if individuals cannot obtain their goals by legitimate means they will pursue the goals in illegitimate ways. Cloward added to the theory that, just as legitimate means are more available to some criminals than others, this is also true of illegitimate means. To be a criminal, the individual must have the opportunity to learn how to be a criminal and the opportunity to commit the crime.

Sutherland is noted for the differential association theory, which is both a learning and an interaction theory.[22] He suggests that criminal deviance is the result of interacting with criminal patterns and isolation from anti-criminal patterns. Basically, individuals become criminal because a preponderance of their associations support criminal activity.

Our discussion of theories of punishment and deviance is a small part of the special knowledge base required of criminal justice social workers. They also need to be familiar with criminal law, substance abuse, AIDS, risk management, prediction of violence literature, inmate classification systems, and drug and alcohol treatment. Since the knowledge generated in this field is so extensive, a double major in criminal justice or criminology can be good preparation for practice. If you are more interested in working with mentally ill or juvenile offenders, you may consider a double major in mental health or juvenile justice.

Effective criminal justice social workers have an eclectic knowledge base. They have substantive knowledge of criminology and knowledge of

Developing social skills is an important part of treatment.

practice methods. The best test for practice knowledge is whether it is useful. Useful knowledge helps us recognize and organize observations in the environment, suggests what things can be changed, and provides direction on how to go about producing change.

For example, we know that treatment activities require the following: (1) a target condition that can be observed and measured; (2) a population at risk; (3) a clearly outlined plan of intervention; and (4) measurement of incidence following the intervention. The problem of transferring an emotionally disturbed inmate to a hospital setting might be referred to the social worker.

The prison social worker must weigh a variety of complex factors in making apparently simple decisions to transfer an inmate from one unit to another. Often, a wise decision in the correctional setting would seem aberrant in the free world.[23] Inmates with minor disorders may be transferred to a special treatment unit for reasons of safety, while other, much more disturbed inmates may have to be treated in the prison unit when the long-term risks of transfer outweigh the short-term benefits of hospitalization.

The target condition is observable and the population at risk is defined in general terms. Both the individual inmate and the hospital population are at risk. For the intervention to be effective, the social worker has to consider both populations. We cannot say the intervention is effective if the individual thrives while three other patients suffer severe traumas. Should the social worker decide to transfer a patient, she will need a baseline measure of incidence of disturbed behavior and the functioning of the hospital unit.

Once the intervention (transfer for treatment) takes place, the outcome must be measured. Based upon the clearly stated goal of the program, the social worker has to determine what intervention would be the most effective, under what conditions, and why. The development of this intervention will draw upon his knowledge of human behavior, prediction of violence, the immediate and larger social environment of the hospital, prognosis for the client's behavior, labeling theory, sensitivity to cultural variables, and knowledge of the statutes regarding right to treatment.

This is not an exhaustive list of the types of knowledge the social worker needs, but rather is intended to convey the importance and complexity of knowledge, particularly in a prison setting, which may lead to a very different intervention than would be chosen in a mental health setting.

ROLES

Criminal justice, more than any other field, presents role conflicts for social workers. Many social workers working in probation and parole or the prison setting are inhibited by the recognition that what the client says in treatment has a tremendous effect on important decisions. What the prison social worker recommends may have important implications for when the inmate is released or what privileges she is allowed.

Some social workers have dealt with this by insisting that treatment would be provided only if no reporting would be done that would ultimately help or hurt the offender. This approach is designed to facilitate open communication and help eliminate the element of manipulation.

Other social workers have taken the opposite view and used their power in the decision-making process as a source of motivation. Knowledge and experience have taught some social workers to recognize and use "conning" as an important variable in treatment. Others find it incompatible with their treatment modality to distrust the client and therefore strive to remove all incentives for deceit.

Based upon the material presented already, you should be able to identify how social workers are likely to be involved in the normal social work roles.

Social workers serve as brokers when they make linkages between the client and a potential employer or other community resource such as the community mental health center. Particularly the probation and parole officer and the public defender advocate will be involved in brokering services. The offender may need help in finding suitable housing, education, financial assistance, or even health care.

The advocate role is familiar to the prison social worker because the complexity of the institution, the fear for safety, the lack of communication with one's family, and the high degree of stratification and depersonalization in a prison can create special problems for even the most knowledgeable and capable inmates.

The enabler role is evident when the social worker assists the client and the family to find strengths and resources within themselves to aid in the rehabilitation. In this role the social worker enables the client to change or achieve the desired goal by concentrating on his own strengths and abilities and helping him apply these strengths to the problems at hand.

The teaching role introduces information to the offender and/or family that was not previously available. A social worker may teach human sexuality to a group of sex offenders. We also see social workers in some settings involved in teaching parenting and communication skills to parents. Employment readiness programs are another setting in which social workers are teachers.

As a mediator the social worker acts to reconcile differences and to intervene between conflicting parties in order to promote reconciliation or compromise. Prison social workers are frequently involved in mediation with families when there is dispute concerning whether the offender will be able to return to the home. For example, a sixty-seven-year-old man was incarcerated for taking indecent liberties with a minor child. Once he completes his prison term, he will be without housing and transportation. Although he does have family, they have been extremely embarrassed by the offense and do not want him in the community, certainly not around their children. While the social worker can understand these feelings, she also realizes that he will not be able to survive outside the institution without some degree of family support.

The social worker can work with the family to identify what types of support they can provide without undue risk to their own families. While the offender is incarcerated this mediation will be done by the prison social worker. At the time of release this role will be assumed by the parole agent.

In Chapter 1 we discussed how the roles of the psychiatrist, psychologist, and social worker sometimes overlap. A brief comparison of the roles in private or public mental hospitals and forensic or correctional settings provides a good illustration.

In most hospital settings, psychiatrists assume major responsibility for managing patients and their treatment through drug therapy and psychotherapy. In correctional or forensic settings, psychiatrists must spend a good deal of time preparing for courtroom testimony. Competency evaluations may be directed more toward legal than therapeutic issues.

Most of the day-to-day program administration and patient management is directed by psychologists or social workers. Since psychiatrists' time is so expensive, it is reserved for tasks for which the law requires a licensed physician. In a forensic setting a psychiatrist's involvement in treatment may be limited to the management of pharmacotherapy.

Pharmacotherapy is behavior management through medication.

This redistribution of roles in correctional settings sometimes leads to job dissatisfaction on the part of the professionals involved. Psychiatrists may feel that their diagnostic work is not being incorporated into treatment and may be frustrated at the lack of opportunity to use psychotherapeutic interventions. The social workers and psychologists who actually do the most critical work are paid much less and do not receive the status deference accorded the psychiatrist. Since correctional settings tend to have fewer resources and less well-trained professionals, it is very difficult to recruit and retain highly skilled individuals.

RELEVANT SOCIAL POLICY/LEGISLATION

The criminal justice system provides a glaring example of how individual attitudes are translated into policy and how that policy then affects service delivery. As we examine recent changes in attitudes toward crime and criminals, it becomes clear that money is going to be spent on building new prisons rather than rehabilitation programs during the 1990s.

Americans overwhelmingly support incarceration as the most appropriate punishment for serious offenders. In a national survey (n = 1,920), 71 percent said a jail or prison sentence was the most suitable penalty for rape, robbery, assault, burglary, theft, property damage, drunk driving, and drug offenses. Survey respondents recommended periods of incarceration that were longer than those typically being served throughout the country.[24]

A new group of people entering the criminal justice system in record numbers is drunk drivers, those who operated a motor vehicle while intoxicated (DWIs). Between 1970 and 1986 arrests for DWI increased nearly 223 percent, while the number of licensed drivers increased by 42 percent. A profile of DWI offenders suggests there are additional problems for this group. About 48 percent had a previous conviction for DWI; approximately 75 percent had previously been convicted of some crime, including DWI. Thirty-three percent were unemployed. Drunk drivers have historically been dealt with by the mental health system, under the assumption that alcoholism is a disease. Now groups such as Mothers Against Drunk Driving are increasingly insisting upon criminal penalties for drunk driving.[25]

The risk of imprisonment for serious crime has also increased in recent years, but it has not yet reached the levels of twenty-five years ago. Of federal offenders convicted between July 1, 1985, and June 30, 1986, 51 percent were sentenced to prison terms, 37 percent to probation only, and the remainder received fines or other sentences.[26]

The Comprehensive Crime Control Act of 1984 has caused serious overcrowding of the jails.

The Comprehensive Crime Control Act of 1984 (CCCA), in which Congress abolished parole for federal offenders, is predicted to raise the federal prison population by 26 percent by 1992 and 50 percent by 1997. Part of this act includes the Bail Reform Act, which enables judicial officers to hold federal suspects in preventive detention before trial if they are considered a threat to the public. The Bail Reform Act has increased the number of federal pretrial detainees by 36 percent between 1984 and 1986.[27]

Louisiana, Texas, Georgia, Mississippi, Alabama, Florida, Utah, and Virginia had executions in 1987.

The Supreme Court reinstated the death penalty in 1977.

Capital punishment has once again become a policy in the criminal justice system. At yearend 1987, 1,984 persons were under a sentence of death in state prisons (a 10.2 percent increase over 1986). All but one had been convicted of murder; one had been convicted of capital rape of a child. At yearend 1987, laws in 37 states authorized the death penalty, and eight states had conducted a total of 25 executions during that year. Between 1977 and 1983 there were a total of 11 executions in seven years. In the four years 1984–88, there were 82 executions.[28]

Mandatory sentences require the imposition of a prison sentence for certain crimes.

Sentencing policies have also undergone drastic changes. States vary in the degree of judicial and parole board discretion in sentencing and release decisions. There has been a strong move toward certain and fixed punishments for crimes through mandatory sentences, determinate sentences, and abolition of parole boards.

The movement away from parole boards is reflected in the fact that in 1977, nearly 72 percent of those discharged from prison exited as a result of a parole board decision; by 1985, this figure had dropped to 43 percent.[29]

In 1983 whites and blacks entering state prisons received the same average sentence, if geographical location and offense distributions are taken into account. A higher proportion of blacks than whites were convicted of a violent crime. Blacks were concentrated in states that gave longer average sentences to all offenders than were given in other states. For each of the major violent crimes, sentences were longer for men than for women.[30]

Recent trends in mental health law have led to an increase in the number of mentally disturbed individuals who end up in prison. Previously, bizarre behaviors that disturbed the community could be dealt with by placing individuals in a mental health institution. Now these individuals cannot be involuntarily committed unless they are a threat to themselves or others. Social workers in their professional role are expected to remove these people for the comfort of the rest of society.

As we already mentioned, this can become a serious ethical problem for the social worker. However, the dilemma does not end merely with protecting a particular individual's rights. If this type of person becomes too disruptive or too plentiful, we may see behaviors criminalized that had not previously been designated as mental illness. The end result will be relabeling mentally ill or perhaps even mentally retarded individuals as criminals. We are already seeing them in overcrowded jails. This is a much worse fate for them than losing their freedom in a hospital equipped to treat their behavior.

The insanity defense is an area of criminal law that social workers need to know. The insanity defense is designed to avoid punishing people for behavior that is out of their control or that they do not have the mental capacity to understand is illegal. To use the insanity defense, the defendant's illness and the resulting impairment must be severe enough to preclude the placing of criminal blame. According to the McNaghten test,

> Every man is presumed to be sane, and . . . to establish a defense on the ground of insanity it must be clearly proved that at the time of committing of the act, the party accused was laboring under such a defect of reason from disease of the mind, as not to know the nature and quality of the act he was doing or if he did know it, that he did not know he was doing what was wrong.[31]

In 1984, part of the Comprehensive Crime Control Act required defendants who wish to raise the defense of insanity to assume the burden of proving this defense by a standard of clear and convincing evidence. All of these policies will have an overwhelming effect on the practice of social work.

THE FUTURE OF CRIMINAL JUSTICE PRACTICE: A SUMMARY

In addition to the roles and functions already identified, criminal justice social workers will increasingly develop new services in the area of victim assistance. While there is less public sentiment favoring rehabilitation of the offender, there is increasing concern for the victims of crime. Teenagers and young adults under age 25 have the highest victimization rates.

Social workers in victim assistance programs work in a variety of settings. Some programs are housed in the district attorney's office, some are attached to the courts, and others operate out of community mental health settings. The victims most likely to use the services have suffered rape or assault. Victim assistance staff also support witnesses during the trial period.

The other expanding areas of practice will be working with people with AIDS, drunk drivers, and mentally ill and mentally retarded offenders. Working with clients with AIDS, social workers will be breaking new ground. As more research is completed and the knowledge base expands, there will be more guidance for practice. At present, literature and practice in the area of terminal illness form the guiding knowledge.

Drunk drivers and mentally ill or retarded offenders will increasingly come into the criminal justice system as new laws are implemented. Social work has a large knowledge base to deal with these clients; however, the problem will be to find the resources to develop the needed services.

CASE STUDY
Social Work Values and Knowledge in Practice

You have been assigned to do a presentence investigation on Judith Brown, age 20, who has just been convicted of murdering her two-day-old infant. Judith is a white, unmarried woman who lives with an unemployed African American who is the father of her two-year-old, as well as of the deceased child.

Judith was the seventh of 11 children. Her father was disabled at the age of 30. Judith and her family received Social Security, AFDC, food stamps, and Medicare when she was growing up. This was the same means of support Judith and her common law husband relied on.

DISCUSSION QUESTIONS

Test your self-awareness.

1. Does the fact that Judith is a second generation welfare client make you hostile?

2. What effect does the fact that this is an interracial relationship have
   a. On your attitude?
   b. On the community's attitude?
   Will this affect your recommendation?

3. You are defined as an expert who can assess this situation and determine what the most effective sanction will be. Identify areas in which knowledge and value judgments might overlap.

4. What general knowledge will you apply in this case? What specific knowledge will you need? How will you go about obtaining that knowledge?

5. Do you see any potential role or value conflicts with other professionals involved in the case? Explain.

6. Who is your client in this case—Judith, the court, or the state? Explain.

7. Even though you are assigned to do the presentence investigation, do you feel other social work roles might be involved? Is your role defined by your task or by your professional expertise?

8. Would you consider that the crime might have been committed during postpartum depression psychosis? If so, would this affect your recommendation? Why or why not?

9. How would you measure the effectiveness of your social work intervention—the presentence report?

NOTES

1. *BJS Sourcebook on Criminal Statistics, 1987* (Washington, D.C.: Bureau of Justice Statistics, April 1988), NCJ-111612, 2.
2. Clemens Bartolas and Stuart Miller, *Correctional Administration* (New York: McGraw, 1978).
3. Michael Serrill, "Determinate Sentencing," *Corrections Magazine* (September 1977): 3–12.
4. Louis Carney, *Corrections: Treatment and Philosophy* (Englewood Cliffs, N.J.: Prentice-Hall, 1980), 15.
5. Seymour Halleck, *The Mentally Disordered Offender* (Rockville, Md.: National Institute of Mental Health, 1986), Pub. No. (ADM) 86–1471, 39.
6. Peter R. Day, *Social Work & Social Control* (New York: Tavistock, 1981), 42.
7. National Coalition for Jail Reform, *Removing the Chronically Mentally Ill from Jail* (Rockville, Md.: NIMH, 1984), Contract #83M02676301D, 13.

8. Anna Laszlo and Marilyn Ayres, *AIDS: Improving the Response of the Correctional System*, National Sheriff's Association, (October 1986), 126–128.
9. William Ryan, *Equality* (New York: Pantheon, 1981), 172.
10. Cesare Lombroso, *Crime: Its Causes and Remedies* (Boston: Little, Brown, 1911).
11. Sheldon and Eleanor Glueck, *Physique and Delinquency* (New York: Harper, 1956).
12. H. Witken, "Criminality in XYY and XXY Men," *Science* 193, 547–555.
13. L. Ellis, "Genetics and Criminal Behavior," *Criminology* 20, 43–66.
14. Seymour Halleck, *Psychiatry and the Dilemmas of Crime* (New York: Harper, 1967), 53–54.
15. R. Ardrey, *The Territorial Imperative* (New York: Atheneum, 1966).
16. Sheldon and Eleanor Glueck, "Mental Pathology and Delinquency," in *The Problem of Delinquency* (Boston: Houghton Mifflin, 1959).
17. J. and W. McCord, *Psychopathology and Delinquency* (New York: Grune and Stratton, 1956).
18. S. Shah and L. H. Roth, "Biological and Psychophysiological Factors in Criminality," in *Handbook of Criminality*, ed. D. Glaser (Chicago: Rand McNally, 1974).
19. S. Yochelson and S. E. Samenow, *The Criminal Personality* (New York: Aronson, 1976).
20. Emile Durkheim, *Suicide* (Glencoe, Ill.: Free Press, 1951).
21. Robert Merton, *Social Theory and Social Structure* (Glencoe, Ill.: Free Press, 1957); Richard Cloward, "Illegitimate Means, Anomie, and Deviant Behavior," in *The Emergence of Social Welfare and Social Work*, 2nd ed., ed. N. Gilbert and H. Specht (Itasca, Ill.: Peacock, 1981).
22. E. H. Sutherland, *Principles of Criminology*, 4th ed. (Philadelphia: Lippincott, 1947).
23. S. Halleck, *The Mentally Disordered Offender*, 146.
24. *BJS Sourcebook*, 35.
25. "Drunk Driving," in *BJS Special Report* (Washington, D.C.: Bureau of Justice Statistics, February 1988), NCJ-109945.
26. *BJS Sourcebook*, 50.
27. "Our Crowded Jails," *BJS Special Report* (Washington, D.C.: Bureau of Justice Statistics, August 1988), NCJ-111846.
28. "Capital Punishment 1987," *BJS Special Report* (Washington, D.C.: Bureau of Justice Statistics, July 1988), NCJ-111939.
29. *BJS Sourcebook*, 47.
30. Ibid.
31. *M'naghten's Case*, Vol. 8 English Reports (1843), 718.

Chapter

19

Gerontology

In 1965 the Older Americans Act (OAA) was adopted. This was a modest beginning for what ultimately has become a wide range of services for the elderly. Advocacy groups and various White House conferences induced the federal government to promote considerable growth in programs and services to the elderly from 1965 to 1980.

The Older Americans Act set forth ten objectives, which can be seen as both goals and values—the conditions we strive for in serving the elderly. How these objectives would be accomplished has never been spelled out, so in reality they function more as value statements than true goals. To discuss social services to the elderly, we need to put them in the context of the Older Americans Act. The objectives of the OAA are listed.

1. An adequate income in retirement, in accordance with the American standard of living.
2. The best possible physical and mental health that science can make available, without regard to economic status.
3. Suitable housing, independently selected, designed, and located with reference to special needs, and available at costs that older citizens can afford.
4. Full restorative services for those who require institutional care.
5. Opportunity for employment with no discriminatory personnel practices because of age.
6. Retirement in health, honor, and dignity, after years of contribution to the economy.
7. Pursuit of meaningful activity within the widest range of civic, cultural, and recreational opportunities.
8. Efficient community services that provide social assistance in a coordinated manner and which are readily available when needed.
9. Immediate benefit from proven research knowledge that can sustain and improve health and happiness.
10. Freedom, independence, and the free exercise of individual initiative in planning and managing their own lives.

This act and these goals set the limits and structure for services to the elderly. Gerontology is a specialized field of social work concerned with providing social services to the elderly and their families and to help them obtain from the community the resources and protections necessary for achieving an adequate quality of life. As people age, services must reinforce, supplement, and substitute some of the functions that can no longer be met by individuals or their families. The elderly frequently need social services to support and strengthen daily functioning, to supplement family care, or to provide long-term care when independent functioning is no longer feasible. Social workers make existing social institutions and programs more responsive to elderly needs, and develop new services when necessary programs do not exist.

HISTORY

Gerontology, the study of the aging process and its effects, is a relatively new multidisciplinary endeavor, marked by the founding of the Gerontological Society in 1945. In 1960 the National Council on Aging was established. It was intended to become "a central national resource that works with and through other organizations to develop interest in work with older people and to design methods that can be used in programs designed to meet their varied needs."[1]

Gerontology was from the outset seen as a multidisciplinary effort. No single profession emerged as the primary care provider. In addition the elderly themselves have insisted on a major role in defining the service delivery system. At the first White House Conference on Aging in 1971, there was a great deal of dissatisfaction with the lack of representation from the elderly. This had to be remedied before progress could be made. One of the concessions made to the elderly was the appointment of Dr. Arthur Flemming, former Secretary of Health, Education, and Welfare (HEW), to chair the conference.

Flemming was successful in increasing the participation of the elderly and calming warring groups at least enough to proceed. Nine needs areas were identified by this group: (1) income, (2) health and mental health, (3) housing and environment, (4) nutrition, (5) education, (6) employment and retirement, (7) retirement roles and activities, (8) transportation, and (9) spiritual well-being.[2] The success of the conference is best measured by the substantial legislative changes that were made in the OAA in 1973, which gave new impetus to governmental services to the elderly.

These nine areas of need all fall within the domain of social work practice.

In the 1973 amendments, the Administration on Aging was moved out of the Social and Rehabilitation Service and made a unit of HEW. The commissioner was now to report directly to the secretary. (This was never implemented.) As a result of these amendments the National Information and Resource Clearing House for the Aging and the Federal Council on the Aging were created. The federal council was created to evaluate the government's policies toward the aging. Each of these administrative structures is discussed under the Knowledge section.

Through expanded grant programs, the states were encouraged to develop "comprehensive and coordinated service systems to serve older persons." This was the beginning of the Area Agencies on Aging (AAAs).

Additionally the amendments provided for model projects: expanded training and research programs, grants to establish senior centers, nutrition programs, and library services. Between 1965 and 1978 the OAA was revised on eight occasions. It was due to expire on September 30, 1978.[3]

The Comprehensive Older Americans Act passed in 1978 included all of the previous services but tried to promote the concept of a single community focal point for all services for the aging. It also provided for another White House Conference to be held in 1981.

Planning for the 1981 conference began under the Carter administration and was completed under the Reagan administration. President Reagan replaced the chairperson of the conference, and many thought the delegates were stacked in support of the administration. Dissatisfaction with conference planning led some formerly appointed delegates to organize an alternative conference. Among the leaders of the alternative conference was Maggie Kuhn, founder of the Gray Panthers.

The Gray Panthers are an excellent example of radical practice.

Dissension was so high among the discussion groups that an estimated 800 people gathered outside the economic well-being committee room and sang "We Shall Overcome." Participants from the alternative conference marched in protest outside the White House and around the committee meetings.

The final report of the conference included five well-written essays that failed to come to grips with the recommendations of the committees. Women's issues were totally ignored, as were many proposals that would have necessitated increased expenditures.[4]

The 1981 amendments reflected the policies of the Reagan administration. The states were given less money and greater control over services. The act also instructed the Department of Labor to establish training programs to help older workers find employment. Funding was authorized for the continuation of the OAA part-time jobs projects.[5]

The 1980s saw a decline in services to the elderly and a new concern with the problem of elderly abuse. In 1985, the Select Committee on Aging's Subcommittee on Health and Long-Term Care, chaired by the late Rep. Claude Pepper, (D–Fla.) issued a report stating that elder abuse was a "full-scale national problem which existed with a frequency and rate only slightly less than child abuse. There was no question that the problem was increasing dramatically from year to year."[6] In a 1981 Harris poll, 79 percent of the public rated elder abuse as "a serious issue" in the country, and 72 percent evaluated it as "a major responsibility" to be assumed by the government.[7]

We have come a long way from the grandiose plans of the 1965 OAA. While social security benefits have increased and fewer elderly now live under the poverty line, we are faced with a very grave social problem that requires new solutions and government resources to contain. Elder abuse, like child abuse, falls within the range of expertise of social workers. Social workers have been and are likely to continue to be prominent among the professionals trying to solve this problem.

VALUES

Working with the elderly can present value conflicts for the social worker. Protective service social workers experience ongoing conflict between rights to privacy and self-determination and the obligation to protect the elderly. As the functioning of the elderly deteriorates there may be a conflict over individual choice versus individual safety. When a 95-year-old woman wants to stay in her home but has set numerous kitchen fires by forgetting to turn off the gas stove, do we insist that she move to a nursing home for her own protection? Does the decision change if she lives in an apartment complex where she might endanger other people and someone else's property? When does quality of life take precedence over longevity, and at what potential cost to others? What is the appropriate social work role? Do we advocate for the client's position, or do we protect the best interests of the client and possibly of society?

The NASW Code of Ethics establishes the ethical responsibilities for social workers with respect to themselves, clients, colleagues, employees, agencies, the profession, and society. Acceptance of these responsibilities guides competent social work practice. The NASW has developed specific standards of practice in two areas that have particular application to the elderly: standards for social work services in long-term care facilities, and standards and guidelines for social work case management for the functionally impaired. Social work values that apply specifically to work with the elderly include those enumerated here.

Acknowledgment of one's own values, attitudes and biases. Social workers must be aware of ethnic and cultural differences, along with awareness of the potential impact of these personal feelings upon professional decision making. They must be committed to providing services without regard to race, ethnicity, or social class. Some recent findings suggest that institutional and individual racism is still an important factor in services to the elderly. In 1982, the Civil Rights Commission issued a report on minority participation in the OAA. They found that minorities were represented at least proportionally on advisory boards and staff of the AAAs; but few of these positions were at a decision-making level. Minority firms were underrepresented in purchased services even when well-established minority firms were available. In each of the six cities evaluated, only a small percentage of eligible minorities were receiving services. The reasons cited were: (1) belief on the part of minorities that they were unwelcome, (2) a feeling that programs were unresponsive to their needs, (3) lack of knowledge about the programs, (4) lack of transportation necessary to participate.[8]

Recognition of the dignity of the older person as an individual with both a right to adequate care/protection and a stake in independent functioning. Related to this is a commitment to the older person's family as a preferred provider of care. When a social worker is faced with a marginally functional family, it may seem easier to place the older person in alternative living arrangements. This can be destructive to a family both emotionally and economically. Even though the family may be experiencing problems, they might need to deal with those problems rather than change the family structure. Families may be devastated emotionally by removal of a parent or grandparent; some families are dependent on pooled economic resources to survive.

Commitment to assist in meeting the physical, emotional, social, transportation, moral, and vocational needs of the elderly. Functionally impaired individuals must have nurturance, care, protection, guidance, and control. Emotionally, they must maintain a sense of trust, belonging, and security. Security needs must be met by adults who will protect them from harm.

Commitment to fostering the rights of the elderly and their families. This includes the right to confidentiality and privacy. Everyone has the right to be protected against abuse, neglect, cruelty, and exploitation; families have the right to determine for themselves, within the limits set by society, how they will care for themselves.

Belief that elderly neglect, abuse, and exploitation are more likely to be symptoms of social and economic deprivations and personal problems rather than of willful, premeditated malice. You will recall that this approach to social problems was identified as one of the unique characteristics of the social work frame of reference. Rather than assuming that elder abuse is a psychological problem of the abuser, the social worker assesses the social environment to determine which social stressors are contributing to the abuse and what resources need to be developed to prevent further abuse.

Recognition of society's responsibility to the elderly and the need for social workers to be accountable to the community. Social workers do not operate in a vacuum in determining what is in the best interests of the client. Social welfare is a socially constructed concept and any intervention in the family system must be socially acceptable. Americans' commitment to family privacy and responsibility at times makes prevention of abuse and neglect more difficult. The whole concept of community sanction can become very difficult when in an individual case, neighbors want the older person removed from what they view as an unacceptable environment. Yet state statutes and social work values protect the family's choices unless significant abuse or neglect can be established in the legal sense.

The quality of the aging process is a combination of good health, economic security, and companionship.

FUNCTIONS

The functions of a social worker in this field are varied. Social workers in long-term care facilities provide direct services to individuals, families, and significant others; health education for residents and families; advocacy; discharge planning; community liaison and services; participation in policy and program planning; quality assurance; development of a therapeutic environment in the facility, and consultation to other members of the long-term care team.[9]

These functions are achieved by preadmission services, which include a social work assessment and participation in an interdisciplinary evaluation of the individual's need for institutional care. The social worker frequently works closely with the family to prepare the incoming resident.

Once the older person is admitted, the social worker designs a social service plan to promote adjustment and lessen the trauma of relocation. This might also include assistance to the elderly person or his family in funding and utilizing financial, legal, and other community resources. As a member of an interdisciplinary team in a long-term care facility the social worker usually has primary responsibility for the psychosocial functioning of the residents. This can include helping them adjust to illness, disability, and institutional living, or helping them cope with interpersonal relationships, separation, death, or dying.

In the community the social worker may fulfill these functions: (1) enhancing the developmental, problem-solving, and coping capacities of the elderly, (2) promoting a comprehensive, humanistic system to provide necessary resources, (3) linking the elderly with the appropriate resources, services, and opportunities, (4) contributing to the development of responsive social policies. For instance, the functionally impaired elderly are usually victims of chronic disease. No amount of medical treatment will reverse these conditions. Therefore, the social worker's role is supportive. The social work goal is to assess the needs of the individual and to assist her in meeting those needs. Many times the frail elderly can remain in the community when we alter their physical environment to compensate for their lost functions. This might include installing walking rails in their home, safety features built into certain rooms such as the bathroom, or ramps to replace stairways. We might also be able to ensure that they have proper nutrition through Meals on Wheels programs without requiring them to sacrifice their independence.

The prevention function is operating when we prevent the elderly from premature and unnecessary institutional placement. It can also refer to programs and policies that are developed to prevent problems in family functioning, such as elder abuse. This may include helping families get the necessary financial and emotional support they need to care for their elderly at home. It might be the development of respite care homes so the caretakers can have time away from the demands of the frail and sometimes demanding parents who require round-the-clock care. By maintaining the mental health of the caretaker you are not only providing the elderly with better care but also preventing abuse or neglect that may occur if the caretaker is overwhelmed by the demands of caring for the older person. If social workers can become involved before the situation deteriorates, intervention is less traumatic for the family. Most families are happy to receive such services.

The protective function has become more central to social work practice in the last decade. A majority of the states have passed some kind of elder abuse legislation since 1980. This legislation varies between states but is usually modeled on child welfare abuse and neglect statutes. No state has developed clear guidelines of what constitutes abuse and neglect. Typically included are such conditions as psychological abuse, exploitation, and self-neglect. One of the paradoxes of elder abuse is that it is increasing at the same time that fewer and fewer elderly are living with their families.

Usually elder abuse cases present multiple functioning problems within the family. It might involve a mentally retarded or mentally ill adult who has become abusive and difficult to handle. These types of cases clearly involve social service needs, not police or court matters. It is important that as mandatory reporting requirements for elder abuse are adopted, the protective function stays within the service area in most cases. This problem usually requires support services as well as protective services.

The support function refers to any statement or action to help individuals or families solve or mitigate personal or social problems. For the social worker attached to an elder abuse unit this may consist of explaining to the overwhelmed caretaker how to obtain financial assistance. The social worker may need to arrange for the caretaker to obtain legal assistance from the Legal Aid Society or day care within the community.

The control function can be important to the gerontological social worker. One elderly woman had to be placed in a nursing home because she was prowling the halls of her apartment building wanting to take people's blood pressure at all hours of the night. This woman was a retired nurse who had provided considerable nursing to other elderly apartment dwellers. When it was impossible to control her in this setting, it was necessary to institutionalize her. Institutions have certain rules that have to be followed. Social workers are frequently called upon to deal with disruptive patients. A plan must be developed that protects the individual's rights but does not interfere with the operation of the facility.

Social work contributions can be in the area of direct service—helping the elderly remain independent and promoting the development and enhancement of self-support and self-sufficiency. However, the profession must continue to play an important role in indirect services—the development of public policy and services that strengthen the ability of the elderly to maintain a high quality of life, economic security, and health care regardless of race or social class.

The primary function of direct practice in gerontology is helping the elderly cope with decreased physical abilities and decreased resources by obtaining the necessary support from their environment and maximizing their social functioning. Our unique expertise in working with the elderly is to assess the social factors contributing to their problems in living, the environmental stressors, and how interpersonal and community relationships are affecting their functioning. Our interventions are based upon knowledge of senescence (the biology of aging), family functioning, the public welfare system, the court system, motivation, and emotional and environmental factors.

KNOWLEDGE

Gerontology, like each field of practice, requires social workers to have knowledge of *general theory* of human behavior and the social environment; *practice theory*, which includes knowledge of policy, services, programs, and institutions and how social work practice relates to each of them, and a *theory of practice*, which is the specific social work methods or interventions they will use. The practice method used will depend upon the systematic interpretation of those principles that help the social worker understand the phenomena and a clear delineation of principles for producing change. In simpler terms, interventions are based on knowledge of what is happening, why it is happening, and how we can change it.

General theories of human behavior and the social environment that contribute to the knowledge base in this field include: theories of aging, the impact and consequences of disability, the cultural implications of age-specific behaviors and family functioning, and the interorganizational structure and process of agency-community resources. The social worker must have the necessary knowledge to contribute to a biopsychosocial assessment of the client and to develop an individualized plan with the client and the client's family based on this assessment and knowledge of service availability in the interorganizational network.

See Chapter 10 for more discussion of interorganizational network theory.

The Aging Network is the administrative structure that has been set up to carry out the objectives of the Older Americans Act.

Practice theory specific to this field includes understanding the general scope, objectives, and administrative structure of the Aging Network; federal and state regulations related to income maintenance, health care, and long term care; characteristics of the aging population; resources available to the elderly; elder abuse; and knowledge of teamwork to deal with other professions in this multidisciplinary field.

Theories of practice such as casework, group work, community organization and research are all important to working with the elderly. The opportunities to work with individuals, groups, and families are very diverse. There are probably more positions in community organization than in any other field of practice. We cannot overlook the importance of understanding how the individual relates to the family, the community, primary and secondary groups, the neighborhood, and wider social systems.

To show application of knowledge to practice, we portray the use of all three levels of knowledge as they relate to assessing elder abuse; we then discuss the primary components of the Aging Network. Space limitations prevent us from presenting a comprehensive overview of the gerontological knowledge base.

Assessment of elder abuse and neglect is a potentially volatile situation. The more professional and well-planned this assessment is, the more likely that it will be done efficiently and effectively. Fortunately, there is an ever-expanding knowledge base to draw from in structuring your assessment. A nurse–social worker team (Mary Joy Quinn, R.N., M.A., and Susan Tomita, M.S.W.) has developed a protocol for the assessment phase.[10] We draw upon their work to present an application of knowledge to effective elder abuse assessment.

The assessment protocol is broken into four phases: (1) assessment of the client's functioning, (2) physical examination of the client, (3) interview of the potential abuser, and (4) collateral contact. Social workers are qualified to perform three of these phases; we address the first phase. This problem exemplifies the importance of teamwork in working with the elderly. The social worker can perform the psychosocial assessment but must rely on medical personnel for the physical examination. The original referral often comes from medical personnel.

Hospital personnel are frequently the first to observe the abused elderly person. Some of the warning signs include: (1) someone other than the caregiver bringing the person to the emergency room, (2) an extended period of time between the injury and seeking treatment, (3) inconsistency between

DIAGNOSTIC QUESTIONS

Steps in Functional Assessment

1. Begin with easy questions to put the client at ease.

   - Address
   - How long have you lived there?
   - Do you live alone?
   - Do you have a car? Do you have a bus pass?
   - Who cooks your meals?
   - What is your income?

2. Ask the client to describe a typical day. Go through an entire day; establish the degree of dependence and who the person has contact with on a daily basis.

3. Assess activities of daily living. There are numerous simple to administer scales that can be used for this.[12]

4. Get the client to describe what expectations he has for the caregiver. You need to assess whether these are realistic and whether they are congruent with the abilities and desires of the caregiver.

5. Determine whether there have been any recent crises in the family. Has the caretaker been under unusual pressure?

6. Determine drug use, alcohol problems, illnesses, or other conditions that could be producing problems in the family.

7. Having established rapport with the client, it is time to ask questions related specifically to the abuse. Make these *yes* and *no* questions. If the answer is *yes*, then ask for specific details.

verbal description and actual injuries, and (4) medications not being taken as prescribed.[11] In the functional assessment the social worker must proceed cautiously.

Your ability to do an accurate assessment of the presence of abuse is directly related to your knowledge of elderly functioning, family dynamics, interviewing, nonverbal communication, and assessment. You need to know how to relate this information to the health care professional to maximize the quality of the examination they can give. You need counseling skills to work with the family; you need to know the resource system to get them financial assistance or medical care if needed; and you need to understand the dynamics of the abusive situation. One of the major things a neophyte social worker needs to know is where to find the appropriate knowledge in the literature and how to use supervision effectively.

Practice theory in gerontology includes familiarity with the Aging Network: the Administration on Aging, the Federal Council on the Aging, state offices of aging, and the area agency on aging. Individual treatment plans as well as potential programs will be limited by policies set by the Aging Network.

The Administration on Aging (AoA) is housed in the Office of Human Development Services. There has been much controversy over the administrative structure, and many people believe that the commissioner on aging should report directly to the secretary of Health and Human Services, as required by the 1981 amendments. The function of the AoA is to establish the organizational framework, to develop the guidelines, and to supply the direction that make a going concern of the specific requirements of the Older Americans Act. Its role has been described as oversight, monitoring, assessing, approving state program plans, authorizing federal funding, and providing technical assistance.[13]

The Federal Council on the Aging was created to advise the president on matters relating to the special needs of older Americans. It was directed to make recommendations on policies for the aging to the president, the secretary of Health and Human Services, the commissioner on aging, and the Congress. It is a fifteen-member body appointed by the president and confirmed by the Senate, which must have at least five older persons. The secretary of HHS and the commissioner on aging are ex officio members.[14] The 1978 amendments reaffirmed a strong commitment that the council provide an evaluation function for programs conducted under the OAA. However, this endorsement was not backed up by the funds necessary to do the evaluation. In fact, in 1982 the council budget was cut by over 50 percent ($481,000 to $200,000).[15]

The state offices of aging are a response to federal requirements that OAA funding be dependent upon designation of an agency that would be the sole unit for developing an annual state plan to be submitted for approval by the governor and then the commissioner on aging. State units are to administer the approved plan and coordinate all state activities funded by the OAA. States can submit two, three, or four year plans. The 1978 amendments said that preference must be given to the elderly with the greatest economic or social need.

The area agency on aging (AAA) is not usually a direct service provider, but the broker or coordinator of services to the elderly in a specifically defined geographic area. Each AAA must submit a "comprehensive and coordinated" plan of services for the elderly. Public hearings are required before the plan can be submitted to the state, and priority must be given to services to the low-income and minority elderly. The AAA has been described as both the end of the line and its beginning.[16] It is the end of the line as far as the Aging Network is concerned; it is the beginning in terms of actual services for the elderly. Neither the federal nor state levels provide or contract for services.

Understanding the cultural, political, and legal structures, processes, and practices is essential. Today, services to the elderly are experiencing drastic

The Administration on Aging interprets the Older Americans Act.

The Council has both an advisory and a watchdog function.

Each state must have an office on aging in order to receive federal funds available to the states through the OAA.

The area agency on aging is the local or community level of administration.

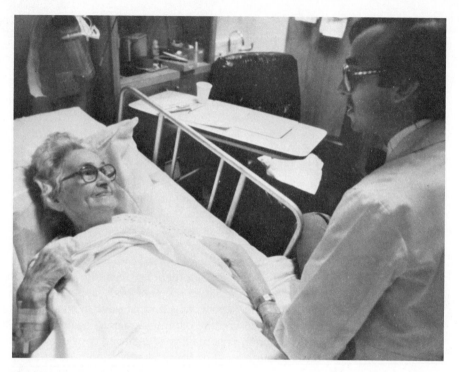

Health care is a major concern of many elderly.

budget cuts at the same time we are seeing an increase in reports of abuse and neglect.

Family functioning is inherently related to the economic factors impinging on individuals and the community in which they live. The cost of living, the standard of living, employment opportunities (or lack thereof), and the accessibility of benefits and services will all affect the degree to which adult children can meet the needs of their parents. Social workers cannot ignore these critical variables.

To address these problems the social worker has to know the purpose and structure of public and private service agencies, the functions of each, how they relate to each other, and on what contingencies their funding is based.

Effective resource linkage requires knowledge of the agency and a professional working relationship between social workers and professionals in the fields of health, mental health, and income assistance programs. Since services never fully meet the needs of the targeted population, it requires knowledge and skill to acquire needed services and resources for your clients. Resource linkage is an important function performed by case managers.

ROLES

Case manager has become one of the most prominent social work roles in the field of gerontology. "Case management is the mechanism for ensuring a comprehensive program that will meet an individual's need for care by co-ordinating and linking the components of a service delivery system."[17] The services are frequently spread throughout various agencies. To be effective, the case manager must have authority to allocate and monitor services. This role became particularly prominent as programs were developed to keep the frail and functionally impaired elderly out of institutions. Case management tasks include assessment and periodic review of client's status, development and implementation of a plan of care, coordination and monitoring of services, advocacy, termination of the case, and follow-up.[18]

Social workers serve as brokers when they make linkages between the client and a community agency such as a day care center. Brokering is a prominent component of the case manager role. Brokered services may include nutrition programs, health care, and transportation, to name a few. As a broker of services, the social worker will have to work with physicians, community nurses, hospice personnel, day care providers, and staff at nutrition sites or Meals on Wheels programs. Each of these professionals has very specific and important roles in serving the needs of the elderly. Social workers need to understand the differences in these roles and to manage the services in such a way that the client gets the correct services at the most appropriate time.

Advocate is a familiar role to the nursing home social worker. Advocacy for the rights of residents can be accomplished through the development and implementation of policies for the facility and getting necessary legal services, including guardianship or conservatorship if necessary. Advocacy is also important since programs are never adequately funded to meet the need identified. Only the most adept at advocating will get the desired services. Most frail and functionally impaired elderly need assistance in this area.

The enabler role is evident when the social worker assists the patient and the family to find strengths and resources within themselves to solve their problems. In this role the social worker enables the family to keep the elderly person in their home by concentrating on their own strengths and abilities and helping them apply these strengths to the problems at hand. On the other hand, the social worker may enable the family to place the older person in a care facility, if that is more appropriate.

The teaching role introduces information to the family that was not previously available. A social worker may teach a stroke victim how to perform daily living tasks in spite of paralysis. He may teach communication skills to a family whose former communication patterns are no longer effective. There are many physical changes the older person experiences that the younger person may not understand; the social worker can teach the caretaker. A social worker might also teach the importance of nutrition and exercise to the elderly. Nursing home social workers are often called upon to teach paraprofessional staff interviewing and communication skills.

As a mediator the social worker acts to reconcile differences and to intervene between conflicting parties in order to promote reconciliation or compromise. Mediation may take place between child and parent or between siblings. With more states adopting policies that require adult children to participate in paying for their parents' care, mediation will probably take a more prominent role. Mediation often takes place in nursing homes when roommates are either inappropriately matched or when an individual is particularly difficult.

Discharge planner is a role that social workers in hospitals or nursing homes are called upon to fill. This role facilitates the patient or resident's integration back into the community by arranging follow-up services. This frequently requires considerable team effort with professionals and agencies in the community. The hospital or nursing home funds the social work position, but they usually do not hire staff with the goal of providing services after discharge. The reality is that such services would not be reimbursed. Therefore, the discharge planner must have a thorough knowledge of community services and track records of agencies that follow through with service provision. Success in this role is based on accurate assessment of older persons' needs, clear articulation of those needs, and appropriate referral.

RELEVANT SOCIAL POLICY/LEGISLATION

The most significant piece of legislation, the Older Americans Act, has fairly dominated our discussion of this field of practice. This has happened naturally, because there is no other field in which a specific piece of legislation has had such an impact on services. Indeed, it is the only field in which there have been so many *services* mandated by the federal government. Now, however, we want to move out of the service arena and present a brief survey of the income programs available to the elderly.

For many elderly, Social Security is the principal source of income. This system has enabled millions of elderly to feel that they can make it on their own—the importance of which should not be underestimated. Of those over age sixty-five, 93 percent have the protection of Social Security.[19] Adequacy has always been one of the goals of the Social Security program, which is one of the reasons why the computation of benefits favors the low-income worker. To receive full benefits, the insured must wait until age sixty-five. Collecting benefits at age 62 reduces the rate collected; working after age 65 earns a delayed retirement credit. At age 65 the spouse is eligible to collect at a rate equal to one-half that of the retiree.

Supplemental Security Income is financial aid for the needy elderly. Rather than being funded from a payroll tax, SSI is funded by general revenues. SSI is the current form of Old Age Assistance that was included in the original Social Security Act. In 1972 the program was renamed and operating control was taken away from state and local governments and placed in the Social Security Administration. Fewer than 10 percent of the elderly receive SSI.

Food stamps are available to the indigent elderly who meet eligibility requirements. Food stamps may be used only for food purchases; they may not be used to buy alcoholic beverages, tobacco, household supplies, or other nonfood items. The elderly may use them for home-delivered meals. Food stamp applications are available at local social service departments; recipients must be recertified once a year.

Medicare and Medicaid (Title XVIII and Title XIX of the SSA) provide the bulk of medical insurance available to the elderly. Although the costs of these programs are so exorbitant that they pose a threat to our economic system, the coverage is far from adequate. Long-term care is extremely labor-intensive and expensive. Today, at minimum it costs $15,000 a year to stay in a nursing home—a cost that Medicare does not cover. The House Select Committee on Aging estimated that nearly two-thirds of all senior citizens living alone would impoverish themselves after only thirteen weeks in a nursing home.[20]

Extensive discussion of the problems of Medicare and Medicaid is included in Chapter 13.

Today Americans spend $35.2 billion a year for nursing home care. This is nearly five times the total amount spent for medical research and nearly $7 billion more than is spent for drugs and medical supplies.[21] In spite of the tremendous amount of tax dollars going into health care for the elderly, only 48 percent of the health care costs for the elderly are picked up by Medicare. Because of medical inflation, the elderly are actually paying more out of their own pockets for health care than they did in 1965 when these programs were first put into place.[22]

Medical assistance legislation holds specific interest for social workers because it is one policy that requires social work services as a prerequisite to Medicaid reimbursement for nursing home care. Some individual states reimburse for social work services in other areas but do not limit reimbursement to social workers. This legislation clearly states that the social worker must have a degree from an accredited social work program or receive supervision from an MSW from an accredited program.

Another way the federal government has worked to augment the financial resources of older people is through special tax provisions for those over sixty-five. This group pays a lower tax, and in the case of poorer older persons, often no income tax at all. Other programs include energy conservation programs, which offer persons with low income assistance in paying their energy bills or in reducing energy costs in other ways. There is free legal assistance to lower-income elderly, which often allows them to secure financial benefits that otherwise would have been denied them. Legal advice itself is a benefit that the elderly would have to pay for if it were not provided by the Legal Assistance program.[23]

There are also federal programs to improve transportation services to the elderly. These fall under the jurisdiction of the Department of Transportation. Congress declared in 1970 that the elderly have the same right as other persons to utilize mass transportation facilities and services, and that special efforts shall be made in the planning and design of mass transportation facilities and services to ensure availability to the elderly and handicapped.[24] Out of this legislation came funds to provide reduced fares, handicap-accessible buses, money for nonprofit groups to purchase vehicles and equipment to meet the needs of the elderly, and a variety of other transportation programs.

There are a number of federal programs designed to provide housing for the elderly. Congregate housing was authorized in 1970 as an amendment to the Housing Act of 1937. It was an attempt to get collaboration from a number of agencies to provide special services to the functionally impaired elderly to keep them in the community. As federal participation in social programs decreases we are likely to see less congregate housing. Other programs that are available to low-income families are also available to the low-income elderly (see Chapter 13). With the tremendous changes taking place in the Department of Housing and Urban Development we cannot know what the future will bring to low-income housing.

THE FUTURE OF GERONTOLOGY PRACTICE: A SUMMARY

The proportion of the elderly in the United States has grown steadily over this century and will likely continue to grow in the near future. One in nine Americans is now over 65 years of age. Women are highly overrepresented, especially in the over age 75 group. They are far less likely to be married and tend to be living economically disadvantaged lives. Minority groups have a significantly shorter life expectancy than whites. The proportion of elderly varies by state from a high of 17.3 percent in Florida to a low of 1.9 percent in Alaska.[25] This means that some states will have to provide more of their tax base for services to the elderly.

For social workers an aging population means increased positions in nursing homes, day care centers, community care programs, and particularly in case management agencies. All of these programs will be competing for limited tax dollars. The elderly seemed to be well on the way to achieving some of the goals of the Older Americans Act prior to the inauguration of Ronald Reagan. His administration not only stopped the march forward but reduced funding of services. There is no evidence that the Bush administration will reverse this trend.

Possibly related to the decrease in services and the cutbacks in economic assistance programs, a whole new service area is being developed in the prevention and treatment of elder abuse. Social workers will be expected to intervene in this problem with minimal resources available to solve the problem. As states develop their elder abuse statutes social workers will play a significant role in their development. This will be an important and significant contribution.

NOTES

1. *Encyclopedia of Social Work*, 16th issue (New York: NASW, 1971), 34.
2. 1971 White House Conference on Aging, *Toward a National Policy on Aging*, Final Report, vol. 1, 9–10.
3. B. Rich and M. Baum, *The Aging: A Guide to Public Policy* (Pittsburgh, Pa.: University of Pittsburgh Press, 1984), 30.
4. Ibid., 35.
5. Ibid.
6. S. Crystal, "Elder Abuse: The Latest 'Crisis'," *The Public Interest* No. 88 (Summer 1987), 56–66.
7. Ibid.
8. *Minority Elderly Services: New Programs, Old Problems, Part II* (Washington, D.C.: U.S. Civil Rights Commission, November 1982), 4.
9. *NASW Standards for Social Work Services in Long-Term Care Facilities.* Policy statement number 9 approved June 1981, prepared by the Long-Term Care Facilities Standards Task Force of the NASW Committee on Aging (Silver Spring, Md.: NASW, 1981).
10. M. Quinn and S. Tomita, *Elder Abuse and Neglect: Causes, Diagnosis, and Intervention Strategies* (New York: Springer, 1986).
11. Ibid.
12. Ibid.
13. *Senior Citizens News* (November 1981), 6.
14. Rich and Baum, *The Aging*, 37.
15. Ibid.
16. Ibid.
17. *NASW Standards and Guidelines for Social Work Case Management for the Functionally Impaired*, professional standard #12, approved November 1984, prepared by the NASW Case Management Task Force (Silver Springs, Md.: NASW, 1984).
18. Ibid.
19. *Social Security Bulletin* 6, 1 (January 1983): 46.
20. House Select Committee on Aging, *The Twentieth Anniversary of Medicare and Medicaid: Americans Still at Risk*, press release, July 30, 1985.
21. *Washington Post*, 30 July, 1986, A6.
22. P. Longman, *Born to Pay: The New Politics of Aging in America* (Boston: Houghton Mifflin, 1987), 99.
23. Rich and Baum, *The Aging*, 122.
24. Public Law 91-453, October 15, 1970.
25. Rich and Baum, *The Aging*.

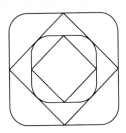

Name Index

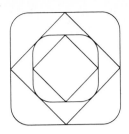

Subject Index

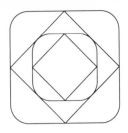

About the Authors

Mary Wirtz Macht received both her M.S.S.W. and Ph.D. from the University of Wisconsin. While a graduate student she studied under a fellowship provided by the National Institute of Mental Health. As a fellow she worked at the Center for Evaluation, Research, and Training. Prior to graduate study, Dr. Macht worked for five years in a county agency carrying a mixed caseload. She was instrumental in developing both the Work Incentive Program and a Day Care Program in that county. After receiving her doctorate Dr. Macht taught in the University of Wisconsin system and Marian College, Fond du Lac, Wisconsin for seven years. She has published articles on corrections, women, child welfare, gerontology, and organizational theory. A generalist planning perspective is the organizing link between these various substantive areas. She is presently the Program Director for the Short Term Treatment and Assessment Unit at Winnebago Mental Health Institute, Division of Care and Treatment Facilities for the State of Wisconsin.

José B. Ashford is an Associate Professor in the School of Social Work and an Associate Faculty member in the Interdisciplinary Doctoral Program in Justice Studies at Arizona State University. Prior to joining the faculty at the Arizona State University, he was a faculty member for four years in the University of Wisconsin System with Dr. Macht. He earned a B.A. from Loyola University of the South in Sociology, a M.S.W. from the Ohio State University, and a Ph.D. in Sociology with a specialization in deviant behavior and criminology from Bowling Green State University. Dr. Ashford has published widely and his primary area of research is in law and mental health with a specific focus on criminal justice and mental health interactions. His other research interests include risk assessment, juvenile justice, parole careers and special offenders.

In addition to his academic work, Dr. Ashford worked for a number of years as a forensic social worker at the Court Diagnostic & Treatment Center in Toldeo, Ohio and for a brief period as an Assistant Director of the Parolee Rehabilitation and Employment Program in Dayton, Ohio. He is widely sought after by attorneys as a consultant in cases requiring either an expert in forensic social work or an expert in risk and treatability assessments. Dr. Ashford is also well recognized as a planning and a research consultant. He co-developed the *Arizona Juvenile Aftercare Decision Making System.* This system formalized risk, needs and placement decisions for parole officers working with juvenile offenders in Arizona. He is presently a consultant to the Drug Testing Technology Focused Offender Disposition Program (DTT/FOD) that was funded by the Bureau of Justice Assistance.